CHILTON'S
REPAIR & TUNE-UP GUIDE

MAZDA
1971 to
1982

RX-2 • RX-3 • RX-4 • 808 (1300) • 808 (1600)
Cosmo • GLC • 626

Managing Editor KERRY A. FREEMAN, S.A.E.
Senior Editor RICHARD J. RIVELE, S.A.E.
Editor RON WEBB

President WILLIAM A. BARBOUR
Executive Vice President JAMES A. MIADES
Vice President and General Manager JOHN P. KUSHNERICK

CHILTON BOOK COMPANY
Radnor, Pennsylvania
19089

SAFETY NOTICE

Proper service and repair procedures are vital to the safe, reliable operation of all motor vehicles, as well as the personal safety of those performing repairs. This book outlines procedures for servicing and repairing vehicles using safe, effective methods. The procedures contain many NOTES, CAUTIONS and WARNINGS which should be followed along with standard safety procedures to eliminate the possibility of personal injury or improper service which could damage the vehicle or compromise its safety.

It is important to note that repair procedures and techniques, tools and parts for servicing motor vehicles, as well as the skill and experience of the individual performing the work vary widely. It is not possible to anticipate all of the conceivable ways or conditions under which vehicles may be services, or to provide cautions as to all of the possible hazards that may result. Standard and accepted safety precautions and equipment should be used during cutting, grinding, chiseling, prying, or any other process that can cause material removal or projectiles.

Some procedures require the use of tools specially designed for a specific purpose. Before substituting another tool or procedure, you must be completely satisfied that neither your personal safety, nor the performance of the vehicle will be endangered.

Although the information in this guide is based on industry sources and is as complete as possible at the time of publication, the possibility exists that the manufacturer made later changes which could not be included here. While striving for total accuracy, Chilton Book Company cannot assume responsibility for any errors, changes, or omissions that may occur in the compilation of this data.

PART NUMBERS

Part numbers listed in this reference are not recommendations by Chilton for any product by brand name. They are references that can be used with interchange manuals and aftermarket supplier catalogs to locate each brand supplier's discrete part number.

ACKNOWLEDGMENTS

The Chilton Book Company expresses its appreciation to the Mazda Technical Center, Inc., Irvine, California 92714; YBH Mazda, Inc., Edgemount, Pennsylvania 19028; Mazda Motors of America (East), Inc., Jacksonville, Florida; and Toyo Kogyo Co., Ltd., Hiroshima, Japan.

CONTENTS

Quick Reference Specifications For Your Vehicle

Fill in this chart with the most commonly used specifications for your vehicle. Specifications can be found in Chapters 1 through 3 or on the tune-up decal under the hood of the vehicle.

 Tune-Up

Firing Order_____

Spark Plugs:

    Type_____

    Gap (in.)_____

Point Gap (in.)_____

Dwell Angle (°)_____

Ignition Timing (°)_____

    Vacuum (Connected/Disconnected)_____

Valve Clearance (in.)

    Intake_____   **Exhaust**_____

Capacities

Engine Oil (qts)

    With Filter Change_____

    Without Filter Change_____

Cooling System (qts)_____

Manual Transmission (pts)_____

    Type_____

Automatic Transmission (pts)_____

    Type_____

Front Differential (pts)_____

    Type_____

Rear Differential (pts)_____

    Type_____

Transfer Case (pts)_____

    Type_____

FREQUENTLY REPLACED PARTS

Use these spaces to record the part numbers of frequently replaced parts.

PCV VALVE	**OIL FILTER**	**AIR FILTER**
Manufacturer_____	**Manufacturer**_____	**Manufacturer**_____
Part No._____	**Part No.**_____	**Part No.**_____

General Information and Maintenance

HOW TO USE THIS BOOK

Chilton's Repair & Tune-Up Guide for the Mazda is intended to help you learn more about the inner workings of your vehicle and save you money on its upkeep and operation. It is designed to aid the owner of both rotary-powered and piston-powdered Mazdas to perform service operations on his or her automobile.

The first two chapters will be the most used, since they contain maintenance and tune-up information and procedures. Studies have shown that a properly tuned and maintained car can get at least 10% better gas mileage than an out-of-tune car. The other chapters deal with the more complex systems of your car. Operating systems from engine through brakes are covered to the extent that the average do-it-yourselfer becomes mechanically involved. This book will not explain such things as rebuilding the differential for the simple reason that the expertise required and the investment in special tools make this task uneconomical. It will give you detailed instructions to help you change your own brake pads and shoes, replace points and plugs, and do many more jobs that will save you money, give you personal satisfaction, and help you avoid expensive problems.

A secondary purpose of this book is a reference for owners who want to understand their car and/or their mechanics better. In this case, no tools at all are required.

Before removing any bolts, read through the entire procedure. This will give you the overall view of what tools and supplies will be required. There is nothing more frustrating than having to walk to the bus stop on Monday morning because you were short one bolt on Sunday afternoon. So read ahead and plan ahead. Each operation should be approached logically and all procedures thoroughly understood before attempting any work.

All chapters contain adjustments, maintenance, removal and installation procedures, and repair or overhaul procedures. When repair is not considered practical, we tell you how to remove the part and then how to install the new or rebuilt replacement. In this way, you at least save the labor costs. Backyard repair of such components as the alternator is just not practical.

Two basic mechanic's rules should be mentioned here. One, whenever the left side of the car or engine is referred to, it is meant to specify the driver's side of the car. Conversely, the right side of the car means the passenger's side. Secondly, most screws and bolts are removed by turning counterclockwise, and tightened by turning clockwise.

Safety is always the most important rule. Constantly be aware of the dangers involved in working on an automobile and take the proper precautions. (See the section in this chapter "Servicing Your Vehicle Safely" and the SAFETY NOTICE on the acknowledgment page.)

Pay attention to the instructions provided. There are 3 common mistakes in mechanical work:

1. Incorrect order of assembly, disassembly or adjustment. When taking something apart or putting it together, doing things in the wrong order usually just costs you extra time; however, it CAN break something. Read the entire procedure before beginning disassembly. Do everything in the order in which the instructions say you should do it, even if you can't immediately see a reason for it. When you're taking apart something that is very intricate (for example, a carburetor), you might want to draw a picture of how it looks when assembled at one point in order to make sure you get everything back in its proper position. (We will supply exploded view whenever possible.) When making adjustments, especially tune-up adjustments, do them in order; often, one adjustment affects another, and you cannot expect even satisfactory results unless each adjustment is made only when it cannot be changed by any other.

2. Overtorquing (or undertorquing). While it is more common for overtorquing to cause damage, undertorquing can cause a fastener to vibrate loose causing serious damage. Especially when dealing with aluminum parts, pay attention to torque specifications and utilize a torque wrench in assembly. If a torque figure is not available, remember that if you are using the right tool to do the job, you will probably not have to strain yourself to get a fastener tight enough. The pitch of most threads is so slight that the tension you put on the wrench will be multiplied many, many times in actual force on what you are tightening. A good example of how critical torque is can be seen in the case of spark plug installation, especially where you are putting the plug into an aluminum cylinder head. Too little torque can fail to crush the gasket, causing leakage of combustion gases and consequent overheating of the plug and engine parts. Too much torque can damage the threads, or distort the plug, which changes the spark gap.

There are many commercial products available for ensuring that fasteners won't come loose, even if they are not torqued just right (a very common brand is "Loctite®"). If you're worried about getting something together tight enough to hold, but loose enough to avoid mechanical damage during assembly, one of these products might offer substantial insurance. Read the label on the package and make sure the product is compatible with the materials, fluids, etc. involved before choosing one.

3. Crossthreading. This occurs when a part such as a bolt is screwed into a nut or casting at the wrong angle and forced. Cross threading is more likely to occur if access is difficult. It helps to clean and lubricate fasteners, and to start threading with the part to be installed going straight in. Then, start the bolt, spark plug, etc. with your fingers. If you encounter resistance, unscrew the part and start over again at a different angle until it can be inserted and turned several turns without much effort. Keep in mind that many parts, especially spark plugs, use tapered threads so that gentle turning will automatically bring the part you're threading to the proper angle if you don't force it or resist a change in angle. Don't put a wrench on the part until it's been turned a couple of turns by hand. If you suddenly encounter resistance, and the part has not seated fully, don't force it. Pull it back out and make sure it's clean and threading properly.

Always take your time and be patient; once you have some experience, working on your car will become an enjoyable hobby.

TOOLS AND EQUIPMENT

Naturally, without the proper tools and equipment it is impossible to properly service your vehicle. It would be impossible to catalog each tool that you would need to perform each or any operation in this book. It would also be unwise for the amateur to rush out and buy an expensive set of tools on the theory that he may need one or more of them at sometime.

The best approach is to proceed slowly, gathering together a good quality set of those tools that are used most frequently. Don't be misled by the low cost of bargain tools. It is far better to spend a little more for better quality. Forged wrenches, 10 or 12 point sockets and fine tooth ratchets are by far preferable to their less expensive counterparts.

As any good mechanic can tell you, there are few worse experiences than trying to work on a car or truck with bad tools. Your monetary savings will be far outweighed by frustration and mangled knuckles.

Begin accumulating those tools that are used most frequently; those associated with routine maintenance and tune-up.

In addition to the normal assortment of screwdrivers and pliers you should have the following tools for routine maintenance jobs:

1. Metric wrenches or SAE/Metric wrenches—sockets and combination open end/box end wrenches in sizes from ⅛ in. (3 mm) to ¾ in. (19 mm); and a spark plug socket ($^{13}/_{16}$ or ⅝ in. depending on plug type).

If possible, buy various length socket drive extensions. One break in this department is that the metric sockets available in the U.S. will all fit the ratchet handles and extensions you may already have (¼, ⅜, and ½ in. drive.)

2. Jackstands—for support;
3. Oil filter wrench
4. Oil filler spout—for pouring oil;
5. Grease gun—for chassis lubrication;
6. Hydrometer—for checking the battery;
7. A container for draining oil;
8. Many rags for wiping up the inevitable mess.

In addition to the above items there are several others that are not absolutely necessary, but handy to have around. These include oil dry, a transmission funnel and the usual supply of lubricants, antifreeze and fluids, although these can be purchased as needed. This is a basic list for routine maintenance, but only your personal needs and desire can accurately determine your list of tools.

The second list of tools is for tune-ups. While the tools involved here are slightly more sophisticated, they need not be outrageously expensive. There are several inexpensive tach-dwell meters on the market that are every bit as good for the average mechanic as a $100.00 professional model. Just be sure that it goes to at least 1,200–1,500 rpm on the tach scale and that it works on 4, 6 or 8 cylinder engines. A basic list of tune-up equipment could include:

1. Tach-dwell meter;
2. Spark plug wrench;
3. Timing light (a DC light that works from the car's battery is best, although an AC light that plugs into 110V house current will suffice at some sacrifice in brightness);

4. Wire spark plug gauge/adjusting tools
5. Set of feeler blades
Here again, be guided by your own needs. A feeler blade will set the points as easily as a dwell meter will read well, but slightly less accurately. And since you will need a tachometer anyway . . . well, make your own decision.

In addition to these basic tools, there are several other tools and gauges you may find useful. These include:

1. A compression gauge. The screw-in type is slower to use, but eliminates the possibility of a faulty reading due to escaping pressure.
2. A manifold vacuum gauge.
3. A test light.
4. An induction meter. This is used for determining whether or not there is current in a wire. These are handy for use if a wire is broken somewhere in a wiring harness.

As a final note, you will probably find a torque wrench necessary for all but the most basic work. The beam type models are perfectly adequate, although the newer click type are more precise.

Special Tools

Normally, the use of special factory tools is avoided for repair procedures, since these are not readily available for the do-it-yourself mechanic. When it is possible to perform the job with more commonly available tools, it will be pointed out, but occasionally, a special tool was designed to perform a specific function and should be used. Before substituting another tool, you should be convinced that neither your safety nor the performance of the vehicle will be compromised.

Some special tools are available commercially from major tool manufacturers. Others can be purchased from your car dealer.

SERVICING YOUR VEHICLE SAFELY

It is virtually impossible to anticipate all of the hazards involved with automotive maintenance and service but care and common sense will prevent most accidents.

The rules of safety for mechanics rang from "don't smoke around gasoline," to "use the proper tool for the job." The trick to avoiding

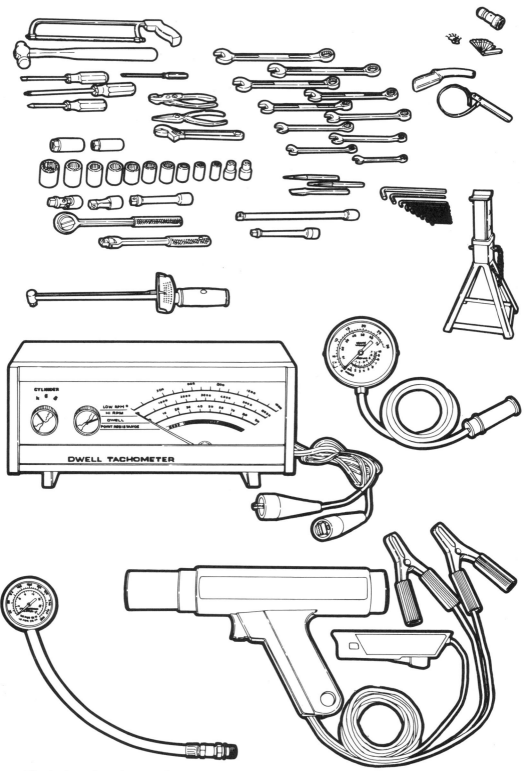

The tools and equipment shown here will handle the majority of the maintenance on a car

injuries is to develop safe work habits and take every possible precaution.

Do's

• DO keep a fire extinguisher and first aid kit within easy reach.

• DO wear safety glasses or goggles when cutting, drilling, grinding or prying, even if you have 20–20 vision. If you wear glasses for the sake of vision, then they should be made of hardened glass that can serve also as safety glasses, or wear safety goggles over your regular glasses.

• DO shield your eyes whenever you work around the battery. Batteries contain sulphuric acid; in case of contact with the eyes or skin, flush the area with water or a mixture of water and baking soda and get medical attention immediately.

• DO use safety stands for any undercar service. Jacks are for raising vehicles; safety stands are for making sure the vehicle stays raised until you want it to come down. Whenever the vehicle is raised, block the wheels remaining on the ground and set the parking brake.

• DO use adequate ventilation when working with any chemicals. Like carbon monoxide, the asbestos dust resulting from brake lining wear can be poisonous in sufficient quantities.

• DO disconnect the negative battery cable when working on the electrical system. The primary ignition system can contain up to 40,000 volts.

• DO follow manufacturer's directions whenever working with potentially hazardous materials. Both brake fluid and antifreeze are poisonous if taken internally.

• DO properly maintain your tools. Loose hammerheads, mushroomed punches and chisels, frayed or poorly grounded electrical cords, excessively worn screwdrivers, spread wrenches (open end), cracked sockets, slipping ratchets, or faulty droplight sockets can cause accidents.

• DO use the proper size and type of tool for the job being done.

• DO when possible, pull on a wrench handle rather than push on it, and adjust your stance to prevent a fall.

• DO be sure that adjustable wrenches are tightly adjusted on the nut or bolt and pulled so that the face is on the side of the fixed jaw.

• DO select a wrench or socket that fits the nut or bolt. The wrench or socket should sit straight, not cocked.

• DO strike squarely with a hammer—avoid glancing blows.

• DO set the parking brake and block the drive wheels if the work requires that the engine be running.

Dont's

• DON'T run an engine in a garage or anywhere else without proper ventilation—EVER! Carbon monoxide is poisonous; it takes a long time to leave the human body and you can build up a deadly supply of it in your system by simply breathing in a little every day. You may not realize you are slowly poisioning yourself. Always use power vents, windows, fans or open the garage doors.

• DON'T work around moving parts while wearing a necktie or other loose clothing. Short sleeves are much safer than long, loose sleeves and hard-toed shoes with neoprene soles protect your toes and give a better grip on slippery surfaces. Jewelry such as watches, fancy belt buckles, beads or body adornment or any kind is not safe working around a car. Long hair should be hidden under a hat or cap.

• DON'T use pockets for toolboxes. A fall or bump can drive a screwdriver deep into your body. Even a wiping cloth hanging from the back pocket can wrap around a spinning shaft or fan.

• DON'T smoke when working around gasoline, cleaning solvent or other flammable material.

• DON'T smoke when working around the battery. When the battery is being charged, it gives off explosive hydrogen gas.

• DON'T use gasoline to wash your hands; there are excellent soaps available. Gasoline may contain lead, and lead can enter the body through a cut, accumulating in the body until you are very ill. Gasoline also removes all the natural oils from the skin so that bone dry hands will suck up oil and grease.

• DON'T service the air conditioning system unless you are equipped with the necessary tools and training. The refrigerant, R-12, is extremely cold and when exposed to the air, will instantly freeze any surface it comes in contact with, including your eyes. Although the refrigerant is normally non-toxic, R-12 becomes a deadly poisonous gas in the presence of an open flame. One good whiff of the vapors from burning refrigerant can be fatal.

History

Toyo Kogyo Co., Ltd., Mazda's parent company, began manufacturing cork products over fifty years ago. In 1927, the company expanded into the machinery and tool business; by 1930 they were producing motorcycles under the Mazda name.

The first three-wheeled trucks appeared in 1931. The first automobile prototype was built in 1940, but it was not until twenty years later that a production car, the Mazda R-360 coupe, was sold.

In the interim, Toyo Kogyo produced light three-wheeled trucks, reaching, in 1957, a peak annual production of 20,000 units.

Shortly after automobile production began in 1960, Toyo Kogyo obtained a license from NSU-Wankel to develop and produce the rotary engine.

The first prototype car powered by this engine was the Mazda 110S, a two passenger sports car which appeared in August 1963. The car did not go on sale until it had been thoroughly tested. The first units were offered for sale in May 1967. The 110S was soon joined by a smaller, cheaper model which put the rotary engine within the reach of the average consumer. Various models powered by the rotary engine were produced for the Japanese home market.

In 1970, Toyo Kogyo began importing Mazda cars (both rotary engined and conventional) into the United States. At first they were available only in the Pacific Northwest, but they have rapidly expanded their market to include almost all of the U.S.

Led by the success of the unique rotary engine powered automobile, Mazda has rapidly climbed into the "top ten" in imported car sales in this country.

DEVELOPMENT OF THE ROTARY ENGINE

Toyo Kogyo was the first auto manufacturer to apply rotary engine technology to successful, mass produced automobiles. This required an unusual degree of courage, but that wasn't enough. The development engineers had to apply a tremendous amount of creative energy to create an engine that would not only perform well, but would be easy to manufacture. This required a greatly accelerated research and development effort

almost unequalled in the annals of mass production autodom. Toyo Kogyo engineers had to produce, in five years, an engine which would compete with a seventy year old cousin. While it can hardly be said that the modern Wankel is as highly refined as the piston engine, the engineers did, indeed, produce a viable competitor, in spite of having only one fourteenth the development time. Having learned about the Wankel engine at a German rotary engine symposium, the Toyo Kogyo engineering staff reached the point, in early 1960, where they could visualize the Wankel rotary in practical automotive use. An initial visit to the NSU works in Germany occurred in October of that year (NSU was the initial Wankel engine developer).

The first prototype engine was built using drawings supplied by NSU. The engine had serious vibration, wear, and oil consumption problems.

And so, the first year was spent studying the fundamentsls: basic behavior and problems of the rotary engine. Then, two years were spent actually mapping these characteristics in detail. Early in 1962, an engine was mounted in a test car to get more practical experience in just how a successful engine should be designed. For example, this work led very soon to a decision to develop a twin rotor engine in order to overcome vibration occurring at low speeds when the throttle was closed. The fourth and fifth years were spent studying means of further improving in-vehicle performance, the basics having been resolved by the end of the third year.

Toyo Kogyo committed itself in dramatic fashion to rotary engine development. Initial investment in a rotary test center was $750,000. Yet in 1964, a completely new test laboratory was built incorporating both basic and endurance test cells. Perhaps even more indicative of the devotion to unqualified success in design of the rotary was the decision to apply the same severe standards applied to the 70 year old piston to the fledgling rotary engine.

The development project's most exciting aspect was the coverage of absolutely new ground. The design of the apex seals on the rotary engine is difficult because of an inherent lubrication problem. The rings in a piston engine separate a combustion space from a lubricated area. Thus, the rings can be coated with oil supplied from below. The apex seal separated two adjacent combustion spaces, and thus can be lubricated only via the mixing of a trace of oil with the fuel. The ultimate solution of the problem of minimizing the amount of oil consumed by the engine was the use of a self lubricating material on the seals. This material (initially carbon impregnated with aluminum) had to be compatible with the working surface on the inside of the rotor housing. That coating, in turn, had to be of a material which could be readily plated onto the aluminum housing.

Other problems that had to be solved included achieving a port design which gave high speed performance with stable combustion at low speeds and stabilizing rotor housing temperatures. The latter problem required finning the water passages selectively so that varying amounts of heat were carried from various portions of the housing, even though housing temperature was almost uniform.

SERIAL NUMBER IDENTIFICATION

Vehicle

All except RX-2

The serial number on these models is on a plate located on the driver's side windshield pillar and is visible through the glass.

A vehicle identification number (VIN) plate, bearing the serial number and other data, is attached to the cowl.

RX-2

The VIN plate location and composition of the serial number for RX-2 models is the same as for RX-3 models, above. The only difference between models is the location of the RX-2 serial number plate which is attached to the upper left-hand side of the instrument panel. The plate is visible through the windshield.

Engine

On piston engines, the serial number and type code is located on a plate mounted at the right/front/top of the block, except on the GLC type TC engine, which has the plate on the front of the cylinder head.

On rotary engines, the type code is located either on the front or rear housing, on the top surface of the housing, left side. The serial number is stamped on the intermediate

housing on engines built before March, 1972, and on the front housing after that date.

ROUTINE MAINTENANCE

Air Cleaner

The air cleaner uses a disposable paper element. The filter can be cleaned by blowing low pressure compressed air through it from the inside out. The air filter should be replaced at least every two years or 24,000–30,000 miles. If the car is driven in a dry, dusty atmosphere clean or replace the air filter twice as often.

PCV Valve

TESTING
RX-2 1971–73
RX-3 1972–73

1. Check and clean (or replace) the air filter element, as necessary.
2. Connect a vacuum gauge into the PCV valve vacuum line with a T-fitting.
3. Start the engine. Increase engine speed to 2,500–3,000 rpm. The vacuum gauge should read 2.4 in. Hg. If the reading on the vacuum gauge is incorrect, replace the valve.

Engine Identification

Year	Model	Code	Engine Displacement Cu In. (CC)
1971–76	RX-2, RX-3	12A	70/1156
1974–78	RX-3SP, RX-4	13B	80/1308
	808	—	96.8/1586
1976–78	808	—	77.6/1272
1977–78	Cosmo	13B	80/1308
	GLC	TC	77.6/1272
1979–80	GLC	—	86.4/1415
	626	—	120.2/1970
1981–82	GLC	—	90.9/1490
	626	—	120.2/1970

Model Identification

Year	Model	Body Type	Code
1971	RX-2	Sedan	—
	RX-2	Coupe	—
1972	RX-3	Sedan	S124 BL
	RX-3	Coupe	M124 B6
	RX-3	Wagon	S124 WL
	RX-2	Sedan	SN1224A-S
	RX-2	Coupe	SN122A-SCA
1973	RX-3	Sedan	2RS 124A
	RX-3	Coupe	2RS 124A
	RX-3	Wagon	2RS 124W
	RX-2	Sedan	2RS 122A
	RX-2	Coupe	2RS 122A
1974	808	Coupe/Sedan	SN3A
	808	Wagon	SN3AV
	RX-2	Coupe/Sedan	S122A
	RX-3	Coupe/Sedan	S124A
	RX-3	Wagon	S124W
	RX-4	Hardtop/Sedan	LA23S
	RX-4	Wagon	LA23W
1975	RX-2	Coupe/Sedan	SS122A
	RX-3	Coupe	SS124A
	RX-3	Wagon	SS124W
	RX-4	Hardtop/Sedan	SLA23S
	RX-4	Wagon	SLA23W
	808	Coupe	SSN3A
	808	Wagon	SSN3AV
1976	RX-3	Coupe	S124A
	RX-3	Wagon	S124W
	RX-4	Hardtop/Sedan	LA23S
	RX-4	Wagon	LA23W
	Cosmo	—	CD23C
	808	1600 Coupe/Sedan	SN3A
	808	1600 Wagon	SN3AV
	808	1300 Coupe/Sedan	STC
	808	1300 Wagon	STCV
1977–78	RX-3	Coupe/Sedan	S124A
	RX-4	Hardtop/Sedan	LA23S
	RX-4	Wagon	LA23W
	Cosmo	—	CD23C
	808	1600 Coupe/Sedan	SN3A
	808	1600 Wagon	SN3AV
	808	1300 Coupe/Sedan	STC
	808	1300 Wagon	STCV
	GLC	Hatchback 3 dr.	FA4TS-3,3P,3T
1978	GLC	Hatchback 5 dr.	FA4TS-5,5P,5T
1979–80	GLC	Hatchback 3 dr.	FA4US-3,3T,3P
	GLC	Hatchback 5 dr.	FA4US-5,5T,5P
	GLC	Station Wagon	FA4UV-5,5T,5P

Year	Model	Body Type	Code
1979–80	626	Sedan	CB2MS-P,T
	626	Hardtop	CB2MS-CP,CT
1981–82	GLC	Station Wagon	BB62,63,64
	GLC	Sedan	BD221
	GLC	Hatchback 3 dr.	BD231
	GLC	Hatchback 5 dr.	BD241
1981–82	626	Sedan	GB211
	626	Hardtop	GB411

Replacing the air cleaner element

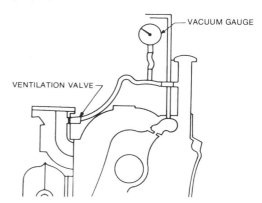

Using a vacuum gauge to test the operation of the PCV valve

1974 All Rotary Engines

1. With the engine idling and fully warmed up, tightly crimp the hose leading to the PCV valve in order to stop airflow to the valve. The engine should slow down slightly. If there is no change in rpm, replace the valve.

1975 RX-3, RX-4

1. With the engine idling and fully warmed up, disconnect the PCV hose at the oil filler pipe.

2. Squeeze the hose coming from the evaporative cannister (at the "X" in the illustration). Engine speed must drop.

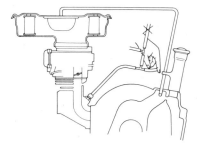

Checking PCV valve—1975 RX-4

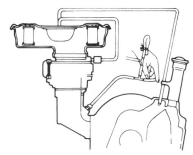

Checking PCV valve—1977–78 Cosmo

3. Close off the open end of the PCV hose. Engine should continue to run.

4. If engine speed does not change when closing off the hose coming from the evaporative cannister, or if the engine stalls when closing off the end of the disconnected hose, replace the valve.

1975–78 808, 1977–82 GLC, 1979–82 626

1. With the engine idling and fully warmed up, unclamp and remove the hose leading to the PCV valve at the valve.

2. Place your finger over the open end of valve to stop airflow. There should be an audible "click" and the engine speed should drop noticeably. Otherwise, replace the valve.

1976–77 RX-3, RX-4, Cosmo

1. On the Cosmo, pinch off the hose which is teed into the PCV line as shown in the illustration.

2. With the engine idling and fully warmed up, disconnect the PCV hose at the oil filler pipe.

3. Close off the end of the PCV hose with your finger. The engine speed should drop.

4. If the engine speed stays the same, replace the PCV valve.

REPLACEMENT

RX-2—1971–73
RX-3—1972–73

1. Remove the air cleaner and its hoses by unfastening the mounting bolts and wing nut inside it.

2. Remove the fuel return valve and the distributor vacuum lines from the carburetor.

3. Disconnect the hose from the PCV valve.

4. Unfasten the PCV valve and withdraw it from the carburetor.

NOTE: *It is difficult to gain access to the*

PCV valve, to get a wrench on it. It is advisable to either purchase the special factory wrench (49 2113 005) or to use a flexible-drive socket wrench.

Installation of a new valve is performed in the reverse order of removal.

All Cars 1974–82

1. On 808, 626, and GLC, remove the air cleaner.

2. Remove the clip fastening the hose to the outer end of the PCV valve, and pull the hose off the valve.

3. Using factory tool 49-1011-120 or a deep well, flex-drive socket on rotary engine cars unscrew the valve from the intake manifold. On GLC, make sure to catch the washer that is located under the valve.

4. Installation is the reverse of removal.

Charcoal Filter

The charcoal filter for the evaporative emission control (EEC) system is located in the top of the air cleaner case on 1972–73 models. It should be checked every 12,000 miles and replaced as necessary.

1. Unfasten the clips and remove the top of the air cleaner case.

Charcoal filter replacement—1972–73 models

2. Inspect the air cleaner element and clean it as necessary.

3. Check the condition of the charcoal filter. If it is saturated with fuel and oil, replace it by unscrewing it from the case. Screw the replacement filter in place.

4. At this time always check the condition of the PCV valve as outlined above.

Charcoal Canister

1971 RX-2

The 1971 RX-2 models use a charcoal canister which is separated from the air cleaner. Check it every 12,000 miles, and replace it as necessary:

1. Be sure that the air cleaner element is not clogged and that the PCV valve is working.

2. Attach a vacuum gauge on the inlet of the PCV valve that connects with the canister, by means of a T-fitting.

3. Increase the engine speed to 2,500–3,000 rpm. The vacuum gauge should read 2.4 in Hg.

If the vacuum gauge reading is not within specification, the PCV valve is functioning properly, and the hoses are not leaking, replace the charcoal canister.

Rotary Engines—1974–78

All rotary engine powered cars except the 1978 RX-4 Wagon built in these years use a charcoal canister which is located in the top of the air cleaner. The entire assembly is replaced if the canister becomes saturated with fuel or oil, or if there are signs that the carbon absorbent material is leaking out. Every 22,000 miles/22 months on 1974–75 vehicles, and every 25,000 miles and 24 months on later vehicles, inspect the unit and then run the vacuum test described below. If the vacuum test is failed, this also indicates that the canister is saturated and should be replaced. On the 1978 RX-4 Wagon, the unit cannot be visually inspected. The vacuum test is the sole basis for replacing the canister on that model.

1. Disconnect the hose leading from the fuel tank, and install a vacuum gauge into the Tee in the oil filler-to-PCV valve line.

2. Operate the engine at 2,500 rpm. The vacuum produced should be 2.4 in. Hg. If vacuum is too high, replace the canister.

Piston Engines—1974–82

All piston engine cars use a canister located separate from the air cleaner in the engine

Charcoal canister 1979 and later model 626

compartment. It should be checked for leakage of either fuel or activated carbon particles, and lightly tapped to check for looseness of internal parts. If there is leakage or an internal rattle, replace the unit by loosening the hose clamps, pulling off the hoses, unbolting the unit, and reversing this procedure to install a replacement. The inspection should be carried out every 22,000 miles/22 months on 1974–75 cars, and every 25,000 miles/24 months on later cars.

Battery

Loose, dirty, or corroded battery terminals are a major cause of "no-start". Every 3 months or so, remove the battery terminals and clean them, giving them a light coating of petroleum jelly when you are finished. This will help to retard corrosion.

Check the battery cables for signs of wear

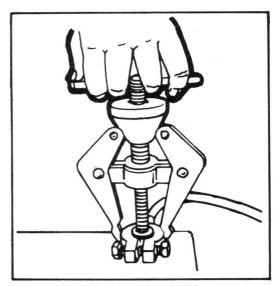
Battery cable removal tool

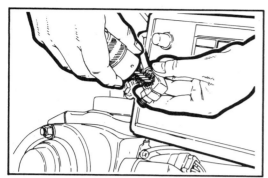

Battery cable connector cleaning tool

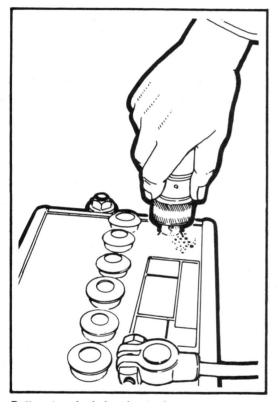

Battery terminal cleaning tool

or chafing and replace any cable or terminal that looks marginal. Battery terminals can be easily cleaned and inexpensive terminal cleaning tools are an excellent investment that will pay for themselves many times over. They can usually be purchased from any well-equipped auto store or parts department. Side terminal batteries require a different tool to clean the threads in the battery case. The accumulated white powder and corrosion can be cleaned from the top of the battery with an old toothbrush and a solution of baking soda and water.

Unless you have a "maintenance-free" battery, check the electrolyte level (see Battery under Fluid Level Checks in this chapter) and check the specific gravity of each cell. Be sure that the vent holes in each cell cap are not blocked by grease or dirt. The vent holes allow hydrogen gas, formed by the chemical reaction in the battery, to escape safely.

REPLACEMENT BATTERIES

The cold power rating of a battery measures battery starting performance and provides an approximate relationship between battery size and engine size. The cold power rating of a replacement battery should match or exceed your engine size in cubic inches.

Belts

TENSION CHECKING AND ADJUSTING

The belts should be inspected and adjusted at 2,000 miles and then every 4,000 miles. First, inspect the belts for cracks. These usually develop on the inner surface and run back into the backing or outer surface of the belt. Check also for glazing—a completely smooth appearance which indicates slippage. A belt that is in good shape will have a slightly grainy appearance like cloth. Replace belts that show cracks or glazing.

Check belt tension. Applying pressure with your thumb at the mid-point between two pulleys, the belt should stretch or deflect about ½ inch. Especially if the belt is loose enough to have actual play, it will require adjustment and should be carefully inspected for signs of slippage.

To adjust belts, first locate the mounting bolt on the air pump or alternator (each has its own belt and adjusts to permit that belt to be tensioned right). This bolt attaches the unit to the engine and has a nut on the back end of it. Put a wrench on either end and loosen the bolt until there is practically no tension on it. Then, loosen the adjusting bolt, which is located on the opposite side of the unit and which passes through a slot. Pull the alternator or air pump away from the engine and tighten the adjusting bolt just enough to hold the unit while you check tension. If possible, it is advisable to avoid the use of a prybar of any kind on the air pump because this can damage the housing. Repeat the adjustment procedure until the belt deflects the right amount, and then fully tighten adjustment and mounting bolts. Avoid too much belt tension or overtightening bolts. A new belt should be tensioned

HOW TO SPOT WORN V-BELTS

V-Belts are vital to efficient engine operation—they drive the fan, water pump and other accessories. They require little maintenance (occasional tightening) but they will not last forever. Slipping or failure of the V-belt will lead to overheating. If your V-belt looks like any of these, it should be replaced.

Cracking or weathering

This belt has deep cracks, which cause it to flex. Too much flexing leads to heat build-up and premature failure. These cracks can be caused by using the belt on a pulley that is too small. Notched belts are available for small diameter pulleys.

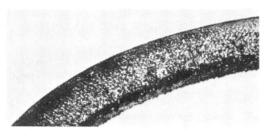

Softening (grease and oil)

Oil and grease on a belt can cause the belt's rubber compounds to soften and separate from the reinforcing cords that hold the belt together. The belt will first slip, then finally fail altogether.

Glazing

Glazing is caused by a belt that is slipping. A slipping belt can cause a run-down battery, erratic power steering, overheating or poor accessory performance. The more the belt slips, the more glazing will be built up on the surface of the belt. The more the belt is glazed, the more it will slip. If the glazing is light, tighten the belt.

Worn cover

The cover of this belt is worn off and is peeling away. The reinforcing cords will begin to wear and the belt will shortly break. When the belt cover wears in spots or has a rough jagged appearance, check the pulley grooves for roughness.

Separation

This belt is on the verge of breaking and leaving you stranded. The layers of the belt are separating and the reinforcing cords are exposed. It's just a matter of time before it breaks completely.

HOW TO SPOT BAD HOSES

Both the upper and lower radiator hoses are called upon to perform difficult jobs in an inhospitable environment. They are subject to nearly 18 psi at under hood temperatures often over 280°F., and must circulate nearly 7500 gallons of coolant an hour—3 good reasons to have good hoses.

A good test for any hose is to feel it for soft or spongy spots. Frequently these will appear as swollen areas of the hose. The most likely cause is oil soaking. This hose could burst at any time, when hot or under pressure.

Swollen hose

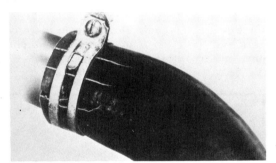

Cracked hoses can usually be seen but feel the hoses to be sure they have not hardened; a prime cause of cracking. This hose has cracked down to the reinforcing cords and could split at any of the cracks.

Cracked hose

Weakened clamps frequently are the cause of hose and cooling system failure. The connection between the pipe and hose has deteriorated enough to allow coolant to escape when the engine is hot.

Frayed hose end (due to weak clamp)

Debris, rust and scale in the cooling system can cause the inside of a hose to weaken. This can usually be felt on the outside of the hose as soft or thinner areas.

Debris in cooling system

just slightly more (about .4 inch deflection) and checked after several hundred miles of operation to make sure tension is still adequate (tension is lost very rapidly until the belt is broken in).

Hose Replacement

1. Remove the radiator cap.

2. Drain the coolant from the radiator by opening the radiator petcock, if so equipped, or by disconnecting the lower radiator hose. If your car is equipped with a petcock it might be a good idea to squirt a little penetrating oil on it first.

3. To replace the bottom hose, drain all the coolant from the radiator. If only the top hose is to be replaced, drain just enough fluid to bring the level down below the level of the top hose. If the fluid is over a year old discard it.

4. Most hoses are attached with screw type hose clamps. If the old clamps are badly rusted or damaged in any way it is always best to replace them with new ones.

5. When installing the new hose slide the clamps over each end of the hose then slide the hose over the hose connections. Position each clamp about ¼″ from the end of the hose and tighten.

CAUTION: *Do not over tighten at the radiator connections as it is very easy to crush the metal.*

6. Close the petcock and refill with the old coolant if it is less than a year old or with a new mixture of 50/50, coolant/water.

7. Start the engine and idle it for 15 minutes with the radiator cap off and check for leaks. Add coolant if necessary and install the radiator cap.

Cooling System

At least once every 2 years, the engine cooling system should be inspected, flushed, and refilled with fresh coolant. If the coolant is left in the system too long, it loses its ability to prevent rust and corrosion. If the coolant has too much water, it won't protect against freezing.

The pressure cap should be looked at for signs of age or deterioration. Fan belt and other drive belts should be inspected and adjusted to the proper tension. (See checking belt tension).

Hose clamps should be tightened, and soft or cracked hoses replaced. Damp spots, or accumulations of rust or dye near hoses,

water pump or other areas, indicate possible leakage, which must be corrected before filling the system with fresh coolant.

CHECK THE RADIATOR CAP

While you are checking the coolant level, check the radiator cap for a worn or cracked gasket. If the cap doesn't seal properly, fluid will be lost and the engine will overheat.

Worn caps should be replaced with a new one.

CLEAN RADIATOR OF DEBRIS

Periodically clean any debris—leaves, paper, insects, etc.—from the radiator fins. Pick the large pieces off by hand. The smaller pieces can be washed away with water pressure from a hose.

Carefully straighten any bent radiator fins with a pair of needle nose pliers. Be careful—the fins are very soft. Don't wiggle the fins back and forth too much. Straighten them once and try not to move them again.

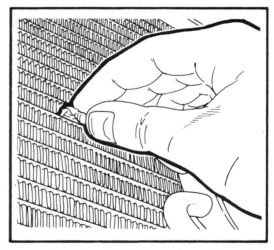

Remove insects and debris from the radiator fins

DRAIN AND REFILL THE COOLING SYSTEM

Completely draining and refilling the cooling system at least every two years will remove accumulated rust, scale and other deposits. Coolant in late model cars is a 50-50 mixture of ethylene glycol and water for year round use. Use a good quality antifreeze with water pump lubricants, rust inhibitors and other corrosion inhibitors along with acid neutralizers.

1. Drain the existing antifreeze and coolant. Open the radiator and engine drain pet-

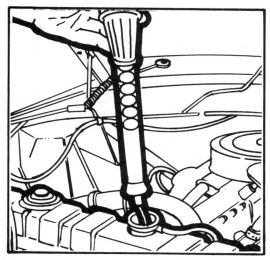

Testing antifreeze effectiveness

cocks, or disconnect the bottom radiator hose, at the radiator outlet.

NOTE: *Before opening the radiator petcock, spray it with some penetrating lubricant.*

2. Close the petcock or re-connect the lower hose and fill the system with water.

3. Add a can of quality radiator flush.

4. Idle the engine until the upper radiator hose gets hot.

5. Drain the system again.

6. Repeat this process until the drained water is clear and free of scale.

7. Close all petcocks and connect all the hoses.

8. If equipped with a coolant recovery system, flush the reservoir with water and leave empty.

9. Determine the capacity of your cooling system (see capacities specifications). Add a 50/50 mix of quality antifreeze (ethylene glycol) and water to provide the desired protection.

10. Run the engine to operating temperature.

11. Stop the engine and check the coolant level.

12. Check the level of protection with an anti-freeze tester, replace the cap and check for leaks.

Air Conditioning

AIR-CONDITIONING SAFETY PRECAUTIONS

There are two particular hazards associated with air conditioning systems and they both relate to the refrigerant gas.

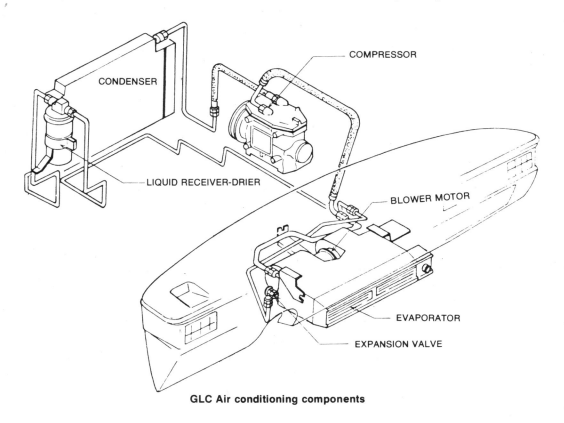

GLC Air conditioning components

First, the refrigerant gas is an extremely cold substance. When exposed to air, it will instantly freeze any surface it comes in contact with, including your eyes. The other hazard relates to fire. Although normally non-toxic, refrigerant gas becomes highly poisonous in the presence of an open flame. One good whiff of the vapor formed by burning refrigerant can be fatal. Keep all forms of fire (including cigarettes) well clear of the air-conditioning system.

Any repair work to an air conditioning system should be left to a professional. Do not, under any circumstances, attempt to loosen or tighten any fittings or perform any work other than that outlined here.

CHECKING FOR OIL LEAKS

Refrigerant leaks show up as oily areas on the various components because the compressor oil is transported around the entire system along with the refrigerant. Look for oily spots on all the hoses and lines, and especially on the hose and tubing connections. If there are oily deposits, the system may have a leak, and you should have it checked by a qualified repairman.

NOTE: *A small area of oil on the front of the compressor is normal and no cause for alarm.*

CHECK THE COMPRESSOR BELT

Refer to the section in this chapter on "Drive Belts."

KEEP THE CONDENSER CLEAR

Periodically inspect the front of the condenser for bent fins or foreign material (dirt, bugs, leaves, etc.) If any cooling fins are bent, straighten them carefully with needle-nosed pliers. You can remove any debris with a stiff bristle brush or hose.

OPERATE THE A/C SYSTEM PERIODICALLY

A lot of A/C problems can be avoided by simply running the air conditioner at least once a week, regardless of the season. Simply let the system run for at least 5 minutes a week (even in the winter), and you'll keep the internal parts lubricated as well as preventing the hoses from hardening.

REFRIGERANT LEVEL CHECK

There are two ways to check refrigerant level, depending on how your model is equipped.

Sight glass location—Model 626 shown

With Sight Glass

The first order of business when checking the sight glass is to find the sight glass. It will either be in the head of the receiver/drier, or in one of the metal lines leading from the top of the receiver/drier. Once you've found it wipe it clean and proceed as follows:

1. With the engine and the air conditioning system running, look for the flow of refrigerant through the sight glass. If the air conditioner is working properly, you'll be able to see a continuous flow of clear refrigerant through the sight glass, with perhaps an occasional bubble at very high temperatures.

2. Cycle the air conditioner on and off to make sure what you are seeing is clear refrigerant. Since the refrigerant is clear, it is possible to mistake a completely discharged system for one that is fully charged. Turn the system off and watch the sight glass. If there is refrigerant in the system, you'll see bubbles during the off cycle. If you observe no bubbles when the system is running, and the air flow from the unit in the car is delivering cold air, everything is OK.

3. If you observe bubbles in the sight glass while the system is operating, the system is low on refrigerant. Have it checked by a professional.

4. Oil streaks in the sight glass are an indication of trouble. Most of the time, if you see oil in the sight glass, it will appear as a series of streaks, although occasionally it may be a solid stream of oil. In either case, it means that part of the charge has been lost.

Without Sight Glass

On vehicles that are not equipped with sight glasses, it is necessary to feel the temperature difference in the inlet and outlet lines at the receiver/drier to gauge the refrigerant level. Use the following procedure:

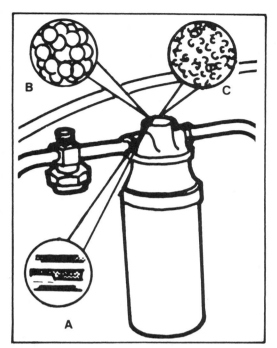

Oil streaks (A), constant bubbles (B) or foam (C) indicate there is not enough refrigerant in the system. Occasional bubbles during initial operation is normal. A clear sight glass indicates a proper charge of refrigerant or no refrigerant at all, which can be determined by the presence of cold air at the outlets in the car. If the glass is clouded with a milky white substance have the receiver/drier checked professionally

1. Locate the receiver/drier. It will generally be up front near the condenser. It is shaped like a small fire extinguisher and will always have two lines connected to it. One line goes to the expansion valve and the other goes to the condenser.

2. With the engine and the air conditioner running, hold a line in each hand and gauge their relative temperatures. If they are both the same approximate temperature, the system is correctly charged.

3. If the line from the expansion valve to the receiver/drier is a lot colder than the line from the receiver/drier to the condenser, then the system is overcharged. It should be noted that this is an extremely rare condition.

4. If the line that leads from the receiver/drier to the condenser is a lot colder than the other line, the system is undercharged.

5. If the system is undercharged or overcharged, have it checked by a professional air conditioning mechanic.

Windshield Wipers

Intense heat from the sun, snow and ice, road oils and the chemicals used in windshield washer solvents combine to deteriorate the rubber wiper refills. The refills should be replaced about twice a year or whenever the blades begin to streak or chatter.

WIPER REFILL REPLACEMENT

Normally, if the wipers are not cleaning the windshield properly, only the refill has to be replaced. The blade and arm usually require replacement only in the event of damage. It is not necessary (except on new Tridon refills) to remove the arm or the blade to replace the regill (rubber part), though you may have to position the arm higher on the glass. You can do this turning the ignition switch on and operating the wipers. When they are positioned where they are accessible, turn the ignition switch off.

There are several types of refills and your vehicle could have any kind, since aftermarket blades and arms may not use exactly the same type refill as the original equipment.

Most Trico styles use a release button that is pushed down to allow the refill to slide out of the yoke jaws. The new refill slides in and locks in place. Some Trico refills are removed by locating where the metal backing strip or the refill is wider. Insert a small screwdriver blade between the frame and metal backing strip. Press down to release the refill from the retaining tab.

The Anco style is unlocked at one end by squeezing 2 metal tabs, and the refill is slid out of the frame jaws. When the new refill is installed, the tabs will click into place, locking the refill.

The polycarbonate type is held in place by a locking lever that is pushed downward out of the groove in the arm to free the refill. When the new refill is installed, it will lock in place automatically.

The Tridon refill has a plastic backing strip with a notch about an inch from the end. Hold the blade (frame) on a hard surface so that the frame is tightly bowed. Grip the tip of the backing strip and pull up while twisting counterclockwise. The backing strip will snap out of the retaining tab. Do this for the remaining tabs until the refill is free of the arm. The length of these refills is molded into the end and they should be replaced with identical types.

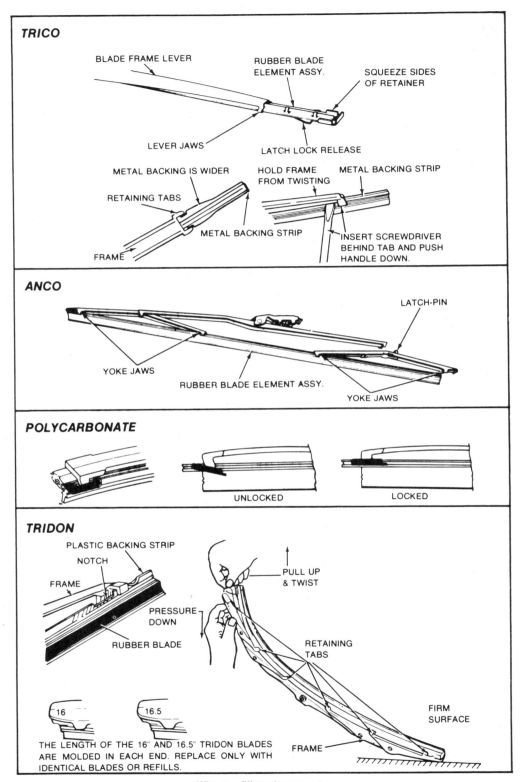

TRICO

BLADE FRAME LEVER

RUBBER BLADE ELEMENT ASSY.

SQUEEZE SIDES OF RETAINER

LEVER JAWS

LATCH LOCK RELEASE

METAL BACKING IS WIDER

HOLD FRAME FROM TWISTING

METAL BACKING STRIP

RETAINING TABS

METAL BACKING STRIP

FRAME

INSERT SCREWDRIVER BEHIND TAB AND PUSH HANDLE DOWN.

ANCO

LATCH-PIN

YOKE JAWS

RUBBER BLADE ELEMENT ASSY.

YOKE JAWS

POLYCARBONATE

UNLOCKED

LOCKED

TRIDON

PLASTIC BACKING STRIP

NOTCH

FRAME

PULL UP & TWIST

PRESSURE DOWN

RUBBER BLADE

RETAINING TABS

16

16.5

FIRM SURFACE

THE LENGTH OF THE 16" AND 16.5" TRIDON BLADES ARE MOLDED IN EACH END. REPLACE ONLY WITH IDENTICAL BLADES OR REFILLS.

FRAME

Wiper refill replacement

No matter which type of refill you use, be sure that all of the frame claws engage the refill. Before operating the wipers, be sure that no part of the metal frame is contacting the windshield.

Fluid Level Checks
ENGINE OIL

Under normal operating contions, the Mazda rotary engine burns about one quart of oil every 1,000–1,400 miles to lubricate the rotor tip seals. Therefore, the oil level should be checked frequently.

Check the oil level, on all models, with the engine cold or as the last procedure at a fuel stop, to allow the oil time to drain back into the sump, (10 minutes).

The dipstick is located on the driver's side of the engine, next to the oil filler tube. It has either a red or green handle, depending upon the engine/transmission combination. Add the proper viscosity oil, as necessary, through the filler tube.

Change the oil at the intervals specified in the "Lubrication" section.

TRANSMISSION/TRANSAXLE
Manual Transmission

Check the transmission oil every 4,000–7,500 miles:

1. Park the car on a level surface.
2. Working from underneath the car, unfasten the filler (upper) plug.
3. Use your finger to check the oil level; it should be up to the bottom of the oil fill hole. Add SAE 90 EP if the temperature is above 0°F or SAE 80 EP if it is below.
4. Replace the filler plug.

CAUTION: *Be careful if you are working under the car when it is warm; the exhaust system (which is protected by wire mesh) gets extremely hot.*

Change the oil as specified under "Lubrication," below.

Manual Transaxle

NOTE: *Checking and replenishing the manual transaxle fluid is accomplished by removing the speedometer driven gear from the top of the transaxle case.*

1. Park the vehicle on level ground.
2. Remove the speedometer cable from the gear assembly by unscrewing the knurled fitting.

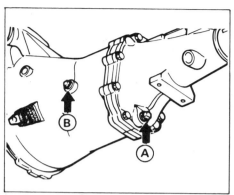

Manual transmission drain plug "A" and filler plug "B". Typical of rear wheel drive cars

Hot and Cold fluid level markings on the automatic transmission dipstick

3. Unbolt and remove the speedometer driven gear.
4. The oil level should cover the gear and gear shoulder.
5. Add gear oil, if necessary, through the speedometer gear mounting hole.
6. Reinstall the speedometer driven gear. Reconnect the speedometer cable.

Automatic

The automatic transmission dipstick is located (rear wheel drive) behind the engine, next to the hood latch, or on the left front side of the engine (front wheel drive). Check fluid level every 4,000–7,500 miles.

There are two levels indicated in the dipstick. One is labeled COLD and the other HOT.

To check the fluid level when the transmission is cold, i.e. when the car has been sitting overnight, proceed as follows:

1. Start the engine and allow it to warm up for at least two minutes.
2. Remove the dipstick and wipe it with a clean cloth.
3. Reinsert the dipstick.
4. Withdraw the dipstick again and note the level on the COLD side. Add Type "F" fluid as necessary. The difference between "L" and "F" is about 0.43 quart.

The procedure for checking the fluid level when the transmission is hot is the same as above, except that the reading should be taken on the HOT side of the dipstick.

Capacities

Year	Model	Engine Displacement Cu In. (cc)	Engine Crankcase (qts) With Filter	Without Filter	Transmission (pts) Manual 4-spd	5-spd	Automatic	Drive Axle (pts)	Gasoline Tank (gals)	Cooling System (qts)
1971–72	RX-2	70/1146	5.8	4.65	3.2	—	11.62	2.6	16.9	8.45
1972–73	RX-3	70/1146	5.5	4.45	3.2	—	11.62	3.0	15.6 ①	8.45
1973	RX-2	70/1146	—	4.8	3.2	—	11.6	2.6	16.9	8.5
1974	RX-2	70/1146	—	4.8	3.6	—	13.2	2.6	16.9	9.9
	808	96.8/1586	—	3.8	3.2	—	13.2 ④	2.6	11.7 ②	7.9
1974–75	RX-3	70/1146	—	4.8	3.6	—	13.2	3.0	15.6 ①	10.2
	RX-4	80/1308	6.8	5.3	3.6	—	13.2	2.8	17.2 ③	10.0
1975	808	96.8/1586	—	3.8	3.2	—	11.6	3.0	11.9 ②	7.9
1976	RX-3	70/1146	5.5	4.4	3.6	4.6	13.2	3.0	15.6 ⑥	9.8
	RX-4	80/1308	—	3.8	3.2	4.6	13.2	2.8	16.9 ⑤	10.0
1976–78	808 (1600)	96.8/1586	3.8	—	3.2	3.6	11.6	3.0	11.9 ②	7.9
	808 (1300)	77.6/1272	3.2	—	2.8	—	—	2.2	11.7 ②	5.8
1977–78	RX-4, RX-3SP	80/1308	6.8	5.3	3.6	4.6	13.2	2.8	16.9 ⑤	10.0
	Cosmo	80/1308	6.8	5.3	—	3.6	13.2	2.6	17.2	10.0
	GLC	77.6/1272 ⑦	—	3.2	2.8	3.6	12.0	1.6	10.0	6.8
1979–80	GLC	86.4/1415	—	3.2	2.8	3.6	12.0	2.2	10.6 ⑧	5.8
	626	120.2/1970	—	4.1	3.0	3.6	13.2	2.6	14.5	7.9
1981–82	GLC	90.9/1490	⑨	⑨	6.8	6.8	12.0	—	11.1	5.8
	GLC Wagon	90.9/1490	⑨	⑨	2.8	3.6	12.0	1.6	11.9	5.8
	626	120.2/1970	⑩	⑩	—	3.6	13.2	2.6	14.5	7.9

① Station wagon—14.3
② Station wagon—10.4
③ Station wagon—17.7
④ 11.6—1975
⑤ Station wagon—17.4
⑥ Station wagon— 14.3
⑦ Also available with 60.1 cu in./985 cc engine—same oil capacity
⑧ Station wagon—11.9
⑨ Add 3.2 qts. run engine, shut off and check level; add to full mark on stick
⑩ Add 3.8 qts. run engine, shut off and check level; add to full mark on stick

BRAKE OR CLUTCH MASTER CYLINDER

Check the level in the brake and clutch master cylinder reservoirs regularly—at least every 4,000–7,500 miles.

NOTE: *If the brake warning light comes on when the brake pedal is depressed and the parking brake if off, stop the vehicle immediately and check the fluid level in the brake master cylinder reservoir.*

Both reservoirs should be kept ⅔ full. Add MUSS 116, DOT-3 or DOT-4, as necessary. Always add fluid *slowly*, so that bubbles do not form in the hydraulic lines.

CAUTION: *Be careful not to spill brake fluid on painted surfaces, as it is an excellent paint remover.*

Bleed the brake system if bubbles are apparent. See the "Brakes" chapter.

Change the brake fluid in both the brake and clutch hydraulic systems yearly on all 1971–73 vehicles. On later models change the fluid every 30,000 miles or 30 months, however, if your vehicle is driven in a mountainous region continuously or when the brakes are used extensively during continuous hard driving or when the climate is extremely humid all of the time the fluid should be changed annually.

COOLANT

The coolant level should be checked regularly. Serious engine damage can occur if the engine overheats.

CAUTION: *Check the coolant level when the engine is cold; serious injury could result from escaping steam or hot water if checked when hot.*

If your car is equipped with an electric cooling fan make sure that the ignition switch is off. The cooling fan will automatically operate if the ignition switch is on and the engine coolant temperature is high or if the wiring connector on the thermostat housing is disconnected.

Models Equipped With Expansion Tank

1. Depress the button on the thermal expansion tank safety cap if there is one. Allow all of the pressure trapped in the system to escape.

CAUTION: *The radiator is not equipped with a safety cap. Do not remove it before removing the expansion tank cap, or when the engine is hot.*

2. Remove the expansion tank cap. The expansion tank should be ½ full on 1971–73 cars, and ⅓ full on later cars.

3. If it is not, carefully remove the cap from the radiator. The radiator should be full.

4. Add a 50-50 solution of ethylene-glycol coolant and clean water. If there was no coolant in the expansion tank, fill the radiator all the way, and then replace the radiator cap. Then, fill the expansion tank to the specified level, and replace the expansion tank cap.

NOTE: *Do not use cooling system additives; they may not mix properly with the coolant.*

Models Without Expansion Tank

1. Push safety button or turn the radiator cap to the first release point and allow any pressure in the system to escape.

2. Remove the radiator cap. The coolant level (when cold) should be just above the gauge or about one inch below the filler neck.

3. Add enough 50/50 water and ethylene glycol anti-freeze (for aluminum engine parts) to maintain the correct level. Do not overfill. If frequent refills are necessary, check the cooling system for leaks.

REAR AXLE

Check the lubricant level in the rear axle every 4,000 miles on cars built in 1975 and earlier years. Periodic checking of the lubricant level is required at 6,000–7,500 mile intervals on 1976 and later cars. However, if you notice oil seepage from the rear axle, or a change in the sound of the axle, it is a good idea to check the oil level and replenish it if necessary. Any significant leaks should be repaired as soon as possible.

1. Park the car on a level surface and set the parking brake.

2. Remove the filler (upper) plug from the differential.

3. Check the oil level; it should be up to the bottom of the filler hole. Add lubricant, as necessary. Use the following:

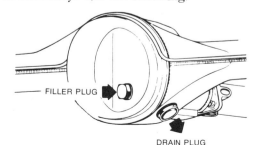

FILLER PLUG

DRAIN PLUG

Rear axle drain and filler plug locations

- Above 0'F—SAE 90 HP
- Below 0°F—SAE 80 HP

The oil in the differential should be changed as specified in the Maintenance Interval Chart or in the lubrication section under fluid changes.

STEERING GEAR

Except Rack and Pinion

Check the lubricant in the steering gear at 6,000 miles and then every 4,000 miles on 1971–75 cars. Cars from 1976–78 require checking after 2,000 miles, and then every 6,000 miles. Cars from 1979–82 every 15,000 miles.

1. Remove the filler plug.
2. The oil level should be up to the bottom of the fill hole.
3. Add SAE EP 90 gear lubricant, as required.
4. Replace the filler plug.

BATTERY

Check the fluid level in the battery at least once a month and more frequently in cold weather. Check the battery first, if the ammeter indicates an abnormality.

The elctrolyte level should be 0.4–0.8 in. above the plates in each cell. Add distilled water, if necessary. Do not overfill.

CAUTION: *Do not smoke around the battery while the caps are removed. Escaping fumes could cause an explosion.*

SUB-ZERO STARTER ASSIST

Check the anti-freeze level in the sub-zero starter assist reservoir every two weeks in cold weather (if so equipped).

The reservoir is located directly beneath the brake master cylinder and is plainly marked.

Replenish the antifreeze in it with a 90% ethylene glycol and 10% water solution, as necessary.

Tires

INFLATION PRESSURE

Tire inflation is the most ignored item of auto maintenance. Gasoline mileage can drop as much as .8% for every 1 pound per square inch (psi) of under inflation.

Two items should be a permanent fixture in every glove compartment; a tire pressure gauge and a tread depth gauge. Check the tire air pressure (including the spare) regularly with a pocket type gauge. Kicking the tires won't tell you a thing, and the gauge on the service station air hose is notoriously inaccurate.

The tire pressures recommended for your car are usually found on the glove box door, the left side door jamb or in the owners manual. Ideally, inflation pressure should be checked when the tires are cool. When the air becomes heated it expands and the pressure increases. Every 10° rise (or drop) in temperature means a difference of 1 psi, which also explains why the tire appears to lose air on a very cold night. When it is impossible to check the tires "cold", allow for pressure build-up due to heat. If the "hot" pressure exceeds the "cold" pressure by more than 15 psi, reduce your speed, load or both. Otherwise internal heat is created in the tire. When the heat approaches the temperature at which the tire was cured, during manufacture, the tread can separate from the body.

CAUTION: *Never counteract excessive pressure build-up by bleeding off air pressure (letting some air out). This will only further raise the tire operating temperature.*

Before starting a long trip with lots of luggage, you can add about 2–4 psi to the tires to make them run cooler, but never exceed the maximum inflation pressure on the side of the tire.

TREAD DEPTH

All tires made since 1968, have 8 built-in tread wear indicator bars that show up as ½" wide smooth bands across the tire when 1/16" of tread remains. The appearance of tread wear indicators means that the tires should be replaced. In fact, many states have laws

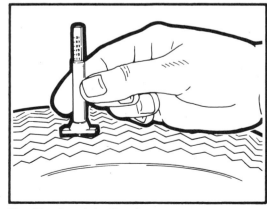

Checking tread depth using a gauge

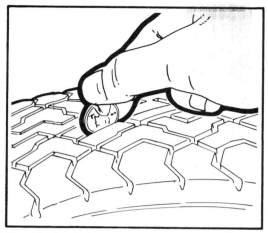

Checking tread depth using a Lincoln head penny

prohibiting the use of tires with less than $1/16''$ tread.

You can check your own tread depth with an inexpensive gauge or by using a Lincoln head penny. Slip the Lincoln penny into several tread grooves. If you can see the top of Lincoln's head in 2 adjacent grooves, the tires have less than $1/16''$ tread left and should be replaced. You can measure snow tires in the same manner by using the "tails" side of the Lincoln penny. If you can see the top of the Lincoln memorial, it's time to replace the snow tires.

TIRE ROTATION

Tire wear can be equalized by switching the position of the tires about every 6000 miles.

Including a conventional spare in the rotation pattern can give up to 20% more tire life.

CAUTION: *Do not include the new "Space-Saver®" or temporary spare tires in the rotation pattern.*

There are certain exceptions to tire rotation, however. Studded snow tires should not be rotated, and radials should be kept on the same side of the car (maintain the same direction of rotation). The belts on radial tires get set in a pattern. If the direction of rotation is reversed, it can cause rough ride and vibration.

NOTE: *When radials or studded snows are taken off the car, mark them, so you can maintain the same direction of rotation.*

TIRE STORAGE

Store the tires at proper inflation pressures if they are mounted on wheels. All tires should be kept in a cool, dry place. If they are stored in the garage or basement, do not let them stand on a concete floor; set them on strips of wood.

Fuel Filter

The fuel filter on all 1971–77 coupes and sedans except the GLC is located behind the trim panel in the luggage compartment. On wagons, except the GLC it is inside the left/rear quarter panel. On the GLC models it is located on the right side of the engine compartment. On the model 626 and late model GLC wagons, it is located under the

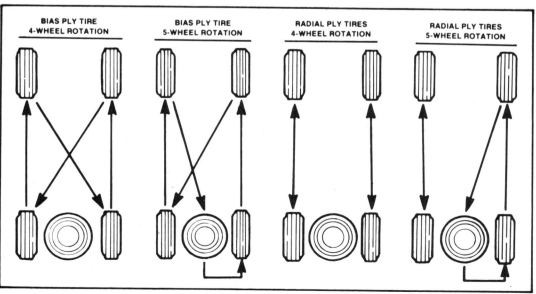

Tire rotation

floor in front of the fuel tank. Replace every 8,000 miles on 1971–73 vehicles, at 10,000 miles and every 12,000 miles thereafter on 1974–75 vehicles, and every 12,000 miles on 1976 and later vehicles. The filter should be replaced immediately if dirty fuel has gotten into the gas tank. To replace the filter, proceed in the following manner:

1. Remove the trim panel by unfastening its two securing screws. On these models so equipped.

2. Detach both hoses from the filter.

3. Unfasten the filter from its mounting bracket.

Install the new filter in the reverse order of removal.

LUBRICATION

Oil and Fuel Recommendations

All Mazda engines require the use of high quality engines oils labeled "SE." Do not use oil that is unlabeled or which has been reprocessed. Oil viscosity should be chosen on the basis of the range of temperatures you expect during the time the oil will be in the crankcase. You need not change oil because of a short period of unusual temperatures. Temperature ranges and related viscosities are as follows:

- 0–85°F.   SAE 10W-30
- 0–100°F.   SAE 10W-40
- 0–120°F.   SAE 10W-50
- 10–100°F.   SAE 20W-40
- 10–120°F.   SAE 20W-50
- Below 0°F. SAE 5W-20
              SAE 5W-30

All engines with catalytic converters require the use of unleaded fuel exclusively, as leaded fuel will amost immediately destroy the effectiveness of the catalytic converter. Unleaded fuel minimizes the accumulation of carbon deposits and corrosion in the engine and exhaust system, thus offering further benefit.

Mazda piston engines not equipped with a catalytic converter require a regular or low lead (.45–2.45 grams of lead per gallon) fuel, rated 91 octane by the Research method.

Mazda rotary engines not equipped with a catalytic converter should be run *only* on low lead or no lead fuel (0–.5 grams of lead per gallon) of 91 Research octane. The use of regular or premium fuels that are fully leaded may cause engine damage.

Oil Changes
ENGINE

On 1971–75 cars, the oil should be changed every 4,000 miles or four months, whichever comes first. On 1971–73 cars, the initial change (with filter) should be performed at 600 miles, while on 1974–75 vehicles, this should be done at 2,000 miles/two months. On 1976 cars, the initial change (with filter) comes at 2,000 miles/two months, and changes are made every 6,000 miles/six months after that. On 1979 and later models change the oil every 7,500 miles. The car should be driven about 10 miles in order to get the oil hot immediately before draining it.

1. Park the car on a level surface. Set the parking brake and block the wheels.

2. Working from underneath the car, remove the oil plug. Have a large, flat container of sufficient capacity ready to catch the oil.

CAUTION: *Be careful not to come into contact with any components of the exhaust system. Serious burns could result.*

3. Allow all of the oil to drain into the container. Wipe off and then replace the drain plug, using care not to damage its threads.

4. Working from the top, add the proper viscosity oil through the filler tube which is on the driver's side of the engine. See the charts above for proper amounts and viscosity.

5. Start the engine without applying throttle and idle it until a few seconds after the oil light goes out. Then, stop the engine and allow it to sit for five minutes or so until all oil has drained back into the crankcase. Then, check the oil level with the dipstick and replenish as necessary.

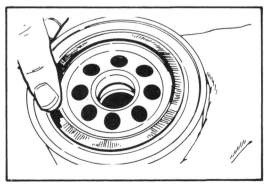

Lubricate the gasket on the new filter with clean engine oil. A dry gasket may not make a good seal and will allow the the filter to leak

Maintenance Interval Chart

Operation	1971–73	1974–75	1976	1977	1978	1979–80	1981–82
	(Number of months or miles in thousands whichever comes first)						
ENGINE							
Air cleaner element—Replace	24	24	24	24	24	30	30
Clean	2	2	2	2	2	2	2
Charcoal canister filter—Check or replace	—	22	25	25	25	25	25
Fuel filter—Replace	8	12	12	12	12	7.5	7.5
Drive belts—Inspect	4	4	4	4	4	15	15
Replace	②	②	②	②	②	②	②
Battery check	4	4	4	4	2	7.5	7.5
Cooling system—Check	4	4	6	6	6	7.5	7.5
Drain and refill	24	24	24	24	24	30	30
Engine oil—Level check	①	①	①	①	①	①	①
Change oil	4	4	6	6	6	7.5	7.5
Change filter	4	4	6	6	6	7.5	7.5
Spark plug replacement	12	12	12.5	12.5	12.5	30	30
Ignition points and condenser	12	12	12.5	12.5	12.5	—	—
Timing adjustment	12	12	12.5	12.5	12.5	30	30
PCV Valve replacement	12	12	12.5	12.5	12.5	30	30
Valve clearance adjustment	—	12.5	12.5	12.5	12.5	15	15
Intake, exhaust and cylinder head bolts adjustment	—	③	③	③	③	③	③
CHASSIS							
Manual transmission fluid level —Check	4	4	4	4	4	7.5	7.5
	④	⑤	⑥	⑥	⑥	⑦	⑦
Automatic transmission fluid level check	4	4	4	4	4	7.5	7.5
Front wheel bearings—Lubricate	32	30	24	24	24	30	30
Rear axle lubricant check	③	⑤	⑥	⑥	⑥	⑦	⑦
Steering gear lubricant check	⑧	⑧	⑨	⑨	⑨	⑩	⑩
Tire pressures	⑪	⑪	⑪	⑪	⑪	⑪	⑪
Tire rotation	4	4	4	4	4	7.5	7.5
Ball joint lubrication	32	24	24	24	—	—	—

Maintenance Interval Chart (cont.)

Operation	1971–73	1974–75	1976	1977	1978	1979–80	1981–82
	(Number of months or miles in thousands whichever comes first)						
ENGINE Front steering linkage inspection	24	24	24	24	30	30	30
Master cylinder fluid	⑫	⑫	⑫	⑫	⑫	⑫	⑫
Brake system inspection (lining)	4	4	4	4	4	7.5	7.5

① Each fuel stop
② Replace as necessary
③ 1st 15,000 miles then every 30,000 miles
④ 1st 600 miles then every 12,000 miles
⑤ 1st 2,000 miles then every 12,000 miles
⑥ 1st 2,000 miles then every 25,000 miles
⑦ 1st 7,500 miles then every 30,000 miles
⑧ 1st 6,000 miles then every 4,000 miles
⑨ 1st 2,000 miles then every 6,000 miles
⑩ 1st 2,000 miles then every 15,000 miles
⑪ once every month
⑫ Check level at least every 4,000 miles. It is recommended by the manufacturer that the fluid be changed every year (1971–73), every 30,000 miles (1979 and later).

Oil Filter Changes

The oil filter should be changed every oil change.

The oil filter is easily accessible; it is located on top of the engine, next to the oil filler tube on rotary engine cars. On cars with piston engines, it is located on the right side or rear of the engine.

1. Use a band-wrench to remove the oil filter.

NOTE: *Place a container underneath the filter as it will leak oil.*

2. Clean the oil filter mounting flange with a cloth.

3. Lubricate the oil filter O-ring and the mounting surface of the filter with engine oil.

4. Install the filter, being careful not to damage the O-ring.

5. Tighten the filter by hand. Do not use the band-wrench to tighten it.

6. If the filter is being replaced in conjunction with an oil change, be sure the crankcase is refilled with the specified total oil capacity (see the "Capacities" chart). If, for some reason, only the filter is being replaced, add the difference between the crankcase capacity "with filter" and "without filter". If this figure is not available, add ½ quart.

7. Start the engine without using the throttle (if possible) and allow it to idle until the oil light goes out. Then, with the engine still running, check for leaks around the base of the filter. Stop the engine, allow it to sit for 5–10 minutes until all the oil has drained back into the crankcase, and then check and fill the crankcase according to the dipstick.

TRANSMISSION

The oil should be changed in the manual transmission at 600 miles and then every 12,000 miles or one year on 1971–73 vehicles. On 1974–75 vehicles, transmission oil should be changed at 2,000 miles and then every 12,000 miles or one year. On 1976–78 vehicles, oil is changed at 2,000 miles and then every 24 months/25,000 miles thereafter. On 1979 and later vehicles the oil should be changed at 7,500 miles then at 30,000 mile intervals. Proceed in the following manner:

1. Start with the engine warm. Park on a level surface. Set the parking brake and block the wheels.

2. Remove the drain (lower) plug from underneath the car.

CAUTION: *Be careful not to come in contact with any components of the exhaust system. Severe burns could result.*

3. Allow the oil to drain into a large, flat container of sufficient capacity.

4. Wipe the magnetic drain plug with a clean cloth, until it is free of particles.

5. Install the drain plug.

6. Remove the filler plug and add one of the following lubricants, depending upon temperature:
- Above 0°F—SAE EP 90
- Below 0°F—SAE EP 80

7. Fill the transmission to capacity (see "Capacities" chart) until the oil level reaches the bottom of the fill hole.

8. Replace the filler plug.

REAR AXLE

The rear axle oil should be changed at 600 miles and then every 12,000 miles or one year on 1971–73 vehicles. On 1974–75 vehicles, it should be changed at 2,000 miles and then every 12,000 miles or one year. On 1976–78 vehicles, oil is changed at 2,000 miles and then every 24 months/25,000 miles thereafter. On 1979 and later vehicles the oil should be changed at 7,500 miles then at 30,000 mile intervals. Proceed as described below:

1. Park the car on a level surface. Set the parking brake and block the wheels.

2. Remove the drain (lower) plug and allow the oil to run into a container of adequate capacity.

3. Clean and replace the drain plug.

4. Unscrew the filler (upper) plug and add one of the following lubricants, depending upon ambient temperature:
- Above 0°F—SAE HP 90
- Below 0°F—SAE HP 80

5. Fill to capacity until the level reaches the bottom of the filler hole. See the "Capacities" chart, above.

6. Replace the filler plug.

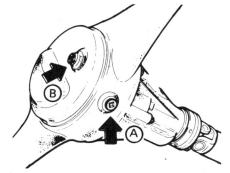

Typical rear axle housing showing drain plug "A" and filler plug "B"

Ball Joint Lubrication

The ball joints should be lubricated: every 32,000 miles or 24 months on 1971–73 cars; on 1974–75 cars, the interval is miles/24

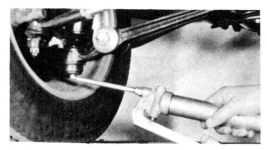

Ball joint lubrication

miles/24 months; on 1976–77 cars (except GLC), the interval is 24,000 miles/24 months; on 1978 cars and all GLC and 626 Models, no lubrication is required. To grease the ball joints, proceed in the following manner:

1. Take the set ring out of the groove on the dust boot. Turn the boot inside out.

2. Remove the plug and install a grease fitting in its place.

3. Use molybdenum disulphide lithium grease, NGLI No. 2, to grease the ball joint. Apply the grease with a grease gun. Drive out the old grease in the dust boot and socket by slowly pumping in new grease.

4. Once the old grease has been completely removed, secure the dust book back in its original position with the set ring.

5. Add grease until the dust boot begins to balloon. Squeeze the boot gently with your fingers until about half of the grease remains in it.

6. Wipe off any excess grease from around the ball joint.

7. Remove the grease fitting and install the plug.

NOTE: *Replace the dust boot if it is worn or damaged. See Chapter Eight.*

Wheel Bearings

The wheel bearings should be repacked with lithium grease, NGLI No. 1, every 32,000 miles or 24 months on 1971–73 cars; 30,000 miles or 24 months on 1974–75 cars; 24,000 miles or 24 months on 1976–78 cars; 30,000 miles or 30 months on 1979 and later cars. For the correct repacking procedure, see Chapter Nine.

PUSHING AND TOWING

CAUTION: *Do not attempt to push start a vehicle equipped with a catalytic converter unless absolutely necessary. Damage to the*

JUMP STARTING A DEAD BATTERY

The chemical reaction in a battery produces explosive hydrogen gas. This is the safe way to jump start a dead battery, reducing the chances of an accidental spark that could cause an explosion.

Jump Starting Precautions

1. Be sure both batteries are of the same voltage.
2. Be sure both batteries are of the same polarity (have the same grounded terminal).
3. Be sure the vehicles are not touching.
4. Be sure the vent cap holes are not obstructed.
5. Do not smoke or allow sparks around the battery.
6. In cold weather, check for frozen electrolyte in the battery.
7. Do not allow electrolyte on your skin or clothing.
8. Be sure the electrolyte is not frozen.

Jump Starting Procedure

1. Determine voltages of the two batteries; they must be the same.
2. Bring the starting vehicle close (they must not touch) so that the batteries can be reached easily.
3. Turn off all accessories and both engines. Put both cars in Neutral or Park and set the handbrake.
4. Cover the cell caps with a rag—do not cover terminals.
5. If the terminals on the run-down battery are heavily corroded, clean them.
6. Identify the positive and negative posts on both batteries and connect the cables in the order shown.
7. Start the engine of the starting vehicle and run it at fast idle. Try to start the car with the dead battery. Crank it for no more than 10 seconds at a time and let it cool off for 20 seconds in between tries.
8. If it doesn't start in 3 tries, there is something else wrong.
9. Disconnect the cables in the reverse order.
10. Replace the cell covers and dispose of the rags.

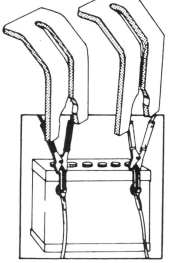

Side terminal batteries occasionally pose a problem when connecting jumper cables. There frequently isn't enough room to clamp the cables without touching sheet metal. Side terminal adaptors are available to alleviate this problem and should be removed after use.

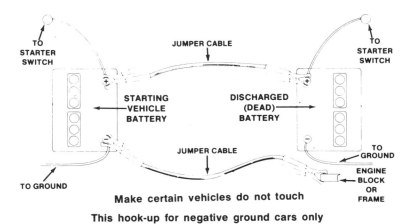

Make certain vehicles do not touch

This hook-up for negative ground cars only

converter will occur caused by raw gas flowing into the converter and then burning at an abnormally high temperature which adversely affects the catalyst.

Mazda models equipped with manual transmissions are started in the same manner as any other car:

1. Place the car in High gear and turn the ignition switch to ON.

CAUTION: *Be sure that the steering column is unlocked.*

2. Have someone push the car until a speed of 10 mph is reached.

CAUTION: *Never attempt to start the automobile by towing it. Once the automobile starts, it could crash into the rear of the tow vehicle.*

3. Slowly let the clutch pedal out until the engine catches. As soon as it has caught, depress the clutch pedal and select First gear.

Mazda models equipped with automatic transmissions cannot be push-started. Not only will pushing the car with the automatic transmission in gear fail to start the car, but it could also cause serious damage to the transmission.

The following precautions should be observed when towing the behicle:

1. Always place the transmission in Neutral and release the parking brake.

2. 1971–72 and 1979–82 models equipped with automatic transmissions may be towed with the transmission in Neutral, but only for short distances at speeds below 20 mph. If the car must be towed beyond this distance or if the transmission is inoperative, tow the car with its drive wheels off the ground or the driveshaft disconnected at the differential end. 1973–78 models with automatic transmissions cannot be towed unless the driveshaft is disconnected or the rear wheels are off the ground.

3. If the rear axle is defective, the car must be towed with the rear wheels off the ground.

4. Always be sure that the steering column is unlocked before towing the car with its front wheels on the ground.

CAUTION: *The steering column lock is not designed to hold the wheels straight while the automobile is being towed. Therefore, if the car is being towed with its front end down, and the wheel cannot be unlocked, place a dolly under the front wheels.*

JACKING

Specific instructions for the use of the jack and the proper jacking points are found on stickers which are attached to the jack and located in the luggage compartment.

There are, however, some general precautions to observe when jacking the automobile:

1. Never climb underneath the car when it is supported only by the jack. Always use jackstands as an additional means of support.

2. Always keep the car on level ground when jacking it. Otherwise, the car may roll or fall off the jack.

3. When raising the *front* of the car, set the parking brake and block the rear wheels.

4. When raising the *rear* of the car, securely block the front wheels.

Tune-Up

TUNE-UP PROCEDURES

Spark Plugs

A typical spark plug consists of a metal shell surrounding a ceramic insulator. A metal electrode extends downward through the center of the insulator and protrudes a small distance. Located at the end of the plug and attached to the side of the outer metal shell is the side electrode. The side electrode bends in at a 90° angle so that its tip is even with, and parallel to, the tip of the center electrode. The distance between these two electrodes (measured in thousandths of an inch) is called the spark plug gap. The spark plug in no way produces a spark but merely provides a gap across which the current can arc. The coil produces anywhere from 20,000 to 40,000 volts which travels to the distributor where it is distributed through the spark plug wires to the spark plugs. The current passes along the center electrode and jumps the gap to the side electrode, and, in so doing, ignites the air/fuel mixture in the combustion chamber.

SPARK PLUG HEAT RANGE

Spark plug heat range is the ability of the plug to dissipate heat. The longer the insulator (or the farther it extends into the engine), the hotter the plug will operate; the shorter the insulator the cooler it will operate. A plug that absorbs little heat and remains too cool will quickly accumulate deposits of oil and carbon since it is not hot enough to burn them off. This leads to plug fouling and consequently to misfiring. A plug that absorbs too much heat will have no deposits, but, due to the excessive heat, the electrodes will burn away quickly and in some instances, preignition may result. Preignition takes place when plug tips get so hot that they glow sufficiently to ignite the fuel/air mixture before the actual spark occurs. This early ignition will usually cause a pinging during low speeds and heavy loads.

The general rule of thumb for choosing the

Checking the electrode gap—note dual electrodes

correct heat range when picking a spark plug is: if most of your driving is long distance, high speed travel, use a colder plug; if most of your driving is stop and go, use a hotter plug. Original equipment plugs are compromise plugs, but most people never have occasion to change their plugs from the factory-recommended heat range.

NOTE: *The spark plugs listed in this chapter are especially designed and built for use in the Mazda rotary engine. They are available from the manufacturers listed.*

CAUTION: *The spark plugs listed are specified for use by Toyo Kogyo Co., Ltd. Use only these plugs, do not substitute a different type of plug.*

REPLACING SPARK PLUGS

A set of spark plugs usually requires replacement after about 10,000 miles on cars with conventional ignition systems and after about 20,000 to 30,000 miles on cars with electronic ignition, depending on your style of driving. In normal operation, plug gap increases about 0.001 in. for every 1,000–2,500 miles. As the gap increases, the plug's voltage requirement also increases. It requires a greater voltage to jump the wider gap and about two to three times as much voltage to fire a plug at high speeds than at idle.

When you're removing spark plugs, you should work on one at a time. Don't start by removing the plug wires all at once, because unless you number them, they may become mixed up. Take a minute before you begin and number the wires with tape. The best location for numbering is near where the wires come out of the cap.

NOTE: *On rotary engines both the distributor and the engine housing are marked to aid in identification of the spark plug and distributor connections. However, to avoid confusion, it is easier to remove one plug at a time.*

1. Twist the spark plug boot and remove the boot and wire from the plug. Do not pull on the wire itself as this will ruin the wire.

2. If possible, use a brush or rag to clean the area around the spark plug. Make sure that all the dirt is removed so that none will enter the cylinder after the plug is removed.

3. Remove the spark plug using the proper size socket. Turn the socket counterclockwise to remove the plug. Be sure to hold the socket straight on the plug to avoid

breaking the plug, or rounding off the hex on the plug.

4. Once the plug is out, check it against the plugs shown in this section to determine engine condition. This is crucial since plug readings are vital signs of engine condition.

5. Use a round wire feeler gauge to check the plug gap. The correct size gauge should pass through the electrode gap with a slight drag. If you're in doubt, try one size smaller and one larger. The smaller gauge should go through easily while the larger one shouldn't go through at all. If the gap is incorrect, use the electrode bending tool on the end of the gauge to adjust the gap. When adjusting the gap, always bend the side electrode. The center electrode is non-adjustable.

6. Squirt a drop of penetrating oil on the threads of the new plug and install it. Don't oil the threads too heavily. Turn the plug in clockwise by hand until is it snug.

7. When the plug is finger tight, tighten it with a wrench. If you don't have a torque wrench, tighten the plug as shown.

8. Install the plug boot firmly over the plug. Proceed to the next plug.

CHECKING AND REPLACING SPARK PLUG CABLES

Visually inspect the spark plug cables for burns, cuts, or breaks in the insulation. Check the spark plug boots and the nipples on the distributor cap and coil. Replace any damaged wiring. If no physical damage is obvious, the wires can be checked with an ohmmeter for excessive resistance. (See the tune-up and troubleshooting section).

When installing a new set of spark plug cables, replace the cables one at a time so there will be no mixup. Start by replacing the longest cable first. Install the boot firmly over the spark plug. Route the wire exactly the same as the original. Insert the nipple firmly into the tower on the distributor cap. Repeat the process for each cable.

Breaker Points

Mazda rotary engines, through 1973, are equipped with two distributors. One distributor operates the leading set of plugs and the other the trailing set. When checking or replacing the points, remember to serve both distributors. 1974 and later rotary engines have a single distributor with either dual or triple point sets.

Most piston engines are equipped with

Spark Plug Usage—Rotary Engine

Year	Manu.	Part Number Hot	Part Number Standard	Part Number Cold
1974–75	NGK	—	B7-EM or B-7EJ	B8-EM or B-8EJ
	Nippondenso	—	W-22EA	W-25EA
	Champion	—	N-80B	N-78B
1976	NGK	—	B-7ET	B-8ET
	Nippondenso	—	W-22EB	W-25EB
	Champion	—	N-278B	N-280B
1977–78	NGK	BJET	B-7ET	B-8ET
	Nippondenso	W-20EB	W-22EB	W-25EB
	Champion	N-278B	N-280B	N-282B

Tune-Up Specifications—Rotary Engine

When analyzing compression test results, look for uniformity among cylinders, rather than specific pressures.

Year	Engine Displace. (cu in.)	Spark Plugs Type	Spark Plugs Gap (in.)	Distributors Point Dwell (deg)	Distributors Point Gap (in.)	Ignition Timing (deg) Leading Normal	Ignition Timing (deg) Leading Retarded	Ignition Timing (deg) Trailing Normal	Idle Speed (rpm) MT	Idle Speed (rpm) AT
1971–73	70	N80B ①	.031–.035	58 ± 3	.018	TDC	10A	10A	900	750 ②
1974	70	N80B ①	.024–.028	58 ± 3	.018	5A	—	15A	900	750 ②
1975	70, 80	N80B ①	.024–.028	58 ± 3	.018	TDC	20A	15A	800–850	750–800 ②
1976	70	RN-278B ①	.039–.043	58 ± 3 ③	.018	TDC	15A	20A	700–750	700–750 ②
1976	80	RN-278B ①	.039–.043	58 ± 3 ③	.018	5A	20A	20A	700–750	700–750 ②
1977	70, 80	RN-278B ①	.039–.043	58 ± 3	.018	5A	—	25A	725–775	725–775 ②
1978	70 ④	RN-278B ①	.039–.043	58 ± 3	.018	0	—	20A	725–775	725–775 ②
1978	80	RN-278B ①	.039–.043	58 ± 3	.018	5A	—	25A	725–775	725–775 ②

① See "Spark Plug Usage" chart above
② Transmission in Drive
③ Leading retarded dwell angle is 53 ± 3
④ Used in RX-35P only
TDC—Top dead center
A—After top dead center
B—Before top dead center

MT—Manual transmission
AT—Automatic transmission
deg—degrees

NOTE: *The underhood specifications sticker often reflects tune-up specification changes made in production. Sticker figures must be used if they disagree with those in this chart.*

Tune-Up Specifications—Piston Engine

When analyzing compression test results, look for uniformity among cylinders, rather than specific pressures.

Year	Engine Displace (cu in.)	Spark Plugs Type	Gap (in.)	Distributor Point Dwell (deg)	Point Gap (in.)	Ignition Timing (deg) MT	AT	Intake Valve Opens (deg)	Fuel Pump Pressure (psi)	Idle Speed (rpm)	Valve Clear (in.) In	Ex
1974	96.8	BP-6ES	.031	49–55	.020	5B	4B ①	13	2.8–3.6	800–850 ②	.012	.012
1975	96.8	BP-6ES	.031	49–55	.020	5B	5B	13	2.8–3.6	800–850 ②	.012	.012
1976–78	96.8	BP-6ES	.031	49–55	.020	5B ③	5B ③	13	2.8–3.6	800–850 ④	.012	.012
	77.6	BP-6ES	.031	49–55	.020	7B ⑤	11B	13	2.84–3.84	700–750 ⑥	.010	.012
1979	86.4	BP-5ES BPR-5ES	.031	49–55	.020	7B ⑦	7B ⑧	15	2.8–3.8	700–750 ⑩⑪	.010	.012
	120.2	BP-5ES BPR-5ES	.031	—	—	8B	8B	10	2.8–3.6	650–700	.012	.012
1980	86.4	BP-5ES BPR-5ES	.031	—	—	5B	5B	15	2.8–3.8	700–750 ⑩	.010	.012
	120.2	BP-5ES BPR-5ES	.031	—	—	5B ⑨	5B ⑨	10	2.8–3.6	650–700	.012	.012
1981–82	90.9	BP-5ES BPR-5ES	.031	—	—	8B	8B	15	2.8–3.8	⑫	.010	.012
	120.2	BP-5ES BPR-5ES	.031	—	—	⑬	⑬	10	2.8–3.6	⑭	.012	.012

① Refers to distributor in retard position—8B in advance position
② In Neutral
③ California—8B
④ Automatic—650–700 in Drive
⑤ California—11B
⑥ Automatic—600–650 in Drive
⑦ California—5B
   Canada—8A
⑧ California—5B
   Canada—8B
⑨ Canada—8B
⑩ Federal:
   Automatic—600–650
⑪ Canada:
   Manual—800–850
   Automatic—700–750
⑫ Manual transmission 800–850 rpm
   Auto transmission 750 rpm in "Drive"
⑬ 1981; USA-5B
      Canada-8B
   1982; All-8B
⑭ Manual transmission 650–700 rpm
   Auto transmission 650 rpm in "Drive"

NOTE: *The underhood specifications sticker often reflects tune-up specification changes made in production. Sticker figures must be used if they disagree with those in this chart.*

breaker point distributors through 1979. GLC models from 1977 use a breakerless distributor except those built for California and Canada 1977–78 and the 1979 Canadian models. The 1979 and later 626 are equipped with breakerless ignition. On the breakerless distributors there are no points or condenser to replace.

ADJUSTMENT

On 1971–75 cars, the ignition points should be checked and gapped every 4,000 miles or four months and replaced every 12,000 miles or 12 months. On 1976 and later cars, the ignition points should be checked and gapped every 12,500 miles or one year.

To check and adjust the point gap, proceed in the following manner:

1. Unfasten the clips and remove the cap from one of the distributors. Leave the leads attached to the cap.

2. Remove the rotor from the distributor.

3. Clean the points with a point file, if they are pitted. If they are badly pitted or burned, replace them as detailed in the section below.

4. Rotate the engine by using a remote starter switch, or have someone inside the car operate the ignition key until the rubbing block is at the top of the cam.

5. Check the point gap with a feeler gauge. The gap should be .018 in. on rotary engine cars, and .020 in. on piston engine cars.

6. Adjust the gap with a screwdriver. Loosen the lockscrew just enough to permit the stationary contact to be moved, using the screwdriver as a lever in the slot provided. The lockscrew must be tight enough, however, to hold the stationary contact in one place while you adjust it. Use a clean, flat type feeler gauge to check the gap, and make sure the blade is sliding straight through the gap—not at an angle. Recheck the gap after tightening the lockscrew to make sure the

Point gap adjustment

gap has not changed, and readjust it as necessary.

7. Make sure the cam follower is properly lubricated. If necessary, wipe dirty grease off the follower and cam and apply high melting point contact point lube to the leading edge of the cam follower and cam.

8. If necessary, repeat these steps for the other set of points. Replace rotor and cap.

9. If there are two distributors, repeat the procedure for the other one. Check the dwell angle as described in the appropriate procedures below.

NOTE: *On 1975–76 rotary engine distributors, the leading-retard points are located on a plate mounted in the top of the distributor. To gain access to the other two sets of points holes are provided in the upper contact plate base or can be reached by disconnecting the wiring and removing the mounting screws for the plate and the connecting screw for the exterior adjusting lever, and removing the plate.*

REMOVAL AND INSTALLATION

New points should be installed on 1971–75 cars at 12,000 miles or 12 months. On 1976 and later models, no set interval for replacement is recommended. Clean, gap, and inspect the points every 12,000 miles and replace them if they're excessively pitted or worn.

1. Perform steps 1 and 2 of the adjustment procedure.

2. Unplug the blade type electrical connector from the contact set.

3. Remove the two mounting screws, noting the location of any condenser lead wires, and remove the contact set.

4. Install the new set of points, any condenser lead wires, and the screws, tightening the screws just enough to hold the contact set in place.

5. Reconnect the blade connector. Then, adjust point gap as described in the procedure above.

6. Repeat the procedure for additional contact sets or the other distributor as required.

7. Check and adjust dwell as described in the appropriate procedure below.

Condenser

The condenser should be replaced every time the points are replaced. If the condenser is suspect, the easiest way to check it is by replacing it with a new one. The condenser capacity is 0.27 mfd. To replace the condenser, perform the following steps:

1. Remove the distributor cap. Leave the wires connected. Withdraw the rotor.

2. Loosen the condenser lead retaining screw from inside the distributor and withdraw the clip.

3. Unfasten the condenser retaining screw which is located on the outside of the distributor housing.

NOTE: *The smaller condenser, mounted next to the ignition condenser, is for radio noise suppression. It need only be replaced if a clicking sound is heard over the radio.*

4. Remove the condensr.

Install the new condenser in the reverse order of removal.

Dwell Angle
ROTARY ENGINES
1971–74

Make separate checks of dwell angle for each distributor, in the following manner:

1. Disconnect the vacuum line from the distributor and plug it with a pencil or a golf tee.

2. Connect the dwell meter in accordance with the manufacturer's instructions. The dwell meter must be connected to the coil which fires the leading plugs to test the leading distributor, and to the coil which fires the trailing plugs to test the trailing distributor. Then, to test the leading retard ignition points (used on 1972–73 RX-2 and RX-3), do the following:

a. Disconnect both the Thermosensor connections (see Chapter 4).

b. Unfasten the idle and/or vacuum switch connections.

c. Detach the choke switch connector. The leading retard points can be identified by the fact that their position on the mounting plate can be rotated to adjust ignition timing. The dwell meter must be connected to the leading coil to test them.

3. Run the engine at idle, after it has warmed up.

4. Observe the dwell meter reading. It should be within the range specified in the tune-up chart.

5. If it is not within specifications, adjust the contact point gap as outlined above.

NOTE: *If dwell angle is above the specified amount, the point gap is too small; if it is below, the gap is too large.*

6. If both the dwell angle and the contact point gap cannot be brought to within specifications, check for one or more of the following:

a. Worn distributor cam

b. Worn rubbing block

c. Bent movable contact arm

Replace any of the parts, as necessary.

7. When the dwell angle check is complete, disconnect the meter and reconnect the vacuum line.

1975–76

1. Run the engine until it is warm.

2. Connect the dwell meter in accordance with the manufacturer's instructions. The dwell meter must be connected to the coil which fires the leading plugs to test the leading contact points, and to the coil which fires the trailing plugs to test the trailing contact points.

3. Run the engine at idle speed and observe the meter reading. It should be within the range specified in the tune-up chart.

4. If dwell is not within the specified range, adjust the contact gap as described above. If dwell angle is too high, the point gap is too small; if dwell angle is too low, the point gap is too wide.

5. After setting dwell of leading and trailing contact points, stop the engine and disconnect the connector in the wiring harness which leads to the distributor. Then, run two jumper wires exactly as shown in the illustration. This will cause the *leading* ignition coil to be operated through the leading-retard contact points, and enable you to read the dwell for those contacts. Dwell for this set of contacts is 58 degrees on 1975 models, and 53 degrees on 1976 models.

6. Be sure to recheck dwell after tightening the adjusting screw, because the point gap (and dwell) sometime change when this is done. If dwell cannot be brought to specification, check for a bent contact arm, worn rubbing block, or worn distributor cam or shaft.

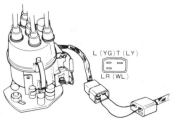

Run jumper wires as shown to set dwell on leading-retard contacts

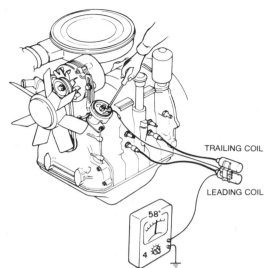

Re-route high tension wiring as shown to set dwell with engine running on 1977–78 rotary cars

1977–78

The method of dwell angle adjustment described here requires that some of the high tension wiring be re-routed to permit the engine to run with the distributor cap and rotor off. While this re-routing process requires some extra time, the dwell adjustment may be made with the engine running, which will save considerable time and make it possible for the dwell to be brought to specification on the first adjustment.

1. Run the engine until it is hot and stop it.
2. Note their locations, and then disconnect high tension leads at leading and trailing ignition coils.
3. Note its location in the distributor cap, and then disconnect the leading spark plug wire for the front rotor at the cap. Connect it to the tower of the leading ignition coil.
4. Note its location in the distributor cap, and then disconnect the leading spark plug wire for the rear rotor at the cap. Connect it to the tower of the trailing ignition coil.
5. Remove the distributor cap and rotor.
6. Check the high tension wiring with the illustration. The plug wires for the top two plugs will still be connected to the rotor, but the bottom two plugs must be wired as shown.
7. Connect the dwell angle tester to the trailing ignition coil. Then, start the engine and read the dwell. If the dwell is incorrect, loosen the set screw for the trailing contact set *only slightly* (or the engine will stop).

Then, very gradually move the stationary contact back and forth until dwell is within the specified range (55–61 degrees).

8. When dwell is correct, tighten the set screw and recheck dwell. Readjust it as necessary.
9. Connect the dwell meter to the leading ignition coil and repeat steps 7 and 8 for the leading contacts.
10. Reconnect all wiring and reinstall the cap and rotor.

PISTON ENGINE CARS

1. Start the engine and run until it is hot and running at normal idle speed.
2. Connect a dwell meter to the ignition coil as described in the manufacturer's instructions. Read the dwell and compare the reading to the specification shown in the "Tune-Up Chart."
3. If dwell is incorrect, stop engine, remove distributor cap and rotor and adjust point gap as described above. If dwell is very far from the specified range, simply set contacts to the specified gap. If dwell is just a little too high, open the contact gap just slightly; if dwell reading is too low, close the point gap just slightly.
4. After contact adjustment, replace cap and rotor, start engine, and read dwell again. Readjust if necessary.

Ignition Timing
ROTARY ENGINES
1971 –73

As in other tune-up procedures involving the ignition system, both distributors must be adjusted separately. Begin with the *leading* distributor when checking the timing:

1. Connect a timing light to the leading distributor spark plug cable which runs to the number one (front) rotor. Check the manufacturer's instructions for specific hook-up details.

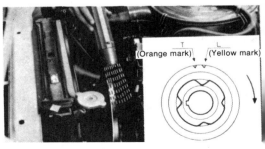

Ignition timing marks

2. Start the engine and run it at idle speed.

3. Loosen the distributor locknuts so that the distributor can be rotated.

4. Aim the timing light at the timing indicator pin in the front housing.

5. The *yellow* mark (0° TDC) should align with the pin on the housing.

6. If it does not, rotate the distributor until it aligns.

7. Tighten the locknuts and recheck the timing.

The ignition timing for the trailing distributor is checked and adjusted in the same manner, except that the timing light lead should be connected to the trailing distributor spark plug cable which runs to the number one rotor.

When the timing light is pointed at the eccentric shaft pulley, the *orange* mark (10° ATDC) should align with the timing pointer.

When the adjustment of normal timing has been completed for both distributors on 1972–73 models, proceed with the next section. On 1972–73 Mazda RX-2 and RX-3 models, the leading distributor is equipped with dual points. One set of points is for normal ignition system operation and the other is used for retarded operation during engine warm-up. To test and adjust retarded timing, proceed in the following manner:

1. Disconnect both of the thermosensor connections (see "Emission Controls," in Chapter Four).

NOTE: *Only manual transmission models have two thermosensors; automatics only have one.*

2. Unfasten the idle and/or vacuum switch connections.

3. Detach the choke switch connector.

4. Connect the timing light to the leading spark plug cable of the number one (front) rotor.

5. Check the timing at idle with the strobe, as above. The pointer should align with the *orange* mark on the timing pulley (10° ATDC ± 2°).

If the retarded timing setting is incorrect, adjust in the following manner:

1. Turn the engine off.

2. Unfasten the clips and remove the distributor cap. Withdraw the rotor.

3. Loosen the adjusting screws and move the point set base to correct the retarded timing setting.

CAUTION: *Do not rotate the distributor housing.*

4. Assemble the distributor and check the retarded timing again with the strobe.

5. When the timing is satisfactory, disconnect the timing light and connect all of the leads which were disconnected for this test.

NOTE: *If the timing cannot be brought to specifications, check the components of the "air flow control system," as detailed in Chapter Four.*

1974

1. Disconnect the vacuum line leading to the distributor and plug it. Connect the timing light to the upper (trailing) plug of the front housing. Warm the engine up and operate it at normal idle speed. This should be checked with a tachometer, which may be read as for a conventional four cylinder engine.

2. Check the trailing timing. If it is not to the specification specified in the tune-up chart, adjust both trailing and leading timing as described in the remaining steps.

3. Loosen the distributor mounting bolt and rotate the distributor to adjust the trailing timing. Tighten bolt and make sure timing has remained correct.

4. Install the timing light on the lower (leading) plug and start the engine. Check the leading timing and estimate how far off specification it is and determine which direction. Then, stop the engine and remove the distributor cap and rotor. Loosen the breaker base setscrews (directly opposite each other near the outside of the distributor body) and turn the base plate the right number of degrees as indicated on the scale inside the distributor. To advance timing, turn the points against the rotation of the rotor. Then, tighten the setscrews.

5. Replace the cap and rotor, recheck timing, and readjust if necessary.

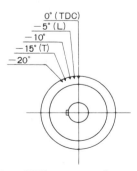

Timing marks—1974 rotary engine

1975

1. Run the engine until it reaches operating temperature. Install a tachometer, and, reading it as for a conventional four cylinder engine, make sure engine is idling at the proper speed. Stop engine and connect a timing light to the leading (lower) spark plug in the front rotor housing. Then, restart the engine.

2. The timing should be 0 degrees—the indicator pin on the front cover should line up with the first notch in the pulley. If timing is not correct, loosen the distributor locknut just slightly and rotate the distributor until the correct reading is obtained. Then, tighten the locknut and recheck.

3. Then, stop the engine and disconnect the distributor wiring connector. Jumper four connectors together as was done to check the dwell for the leading-retard contacts in the appropriate procedure above.

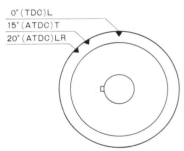

Timing marks—1975 rotary engine

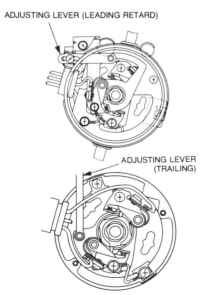

Adjusting points for leading retard and trailing ignition timing—1975–76 rotary engines

Then, start the engine and run it at idle speed and check timing again. The timing should now be 20 degrees After Top Center—the pin should line up with the last notch in the pulley. If not, loosen the screw (see illustration) located on the external adjusting lever for leading-retard timing, and gradually move the lever back and forth until the correct timing is obtained. Then, retighten the screw and recheck timing.

4. Finally, stop the engine and move the timing light over to the trailing (upper) spark plug for the front rotor.

5. Start the engine and check timing again. It should be 15 degrees After Top Center—lined up with the middle mark on the pulley. If necessary, adjust the timing by loosening the lockscrew and moving the trailing contacts adjusting lever. When the timing is correct, tighten the lockscrew and recheck the timing.

6. Stop the engine and remove the timing light.

1976

1. Connect a tachometer to the engine, and run the engine until it is warmed up. Reading the tach as for a conventional four cylinder engine, verify that the engine is operating at its normal idle speed. Then, stop the engine and hook up the timing light to the leading (lower) spark plug for the front rotor.

2. Aim the timing light at the indicator pin on the front cover and check to see if spark occurs when the pin is lined up with the first notch. If not, loosen the distributor locknut, and slowly turn the distributor back and forth until the timing is correct. Then, tighten the distributor locknut and recheck.

3. Stop the engine and move the timing light to the trailing (upper) plug for the front rotor. Start the engine and check to see if the spark occurs at the last notch on the pulley. If not, note the direction timing is off and stop the engine. Remove the cap and rotor. Disconnect the primary wire from the leading retard points located in the top of the distributor, remove the attaching screws for the upper breaker base plate and external adjusting lever, and remove the upper base plate. Then, loosen the lower base plate attaching screws and rotate the plate and trailing contacts. If timing is too far advanced, turn the plate in the direction of distributor shaft rotation; otherwise, turn it the opposite way. Then, completely reassemble the distributor

and recheck trailing timing. Repeat this adjustment until trailing timing is correct.

4. Stop the engine and disconnect the distributor wiring connector. Jumper four of the connectors together as was done to check the dwell for the leading-retard contacts in the appropriate procedure above. Then, start the engine and recheck timing. Timing should be 20 degrees After Top Center again, as in the preceding step on RX-4 engines, or 15 degrees After Top Center (middle notch), on RX-3 engines. If not, loosen the setscrew on the external adjusting lever, and move the lever until the timing if correct. Tighten the setscrew and verify that timing is still correct or readjust as necessary.

1977–78

1. Warm the engine up until it reaches operating temperature. Connect a tachometer. On automatic transmission cars, securely apply the handbrake, block the wheels, and put the car in Drive. Reading the tach as for a conventional four cylinder engine, verify that the engine is running at its normal idle speed. If not, adjust idle speed to specification.

2. Stop the engine and connect a timing light to the leading (lower) spark plug on the front rotor. Then, restart the engine. Aim the timing light at the pin on the front housing cover, and observe timing. If spark does not occur when the pin is lined up with the first mark to pass it, loosen the distributor locknut and rotate the distributor back and forth until

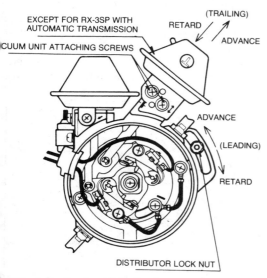

Method of adjusting 1978 distributors with external trailing timing adjustment

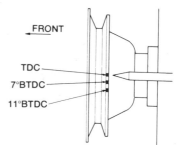

Timing mark—1978–79 GLC

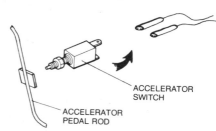

Disconnect connectors shown to check advance timing (1978 GLC)

timing is correct. Tighten the locknut and check that timing is still correct.

3. Stop the engine and switch the timing light to the trailing (upper) spark plug on the front rotor. Start the engine (putting automatic transmission cars in Drive), and check trailing timing. On 1978 cars except RX-3SP with automatic, if timing does not occur at the second notch on the pulley, loosen the vacuum advance attaching screws and pull the unit in or out to correct timing. Then, tighten screws and recheck timing. In 1977 cars, and 1978 RX-3SP with automatic, stop the engine and remove distributor cap and rotor. Then, slightly loosen the set screws which fasten the slotted breaker plate in place and turn the plate in the direction of distributor shaft rotation to retard timing, or against shaft rotation to advance. Tighten screws, replace cap and rotor, and restart engine and check timing. Repeat this adjustment until timing is correct.

PISTON ENGINE

NOTE: *Some 1977 and most 1978 and later models require the ignition timing adjusted with the vacuum line connected to the distributor. Refer to the emission sticker (under the hood) to determine if the vacuum line is to be connected or disconnected and plugged.*

1. If required; disconnect and plug the distributor vacuum line.

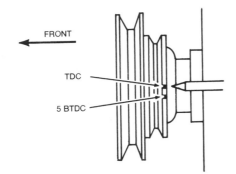

FRONT

TDC

5 BTDC

Timing mark—1980 GLC

2. Set the parking brake and block the front wheels. Start and run the engine until it reaches the normal operating temperature. Shut off the engine and connect a tachometer. Restart and check engine idle speed. Adjust if necessary. Shut off engine.

NOTE: *Prior to starting the engine, clean off any grease or oil that will prevent seeing the timing marks on the crankshaft pulley. Mark the pulley notches with chalk or paint.*

3. Connect a timing light to the engine following the manufacturer's instructions. Start the engine and observe the timing by pointing the light at the timing marks on the crankshaft pulley.

NOTE: *If the car is equipped with an automatic transmission put the lever in "D"; check emission sticker of tune-up "specs" for requirement.*

4. If the timing is not correct, loosen the distributor mounting bolt and rotate the distributor as necessary to produce the correct timing mark alignment. Recheck the timing after tightening the lock bolt. Readjust if necessary. Check idle speed.

5. On 1978 non-California cars with manual transmissions, the advance timing may be checked by disconnecting the leads to the switch which is operated by the accelerator pedal. If the advance setting is not at 11° BTC, check the dwell angles of both sets of points. If the advance setting is not correct, it indicates unequal dwell angles, or, more rarely, faulty parts in one or both contact sets or a worn distributor shaft or cam.

NOTE: *Some Canadian models require the bullet connectors at the water temperature connector disconnected before timing the ignition; check the emission sticker for requirements.*

6. Reconnect the vacuum line, accelerator switch or bullet connectors if disconnected. Recheck idle speed, readjust if necessary.

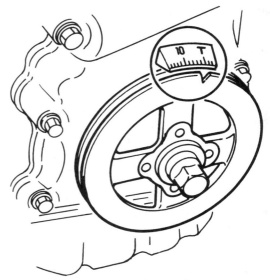

GLC front wheel drive, timing marks

Compression

Because of the unusual shape of the combustion chamber, the lack of valves, and because there are three chambers for each rotor, a normal gauge is useless for the measurement of rotary engine compression.

Mazda makes a special recording compression tester which produces a separate graph for each of the three chambers.

This is a fairly expensive piece of equipment and not one that back yard mechanics are likely to have around. If low compression is suspected, your best bet is to take the car to your local Mazda dealer, who does have this instrument.

Compression may be checked on piston engines in the conventional manner; that is, with engine hot, all spark plugs removed, and cranking the engine with the starter until

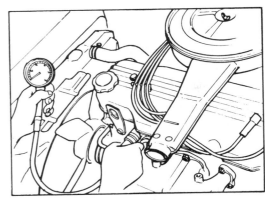

Checking engine compression

the compression gauge reading ceases to rise. Follow this procedure for each cylinder.

Valve Lash Adjustment

Valve lash adjustment is performed on piston engines at 2,000 miles and then at 12,500 miles, 25,000 miles, etc. on 1978 and earlier models and every 15,000 miles on 1979 and later. This adjustment is performed to correct for wear in the valve train and changes in dimensions of various engine parts that occur during normal engine operation, and, at a faster rate, during the break-in process. Failure to keep valves properly adjusted can result in excessive wear or burning of valves or valve train parts, poor performance, and/or noisy operation of the valve train. To perform valve adjustment, proceed as follows:

1. Operate the engine until several miles after temperature gauge indicates operating temperature has been reached. Then, stop engine and remove the valve cover.

2. Rotate the engine with a wrench on the crankshaft pulley bolt or with the starter until the mark on the crankshaft pulley indicates it has reached Top Dead Center, and the valves for Number 1 cylinder (at front) are both fully closed (are not moving as the crankshaft is turned). If engine is at TDC and these valves are still open, rotate the crankshaft one full turn until it is again at Top Dead Center.

3. Insert a flat feeler gauge of proper dimension (see tune-up chart) between the exhaust valve and the exhaust valve rocker lever for No. 1 cylinder. The exhaust valve is in line with the front exhaust manifold passage. The gauge should slide between these two parts with a slight pull. If the gauge will not slide readily, or there is no resistance in pulling it through, loosen the locknut and use a screwdriver to rotate the adjusting screw clockwise to tighten the adjustment or counterclockwise to loosen it. When a slight pull is obtained, hold the adjusting screw in place with a screwdriver and use a box wrench or open end wrench to tighten the locknut. If the adjustment has tightened up, readjust the position of the adjusting screw. *If a great deal of effort is required to pull the gauge (adjustment too tight) burned valves may result.*

4. Select the gauge for the adjusting dimension of the intake valves (see the Tune-up chart). Repeat Step 2 for the front intake valve (lined up with the front intake manifold passage).

5. Turn the crankshaft one half turn forward. Repeat Steps 2 and 3 for cylinder No. 3. When the valves for No. 3 have been adjusted, continue in the same manner for cylinders 4 and 2, turning the crankshaft one half turn forward before adjusting the valves for each of these cylinders.

Idle Speed and Mixture Adjustment

1971–73 ROTARY ENGINES

1. Start the engine and allow it to warm up. Remove the air cleaner assembly.

2. Operate the secondary throttle valve. Be sure that it returns full.

3. Connect a tachometer to the engine in accordance with its manufacturer's instructions, or if none is available, have someone sit in the car and watch the tachometer on the instrument panel.

4. Adjust the mixture by seating the mixture control screw lightly and then unscrewing it four or five turns.

5. Turn the idle screw until the specified idle is obtained; it may also be necessary to turn the mixture control screw slightly.

CAUTION: *The carburetor is equipped with an idle limiter screw, as an aid in controlling emissions; do not attempt to defeat its purpose by adjusting it.*

6. Remove the tachometer (if used) and install the air cleaner once idle adjustments are completed.

1974–78 ROTARY AND 1974 AND LATER PISTON ENGINES

Idle speed adjustments are easily performed, but you must be careful to perform them

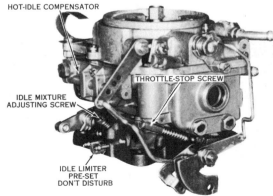

HOT-IDLE COMPENSATOR

THROTTLE-STOP SCREW

IDLE MIXTURE ADJUSTING SCREW

IDLE LIMITER PRE-SET DON'T DISTURB

Carburetor idle adjustment screws—typical 1971–73

under the proper conditions. The engine must be fully warmed up—the best procedure is to drive the vehicle for several miles after the temperature gauge indicates that the cooling water has reached operating temperature. The gas tank cap should be removed on 1975 and later rotary engine Mazdas, but all other normal operating conditions should be maintained. For example, the air cleaner and all vacuum hoses should be installed or connected, the choke should be wide open, and all accessories should be off. Also, avoid extremes of outside temperature, and replace a thermostat that makes the engine operate too hot or too cold before proceeding. On the 1978–79 GLC and the 1979 626 models disconnect the canister purge hose between the canister and the air cleaner.

Identify the idle speed screw on the carburetor. This screw acts directly on a flange which is integral with the throttle shaft; it does not act through any cams or levers. Connect a reliable tachometer according to manufacturer's instructions (usually between the coil "−" terminal and ground). Read the tach as for a 4 cylinder engine on all engines—both rotary and piston. If the tach has a six cylinder scale and an eight cylinder scale, read the eight cylinder scale and *be sure* to multiply all readings by two to get the correct rpm. For example, if the specified rpm is 700, set the idle speed at 350 rpm on the right cylinder scale.

Idle mixture adjustment for all Mazda cars built after 1973 requires the use of an HC/CO analyzer. Since this is an extremely expensive piece of equipment, the adjustment procedure is complex, and this adjustment is not required as a part of ordinary maintenance, no procedures are included here. This adjustment can, however, be checked at reasonable cost at many diagnostic centers or may be checked as a matter of routine during required vehicle inspection procedures. If the engine exhibits rough idle and/or smoke combined, in some cases, with hesitation or poor running at low speeds, idle mixture might be at fault. You should first check all the basic tune-up adjustments such as dwell, ignition timing, and spark plug condition and verify that there are no vacuum leaks due to disconnected or leaking hoses. Then, if these symptoms persist, the next step would be to have the idle mixture checked with an HC/CO meter at a dealer or diagnostic center. If incorrect readings are uncovered, we suggest you take the vehicle to a shop or dealer familiar with Mazdas and have the mixture adjusted according to the procedure specified by the factory.

Engine and Engine Rebuilding

3

ENGINE ELECTRICAL

Electronic Ignition

TROUBLESHOOTING

1978 GLC—California and Canada
1979 626
1979 GLC Except Canada
1980 and Later—All Models

Electronic ignition replaces the contact points with an electromagnetic generator, consisting of a rotating pole piece and a stationary pickup. As the rotating piece, mounted on the distributor shaft, passes the pickup, current is generated, much as in the car's main electrical system generator. The spikes of current produced as each of the four corners on the pole piece pass the pickup operate transistors in the ignitor mounted on the coil. This provides the switching actions ordinarily handled by the contact points, but without the arcing and stress of opening and closing associated with their operation.

There are two checks unique to this system that can be made to locate or repair trouble. The gap between the pole piece and pickup can be checked and adjusted, and the electrical resistance of the pickup can be checked. The resistance of the coil can also be checked.

ADJUSTING PICKUP GAP

1. Remove the distributor cap and rotor. Turn the engine over with the starter or by using a socket wrench on the crankshaft pulley bolt until one of the four high points on the pole piece lines up directly with the metallic portion of the pickup.

2. Using a non-magnetic (i.e. brass or paper) feeler gauge, check the gap. If it is not .010 in.–.018 in. (GLC) or .008 in. or more (626) wide loosen the two adjusting screws and slide the pickup in or out until the dimension is correct. Tighten screws and recheck the gap. Readjust if necessary.

Adjusting pickup gap

CHECKING PICKUP COIL RESISTANCE

1. Unplug the primary ignition wire connector, and connect an ohmmeter between the two prongs of the connector on the distributor side. The resistance of the pickup coil should be 670–790 ohms (GLC) or 720–1,050 ohms (626) as measured at room temperature. If resistance is incorrect, replace the pickup.

CHECKING IGNITION COIL RESISTANCE

1. Run the engine until it reaches operating temperature (coil must be hot). Pull the high tension lead out of the coil tower.

2. Measure primary resistance with an ammeter, connecting between coil minus and plus primary terminals. Resistance should be 1.15–1.28 ohms (GLC) or 0.9–1.15 ohms (626).

3. Measure secondary resistance, connecting the ohmmeter between the coil tower and the plus primary terminal. Resistance should be 13,500 ohms (GLC) or 7,000 ohms (626).

4. Replace the coil if resistances are incorrect by plus or minus 10%.

Distributors

REMOVAL AND INSTALLATION

1971–73 Rotary Engines

The removal procedure for both the leading and the trailing distributor is the same. To remove either or both of them, proceed in the following manner:

NOTE: *It is a good idea to remove and install the distributors separately, to avoid confusion.*

1. Disconnect the vacuum advance line at the distributor.

2. Unfasten the vacuum advance switch connector (trailing distributor).

3. Disconnect the primary wire at the coil.

4. Note the letters and numbers identifying them, and remove the spark plug cables.

5. Matchmark the distributor housing and sockets. Matchmark the position of the rotor, in relation to the distributor housing. These marks are to be used as an aid when installing the distributor in a properly timed engine.

6. Remove the distributor clamping screw and carefully lift the distributor out of its socket.

NOTE: *Try to avoid rotating the engine while the distributors are removed. Unnec-*

essary rotation of the engine under these conditions only means more work.

If the engine has not been rotated with either of the distributors removed, their installation is performed in the reverse order of removal. Use the matchmarks made during removal to correctly position the distributors in their sockets.

NOTE: *If both distributors were removed at the same time, use care to see that they are returned to their proper sockets. Both the distributors and the front cover are marked to aid in correct installation.*

Once the distributors are installed, adjust the point gap, the dwell angle, and the timing, as detailed in Chapter Two.

If the engine was rotated, or otherwise disturbed, such as for engine rebuilding, install the distributors in the following manner:

1. Turn the engine until the white mark on the eccentric shaft pulley is aligned with the pointer on the front cover. This will always be top dead center (TDC) of the number one rotor's compression cycle, because each rotor only makes ⅓ of a turn for each full rotation of the eccentric shaft.

NOTE: *TDC cannot be found by feeling for compression at the number one spark plug hole, as in a conventional piston engine.*

2. Align the marks stamped on each distributor housing and driven gear.

3. Install either distributor, so that the key on the end of its drive engages with the slot in the socket.

NOTE: *If both distributors were removed*

Align the distributor identification marks prior to installation

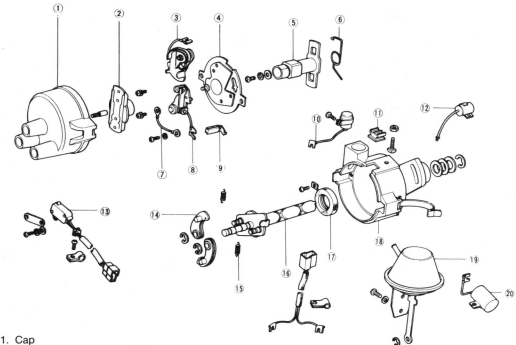

1. Cap
2. Rotor
3. Point set
4. Breaker plate
5. Cam
6. Spring
7. Ground wire
8. Point set
9. Felt
10. Ignition condenser
11. Terminal
12. Radio suppression
       condenser
13. Vacuum switch—
       trailing distributor
       only
14. Governor
15. Governor spring
16. Shaft
17. Oil seal
18. Distributor housing
19. Vacuum advance unit
20. Ignition condenser

Distributor components

at the same time, be careful not to mix their parts or confuse them upon installation. Both distributor and the front housing are marked with a "T" or an "L"; insert the distributor having the same letter as the housing into its proper socket.

4. Rotate each distributor slightly, until its points just start to open and then tighten its locknut.

5. Check the point gap and install the cap.

6. Connect all of the vacuum lines and the wires carefully, to ensure their connection to the proper distributor.

NOTE: *Spark plug position and leads are marked, as is each distributor cap, to aid in installation.*

7. Check and adjust the dwell angle and ignition timing, using the procedures outlined above in Chapter Two.

8. Connect the vacuum advance lines to the distributors.

1974–78 Rotary Engines

1. Rotate the engine in normal direction of rotation until the first ("TDC" or "Leading")

timing mark aligns with the pin on the front cover. Matchmark the body of the distributor and the engine rotor housing.

2. The easiest way to clear the high tension wires out of the way is to simply remove the cap and set it aside with the wires still attached. However, if you wish to keep the cap with the distributor, pull the wires out of the cap, observing markings.

3. Disconnect vacuum advance and, if so equipped, retard hoses. Disconnect the primary electrical connector.

4. Remove the distributor adjusting bolt. Pull the distributor vertically out of the engine.

5. To install the distributor, first make sure the engine has not been disturbed. If it has been moved, again turn the crankshaft until the first timing mark lines up with the pin on the front cover. Then align the dimple in the distributor gear with the notch or line cast into the body of the distributor (see illustrations).

6. Insert the distributor carefully and slowly into the engine with distributor body

Distributor alignment marks—1974–76 rotary engines

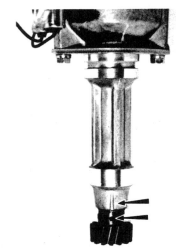

Distributor alignment marks—1977–78 rotary engines

2. Rotate the engine with the starter or by using a socket wrench on the bolt which retains the front pulley until the timing mark on the pulley is aligned with the pin on the front cover. Check to see if the contact on the rotor is pointing toward the No. 1 spark plug wire. If the rotor is half a turn away from the No. 1 plug wire, turn the crankshaft ahead one full turn until the timing mark is again aligned with the pin. Match mark the distributor body with the cylinder head.

3. Disconnect the vacuum advance line at the advance unit and disconnect the primary wire at the connector near the distributor.

4. Remove the adjusting bolt, and pull the distributor out of the engine.

5. To install the distributor, first align the dimple on the distributor drive gear with the mark cast into the base of the distributor body by rotating the shaft. Then, being careful not to rotate the shaft, insert the distributor back into the cylinder head with distributor body and cylinder head match marks aligned and seat it.

6. Install the mounting bolt, but do not tighten it. Rotate the distributor until the points are just opening, and tighten the mounting bolt.

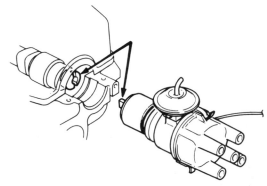

On GLC front wheel drive models, the distributor engages a notch in the rear of the camshaft. Do not remove the seal block (not shown) at the rear of the valve cover

7. Install the distributor cap, and reconnect the vacuum advance line and the primary connector.

8. If the ignition points have been disturbed, set the dwell as described in the previous chapter. Set timing.

NOTE: *If the engine has been rotated while the distributor was out, it will be necessary to turn the crankshaft until the point where No. 1 cylinder is just about to fire. To do this, remove No. 1 spark plug*

and rotor housing matchmarks aligned. Avoid allowing the shaft to turn and be careful not to damage the housing when inserting the gear into it.

7. Install the adjusting bolt, but do not tighten. Turn the distributor until the leading points just start to open, and then tighten the locking bolt.

8. Install vacuum hoses, electrical connectors, and high tension wires in reverse of the removal procedure.

9. If ignition points have been disturbed or replaced, set the dwell as described in the previous chapter. Set ignition timing.

Piston Engines

1. Unfasten the clips which hold the distributor cap to the top of the distributor, and remove the cap. Note the location of the wire going to No. 1 (the front) cylinder where it enters the cap.

and rotate the engine until you can feel compression pressure building (with your finger over the spark plug hole) as the engine is turned forward. Then, turn the engine until the timing mark on the front pulley is aligned with the pin on the front cover, and proceed with step 5.

Firing Order

To avoid confusion, replace spark plug wires one at a time.

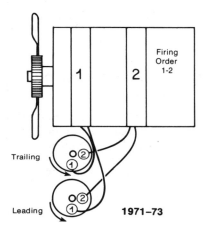

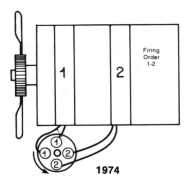

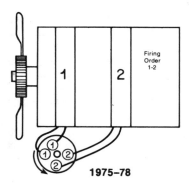

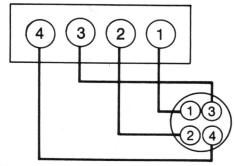

Firing order; 1-3-4-2. All models except the GLC front wheel drive. Number one distributor tower location may vary, depending on model

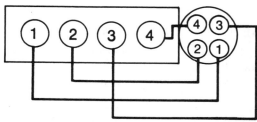

Firing order; 1-3-4-2. GLC front wheel drive models

Alternator

ALTERNATOR SERVICE PRECAUTIONS

Because of the nature of alternator design, special care must be taken when servicing the charging system.

1. Battery polarity should be checked before any connections, such as jumper cables or battery charger leads, are made. Reversed battery connections will damage the diode rectifiers.

2. The battery must never be disconnected while the alternator is running, because the regulator will be ruined.

3. Always disconnect the battery ground cable before replacing the alternator.

4. Do not attempt to polarize an alternator.

5. Do not short across or ground any alternator terminals.

6. Always disconnect the battery ground cable before removing the alternator output cable whether the engine is running or not.

7. If electric arc welding equipment is to be used on the car, first disconnect the battery and alternator cables. Never operate the car with the electric arc welding equipment attached.

8. If the battery is to be "quick charged," disconnect the positive cable from the battery.

REMOVAL AND INSTALLATION

1. Disconnect the battery ground cable at the negative (−) terminal.

2. Remove the air cleaner. Remove the nut, and disconnect the alternator "B" terminal. Unplug the connector from the rear of the alternator.

3. Remove the alternator adjusting link bolt. Do not remove the adjusting link.

4. Remove the alternator securing nuts and bolts. Withdraw the drive belt and remove the alternator.

Installation is performed in the reverse order of removal. Adjust the drive belt tension as detailed below.

BELT TENSION ADJUSTMENT

1. Check the drive belt tension by applying about 22 lbs of thumb pressure to the belt, midway between the eccentric shaft and alternator pulleys. The belt should deflect to the following specifications:

Old belt: approximately .6 in.
New belt: approximately .5 in.

2. If belt deflection is not within specifications, loosen, but do not remove, the bolt on the adjusting link.

3. Push the alternator in the direction required to obtain proper belt deflection.
CAUTION: *Do not pry or pound on the alternator housing.*

4. Tighten the adjusting link bolt to 20 ft. lbs.

Regulator

NOTE: *Some later models have the voltage regulator mounted within the alternator as part of the unit. No adjustments can be made to the regulator and the alternator must be removed and disassembled to replace the regulator.*

REMOVAL AND INSTALLATION

1971–79 except 626

1. Disconnect the battery ground cable at the negative (−) battery terminal.

2. Disconnect the wiring from the regulator.

3. Remove the regulator mounting screws.

4. Remove the regulator.

Installation is performed in the reverse order of removal.

Alternator and Regulator Specifications

		Alternator		Regulator							
					Regulator			Field Relay			
Year	Model	Field Current @ 14 v	Output (amps)	Air Gap (in.)	Point Gap (in.)	Back Gap (in.)	Air Gap (in.)	Point Gap (in.)	Back Gap (in.)	Volts @ 75°
1971–73	RX-2, RX-3	32	40	—	—	—	.028–.043	.012–.016	.028–.043	14
1974	All Rotary	—	56	.035–.047	.028–.043	.028–.043	.028–.043	.012–.016	.028–.043	14
1975–76	RX-3, RX-4	—	56	.035–.055	.028–.043	.028–.059	.028–.051	.012–.018	.028–.059	14–15
1974–78	808	—	40 ①	.035–.055	.028–.043	.028–.059	.028–.051	.012–.018	.028–.059	14–15
1977–78	All Rotary	—	63	.035–.055	.028–.043	.028–.049	.028–.051	.012–.018	.028–.059	14
1977–80	GLC	—	30	.039–.059	.020–.035	.028–.059	.028–.051	.012–.018	.028–.059	14–15

①—1974 808—50

VOLTAGE ADJUSTMENTS

1971–79 except 626

1. Remove the cover from the regulator.
2. Check the air gap, the point gap, and the back gap with a feeler gauge (see illustration).
3. If they do not fall within the specifications given in the "Alternator and Regulator" chart above, adjust the gaps by bending the stationary contact bracket.
4. Connect a voltmeter between the "A" and the "E" terminals of the regulator, except on GLC. On GLC, connect a voltmeter between the top terminal of the alternator and the coil mounting bolt.

   NOTE: *Be sure that the car's battery is fully charged before proceeding with this test.*

5. Start the engine and run it at the rpm specified in the chart below. The voltage reading should be to the specification shown in the chart below.
6. Stop the engine.
7. Bend the upper plate *down* to decrease the voltage setting, or *up* to increase the setting, as required.
8. If the regulator cannot be brought within specifications, replace it.
9. When the test is completed, disconnect

Regulated Voltage Test Chart

Model/Year	Alternator rpm	Engine rpm	Regulated Voltage
1971–73 RX-2, RX-3	4000	2000	13.5–14.5
1974–75 All Rotary	4000	1800	14–15
1974–78 808	4000	2000	14–15
1976–78 All Rotary	4000	2000	14–15
1977–82 GLC ①	—	2000	14–15
1981–82 GLC ② 626	5000	2000	14.1–14.7

① without internal regulator
② with internal regulator

the voltmeter and replace the regulator cover.

Starter

REMOVAL AND INSTALLATION

There are two possible locations for the starter motor; one is the lower right-hand side of the engine and the other is on the upper right-hand side.

1. Remove the ground cable from the negative (−) battery terminal.
2. If the car is equipped with the lower mounted starter, remove the gravel shield from underneath the engine. On 1976 and later vehicles equipped with automatic transmission, remove the two bolts attaching the starter bracket to the transmission.

   CAUTION: *Be extremely careful not to contact the hot exhaust pipe, while working underneath the car.*

3. Remove the battery cable from the starter terminal.
4. Disconnect the solenoid leads from the solenoid terminals.
5. Remove the starter securing bolts and withdraw the starter assembly.

Installation is the reverse of the above steps.

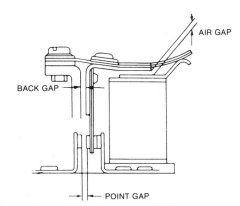

Regulator mechanical adjustments

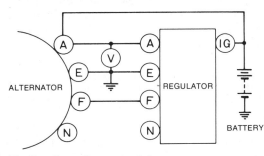

Testing the voltage regulator

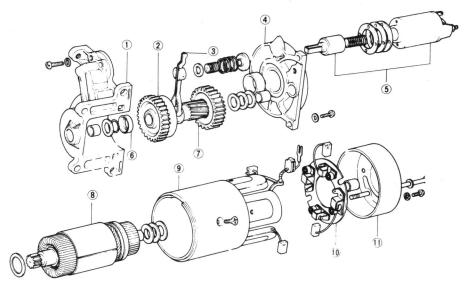

1. Front housing
2. Overrunning clutch
3. Engagement fork
4. Center frame
5. Solenoid
6. Stop
7. Idler gear
8. Armature
9. Field coil
10. Brush holder
11. End frame

Starter components

SOLENOID REPLACEMENT

Perform solenoid replacement with the starter motor removed from the car.

1. Detach the field strap from the solenoid terminals.

2. Remove the solenoid securing screws.

3. Withdraw the solenoid spring and washers from the starter drive housing.

Solenoid installation is performed in the reverse order of removal.

Starter solenoid removal

STARTER DRIVE REPLACEMENT

1971–73

1. Perform the solenoid removal procedure, above.

2. Remove the plunger from the drive engagement fork.

3. Unfasten the nuts from the thru-bolts. NOTE: *Unless further disassembly of the starter is desired, do not remove the thru-bolts.*

4. Remove the drive housing from the front of the starter.

5. Remove the engagement fork, spring, and spring seat.

6. Withdraw the over-running clutch from the armature shaft.

Assembly is performed in the reverse order of disassembly. Check the clearance between the pinion and the stop collar with the solenoid closed. It should be 0.0012–0.0060 in.

1974 and Later

1. On 1976 and later cars with automatic transmissions, remove the bracket from the rear of the starter.

2. Disconnect the field strap from the terminal on the solenoid, remove the solenoid attaching screws, and remove the solenoid, spring, and washers.

3. Detach the plunger at the drive lever, and remove it.

4. Remove the starter through bolts and the brush holder attaching screws. Remove the rear cover.

5. Remove the insulator and washers from the rear end of the armature shaft. Remove the brush holder.

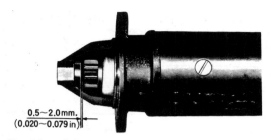

0.5~2.0mm.
(0.020~0.079 in.)

Checking pinion-to-stop collar clearance

6. Pull the yoke off the drive housing. Remove the rubber packing, spring, and spring seat.

7. Pull the armature, drive lever, and overrunning clutch assembly from the drive housing.

8. Position the armature with the front end upward in a soft jawed vise. Drive the pinion stop collar rearward until the stop ring can be removed. Then, remove the stop ring, stop collar, and overrunning clutch.

9. Assemble in exact reverse order. Then, energize the solenoid by connecting the "M" terminal on the solenoid to the battery "+" terminal, and grounding the solenoid housing to the battery "−" terminal. Check the clearance between pinion and stop collar with a feeler gauge—it should be .020–.079 in. If the clearance is incorrect, adjusting washers are available for insertion between the solenoid and drive housing.

STARTER BRUSH REPLACEMENT

Inspect the brushes for excessive wear (limit is .45 in.). If worn beyond the limit, they must be replaced.

1. Remove the brush from the holder. Smash the brush in order to free the lead from it. Clean old solder and corrosion from the lead.

2. Insert the lead into the new brush, going into the end with the smaller chamfer.

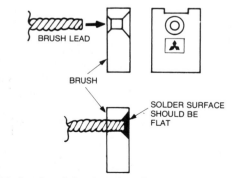

BRUSH LEAD

BRUSH

SOLDER SURFACE
SHOULD BE
FLAT

Soldering brush leads to brushes

3. Solder the lead into the brush by filling the large chamfer with rosin core solder. The factory recommends a small soldering iron—about 150 watts. Smooth the outer surface of the soldered connection.

4. Install the brush in the brush holder under the spring.

Battery

REMOVAL AND INSTALLATION

1. Protect the paint finish with fender covers.

2. Disconnect the battery cables from the battery terminal posts.

3. Remove the battery hold-down clamp and remove the battery from the vehicle.

4. Inspect the battery carrier and the fender panels for damage caused by loss of acid from the battery.

5. If the battery is to be reinstalled, clean its top with a solution of clean, warm water and baking soda. Scrub heavily deposited areas with a stiff bristle brush, being careful not to scatter corrosion residue.

6. Rinse off the top of the battery with clean, warm water.

NOTE: *Keep the cleaning solution and water out of the battery cells.*

7. Examine the battery case and cover for cracks.

8. Clean the battery posts and cable connectors with a wire brush. Replace damaged or worn cables.

9. Install the battery in the car. Tighten the hold-down clamp nuts.

10. Connect the cables to their correct battery terminals and, after tightening the connections, coat all connections with petroleum jelly to prevent corrosion.

11. If the electrolyte level is low, fill the battery to the recommended level with distilled water.

ENGINE MECHANICAL

Design

ROTARY ENGINE

The Mazda rotary engine replaces conventional pistons with three-cornered rotors which have rounded sides. The rotors are mounted on a shaft which has eccentrics rather than crank throws.

Battery and Starter Specifications

All cars use 12 volt, negative ground electrical systems

| Year | Model | Battery Amp Hour Capacity | Starter | | | | | | | Brush Spring Tension * (oz) | Min. Brush Length (in.) |
| | | | Lock Test | | Torque (ftllbs) | No Load Test | | | | |
			Amps	Volts		Amps	Volts	RPM		
1971	RX-2	60	600	6	19.5	70	12	3,600	40.0	.45
1972–75	RX-2 and RX-3 w/MT	70	600	6	19.5	70	12	3,600	56.3	.45
	RX-2 and RX-3 w/AT	70	1,200	4	19.5	100	12	5,400	56.3	.45
1974–78	RX-4 w/MT	70	780	5	7.96	75	11.5	4,900	56	.45
	RX-4 w/AT	70①	1,100	5	17.36	100	11.5	7,800	56	.45
1975–77	808	60	400	6	6.7	53	10.5	5,000	56	.45
1976	RX-3 w/MT	60	780	5	8.0	75	11.5	4,900	56	.45
	RX-3 w/AT	60	1,100	5	17.4	100	11.5	7,800	56	.45
1977–78	Cosmo w/MT	45	600	5	6.9	50	11.5	5,600	56	.45
	Cosmo w/AT	70	1,050	5	15.9	100	11.5	6,600	56	.45
1977–82	GLC	45②	310	5	5.4	53	11.5	6,800	56	.45
1979–82	626	45	310	5	5.4③	53④	11.5	6,800	56	.45

MT—Manual transmission
AT—Automatic transmission
① —60 amp w/MT
② —1977   Canada 45 amp
              Exc Calif. 60 amp
              Calif. 35 amp
    1978   Calif. 35 amp
    1979–80 Calif. 33 amp
③ 1982; 8.3
④ 1982; 60 amp or less

The chamber in which the rotor travels is roughly oval-shaped, but with the sides of the oval bowed in slightly. The technical name for this shape is a two-lobe epitrochoid.

As the rotor travels its path in the chamber, it performs the same four functions as the piston in a regular four-cycle engine:
1. Intake
2. Compression
3. Ignition
4. Exhaust
But all four functions in a rotary engine are happening concurrently, rather than in four separate stages.

Ignition of the compressed fuel/air mixture occurs each time a side of the rotor passes the spark plugs. Since the rotor has three sides there are three complete power impulses for each complete revolution of the rotor.

As it moves, the rotor exerts pressure on the cam of the eccentric shaft, causing the shaft to turn.

Because there are three power pulses for every revolution of the rotor, the eccentric

How the Rotary Engine Works

1. INTAKE.
Fuel/air mixture is drawn into combustion chamber by revolving rotor through intake port (upper left). No valves or valve-operating mechanism needed.

2. COMPRESSION.
As rotor continues revolving, it reduces space in chamber containing fuel and air. This compresses mixture.

3. IGNITION.
Fuel/air mixture now fully compressed. Leading sparkplug fires. A split-second later, following plug fires to assure complete combustion.

4. EXHAUST.
Exploding mixture drives rotor, providing power. Rotor then expels gases through exhaust port.

How Your Piston Engine Works

1. INTAKE.   2. COMPRESSION.   3. IGNITION.   4. EXHAUST.

shaft must make three complete revolutions for every one revolution of the rotor. To maintain this ratio, the rotor has an internal gear that meshes with a fixed gear in a three-to-one ratio. If it was not for this gear arrangement, the rotor would spin freely and timing would be lost.

The Mazda rotary engine has two rotors mounted 60 degrees out of phase. This produces six power impulses for each complete revolution of both rotors and two power impulses for each revolution of the eccentric shaft.

Because of the number of power impulses for each revolution of the rotor and because all four functions are concurrent, the rotary engine is able to produce a much greater amount of power for its size and weight than a comparable reciprocating piston engine.

Instead of using valves to control the intake and exhaust operations, the rotor uncovers and covers ports on the wall of the chamber, as it turns. Thus, a complex valve train is unnecessary. The resulting elimination of parts further reduces the size and

weight of the engine, as well as eliminating a major source of mechanical problems.

Spring-loaded carbon seals are used to prevent loss of compression around the rotor apexes and cast iron seals are used to prevent loss of compression around the side faces of the rotor. These seals are equivalent to compression rings on a conventional piston, but must be more durable because of the high rotor rpm to which they are exposed.

Oil is controlled be means of circular seals mounted in two grooves on the side face of the rotor. These oil seals function to keep oil out of the combustion chamber and gasoline out of the crankcase, in a similar manner to the oil control ring on a piston.

The rotor housing is made of aluminum and the surfaces of the chamber are chrome-plated.

PISTON ENGINE

The Mazda piston engines incorporate many of the design features used to make small and efficient engines both clean and willing performers. They incorporate a slightly un-

General Engine Specifications—Rotary Engine

Model	Engine Displacement Cu In. (cc)	Carburetor Type	Net Horsepower @ rpm	Net Torque @ rpm	Rotor Displacement (cu in.)	Compression Ratio	Oil Pressure @ rpm (psi)
RX-3	70/1,146	4-bbl	90 @ 6,000	96 @ 4,000	35	9.4 : 1	71.1 @ 3,000
RX-2, RX-3SP	70/1,146	4-bbl	97 @ 6,500	98 @ 4,000	35	9.4 : 1	71.1 @ 3,000
RX-4, Cosmo	80/1,308	4-bbl	110 @ 6,000	120 @ 4,000	40	9.2 : 1	71.1 @ 3,000

General Engine Specifications—Piston Engine

Year	Engine Displacement Cu In. (cc)	Carburetor Type	Horsepower (@ rpm)	Torque @ rpm (ft. lbs.)	Bore x Stroke (in.)	Compression Ratio	Oil Pressure @ rpm (psi)
1975–78	96.8 (1,586)	2-bbl	64 @ 5,000	78 @ 3,000	3.07 x 3.27	8.6 : 1	57 @ 3,000
1976–78	77.6 (1,272)	2-bbl	—	—	2.87 x 2.99	9.2 : 1	57 @ 3,000
1979–82	86.4 (1,415)	2-bbl	—	—	3.03 x 2.99	9.0 : 1	57 @ 3,000
	90.9 (1,490) ①	2-bbl	—	—	3.03 x 3.15	9.0 : 1	57 @ 3,000
	120.2 (1,970)	2-bbl	—	—	3.15 x 3.86	8.6 : 1	57 @ 3,000

① 1981 and later

Eccentric Shaft Specifications—Rotary

All measurements are given in inches.

Model	Journal Diameter		Oil Clearance		Eccentric Shaft End-Play		Min. Shaft Runout
	Main Bearing	Rotor Bearing	Main Bearing	Rotor Bearing	Normal	Limit	
All	1.6929	2.9134	0.0016–0.0028	0.0016–0.0031 ①	0.0016–0.0028	0.0035	0.0008

① 1971—0.0020–0.0035

dersquare (Stroke slightly longer than bore) design in combination with hemispherical combustion chambers for minimal hydrocarbon emissions. The hemi-head also provides room for large valves, and these, in combination with the crossflow cylinder head design, permit free breathing and high output for the engine's size. Because the exhaust manifold is on the opposite side from the intake, engine coolant is used to warm the intake passages instead of exhaust gas.

Free breathing is aided further through the use of a progressive, 2 venturi carburetor. An overhead camshaft design minimizes valve train mass so that the engine's breathing ability can be translated into higher rpm and the higher maximum output this creates. The use of rocker levers not only allows a single camshaft to operate both intake and exhaust valves, but ensures easy adjustment of valve clearances without the use of special tools or shims or spacers. The camshaft is operated via a chain for maximum durability.

Crankcraft and Connecting Rod Specifications—Piston Engine

All measurements given in inches.

Year	Engine Displacement Cu In. (cc)	Crankshaft				Connecting Rod		
		Main Brg Journal Dia	Main Brg Oil Clearance	Shaft End-Play	Thrust on No.	Journal Dia	Oil Clearance	Side Clearance
1972–78	96.8 (1,586)	2.4804	0.001–0.002	0.003–0.009	5	2.0866	0.001–0.003	0.004–0.008
1976–78	77.6 (1,272)	2.4804	0.0012–0.0024	0.003–0.009	5	1.7717	0.0011–0.0029	0.004–0.008
1979–82	86.4 (1,415)	1.9685	0.0009–0.0017	0.004–0.006	5	1.5748	0.0009–0.0019	0.004–0.008
	90.9 (1,490) ①	1.9668	0.0009–0.0017	0.004–0.006	5	1.5734	0.0009–0.0019	0.004–0.010
	120.2 (1,970)	2.4804	0.0012–0.0020	0.003–0.009	5	2.0866	0.001–0.003	0.004–0.008

① 1981 and later

Rotor and Housing Specifications—Rotary Engine

All measurements are given in inches.

Model	Rotor			Housings						
				Front and Rear		Rotor		Intermediate		
	Side Clearance	Standard Protrusion of Land	Limit of Protrusion of Land	Distortion Limit	Wear Limit	Width	Distortion Limit	Distortion Limit	Wear Limit
RX-3, RX-3SP, and RX-2	0.0051–0.0067	0.004–0.006	0.003	0.002	0.004	2.7539	0.002	0.002	0.004
1974 RX-4	0.0047–0.0083	—	—	0.002	0.004	3.1438	0.002	0.002	0.004
1975–78 RX-4, Cosmo	0.0039–0.0083	—	—	0.0016	0.0039	3.150	0.0024	0.0016	0.0039

Seal Clearances—Rotary Engine

All measurements are given in inches.

Model	Apex Seals				Corner Seal to Rotor Groove		Side Seal			
	To Side Housing		To Rotor Groove				To Rotor Groove		To Corner Seal	
	Normal	Limit	Normal	Limit	Normal	Limit	Normal	Limit	Normal	Limit
RX-2, RX-3, RX-3SP	0.0020–0.0028 ①	0.0039	0.0014–0.0029	0.0039	0.0008–0.0019	0.0031	0.0016–0.0028	0.0039	0.002–0.006	0.016
RX-4, Cosmo	0.0051–0.0067	0.0118	0.0020–0.0035	0.006	0.0008–0.0019 ②	0.0031 ②	0.0016–0.0028	0.0040	0.0020–0.0059	0.016 ③

① Arctic Specifications—0.0004–0.0020   ② Applies only to 1974 models   ③ 1975–78 models—0.0157

Seal Specifications—Rotary Engine
All measurements are given in inches.

Model	Apex Seal		Corner Seal Width (OD)	Side Seal		Oil Seal Contact Width of Lip	
	Normal Height	Height Limit		Thickness	Width	Normal	Limit
RX-2, RX-3, RX-3SP	0.03937	0.03150	0.2756	0.0394	0.1378	0.008	0.031
RX-4, Cosmo	0.33500	0.27600	0.4331	0.0394	0.1378	0.008	0.031

Piston and Ring Specifications
All measurements are given in inches.

Year	Engine Displacement Cu In. (cc)	Piston Clearance	Ring Gap			Ring Side Clearance		
			Top Compression	Bottom Compression	Oil Control	Top Compression	Bottom Compression	Oil Control
1972–78	96.8 (1586)	0.0022–0.0028	0.008–0.016	0.008–0.016	0.008–0.016	0.0014–0.0028	0.0012–0.0025	0.008–0.016
1976–78	77.6 (1272)	0.0021–0.0026	0.008–0.016	0.008–0.016	0.008–0.016	0.0014–0.0028	0.0012–0.0025	0.008–0.016
1979–80	86.4 (1415)	0.0021–0.0026	0.008–0.016	0.008–0.016	0.012–0.035	0.0012–0.0025	0.0012–0.0025	0.008–0.016
1981–82	90.9 (1490)	0.0010–0.0026	0.008–0.016	0.008–0.016	0.012–0.035	0.0012–0.0028	0.0012–0.0028	0.008–0.016
1979–82	120.2 (1970)	0.0014–0.0030	0.008–0.016	0.008–0.016	0.012–0.035	0.0012–0.0028	0.0012–0.0028	0.008–0.016

Valve Specifications—Piston Engine

Year	Engine Displacement Cu In. (cc)	Seat Angle (deg)	Face Angle (deg)	Spring Test Pressure (lbs. @ in.)	Spring Installed Height (in.)	Stem-to-Guide Clearance (in.)		Stem Diameter (in.)	
						Intake	Exhaust	Intake	Exhaust
1972–78	96.8 (1586)	45	45	①	②	0.0007 0.0021	0.0007–0.0023	0.3150	0.3150
1976–78	77.6 (1272)	45	45	③	④	0.0007–0.0021	0.0007–0.0023	0.3150	0.3150
1979–80	86.4 (1415)	45	45	③	④	0.0007–0.0021	0.0007–0.0023	0.3150	0.3150
1981–82	90.9 (1490)	45	45	⑤	1.319	0.0007–0.0021	0.0007–0.0021	0.3150	0.3150
1979–82	120.2 (1970)	45	45	①	②	0.0007–0.0021	0.0007–0.0023	0.3150	0.3150

① Outer: 31.4 @ 1.339 Inner: 20.9 @ 1.260   ② Outer: 1.339 Inner: 1.260   ③ Outer: 43.7 @ 1.319 Inner: 20.9 @ 1.260   ④ Outer: 1.319 Inner: 1.260   ⑤ 63.3 @ 1.319

Torque Specifications—Rotary Engine
(All figures in ft lbs)

Engine Displacement Cu In. (cc)	Front Cover	Bearing Housing	Rear Stationary Gear	Eccentric Shaft Pulley Bolt	Flywheel to Eccentric Shaft Nut	Manifolds		Oil Pan	Tension Bolts
						Intake	Exhaust		
70 (1,156)	15	15	15	45	350	15	30	7	20
80 (1,308)	—	—	—	54–69 ①	289–362	15	32–43 ②	5–7	23–27

① 1977–78—72–87
② 1975–78—22–40

Torque Specifications—Piston Engine
(All figures in ft. lbs.)

Year	Engine Displacement Cu In. (cc)	Cylinder Head Bolts (cold)	Rod Bearing Bolts	Main Bearing Bolts	Crankshaft Pulley Bolt	Flywheel-to-Crankshaft Bolts	Manifolds	
							Intake	Exhaust
1974–78	1600	56–60	36–40	61–65	101–108	112–118	14–19	16–21
1976	1300	56–60	36–40	61–65	101–108	112–118	14–19	16–21
1977–78	1300	47–51	29–33	43–47	80–87	60–65	14–19	12–17
1979–82	1415	47–51	22–25	43–47	80–87	60–65	14–19	12–17
	1490	56–59	22–25	48–51	80–87	60–65 ①	14–19	14–17
	1970	59–64	29–33	61–65	101–108	112–118	14–19	16–21

① Autotransaxle 51–61

Engine Removal and Installation

ROTARY ENGINES

Be sure that the engine has completely cooled before attempting to remove it.

1. Scribe matchmarks on the hood and hinges. Remove the hood from the hinges.

2. Working from underneath the car, remove the gravel shield then drain the cooling system and the engine oil.

3. Disconnect the cable from the negative (−) battery terminal.

4. Remove the air cleaner, its bracket, and its attendant hoses.

5. Detach the accelerator cable, choke cable, and fuel lines from the carburetor.

6. Remove the nuts which secure the thermostat housing. Disconnect the ground cable from the housing and install the housing again after the cable is removed.

7. Disconnect the power brake vacuum line from the intake manifold.

8. Remove the fan shroud securing bolts and then the shroud itself.

9. Remove the bolts which secure the fan clutch to the eccentric shaft pulley. Withdraw the fan and clutch as a single unit.

CAUTION: *Keep the fan clutch in an upright position so that its fluid does not leak out.*

10. Unfasten the clamps and remove both radiator hoses.

11. Note their respective positions and remove the spark plug cables. Disconnect the primary leads from the distributors and remove both distributor caps.

12. Detach all of the leads from the alternator, the water temperature sender, the oil pressure sender, and the starter motor.

13. Disconnect all of the wiring from the

emission control system components. See Chapter Four.

14. Detach the heater hoses at the engine.

15. Detach the oil lines from the front and the rear of the engine.

16. Disconnect the battery cable from the positive (+) battery terminal and from the engine.

17. Unfasten the clutch slave cylinder retaining nuts from the clutch housing and tie the cylinder up and out of the way.

NOTE: *Do not remove the hydraulic line from the slave cylinder.*

18. Remove the exhaust pipe and the thermal reactor.

CAUTION: *Be sure that the thermal reactor has completely cooled; severe burns could result if it has not.*

19. Remove the nuts and bolts, evenly and in two or three stages, which secure the clutch housing to the engine.

20. Support the transmission by a jack placed underneath it.

21. Remove the nuts from each of the engine mounts.

22. Attach a lifting sling to the lifting bracket on the rear of the engine housing.

23. Use a hoist to take up the slack on the sling.

CAUTION: *Be sure that the hoist is secure to prevent personal injury or damage to the engine.*

24. Pull the engine forward until it clears the transmission input shaft. Lift the engine straight up and out of the car.

CAUTION: *Be careful not to damage any of the components remaining in the car.*

25. Remove the heat stove from the exhaust manifold.

26. Remove the thermal reactor as outlined below.

27. Mount the engine on a workstand.

NOTE: *A special three part workstand, designed for the rotary engine, is available from Mazda.*

Engine installation is performed in the reverse order of removal. Remember to refill all fluids according to specifications and to adjust the ignition after installation.

PISTON ENGINES

808

1. Remove the hood.
2. Remove the oil pan cover.
3. Drain coolant from radiator and cylinder block drain cocks (located on right rear). Drain engine oil.

4. Disconnect battery cables, remove clamp bolts and nuts, and remove battery.

5. Disconnect air control valve air hose and vacuum sensing tubes.

6. Disconnect primary and high tension wires at distributor and alternator wiring at the connector and "B" terminal.

7. Disconnect oil pressure switch wire and engine ground wire. Disconnect the wiring connector located near the rear of the cylinder head.

8. Remove the radiator water hoses. Remove the radiator cowling bolts and radiator attaching bolts, and remove both cowling and radiator from the car.

9. Remove the hot air hose. Remove air cleaner mounting bolts, and remove the air cleaner.

10. Disconnect the choke wire and throttle linkage at the carburetor.

11. Disconnect fuel supply and return lines at the carburetor, noting which is which.

12. Disconnect heater hoses from the manifold.

13. Disconnect the wires at the water temperature sending unit and carburetor solenoid.

14. Disconnect the power brake unit vacuum sensing tube at the intake manifold.

15. On California cars, disconnect the vacuum sensing tubes from the three way solenoid.

16. Disconnect the acclerator switch wiring.

17. Disconnect all starter motor wiring, and remove the starter.

18. Disconnect the exhaust pipe at the manifold.

19. Remove the clutch cover and brackets.

20. Support the transmission with a suitable jack. Then, install a suitable lifting sling to the engine hanger brackets, and connect the sling to a suitable hoist, and take up all slack.

21. Remove the nuts and bolts which connect the transmission to the engine, and the engine mount through bolts on both sides.

22. Pull the engine forward until it clears the clutch shaft. Then, lift the engine from the vehicle.

23. Installation is the reverse of the removal procedure.

GLC—Rear Wheel Drive

1. Remove the hood.
2. Disconnect the negative battery cable.
3. Drain the cooling system by opening radiator drain cock.
4. Disconnect upper and lower water hoses.
5. Remove radiator.
6. Remove air cleaner.
7. Disconnect: ECS hoses, heater hose, accelerator an choke cables, fuel lines, vacuum hoses, and distributor, starter, temperature sending unit, thermostatic switch, and alternator wiring.
8. Disconnect the exhaust pipe at the exhaust manifold.
9. Remove the starter.
10. Support the car on axle stands. Support the transmission with a jack. Connect a suitable lifting sling to the engine hanger brackets and to a hoist, and remove slack. Then, remove engine mount bolts.
11. Remove transmission mounting bracket from left side, and transmission-to-engine bolts from right side.
12. Pull the engine forward until it clears the clutch shaft, and then remove it from the vehicle.
13. Installation is the reverse of the removal procedure.

GLC—Front Wheel Drive

NOTE: *The factory recommends that the engine and transaxle be removed from the car as a unit.*

1. Mark the outline of the hood hinges for reinstallation alignment. Remove the hood.
2. Disconnect the battery cables from the battery; negative cable first. Remove the battery.
3. Loosen the front wheels lugs. Jack up the car and safely support it on jackstands. (Refer to Chapter 1 for jacking instructions).
4. Remove the two front wheels. Remove the bottom and side splash shields. Drain the coolant, engine oil and transaxle fluid.
5. Remove the air cleaner assembly. Remove the radiator hoses and the radiator shroud and electric fan assembly.
6. Connect an engine lifting sling to the engine. Connect a chain hoist or portable engine crane to the lifting sling and apply slight upward pressure to the engine and transaxle assembly.

7. Remove the mounting bolts from the engine crossmember. Remove the crossmember.
8. Disconnect the lower ball joints. Dismount the steering knuckles and drive axles. (See Chapters 7 and 8).
9. Cars equipped with manual transaxles: Disconnect the shifting rod and extension bar. Cars equipped with an automatic transaxle: Disconnect the selector rod and counter rod.
10. Remove the front and rear transaxle mounting bushings. Disconnect the exhaust pipe from the converter. Remove the transaxle crossmember.
11. Disconnect all wires and hoses from under the engine and transaxle. Label them for identification.
12. Disconnect all wires, heater hoses and vacuum hoses from the upper side of the engine and transaxle. Label them for correct installation.
13. Disconnect the accelerator cable, speedometer cable, clutch cable, power brake booster line and fuel lines.
14. Check to be sure all remaining hoses and wiring are disconnected. Remove the evaporative canister. Remove the right side upper engine mount through bolt.
15. Lift the engine and transaxle assembly from the car. Take care not to allow the assembly to swing forward into the radiator.
16. If the car must be moved from underneath the engine: Remount the steering knuckles, secure the drive axles so that they can still turn, mount the front wheels and lower the car from the jackstands.
17. Installation is in the reverse order of removal.

626

1. Remove the hood.
2. Disconnect the negative battery cable.
3. Drain the cooling system.
4. Remove the upper and lower radiator hoses.
5. On cars equipped with an automatic transmission disconnect the cooler lines.
6. Remove the radiator cowling and fan.
7. Remove the radiator.
8. Remove the air hoses from the air cleaner and remove the air cleaner.
9. Disconnect the wiring from the distributor primary, coil wire, oil pressure gauge unit, alternator "B" terminal, alternator wiring coupler, and the right side engine mounting nut.
10. Disconnect the wiring from the water

temperature gauge unit, fuel cut solenoid, automatic choke, starter motor.

11. Disconnect the air hoses (reed valve), vacuum hoses (three way solenoid valve), fuel hoses, acceleration wire, master vacuum hose, and the left side engine mounting nut.

12. Raise the front of the vehicle and support with jack stands.

13. Remove the under cover.

14. Disconnect the exhaust pipe.

15. Remove the clutch under cover plate.

16. On cars equipped with automatic transmission, remove the torque converter and driving plate support bolts.

17. Support the transmission with a suitable jack and remove the transmission support belts and nuts.

18. Remove the starter motor and the clutch release cylinder.

19. Connect a suitable lifting sling to the engine hanger brackets and to a hoist, and remove the slack.

20. Pull the engine forward until it clears the clutch shaft, then lift the engine from the vehicle.

21. To install reverse the removal procedure.

4. Rotate the crankshaft to put the No. 1 cylinder at TDC on the compression stroke.

5. Remove the distributor.

6. Remove the rocker arm cover.

7. Raise and support the car. Disconnect the exhaust pipe from the manifold.

8. Remove the acclerator linkage.

9. Remove the nut, washer and the distributor gear from the camshaft, if equipped.

10. Front wheel drive (1490cc); remove the tensioner from the timing case cover. On other models remove the nut and washer and disconnect the camshaft gear from the camshaft. Support the timing chain so the tensioner will not come apart.

11. Remove the cylinder head bolts in several stages, reversing the torquing sequence. Remove the cylinder head-to-front cover bolt.

12. Remove the rocker arm assembly.

13. Remove the camshaft.

14. Lift off the cylinder head.

15. Remove all tension from the timing chain.

16. Check the cylinder head for warpage, as shown, by running a straightedge diagonally across the cylinder head and across either end, and attempting to insert a feeler

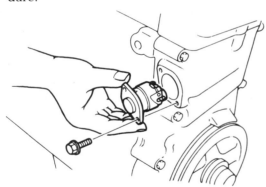

Removing the tensioner. GLC front wheel drive models

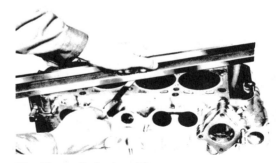

Checking cylinder head for warpage

Cylinder Head

REMOVAL AND INSTALLATION

Be sure that the cylinder head is cold before removal. This will prevent warpage. Do not remove the cam gear from the timing chain. The relationship between the chain and gear teeth should not be disturbed. Wire the chain and gear together.

1. Drain the cooling system.

2. Remove the air cleaner.

3. Disconnect all applicable electrical wires and leads.

Cylinder head torque sequence—all engines

gauge between the head surface and the straightedge. Permissible limit is .015 in. If distortion exceeds the limit, grind the head with a surface grinder.

17. Installation is in reverse of removal. Be sure to torque bolts in several stages using the proper sequence. Adjust timing chain tension and valves.

OVERHAUL

1. Check the cylinder head for distortion as described in the cylinder head removal and installation procedure above. Inspect water passages to make sure they are fully open and, if necessary, hot tank head in a solution that is compatible with aluminum to clean them. Repair or replace any damaged threads or broken studs.

2. Check the intake and exhaust mani-

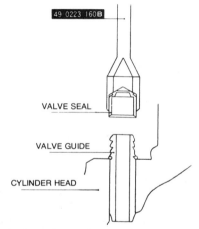

Replacing the valve seal on the 1600 engine—The procedure is for all the other engines is the same, but the special tool is numbered 49 0223 160C

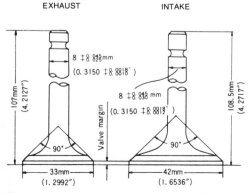

Valve face angles and dimensions—1600 and 1970 cc engines

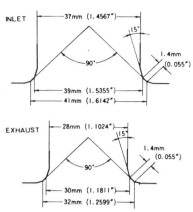

Valve seat angles and dimensions—1600 and 1970 cc engines

folds for distortion with a straightedge, or by placing them against a surface plate. The limit is .006 in. Regrind the surface of the manifold if excessive distortion is found.

3. Inspect valve springs for breakage or corrosion, and replace as necessary. Measure free length for conformity to specification, and replace as necessary. Limits are: 1970 and 1600 engine—1.449 inner, 1.469 outer; 1300 engine—1.406 inner, 1.539 outer; 1500 engine—1.705. Also, check spring pressure at specified length.

4. Remove all carbon from the valves and inspect for warpage, cracks, or excessive burning. Replace valves that cannot be cleaned up and refaced. Measure stem diameter at three places, and check stem-to-guide clearance with the valve in the guide using a dial indicator. Replace the guide and valve if stem-to-guide clearance is excessive, replace the valve if stem diameter is under specification, but a new valve will provide proper stem-to-guide clearance.

5. Press out valve guides that require replacement with a valve guide removing tool and hammer. Press in a new guide in a similar manner, stopping when the rim on the guide touches the head. Be sure to hit the end of the tool as squarely as possible. Install a new seal onto replaced guides with a special tool.

6. Reface the valves with a refacing tool, following the instructions of the tool manufacturer. See illustrations for dimensions and angles. Remove just enough metal to clean up faces and sets. If, during the refacing process, valve margin becomes less than .039 in. the valve must be replaced.

7. If valve seats have cracks, burrs, or ridges, or angles and dimensions are not cor-

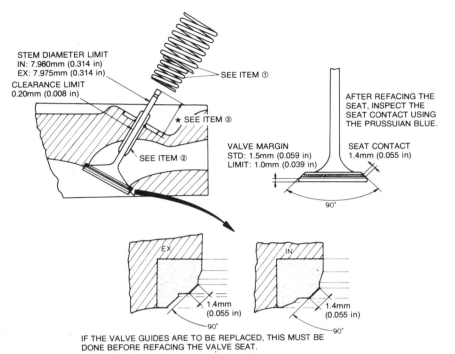

STEM DIAMETER LIMIT
IN: 7.980mm (0.314 in)
EX: 7.975mm (0.314 in)

CLEARANCE LIMIT
0.20mm (0.008 in)

SEE ITEM ①

★ SEE ITEM ③

SEE ITEM ②

AFTER REFACING THE
SEAT, INSPECT THE
SEAT CONTACT USING
THE PRUSSUIAN BLUE.

VALVE MARGIN
STD: 1.5mm (0.059 in)
LIMIT: 1.0mm (0.039 in)

SEAT CONTACT
1.4mm (0.055 in)

90°

EX

IN

1.4mm
(0.055 in)

1.4mm
(0.055 in)

90°

90°

IF THE VALVE GUIDES ARE TO BE REPLACED, THIS MUST BE
DONE BEFORE REFACING THE VALVE SEAT.

Valve seat and face angles and dimensions—1300 and 1415 cc engines

rect, remove the minimum amount of metal that will correct them with a valve seat grinder. Note that seat grinding *must* be done *after* valve guide replacement, where it is required. Also note that, while some engines use a pressed in seat, it cannot be replaced. Contact of valve and seat must be checked by applying Prussian Blue dye to

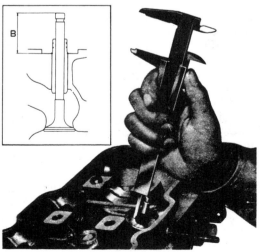

Check spring seat to top-of-valve-stem dimension ("B") with vernier calipers as shown

seat, seating valve, and repeatedly seating the valve while rotating it. If the dye marking on the valve is uneven, the valve must be lapped in.

8. When valve/seat machining has been performed, it is necessary to check the distance between the valve spring seat on the cylinder head and the top of the valve stem so that adequate spring tension is assured. Check dimension using vernier calipers as shown. Standard dimensions are: 1970 and 1600—intake 1.59 in., exhaust 1.48 in.; 1300 and 1500—1.555 in. If this dimension is exceeded by more than .020 in., shims must be inserted on the spring seat so as to bring the dimension to within the dimension. If the dimension is greater than .069 in., replace the valve.

9. Check clearance between rocker arms and shafts with rockers assembled to shafts. Limit is .004 in. Replace rocker or shaft, depending on characteristics of the wear (e.g., if all clearances are wide on a rocker shaft, replace the shaft; if clearance is wide under only one rocker, replace rocker, etc.).

10. Inspect the camshaft cam faces and bearing journals for roughness or obvious excessive wear. Measure the cam height with a micrometer. It should be:

Year	Engine	Intake	Exhaust
1975–78	1600	1.7256 in.	1.7592 in.
1976	1300	1.7290 in.	1.7290 in.
1977	1300	1.7288 in.	1.7288 in.
1978	1300	1.7290 in.	1.7290 in.
1979–80	1415	1.7291 in.	1.7291 in.
1979–80	1970	1.7731 in.	1.7784 in.
1981–82	1970	1.7731 in.	1.7718 in.
1981–82	1490	1.7367 in.	1.7288 in.

Replace the camshaft if it is obviously worn or damaged or if cam height is worn beyond limits.

11. Measure camshaft bearing journals with a micrometer. Wear limits are:

Year	Engine	Front	Center	Rear
1975–78	1600	1.7675 in.	1.7671 in.	1.7675 in.
1976–78	1300	1.6516 in.	1.6516 in.	1.6516 in.
1979–80	1415	1.6516 in.	1.6516 in.	1.6516 in.
1979–82	1970	1.7695 in.	1.7691 in.	1.7695 in.
1981–82	1490	1.6516 in.	1.6516 in.	1.6516 in.

On 1300 and 1500 cc engines, camshaft must be replaced if worn beyond limits. On 1600 and 1970 cc engines, the journals may be ground to undersize of .010 in., .020 in., or .030 in., and undersize bearings may be installed.

12. Check camshaft runout with a dial indicator, taking the measurement at the center bearing. Limit is .0012 in.

13. Check camshaft bearing clearance (1600 and 1970 engine only). See the Engine Rebuilding Section under plastigauging connecting rod bearings. Torque rocker assembly bolts to 56–60 ft. lb., and check clearance—it should be .0007–.0027 in. for front and rear bearings, and .0011–.0031 in. for the center bearing.

14. Measure camshaft end play by inserting a feeler gauge between the camshaft sprocket surface and the surface of the thrust plate. Clearance should be .001–.007 in. If clearance is excessive, replace the thrust plate.

Rocker Shafts
REMOVAL AND INSTALLATION

This operation should only be performed when the engine is cold; the bolts which hold the rocker shafts in place also hold the cylinder head to the block, and releasing the head when hot can cause it to warp.

1. Disconnect choke cable and, if so equipped, the air bypass valve cable.
2. Remove the rocker cover.
3. Remove the rocker shaft bolts, going in reverse of the cylinder head torquing sequence in several stages.
4. Remove the rocker shaft assembly.
5. Installation is generally in reverse of removal. Make sure all the spherical valve operators at the outer ends of the rocker levers are positioned so the flat surface is against the top of the valve stem. Then, position the rocker assembly toward the exhaust side of the engine so that the exhaust valve rocker arms are offset .04 in. from the centers of the

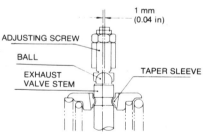

Position of valve actuating ball and offset of rocker arms—1600 and 1970 engines

valve stems (see illustration). Then, torque head bolts in several stages using the torquing pattern shown under "Cylinder Head Installation."

Rotary Engine Intake Manifold
REMOVAL AND INSTALLATION

To remove the intake manifold and carburetor assembly, with the engine remaining in the automobile, proceed in the following manner:

1. Perform Steps 2, 3, 4, 5, 7, and 13 of

"Engine Removal and Installation," above. Do not remove the engine.

2. Perform Steps 1, 2, 3, and 4 of "Engine Disassembly," above.

Install the intake manifold and carburetor assembly in the reverse order of removal. Tighten the manifold securing nuts working from the inside out, and in two or three stages, to specification.

Rotary Engine Thermal Reactor
REMOVAL AND INSTALLATION

To remove the thermal reactor, which replaces the exhaust manifold, proceed in the following manner:

CAUTION: *The thermal reactor operates at extremely high temperatures. Allow the engine to cool completely before attempting its removal.*

1. Remove the air cleaner assembly from the carburetor.

2. Unbolt and remove the air injection pump, as outlined in "Emission Controls."

3. Remove the intake manifold assembly, complete with the carburetor. See the section above.

4. Remove the heat stove from the thermal reactor.

5. Unfasten the thermal reactor securing nuts.

NOTE: *The bottom nut is difficult to reach. Mazda makes a special wrench (part number 49 213 001) to remove it. If the wrench is unavailable, a flexible drive metric socket wrench may be substituted.*

6. Lift the thermal reactor away from the engine.

Installation of the thermal reactor is performed in the reverse order of removal.

Piston Engine Intake Manifold
REMOVAL AND INSTALLATION

1. Drain the cooling system and remove the air cleaner.

2. Disconnect: throttle and choke linkage; fuel line(s); PCV valve hose; heater hoses; distributor vacuum line; ventilation valve hose (at the manifold); air pump hose at the anti afterburn valve.

3. Remove bolts attaching the manifold and remove it and gaskets from the head.

4. Replace gaskets, make sure all surfaces are clean and smooth, and check manifold for warpage as described in the Cylinder head overhaul procedures. Repair if necessary.

5. Install the manifold and tighten bolts gradually and in several stages, going from the center outward, to 14–19 ft. lb.

6. Install auxiliaries in reverse of the above procedure. Refill cooling system with engine idling.

Piston Engine Exhaust Manifold
REMOVAL AND INSTALLATION

1. Make sure engine is cold. Disconnect the inlet hose going to the anti-afterburn valve on the air injection manifold.

2. Disconnect the heat stove air pipe and remove the heat stove.

3. Disconnect the exhaust pipe or converter attaching nuts, and disconnect the exhaust pipe or converter.

4. Remove exhaust manifold attaching bolts, and remove the manifold and port liners.

5. Check the manifold for distortion as described under "Cylinder Head Overhaul" and repair it as necessary.

6. Install manifold with new gaskets, and torque bolts in several stages, going from the center outwards. Install auxiliaries in reverse of the above.

NOTE: *On California 1600 engines, a thermal reactor may be used in place of a manifold. Removal and installation procedures are the same.*

Front Cover, Timing Chain and Tensioner
REMOVAL AND INSTALLATION

NOTE: *On front wheel drive GLC models, the engine must be removed from the car. Start procedure at Step 5.*

1. Bring number one piston to TDC (timing marks aligned). Drain the cooling system. Remove the radiator hoses, thermostat housing, thermostat, fan, water pump and radiator.

2. Remove all lower and side splash or skid shields. Remove the crankshaft pulley and any driven units (alternator, air pump etc.) that will interfere with front cover removal.

3. Remove the blind cover (small plate retained by two or three bolts that covers the chain adjuster). Install the special clamping tool or make a simple device to prevent the slipper head of the chain adjuster from popping out.

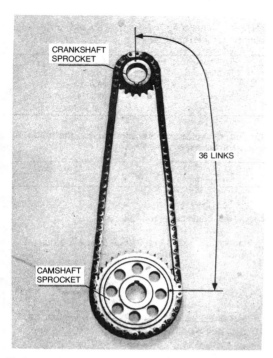

Timing chain and gear alignment; 1978—1300cc engine, 1979–80—1415cc engine and 1981–82 GLC station wagon with the 1490cc engine

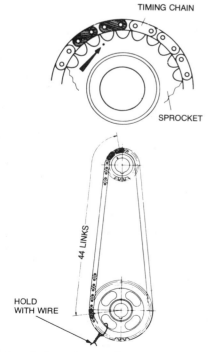

Timing chain and gear alignment; 1970cc engine

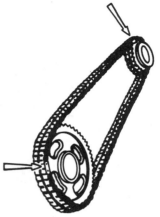

Timing chain and gear alignment; 1586cc engine. Align the bright links and marks

4. Remove the cylinder head, oil pan and timing chain front cover.

5. On GLC front wheel drive models: Remove the chain tensioner (located on the left upper corner of the timing cover) before removing the cylinder head. Remove the crankshaft pulley and proceed as follows.

6. Remove the oil slinger from the crankshaft. Depending on engine remove; the oil pump pulley and chain or the timing chain with sprockets first, the remaining sprockets and chain second. Loosen the timing chain guide strip and remove the chain tensioner if necessary.

7. Installation is in the reverse order of removal.

8. When installing the oil pump sprocket and chain check for excessive slack. Replace the chain if necessary. On the 626 models slack should be 0.015 in. Adjusting shims (between the oil pump and mounting) are available in thicknesses of 0.006 in.

9. Inspect the slipper head of the chain adjuster, the chain guide strip and the vibration damper for wear or damage. Check the adjuster spring for loss of tension. Replace parts as necessary.

10. Place the camshaft sprocket into the timing chain as shown on the appropriate illustration. Wire the sprocket and chain in position.

11. Install the timing chain onto the crankshaft sprocket as illustrated. Tighten the chain guide. Install the timing chain tensioner (except GLC—front wheel drive). Make sure the snubber spring is fully compressed. Install clamping tool.

12. Install a new timing cover oil seal. Install the timing chain front cover, oil pan and

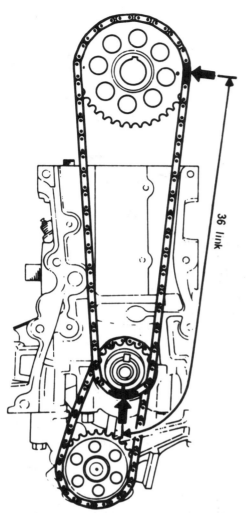

Timing chain and gear alignment; 1490cc engine, GLC front wheel drive

cylinder head. When installing the front cover be sure tension is applied to the timing chain to prevent it from coming off of the crankshaft sprocket. If the chain comes off of the sprocket, incorrect timing and engine damage will occur.

13. Install the sprocket and timing chain on the camshaft. Refer to illustrations. Adjust the timing chain tension.

14. Further installation is the reverse of removal.

Timing Chain Tensioner
REMOVAL, INSTALLATION AND ADJUSTMENT
Except GLC—Front Wheel Drive

1. Remove the water pump.
2. Remove the tensioner cover.

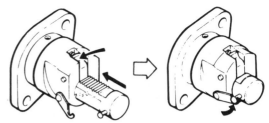

Adjusting the tensioner before installation. GLC front wheel drive

3. Remove the attaching bolts from the tensioner. Remove the tensioner.

To install the tensioner.

4. Fully compress the snubber spring. Insert a screwdriver into the tensioner release mechanism on 1600 cc engines. On 1300, 1415, 1490 GLC wagon and 1970 cc engines, clamp the parts of the tensioner together with an appropriate tool (see illustration above).

5. Without removing the screwdriver, insert the tensioner and align the bolt holes. Install and torque the bolts.

6. Adjust the chain tension as follows:

   a. Remove the two blind plugs and aluminum washers from the front cover.

   b. Loosen the guide strip attaching screws.

   c. Press the top of the chain guide strip through the adjusting hole in the cylinder head.

   d. Tighten the guide strip attaching screws.

   e. Remove the screwdriver or clamping tool from the tensioner and let the snubber take up the slack in the chain.

   f. Install the blind plugs and aluminum washers.

   g. Install the tensioner cover and gasket.

   h. Install a new gasket and water pump. Install the crankshaft pulley and drive belt and adjust the tension. Check the cooling system level.

GLC—Front Wheel Drive

The chain tensioner is located on the left upper side of the timing case cover, it is operated by spring plus hydraulic pressure. The tensioner has a one-way locking system and an automatic release device. After assembly, it will automatically adjust when the engine is rotated one or two times. No disassembly of the tensioner is required.

1. The tensioner is retained by two bolts. Remove the bolts and the tensioner.

2. Check the number of teeth showing on

the sleeve of the tensioner. If thirteen or more notches are showing the timing chain is stretched and must be replaced.

3. To install the tensioner; push the sleeve back into the body and lock it with the swivel catch on the tensioner body. Install the tensioner into the timing cover. After installation the catch is released by the action of the timing chain when the engine is rotated one to two revolutions. The sleeve projects automatically providing the proper chain adjustment.

Front Cover Oil Seal
REMOVAL AND INSTALLATION

The front cover oil seal can be replaced, in most cases, without removing the front cover.

1. Drain the cooling system (except GLC front wheel drive).
2. Remove the radiator (except GLC front wheel drive).
3. Remove the drive belts and crankshaft pulley.
4. Pry the front oil seal carefully from the timing case cover.
5. Install the new oil seal. The rest of the installation is in the reverse order of removal.

Camshaft
REMOVAL AND INSTALLATION

Perform this operation on a cold engine only. Do not remove the camshaft gear from the timing chain. Be sure that the gear teeth and chain relationship is not disturbed. Wire the chain and cam gear to a place so that they will not fall into the front cover.

1. Remove the water pump (except GLC front wheel drive).
2. Rotate the crankshaft to place the No. 1 cylinder on TDC of the compression stroke.
3. Remove the distributor.
4. Remove the valve cover.
5. Release the tension on the timing chain by using a screwdriver or clamping tool (see "Timing Chain Tensioner" above).
6. Remove the cylinder head bolts in reverse of torquing sequence, in several stages.
7. Remove the rocker arm assembly.
8. Remove the nut, washer and distributor gear from the camshaft.
9. Remove the nut and washer holding the camshaft gear.
10. Remove the camshaft.
11. Installation is the reverse of removal. Torque in several stages using the torquing

sequence shown under "Cylinder Head Overhaul." Camshaft end-play should be 0.001–0.007 in.

Pistons and Connecting Rods
REMOVAL AND INSTALLATION

Refer to the "Piston Engine Rebuilding" section. Pistons are installed with the "F" marking toward the front of the engine. Rings are installed with markings facing upward.

PISTON ENGINE LUBRICATION

Oil Pan
REMOVAL AND INSTALLATION

1. Jack up the front of the car and safely support on jackstands. Disconnect negative battery cable. Remove the engine splash shield or skid plate.
2. Remove the clutch slave cylinder, if equipped. Do not disconnect the hydraulic line, let the cylinder hang.
3. Remove the engine rear brace attaching bolts and loosen the bolts on the left side, if equipped.
4. Disconnect the emission line from the oil pan, if equipped.
5. Loosen the front motor mounts, raise the front of the engine and block up to gain clearance if necessary. (Except GLC—front wheel drive).
6. Remove the oil pan and allow it to rest on the crossmember. Remove the oil pump pickup tube, if necessary, to remove the oil pan.
7. Install in the reverse order of removal.

Rear Main Oil Seal
REPLACEMENT

If the rear main oil seal is being replaced independently of any other parts, it can be done with the engine in place. If the rear main oil seal and the rear main bearing are being replaced, together, the engine must be removed

1. Remove the transmission.
2. Remove the clutch disc, pressure plate and flywheel.
3. Punch two holes in the crankshaft rear oil seal. They should be punched on opposite sides of the crankshaft, just above the bearing cap-to-cylinder block split line.
4. Install a sheet metal screw in each hole.

Pry against both screws at the same time to remove the oil seal.

5. Clean the oil recess in the cylinder block and bearing cap. Clean the oil seal surface on the crankshaft.

6. Coat the oil seal surfaces with oil. Coat the oil surface and the steal surface on the crankshaft with Lubriplate. Install the new oil seal and make sure that it is not cocked. Be sure that the seal surface was not damaged.

7. Install the flywheel. Coat the threads of the flywheel attaching bolts with oil-resistant sealer.

8. Install the clutch, pressure plate and transmission.

Oil Pump

CHECKING OIL PUMP

1. Measure the clearance between the lobes of the rotors. If the clearance exceeds 0.010 in., replace both rotors.

2. Check the clearance between the outer rotor and the pump body. Clearance should be 0.006–0.010 in. If it exceeds 0.012 in., replace the pump on 1600 engines, or the rotor on 1300, 1415, 1490 1970 engines. If a new rotor will not bring the dimension within specification on 1300 engines, the block must be replaced.

3. Place a straight-edge across the pump body and measure the clearance between the rotor and the straight-edge. Place a straight-edged across the pump cover and measure the clearance between the straight-edge and the cover. The combined clearance is the rotor end-play. If it is 0.006 in. or more, correct it by grinding the cover. End-play should be 0.002–0.004 in.

NOTE: *When replacing rotors, install them so the marks face outward.*

REMOVAL AND INSTALLATION

1490 GLC—Front Wheel Drive, 1600 and 1970 cc Engines

Remove the oil pan. Remove the oil pump gear attaching nut. Remove the bolts attaching the oil pump to the block. Loosen the gear on the pump. Remove the oil pump and gear.

1300, 1415 and 1490 cc GLC Wagon

1. Remove the front cover as described.
2. Remove oil pump drive sprocket retaining nut and lockwasher. Slide both oil pump

drive sprockets and drive chain off crankshaft and oil pump shaft.

3. Remove oil pump cover, and pull out pump shaft and rotors.

4. Installation is the reverse of the removal procedure. Oil pump drive sprocket retaining nut is torqued to 22–25 ft. lbs.

ROTARY ENGINE LUBRICATION

Oil Pan

REMOVAL AND INSTALLATION

1. Drain engine oil. Remove attaching bolts, and remove the gravel shield.

2. Disconnect the oil level sensor and, if so equipped, the oil temperature sending unit.

3. Remove oil pan bolts and remove the pan.

4. Coat both sides of a new gasket with a sealer before installing the pan. Install bolts and torque to 5–7 ft. lbs. Reverse the remaining removal procedures.

Metering Oil Pump

OPERATION

A metering oil pump, mounted on the top of the engine, is used to provide additional lubrication to the engine when it is operating under a load. The pump provides oil to the carburetor, where it is mixed in the float chamber with the fuel which is to be burned.

The metering pump is a plunger type and is controlled by throttle opening. A cam arrangement, connected to the carburetor throttle lever, operates a plunger. The plunger, in turn, acts on a differential plunger, the stroke of which determines the amount of oil flow.

When the throttle opening is small, the amount of the plunger stroke is small; as the throttle opening increases, so does the amount of the plunger stroke.

TESTING

1. Disconnect the oil lines which run from the metering oil pump to the carburetor, at the carburetor end.

2. Use a container which has a scale calibrated in cubic centimeters (cc) to catch the pump discharge from the oil lines.

NOTE: *Such a container is available from a scientific equipment supply house.*

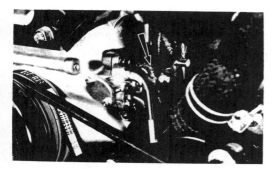

Arrow indicates metering oil pump adjusting screw

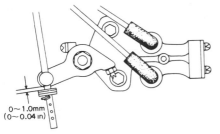

0~1.0mm
(0~0.04 in)

Checking metering oil pump lever-to-washer clearance

3. Run the engine at 2,000 rpm for six minutes.

4. At the end of this time, 2.4–2.9 cc of oil should be collected in the container on vehicles built up to 1976, and 2.0–2.5 cc on 1977 and later vehicles. If not, adjust the pump as explained below.

ADJUSTMENTS

Rotate the adjusting screw on the metering oil pump to obtain the proper oil flow. Clockwise rotation of the screw *increases* the flow; counterclockwise rotation *decreases* the oil flow. After adjustment is completed, tighten the locknut.

If necessary, on 1971–76 vehicles, the oil discharge rate may further be adjusted by changing the position of the cam in the pump connecting rod. The shorter the rod throw the more oil will be pumped. Adjust the throw by means of the three holes provided.

On 1977 and later vehicles, after adjusting the adjusting screw, check the clearance between the pump lever and washer as shown, and, if necessary, install washer(s) to create the proper clearance.

Oil Pump

REMOVAL AND INSTALLATION

Oil pump removal and installation is contained in the "Engine Overhaul" section.

Perform only those steps needed in order to remove the oil pump.

Oil Cooler

REMOVAL AND INSTALLATION

1. Raise the car and support it with jackstands.
   CAUTION: *Be sure that the car is securely supported.*
2. Drain the engine oil.
3. Unfasten the screws which retain the gravel shield and remove the shield.
4. Unfasten the oil lines from the oil cooler.
5. Unfasten the nuts which secure the oil cooler to the radiator.
6. Remove the oil cooler.

Examine the oil cooler for signs of leakage. Solder any leaks found. Blow the fins of the cooler clean with compressed air.

Installation is performed in the reverse order of removal.

PISTON ENGINE COOLING

Radiator

REMOVAL AND INSTALLATION

1. Drain the coolant from the radiator.
2. Remove the fan blades and shroud or disconnect the electric harness from the electric fan motor and remove the fan and cowling mount.
3. Remove the upper and lower hoses. Disconnect the transmission cooler lines, if equipped.
4. Remove the radiator mounting bolts and remove the radiator.
5. Install the radiator by reversing the removal procedure. Refer to Chapter 1 for coolant refill.

Water Pump

REMOVAL AND INSTALLATION

1. Drain the coolant from the radiator.
2. On GLC front wheel drive models, jack up the front of the car and safely support it on jackstands. Remove the splash shield. Remove the drive belt, lower hose and by-pass pipe with O-ring. Remove the water pump.
3. On other models, remove the air pump if interfering. Remove the fan from the fan pulley if not equipped with electric fan assembly. Loosen and remove the fan drive belt. Remove the radiator hose.

4. Loosen and remove the water pump mounting bolts, remove the water pump.

5. Clean all gasket surfaces. Mount the new water pump and gasket. Tighten the mounting bolts evenly in several stages. The rest of the installation is in the reverse order of removal.

Thermostat

REMOVAL AND INSTALLATION

1. Drain several quarts of coolant from the radiator so that the coolant level is below the thermostat.

2. Disconnect the radiator hose from the thermostat housing.

3. Remove the thermostat housing mounting bolts, housing, gasket and thermostat.

4. Clean all gasket surfaces. Install the new thermostat with the temperature sensing pellet downwards. Use a new mounting gasket and install the housing.

5. The rest of the installation is in the reverse order of removal.

ROTARY ENGINE COOLING

Radiator

REMOVAL AND INSTALLATION

1971–76

1. Drain the engine coolant.
2. Remove the shroud.
3. Remove the upper, lower, and expansion tank hoses.
4. Remove the oil cooler.
5. Withdraw the radiator.
6. Install in the reverse order of removal.

1977–78

1. Drain the cooling system.
2. Remove the fan drive attaching bolts, and remove fan and fan drive as an assembly.
3. Loosen hose clamps, and disconnect inlet and outlet hoses and heater hose at radiator.
4. Disconnect oil cooler hoses at radiator, if the vehicle has an automatic transmission.
5. Remove oil cooler mounting brackets from the radiator. Remove radiator shroud from the radiator.
6. Remove mounting bolts, and remove the radiator.
7. To install, reverse the removal procedure.

Water Pump

REMOVAL AND INSTALLATION

1971–75

1. Drain the engine coolant.
2. Remove the air cleaner.
3. Loosen, but do not remove, the water pump pulley bolts.
4. Remove the alternator drivebelt.
5. Remove the water pump pulley.
6. Remove the pump.
7. Separate the pump body from the casing.
8. Installation is the reverse of removal.

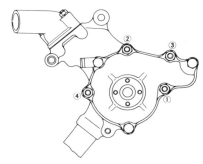

Late model rotary engine water pump tightening sequence

1976–78

1. Drain the cooling system and remove the air cleaner.
2. Disconnect the water temperature sending unit.
3. Remove alternator and air pump and their belts.
4. Disconnect the upper radiator hose at the thermostat housing. Remove the upper fan shroud.
5. Remove the attaching bolts, and remove the fan and fan drive as an assembly.
6. Installation is in reverse order. Coat a new water pump gasket with sealer on both sides, and torque water pump attaching bolts, a little at a time, in the order shown to 13–20 ft. lb.

Thermostat

REMOVAL AND INSTALLATION

1. Drain the engine coolant.
2. Remove the thermostat housing and the thermostat.

Installation is the reverse of removal.

CAUTION: *The thermostat is equipped with a plunger which covers and uncovers*

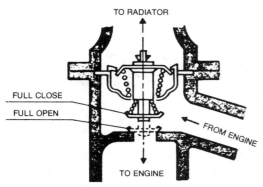

Rotary engine thermostat installation

Mark the front and rear rotor housings to prevent confusion during assembly

a by-pass hole at its bottom. Because of this unusual construction, only the specified Mazda thermostat should be used for replacement. A standard thermostat will cause the engine to overheat.

ROTARY ENGINE OVERHAUL

1971–73

DISASSEMBLY

Engine disassembly should be performed in the following order, after it has been removed from the automobile and placed on a workstand:

1. Remove all of the components of the emission control system. See "Emission Controls" in Chapter Four.
2. Detach the metering oil pump linkage, oil lines, and vacuum sensing lines from the carburetor.
3. Remove the intake manifold securing nuts, evenly and in several stages.
4. Remove the intake manifold assembly, complete with the carburetor.
5. Remove the alternator adjusting link bolt, but do not remove the adjusting link, itself.
6. Unfasten the alternator attaching bolts, then remove the alternator and its drive belt.
7. Remove the pulley from the water pump.
8. Unfasten the five nuts and two bolts which secure the water pump and remove the pump.
9. Remove the clamping nuts from both of the distributors and withdraw the distributors from their sockets.
10. Mark the distributor sockets for identification during assembly. Remove the nuts and withdraw the distributor sockets from the front housing.

11. Attach a brake to keep the ring gear from turning (Mazda tool, part number 49 0820 060A).
12. Unfasten the eccentric shaft pulley bolt. Remove the pulley and the key from the eccentric shaft.
13. Unfasten the clutch cover attachment bolts.
14. Remove the clutch assembly from the flywheel.
15. Straighten the tabs on the flywheel nut lockwasher.
16. Remove the flywheel nut with a wrench of a suitably large size.
   CAUTION: *Do not use locking pliers or a hammer and chisel to remove the flywheel nut.*
17. Remove the flywheel with a puller.
18. Invert the engine on the workstand.
19. Remove the oil pan bolts and take the oil pan off the engine along with its gasket.
20. Remove the oil strainer bolts, the oil strainer, and its gasket.
21. Mark the front and rear rotor housings, which are identical in appearance, so that they will not be confused upon assembly.
22. With the front of the engine facing up in the stand, unfasten the front engine mount securing nuts and remove the mounts.

Tension bolt removal sequence

23. Remove the front engine cover securing bolts. Lift off the cover and its gasket.

24. Withdraw the O-ring from the passage on the front of the housing.

25. Remove the oil pump drive chain and related components from the engine on 1972–73 models, in the following manner:

　　a. Slide the oil slinger, spacer, and distributor drive gear off the eccentric shaft.

　　b. Remove the chain tensioner nuts and the chain tensioner.

　　c. Remove the locknut and washer from the oil pump sprocket.

　　d. Slide the sprockets off the eccentric shaft and oil pump drive shaft simultaneously, complete with the chain.

　　e. Remove the key from the eccentric shaft.

26. Slide the oil pump drive gear (1971 models), balancing weight, thrust washer, and the first needle bearing off the eccentric shaft.

27. Unfasten the bearing housing securing bolts.

28. Remove the bearing housing, second needle bearing, spacer, and thrust washer.

29. Turn the engine on the workstand so that the top side of it is facing upward.

30. Loosen the engine housing tension bolts in the order illustrated.

CAUTION: *Do not loosen the tension bolts one at a time. Loosen the bolts evenly and in two or three stages.*

31. With the front of the engine facing up, lift the front housing off the eccentric shaft.

32. Remove any side seals which are sticking to the surface of the front housing and place them in their original position on the rotor.

33. Remove the rotor seals and related components in the following order, after not-

Identify each apex seal by marking its bottom with a felt-tipped pen

ing their original positions so that they will not be confused during assembly.

　　a. Three corner seals

　　b. Three corner seal springs

　　c. Six side seals

　　d. Six side seal springs

NOTE: *Each seal has its own installation mark next to its groove on the rotor. Mazda has a special seal tray (part no. 49 0813 250) which uses the same marks so that the seals will not be confused during storage and assembly.*

34. Remove the oil seals and O-rings from the grooves in the rotor face.

35. Hold the front rotor housing down while threading a nut and bolt of the proper *metric* size into each of the hollow dowels on the engine housing.

36. Remove the dowels by holding the bolt with a wrench while tightening the nut. Once the dowel contacts the nut, back off on the nut and insert a spacer between the nut and the housing. Continue tightening the nut and inserting spacers until each dowel is out of the housing.

37. Lift the front housing away from the rotor.

CAUTION: *Use care when lifting the housing off the rotor, so that the apex seals do not fall off. If they strike a hard surface they will shatter.*

38. Remove the air injection nozzles, the O-rings, and the rubber seals from the front housing.

39. Remove the apex seals and their springs from the front rotor. When removing each seal, place an identification mark on the *bottom*, with a felt-tipped pen, so that it can be installed in the proper location and direction. If any of the seals have come off, be sure to note their proper location.

CAUTION: *When marking the seals, do not use a punch or scratch the surface of the seal.*

Remove any side seals which adhere to the front housing

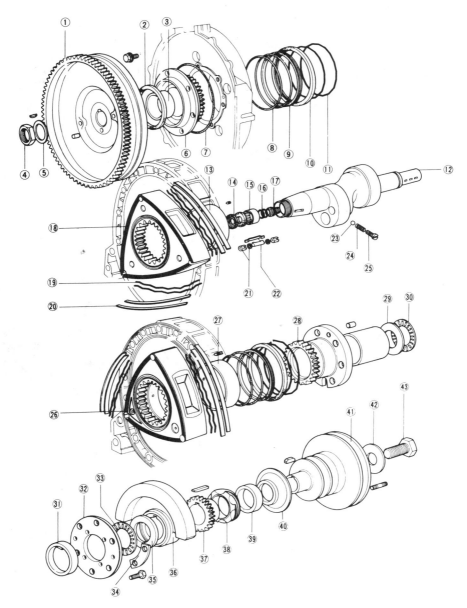

1. Flywheel	16. O-ring	31. Spacer
2. Oil seal	17. Blind plug	32. Bearing housing
3. Main bearing	18. Front rotor	33. Needle bearing
4. Locknut	19. Side seal spring	34. Washer
5. Washer	20. Side seal	35. Thrust plate
6. Rear stationary gear	21. Corner seal and spring	36. Balance weight
7. O-ring	22. Apex seal w/spring	37. Oil pump drive sprocket
8. Oil seal O-ring	23. Steel ball	—1972–73
9. Oil seal	24. Spring	38. Distributor drive gear
10. Oil seal	25. Oil nozzle	39. Spacer
11. Oil seal spring	26. Rear rotor	40. Oil slinger
12. Eccentric shaft	27. Rotor bearing	41. Eccentric shaft pulley
13. Rotor bearing	28. Front stationary gear	42. Washer
14. Grease seal	29. Thrust washer	43. Bolt
15. Needle bearing	30. Thrust bearing	

Rotor and eccentric shaft components

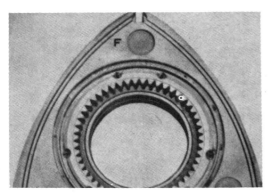

The front rotor is marked with an "F" on its internal gear side and the rear with an "R" in the same manner

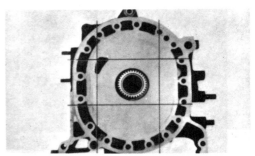

Measure the housing distortion along the axes indicated

Measure the housing wear with a dial indicator

40. Remove the front rotor from the eccentric shaft and place it face down on a clean, soft cloth.

NOTE: *The internal gear side of the front rotor is marked with an "F" to ensure installation in the proper rotor housing.*

41. Remove the seals and springs from the rear side of the rotor in the same manner as detailed for the front side in Step 38.

42. Hold the intermediate housing down and remove the hollow dowels, as outlined for the front rotor housing in Steps 35–36.

43. Lift the intermediate housing off the eccentric shaft by sliding it beyond the front rotor journal while pushing up on the shaft. Use care not to damage the eccentric shaft.

44. Withdraw the eccentric shaft.

45. Repeat Steps 35–41 to remove the rear rotor housing and rotor.

NOTE: *The internal gear side of the rear rotor is marked with a "R" to ensure installation in the proper rotor housing.*

INSPECTION AND REPLACEMENT

Front Housing

1. Check the housing for signs of gas or water leakage.

2. Remove the carbon deposits from the front housing with an extra fine emery cloth.

NOTE: *If a carbon scraper must be used, be careful not to damage the mating surfaces of the housing.*

3. Remove any old sealer which is adhering to the housing using a brush or a cloth soaked in ketone.

4. Check for distortion by placing a straightedge on the surface of the housing. Measure the clearance between the straightedge and the housing with a feeler gauge. If

the clearance is greater than 0.002 in. at any point, replace the housing.

5. Use a dial indicator to check for wear on the rotor contact surfaces of the housing. If the wear is greater than 0.004 in., replace the housing.

NOTE: *The wear at either end of the minor axis is greater than at any other point on the housing. However, this is normal and should be no cause for concern.*

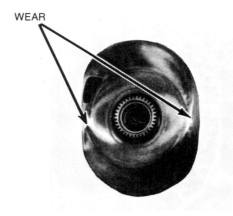

WEAR

Most of the front and rear housing wear occurs at the ends of the minor axis, as indicated

Front Stationary Gear and Main Bearing

1. Examine the teeth of the stationary gear for wear or damage.

2. Be sure that the main bearing shows no signs of excessive wear, scoring, or flaking.

3. Check the main bearing-to-eccentric journal clearance by measuring the journal with a vernier caliper and the bearing with a pair of inside calipers. The clearance should be between 0.0018–0.0028 in., and the wear limit is 0.0039 in. Replace either the main bearing or the eccentric shaft if it is greater than this. If the main bearing is to be replaced, proceed as detailed in the following section.

Align the slot in the stationary gear flange with the pin on the housing (arrow)

Main Bearing Replacement

1. Unfasten the securing bolts, if used. Drive the stationary gear and main bearing assembly out of the housing with a brass drift.

2. Press the main bearing out of the stationary gear.

3. Press a new main bearing into the stationary gear so that it is in the same position as the old bearing before it was removed.

4. Align the slot in the stationary gear flange with the dowel pin in the housing and press the gear into place. Install the securing bolts, if required.

NOTE: *To aid in stationary gear and main bearing removal and installation, Mazda supplies a special tool, part number 49 0813 235.*

Intermediate and Rear Housings.

Inspection of the intermediate and rear housings is carried out in the same manner as detailed for the front housing above. Replacement of the rear main bearing and stationary gear (mounted on the rear housing) is given below.

Rear Stationary Gear and Main Bearing

Inspect the rear stationary gear and main bearing in a similar manner to the front. In addition, examine the O-ring, which is located in the stationary gear, for signs of wear or damage. Replace the O-ring, if necessary.

If required, replace the stationary gear in the following manner:

1. Remove the rear stationary gear securing bolts.

2. Drive the stationary gear out of the rear housing with a brass drift.

Position the o-ring in the groove on the stationary gear (arrow)

3. Apply a light coating of grease on a new O-ring and fit it into the groove on the stationary gear.

4. Apply sealer to the flange of the stationary gear.

5. Install the stationary gear on the housing so that the slot on its flange aligns with the pin on the rear housing.

CAUTION: *Use care not to damage the O-ring during installation.*

6. Tighten the stationary gear bolts evenly, and in several stages, to 15 ft. lbs.

Rotor Housings

1. Examine the inner margin of both housings for signs of gas or water leakage.

2. Wipe the inner surface of each housing with a clean cloth to remove the carbon deposits.

NOTE: *If the carbon deposits are stubborn, soak the cloth in a solution of ketone. Do not scrape or sand the chrome plated surfaces of the rotor chamber.*

3. Clean all of the rust deposits out of the cooling passages of each rotor housing.

Measure the rotor housing distortion along the axes indicated

Normal shading of deposits on the rotor

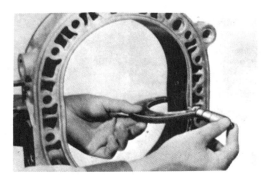

Check the rotor housing width at eight points along the trochoid surfaces

4. Remove the old sealer with a cloth soaked in ketone.

5. Examine the chromium plated inner surfaces for scoring, flaking, or other signs of damage. If any are present, the housing must be replaced.

6. Check the rotor housings for distortion by placing a straightedge on the areas illustrated.

7. Measure the clearance between the straightedge and the housing with a feeler gauge. If the gap exceeds 0.002 in., replace the rotor housing.

8. Check the widths of both rotor housings, at a minimum of eight points near the trochoid surfaces of each housing, with a vernier caliper.

If the difference between the maximum and minimum values obtained is greater than 0.0031 in., replace the housing. A housing in this condition will be prone to gas and coolant leakage.

NOTE: *Standard rotor housing width is 2.7559 in.*

Rotors

1. Check the rotor for signs of blow-by around the side and corner seal areas.

2. The color of the carbon deposits on the rotor should be brown, just as in a piston engine.

NOTE: *Usually the carbon on the leading side of the rotor is brown, while carbon on the trailing side tends toward black, as viewed from the direction of rotation.*

3. Remove the carbon on the rotor with a scraper or extra fine emery paper. Use the scraper carefully when doing the seal grooves, so that no damage is done to them.

4. Wash the rotor in solvent and blow it dry with compressed air after removing the carbon.

5. Examine the internal gear for cracks or damaged teeth.

NOTE: *If the internal gear is damaged, the rotor and gear must be replaced as a single assembly.*

6. With the oil seal removed, check the land protrusions by placing a straightedge over the lands. Measure the gap between the rotor surface and the straightedge with a feeler gauge. The standard specification is 0.004–0.006 in.; if it is less than this, the rotor must be replaced.

7. Check the gaps between the housings and the rotor on both sides.

    a. Measure the rotor width with a vernier caliper. The standard rotor width is 2.7500 in.

    b. Compare the rotor width with the

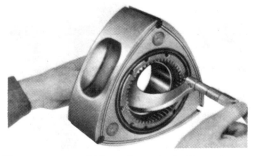

Measure rotor width at the point indicated

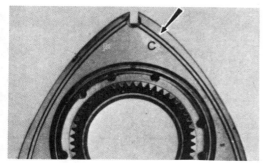

Weight classification letter placement

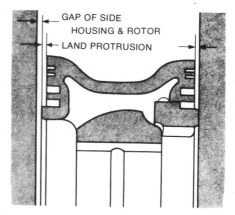

Oil Seal protrusion

width of the rotor housing measured above. The standard rotor housing width is 2.7559 in.

c. Replace the rotor if the difference between the two measurements is not within 0.0051–0.0067 in.

8. Check the rotor bearing for flaking, wearing, or scoring and proceed as indicated in the next section, if any of these are present.

The rotors are classified into five lettered grades, according to their weight. A letter between A and E is stamped on the internal gear side of the rotor. If it becomes necessary to replace a rotor, use one marked with a "C" because this is the standard replacement rotor.

Rotor Bearing Replacement

Special service tools are required to replace a rotor bearing. Replacement is also a tricky procedure which, if done improperly, could result in serious damage to the rotor and could even make replacement of the entire rotor necessary. Therefore, this service procedure is best left to an authorized service facility or a qualified machine shop.

Oil Seal Inspection

NOTE: *Inspect the oil seal while it is mounted in the rotor.*

1. Examine the oil seal for signs of wear or damage.

2. Measure the width of the oil seal lip. If it is greater than 0.031 in., replace the oil seal.

3. Measure the protrusion of the oil seal, it should be greater than 0.020 in. Replace the seal, as detailed below, if it is not.

Oil Seal Replacement

NOTE: *Replace the rubber O-ring in the oil seal as a normal part of engine overhaul.*

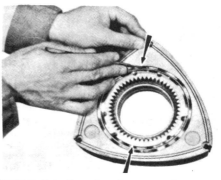

Position the oil seal spring gaps at arrows

1. Pry the seal out gently by inserting a screwdriver in the slots on the rotor. Do not remove the seal by prying it at only one point as seal deformation will result.

CAUTION: *Be careful not to deform the lip of the oil seal if it is to be reinstalled.*

2. Fit both of the oil seal springs into their respective grooves, so that their ends are facing upward and their gaps are opposite each other on the rotor.

3. Insert a new rubber O-ring into each of the oil seals.

NOTE: *Before installing the O-rings into the oil seals, fit each of the seals into its proper groove on the rotor. Check to see that all of the seals move smoothly and freely.*

4. Coat the oil seal groove and the oil seal with engine oil.

5. Gently press the oil seal into the groove with your fingers. Be careful not to distort the seal.

NOTE: *Be sure that the white mark is on the bottom side of each seal when it is installed.*

6. Repeat the installation procedure for the oil seals on both sides of each rotor.

Apex Seals

CAUTION: *Although the apex seals are extremely durable when in service, they are easily broken when they are being handled. Be careful not to drop them.*

1. Remove the carbon deposits from the apex seals and their springs. Do not use emery cloth on the seals as it will damage their finish.

2. Wash the seals and the springs in cleaning solution.

3. Check the apex seals for cracks and other signs of wear or damage.

4. Test the seal springs for weakness.

5. Use a micrometer to check the seal height. Replace any seal if its height is less than 0.3150 in.

6. With a feeler gauge, check the side clearance between the apex seal and the groove in the rotor. Insert the gauge until its tip contacts the bottom of the groove. If the gap is greater than 0.004 in., replace the seal.

7. Check the gap between the apex seals and the side housing, in the following manner:

    a. Use a vernier caliper to measure the length of each apex seal.

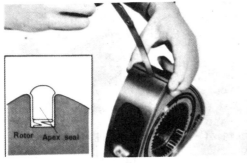

Check the gap between the apex seal and groove with a feeler gauge

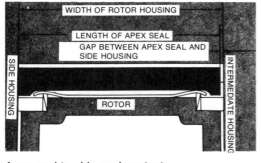

Apex seal to side seal contact

    b. Compare this measurement to the *minimum* figure obtained when rotor housing width was being measured.

    c. If the difference is more than 0.0059 in., replace the seal.

    d. If, on the other hand, the seal is too long, stand the ends of the seal with emery cloth until the proper length is reached.

CAUTION: *Do not use the emery cloth on the faces of the seal.*

Side Seals

1. Remove the carbon deposits from the side seals and their springs with a carbon scraper.

2. Check the side seals for cracks or wear. Replace any of the seals found to be defective.

3. Check the clearance between the side seals and their grooves with a feeler gauge. Replace any side seals if they have a clearance of more than 0.0039 in. The standard clearance is 0.002–0.003 in.

4. Check the clearance between the side seals and the corner seals with both of them installed in the rotor.

    a. Insert a feeler gauge between the end of the side seal and the corner seal.

NOTE: *Insert the gauge against the direction of the rotor's rotation.*

    b. Replace the side seal if the clearance is greater than 0.016 in.

5. If the side seal is replaced, adjust the clearance between it and the corner seal as follows:

    a. File the side seal on its reverse side, in the same rotational direction of the rotor, along the outline made by the corner seal.

    b. The clearance obtained should be 0.002–0.006 in. If it exceeds this, the performance of the seals will deteriorate.

CAUTION: *There are four different types*

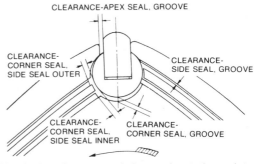

Check the clearance of the seals at the points indicated

of side seals, depending upon their location. Do not mix the seals up and be sure to use the proper type of seal for replacement.

Corner Seals

1. Clean the carbon deposits from the corner seals.
2. Examine each of the seals for wear or damage.
3. Measure the clearance between the corner seal and its groove. The clearance should be 0.0008–0.0019 in. The wear limit of the gap is 0.0031 in.
4. If the wear between the corners seal and the groove is uneven, check the clearance with the special "bar limit gauge" (Mazda part number 49 0839 165). The gauge has a "go" end and a "no go" end. Use the gauge in the following manner:

    a. If neither end of the gauge goes into the groove, the clearance is within specifications.

    b. If the "go" end of the gauge fits into the groove, but the "no go" end does not, replace the corner seal with one that is 0.0012 in. oversize.

    c. If both ends of the gauge fit into the groove, then the groove must be reamed out as detailed below. Replace the corner seal with one which is 0.0072 in. oversize, after completing reaming.

NOTE: *Take the measurement of the groove in the direction of maximum wear, i.e., that of rotation.*

Corner Seal Groove Reaming

NOTE: *This procedure requires the use of special tools; if attempted without them, damage to the rotor could result.*

1. Carefully remove all of the deposits which remain in the groove.
2. Fit the jib (Mazda part number 2113 99 900) over the rotor. Tighten its adjusting bar, being careful not to damage the rotor bearing or the apex seal grooves.
3. Use the corner seal groove reamer (Mazda part number 49 0839 170) to ream the groove.
4. Rotate the reamer at least 20 times while applying engine oil as a coolant.

NOTE: *If engine oil is not used, it will be impossible to obtain the proper groove surfacing.*

5. Remove the reamer and the jib.
6. Repeat Steps 1–5 for each of the corner seal grooves.

Reaming the corner seal groove

7. Clean the rotor completely and check it for any signs of damage.
8. Fit a 0.0079 in. oversize corner seal into the groove and check its clearance. Clearance should be 0.0008–0.0019 in.

Seal Springs

Check the seal springs for damage or weakness. Be exceptionally careful when checking the spring areas which contact either the rotor or the seal.

Eccentric Shaft

1. Wash the eccentric shaft in solvent and blow its oil passages dry with compressed air.
2. Check the shaft for wear, cracks, or other signs of damage. Make sure that none of the oil passages are clogged.

Position the dial indicator as shown, in order to measure shaft runout

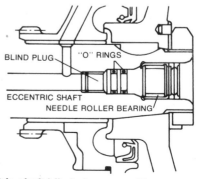

Eccentric shaft blind plug assembly

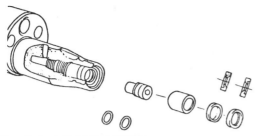

Needle bearing components

Corner seal installation

3. Measure the shaft journals with a vernier caliper. The standard specifications are:

Main journals—1.6929 in.
Rotor journals—2.9134 in.

Replace the shaft if any of its journals show excessive wear.

4. Check eccentric shaft runout by placing the shaft on V-blocks and using a dial indicator as shown. Rotate the shaft slowly and note the dial indicator reading. If runout is more than 0.0008 in., replace the eccentric shaft.

5. Check the blind plug at the end of the shaft. If it is loose or leaking, remove it with an allen wrench and replace the O-ring.

6. Check the operation of the needle roller bearing for smoothness by inserting a mainshaft into the bearing and rotating it. Examine the bearing for signs of wear or damage.

7. Replace the bearing, if necessary, with the special bearing replacer (Mazda part number 49 0823 073 and 49 0823 072).

ASSEMBLY

1. Place the rear rotor on a rubber pad or a clean, thick cloth.

2. Install the oil seals on both sides of the rotor, if you have not already done so. Follow the procedure outlined in the appropriate section under "Inspection and Replacement," below.

3. Place the rear rotor on the pad or cloth, so that its internal gear is facing upward.

NOTE: *When installing the various seals, consult the marks made during engine disassembly in order to ensure installation of the seals in their proper location.*

4. Place each of the apex seals into their respective grooves without fitting the springs.

5. Place each of the corner seal springs, followed by the corner seals, into the grooves on the rotor. Lubricate them with engine oil.

6. Check to see that the upper surface of the corner seal is 0.05–0.06 in. higher than

the rotor. The corner seal should also move freely when finger-pressure is applied to it.

7. Place the side seal springs into their grooves with both ends facing upward. Coat them with engine oil.

8. Install each of the side seals into the proper groove.

9. Be sure that each seal protrudes about 0.04 in. from the surface of the rotor. Test free movement of the seals by pressing them with your finger.

10. Lubricate all of the seals and the internal gear with engine oil.

11. Mount the rear housing in the workstand so that the top of it is facing upward.

12. Place the rotor on the rear housing so that both its rotor contact surface and the rotor are facing upward.

CAUTION: *Be sure that none of the seals fall off while the rotor is being moved.*

13. Mesh the rotor internal gear with the stationary gear on the housing so that the apexes of the rotor are positioned as illustrated.

NOTE: *When positioning the rotor, be sure that none of the corner seals drop into the parts.*

The rear rotor must be positioned exactly as shown for installation

14. Remove the three apex seals from the rotor and place them so that they are near their proper installation positions.

15. Lubricate the eccentric shaft rear rotor and main bearing journals with engine oil.

16. Insert the eccentric shaft into the rotor and rear housing using care not to damage any of the bearings or journals.

17. Fit the air injection nozzles into place and apply sealer to the back of the rear rotor housing.

NOTE: *Use care not to get any sealer into the water or oil passages of the rear housing.*

18. Apply a small amount of rubber lubricant on new O-rings and rubber seals, then install them into the rear side of the rotor housing.

19. Invert the rear rotor housing, fit it over the rotor, and then onto the rear housing. Be sure that none of the O-rings or rubber seals fall out of the housing.

20. Coat the hollow dowels with engine oil. Fit the dowels through the holes in the rotor housing and into the holes on the rear housing.

21. Install the apex seals, complete with springs, in their proper positions and directions in the rotor.

22. Fit the corner and side seals, with their springs, into the proper grooves. Be sure that they are facing in the correct direction.

23. Lightly lubricate the rotor and the rotor contact surface of the rear housing, with engine oil.

24. Apply sealer to the O-rings and rubber seals. Install them on the intermediate housing in a similar manner to that outlined in Steps 17–18 above.

25. Hold the back end of the eccentric shaft up, so that the front end of the rear rotor journal does not extend beyond the front side of the rotor bearing.

26. Fit the intermediate housing on the rear rotor housing, while holding the eccentric shaft, as explained in the step above.

27. Install the front rotor and rotor housing in the same manner outlined for the rear rotor and housing in Steps 1–23.

NOTE: *The proper relationship between the timing of the front and rear rotors will be obtained when the front rotor is placed over the rotor journal on the eccentric shaft and positioned as the rear rotor is in Step 13.*

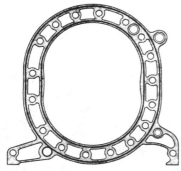

Apply sealer to the grey-shaded areas of the rotor housing

ntermediate housing installation

Installation of the apex seal and spring

Tension bolt tightening sequence

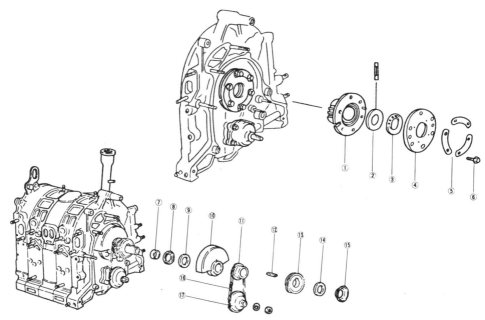

1. Stationary gear
2. Thrust-plate
3. Needle bearing
4. Bearing housing
5. Lockwasher
6. Bolt
7. Spacer
8. Needle bearing
9. Thrust washer
10. Balance weight
11. Oil pump drive sprocket
12. Key
13. Distributor drive gear
14. Spacer
15. Oil slinger
16. Drive chain
17. Oil pump drive sprocket

Bearing housing assembly—1972–73 illustrated

Flywheel installation

Use a dial indicator attached to the flywheel to measure eccentric shaft end-play

28. Apply engine oil to the front housing stationary gear and main bearing. Place the front housing over the front rotor housing. If necessary, turn the front rotor slightly to engage its internal gear with the front housing stationary gear.

29. Install the tension bolts in the following manner:

　a. Fit each bolt through the housings and turn it two or three times.

　b. Rotate the engine in the stand so that its top is facing upward.

　c. Tighten the bolts evenly and in two or three stages. Use the sequence illustrated below and the torque figure listed in the torque specifications chart.

CAUTION: *Do not tighten the bolts one at a time.*

　d. Rotate the eccentric shaft to see that it operates lightly and smoothly.

30. Coat the rear oil seal with engine oil. Apply Loctite® to the threads on the eccentric shaft through the key.

31. Install the flywheel on the rear of the eccentric shaft with its keyway over the key on the shaft.

32. Coat both sides of the flywheel lockwasher with sealer, then fit the washer on the eccentric shaft.

33. Finger-tighten the flywheel locknut. Use a brake on the flywheel to keep it from rotating while tightening the nut on the flywheel to 350 ft. lbs.

34. Turn the engine on the workstand so that its front end is facing up.

35. Slip the thrust plate, spacer, and the rear needle bearing over the front of the eccentric shaft. Lubricate the parts which were just installed, with engine oil.

36. Install the bearing housing, tighten its securing bolts, and bend up the lockwasher tabs on the bolts.

37. Fit the front needle bearing and thrust washer on the shaft, then coat them with engine oil. Install the balance weight on the shaft.

38. On 1972–73 models, fit the oil pump drive chain over both of the sprockets. Install the sprocket and chain assembly over the eccentric and oil pump shafts simultaneously. Place the key on the eccentric shaft.

NOTE: *Be sure that both of the sprockets are engaged by the chain before installing them over the shafts.*

39. Slip the oil pump drive gear (1971), distributor drive gear, the spacer, and the oil slinger over the eccentric shaft.

40. Align the keyway on the eccentric shaft pulley with the key on the shaft and install the pulley. Tighten the pulley securing bolt to 47 ft. lbs. while holding the flywheel with the brake.

41. Check eccentric shaft end-play in the following manner:

  a. Attach a dial indicator to the flywheel. Move the flywheel forward and backward.

  b. Note the reading on the dial indicator; it should be 0.0016–0.0018 in.

  c. If the end-play is not within specifications, adjust it by replacing the front spacer. Spacers come in four sizes, ranging from 0.3151–0.3181 in.

  d. Check the end-play again and, if it is now within specifications, proceed with the next step.

42. Remove the pulley from the front of the eccentric shaft. Tighten the oil pump drive sprocket nut and bend the locktabs on the lockwasher.

43. Fit a new O-ring over the front cover oil passage.

44. Install the chain tensioner and tighten its securing bolts, if so equipped.

45. Position the front cover gasket and the front cover on the front housing, then secure the front cover with its attachment bolts.

46. Install the eccentric shaft pulley again. Tighten its bolt to 47 ft. lbs.

47. Use a spare mainshaft or an arbor to hold the clutch disc in place.

48. Install the clutch cover and pressure plate assembly over the flywheel.

NOTE: *Align the O-mark on the clutch cover with the hole in the flywheel.*

49. Tighten the clutch cover bolts to 15 ft. lbs., while holding the ring gear with a brake. Install the self-tapping bolt into the reamed hole.

50. With the bottom of the engine pointing upward in the workstand, cut the excess front cover gasket at the oil pan mounting flange.

51. Install the oil strainer gasket and the strainer. Bolt them to the front housing.

52. Apply sealer to the oil pan and housing mounting flanges. Install the oil pan and gasket. Tighten the bolts evenly and in several stages, to 7 ft. lbs.

53. Align the white mark on the eccentric shaft pulley with the pointer on the front housing to obtain top dead center (TDC) of the number one rotor's compression cycle.

54. Place the distributor socket gaskets on

Cut off the excess front cover gasket

Position the distributor drive slot as shown

the housing. Install the trailing distributor socket into the housing so that the driveshaft groove is inclined 34° to the right of the longitudinal axis of the engine.

55. Install the leading distributor socket in a similar manner, except that its driveshaft groove should be inclined 17° to the right of the longitudinal axis of the engine.

56. Install both distributors as outlined under "Engine Electrical," above.

57. Install the water pump as detailed under "Cooling System," below.

58. Bolt the engine mounts on the front housing.

59. Perform alternator installation and drivebelt tension adjustments as detailed under "Engine Electrical," above.

60. Position the intake manifold/carburetor assembly and gaskets on the engine. Tighten the manifold securing nuts evenly, and working in two or three stages, to the specifications in the "Torque Chart."

NOTE: *Start from the inside and work out when tightening the bolts.*

61. Attach the oil lines, the vacuum lines, and the metering oil pump linkage to the carburetor.

62. Remove the engine from the workstand.

63. Install the gaskets and then the thermal reactor on the engine. Tighten its securing nuts evenly, and working in two or three stages, to the specifications in the "Torque Chart."

64. Place the heat stove over the thermal reactor and secure it with its mounting nuts.

65. Install the components of the emission control system as detailed in "Emission Controls," below. See Chapter Four.

66. Install the engine in the car.

1974–78
DISASSEMBLY

Because of the design of the rotary engine, it is not practical to attempt component removal and installation. It is best to disassemble and assemble the entire engine, or, go as far as necessary with the disassembly procedure.

1. Mount the engine on a stand.

2. Remove the oil hose support bracket from the front housing.

3. Disconnect the vacuum hoses, air hoses and remove the decel valve.

4. Remove the air pump and drive belt. Remove the air pump adjusting bar.

5. Remove the alternator and drive belt.

6. Disconnect the metering oil pump connecting rod, oil tubes and vacuum sensing tube from the carburetor.

7. Remove the carburetor and intake manifold as an assembly.

8. Remove the gasket and two rubber rings.

9. Remove the thermal reactor and gaskets.

10. Remove the distributor.

11. Remove the water pump.

12. Invert the engine.

13. Remove the oil pan.

14. Remove the oil pump.

15. Identify the front and rear rotor housing with a felt tip pen. These are common parts and must be identified to be reassembled in their respective locations.

16. Turn the engine on the stand so that the top of the engine is up.

17. Remove the engine mounting bracket from the front cover.

18. Remove the eccentric shaft pulley.

19. Turn the engine on a stand so that the front end of the engine is up.

20. Remove the front cover.

21. Remove the O-ring from the oil passage on the front housing.

22. Remove the oil slinger and distributor drive gear from the shaft.

23. Unbolt and remove the chain adjuster.

24. Remove the locknut and washer from the oil pump drive sprocket.

25. Slide the oil pump drive sprocket and driven sprocket together with the drive chain off the eccentric shaft and oil pump simultaneously.

26. Remove the keys from the eccentric and oil pump shafts.

27. Slide the balance weight, thrust washer and needle bearing from the shaft.

28. Unbolt the bearing housing and slide the bearing housing, needle bearing, spacer and thrust plate off the shaft.

29. Turn the engine on the stand so that the top of the engine is up.

30. If equipped with a manual transmission, remove the clutch pressure plate and clutch disc. Remove the flywheel with a puller.

31. If equipped with an automatic transmission, remove the drive plate. Remove the counterweight.

32. Working at the rear of the engine, loosen the tension bolts.

NOTE: *Do not loosen the tension bolts one at a time. Loosen the bolts evenly in small stages to prevent distortion.*

33. Lift the rear housing off the shaft.

34. Remove any seals that are stuck to the rotor sliding surface of the rear housing and reinstall them in their original locations.

35. Remove all the corner seals, corner seal springs, side seal and side seal springs from the rear side of the rotor. Mazda has a special tray which holds all the seals and keeps them segregated to prevent mistakes during reassembly. Each seal groove is marked to prevent confusion.

36. Remove the two rubber seals and two O-rings from the rear rotor housing.

37. Remove the dowels from the rear rotor housing.

38. Lift the rear rotor housing away from the rear rotor, being very careful not to drop the apex seals on the rear rotor.

39. Remove each apex seal, side piece and spring from the rear rotor and segregate them.

40. Remove the rear rotor from the eccentric shaft and place it upside down on a clean rag.

41. Remove each seal and spring from the other side of the rotor and segregate these.

42. If some of the seals fall off the rotor, be careful not to change the original position of each seal.

43. Identify the rear rotor with a felt tip pen.

44. Remove the oil seals and the springs. Do not exert heavy pressure at only one place on the seal, since it could be deformed. Replace the O-rings in the oil seal when the engine is overhauled.

45. Hold the intermediate housing down and remove the dowels from it.

46. Lift off the intermediate housing being careful not to damage the eccentric shaft. It should be removed by slidin g it beyond the rear rotor journal on the eccentric shaft while holding the intermediate housing up and, at the same time, pushing the eccentric shaft up.

47. Lift out the eccentric shaft.

48. Repeat the above procedures to remove the front rotor housing and front rotor.

INSPECTION

The illustrations below detail and illustrate engine inspection procedures, and, in some cases, show usage and give the factory part numbers of special tools, or describe particular aspects of the assembly operation.

ASSEMBLY

1. Place the rotor on a rubber pad or cloth.

2. Install the oil seal rings in their respective grooves in the rotors with the edge of the spring in the stopper hole. The oil seal springs are painted cream or blue in color. The cream colored springs must be installed on the front faces of both rotors. The blue colored springs must be installed on the rear faces of both rotors. When installing each oil seal spring, the painted side (square side) of the spring must face upward (toward the oil seal).

3. Install a new O-ring in each groove. Place each oil seal in the groove so that the square edge of the spring fits in the stopper hole of the oil seal. Push the head of the oil seal slowly with the fingers, being careful that the seal is not deformed. Be sure that the oil seal moves smoothly in the groove before installing the O-ring.

4. Lubricate each oil seal and groove with engine oil and check the movement of the seal. It should move freely when the head of the seal is pressed.

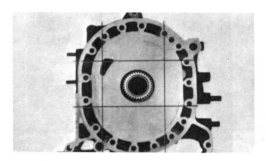

Measure the housing distortion along the axes indicated

Measuring housing wear with a dial indicator

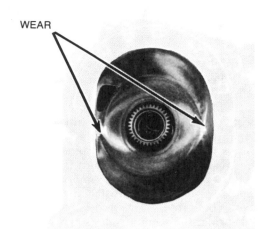

Most of the front and rear housing wear occurs at the end of the minor axis as shown

Measure the rotor housing distortion along the axes indicated

Check the rotor housing width at eight points near the trochoid surface

Normal shading of carbon deposits on rotor

Measure the rotor width at the point indicated

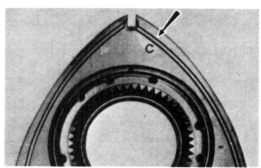

Weight classification letter placement (arrow)

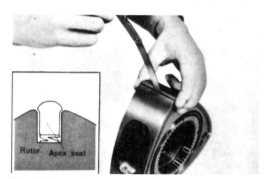

Check the gap between the apex seal and groove with a feeler gauge

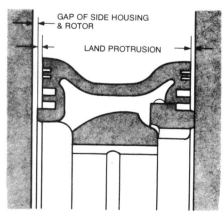

Oil seal protrusion

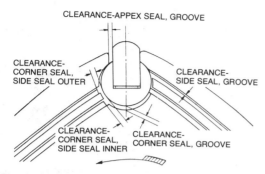

Check the clearance of the seals at the points indicated

Position the oil seal spring gaps at arrows

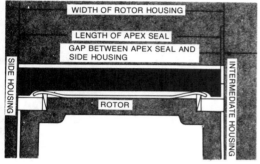

Apex seal-to-side seal housing gap

Insert the special bearing expander into the rotor

Reaming the corner seal groove

Installing a new rotor bearing

Corner seal installation

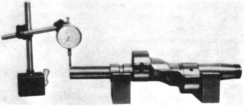

Position the dial indicator as shown in order to measure shaft runout

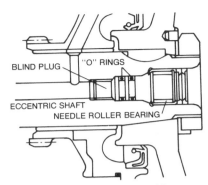

Eccentric shaft blind plug assembly

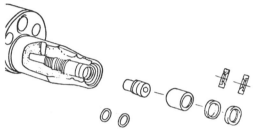

Needle bearing components

Align the slot in the stationary gear flange with the pin in the housing (arrow)

Position the o-ring in the groove on the stationary gear (arrow)

The rear rotor must be positioned as shown during engine assembly

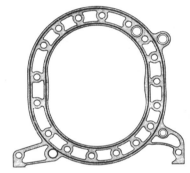

Apply sealer to the gray shadowed areas of the rotor housing

Intermediate housing installation

Installing oil pump

Use a dial indicator attached to the flywheel to measure eccentric shaft end-play

5. Check the oil seal protrusion and install the seals on the other side of each rotor.

6. Install the apex seals without springs and side pieces into their respective grooves so that each side piece positions on the side of each rotor.

7. Install the corner seal springs and corner seals into their respective grooves.

8. Install the side seal springs and side seals into their respective grooves.

9. Apply engine oil to each spring and check each spring for smooth movement.

10. Check each seal protrusion.

11. Invert the rotor being careful that the seals do not fall out, and install the oil seals on the other side in the same manner.

12. Mount the front housing on a workstand so that the top of the housing is up.

13. Lubricate the internal gear of the rotor with engine oil.

14. Hold the apex seals with used O-rings to keep the apex seals installed and place the rotor on the front housing. Be careful not to drop the seals. Turn the front housing so that the sliding surface faces upward.

15. Mesh the internal and stationary gears so that the one of the rotor apexes is at any one of the four places shown and remove the old O-ring which is holding the apex seals in position.

16. Lubricate the front rotor journal of the eccentric shaft with engine oil and lubricate the eccentric shaft main journal.

17. Insert the eccentric shaft. Be careful that you do not damage the rotor bearing and main bearing.

18. Apply sealing agent to the front side of the front rotor housing.

19. Apply a light coat of petroleum jelly onto new O-rings and rubber seals (to prevent them from coming off) and install the O-rings and rubber seals on the front side of the rotor housing.

NOTE: *The inner off) seal is of the square type. The wider white line of the rubber seal should face the combustion chamber and the seam of the rubber seal should be positioned as shown. Do not stretch the rubber seal.*

20. If the engine is being overhauled, install the seal protector to only the inner rubber seal to improve durability.

21. Invert the front rotor housing, being careful not to let the rubber seals and O-rings fall from their grooves, and mount it on the front housing.

22. Lubricate the dowels with engine oil and insert them through the front rotor housing holes and into the front rotor housing.

23. Apply sealer to the front side of the rotor housing.

24. Install new O-rings and rubber seals on the front rotor housing in the same manner as for the other side.

25. Insert each apex spring seal, making sure that the seal is installed in the proper direction.

26. Install each side piece in its original position and be sure that the springs seat on the side piece.

27. Lubricate the side pieces with engine oil. Make sure that the front rotor housing is free of foreign matter and lubricate the sliding surface of the front housing with engine oil.

28. Turn the front housing assembly with the rotor, so that the top of the housing is up. Pull the eccentric shaft about 1 in.

29. Position the eccentric portion of the eccentric shaft diagonally, to the upper right.

30. Install the intermediate housing over the eccentric shaft onto the front rotor housing. Turn the engine so that the rear of the engine is up.

31. Install the rear rotor and rear rotor housing following the same steps as for the front rotor and the front housing.

32. Turn the engine so that the rear of the engine is up.

33. Lubricate the stationary gear and main bearing.

34. Install the rear housing onto the rear rotor housing. If necessary, turn the rear rotor slightly to mesh the rear housing stationary gear with the rear rotor internal gear.

35. Install a new washer on each tension bolt, and lubricate each bolt with engine oil.

36. Install the tension bolts and tighten them evenly, in several stages following the sequence shown. The specified torque is 23–27 ft.lbs.

37. After tightening the bolts, turn the eccentric shaft to be sure that the shaft and rotors turn smoothly and easily.

38. Lubricate the oil seal in the rear housing.

39. On vehicles with manual transmission, install the flywheel on the rear of the eccentric shaft so that the keyway of the flywheel fits the key on the shaft.

40. Apply sealer to both sides of the flywheel lockwasher and install the lockwasher.

41. Install the flywheel locknut. Hold the flywheel SECURELY and tighten the nut to THREE HUNDRED AND FIFTY FT. LBS. (350 ft. lbs.) of torque.

NOTE: *350 ft. lbs. is a great deal of torque. In actual practice, it is practically impossible to accurately measure that much torque on the nut. At least a 3 ft bar will be required to generate sufficient torque. Tighten it as tight as possible, with no longer than 3 ft of leverage. Be sure the engine is held SECURELY.*

42. On vehicles with automatic transmission, install the key, counterweight, lockwasher and nut. Tighten the nut to 350 ft. lbs. SEE STEP 41. Install the drive plate on the counterweight and tighten the attaching nuts.

43. Turn the engine so that the front faces up.

44. Install the thrust plate with the tapered face down, and install the needle bearing on the eccentric shaft. Lubricate with engine oil.

45. Install the bearing housing on the front housing. Tighten the bolts and bend up the lockwasher tabs.

The spacer should be installed so that the center of the needle bearing comes to the center of the eccentric shaft and the spacer should be seated on the thrust plate.

46. Install the needle bearing on the shaft and lubricate it with engine oil.

47. Install the balancer and thrust washer on the eccentric shaft.

48. Install the oil pump drive chain over both of the sprockets. Install the sprocket and chain assembly over the eccentric shaft and oil pump shafts simultaneously. Install the key on the eccentric shaft.

NOTE: *Be sure that both of the sprockets are engaged with the chain before installing them over the shafts.*

Eccentric Shaft Spacer Thickness Chart

Marking	Thickness
X	8.08 ± 0.01 mm (0.3181 ± 0.0004 in.)
Y	8.04 ± 0.01 mm (0.3165 ± 0.0004 in.)
V	8.02 ± 0.01 mm (0.3158 ± 0.0004 in.)
Z	8.00 ± 0.01 mm (0.3150 ± 0.0004 in.)

49. Install the distributor drive gear onto the eccentric shaft with the "F" mark on the gear facing the front of the engine. Slide the spacer and oil slinger onto the eccentric shaft.

50. Align the keyway and install the eccentric shaft pulley. Tighten the pulley bolt to 60 ft. lbs.

51. Turn the engine top of the engine faces up.

52. Check eccentric shaft end-play in the following manner:

a. Attach a dial indicator to the flywheel. Move the flywheel forward and backward.

b. Note the reading on the dial indicator: it should be 0.0016–0.0028 in.

c. If the end-play is not within specifications, adjust it by replacing the front spacer. Spacers come in four sizes, ranging from 0.3150–0.3181 in. If necessary, a spacer can be ground on a surface plate with emery paper.

d. Check the end-play again and, if it is now within specifications, proceed with the next step.

53. Remove the pulley from the front of the eccentric shaft. Tighten the oil pump drive sprocket nut and bend the locktabs on the lockwasher.

54. Fit a new O-ring over the front cover oil passage.

55. Install the chain tensioner and tighten its securing bolts on 1974–77 engines. On 1978 engines, depress the oil pump drive chain in the center of its length between sprockets and measure slack. If it is greater than .51 in., replace the chain, as there is no tensioner.

56. Position the front cover gasket and the front cover on the front housing, then secure the front cover with its attachment bolts.

57. Install the eccentric shaft pulley again. Tighten its bolt to 60 ft. lbs.

58. Turn the engine so that the bottom faces up.

59. Cut off excess gasket on the front

cover along the mounting surface of the oil pan.

60. Install the oil strainer gasket and strainer on the front housing and tighten the attaching bolts.

61. Apply sealer to the joint surfaces of each housing.

62. Install the oil pan.

63. Turn the engine so that top is up.

64. Install the water pump.

65. Rotate the eccentric shaft until the yellow mark (leading side mark) aligns with the pointer on the front cover.

66. Align the marks on the distributor gear and housing and install the distributor so that the lockbolt is in the center of the slot.

67. Rotate the distributor until the leading points start to separate and tighten the distributor locknut.

68. Install the gaskets and thermal reactor.

69. Install the hot air duct.

70. Install the carburetor and intake manifold assembly.

71. Connect the oil tubes, vacuum tube and metering oil pump connecting rod to the carburetor.

72. Install the decel valve and connect the vacuum lines, air hoses and wires.

73. Install the alternator bracket, alternator and bolt and check the clearance. If the clearance is more than 0.006 in., adjust the clearance using a shim. Shims are available in three sizes: 0.0059 in., 0.0118 in., and 0.0197 in.

74. Install the alternator drive belt.

75. Install the air pump.

76. Install the engine hanger bracket.

77. Remove the engine from the stand.

78. Install the engine.

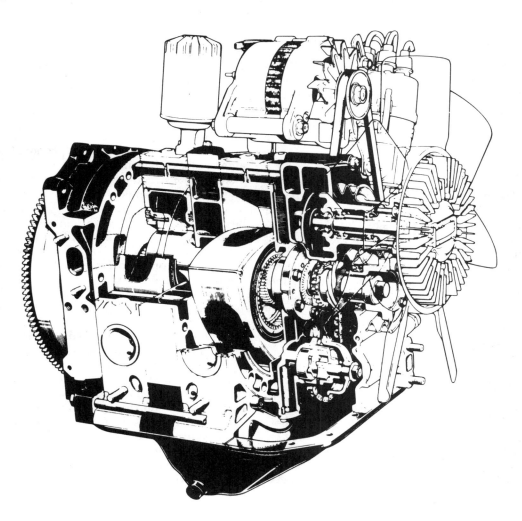

ENGINE REBUILDING

Most procedures involved in rebuilding an engine are fairly standard, regardless of the type of engine involved. This section is a guide to accepted rebuilding procedures. Examples of standard rebuilding practices are illustrated and should be used along with specific details concerning your particular engine, found earlier in this chapter.

The procedures given here are those used by any competent rebuilder. Obviously some of the procedures cannot be performed by the do-it-yourself mechanic, but are provided so that you will be familiar with the services that should be offered by rebuilding or machine shops. As an example, in most instances, it is more profitable for the home mechanic to remove the cylinder heads, buy the necessary parts (new valves, seals, keepers, keys, etc.) and deliver these to a machine shop for the necessary work. In this way you will save the money to remove and install the cylinder head and the mark-up on parts.

On the other hand, most of the work involved in rebuilding the lower end is well within the scope of the do-it-yourself mechanic. Only work such as hot-tanking, actually boring the block or Magnafluxing (invisible crack detection) need be sent to a machine shop.

Tools

The tools required for basic engine rebuilding should, with a few exceptions, be those included in a mechanic's tool kit. An accurate torque wrench, and a dial indicator (reading in thousandths) mounted on a universal base should be available. Special tools, where required, are available from the major tool suppliers. The services of a competent automotive machine shop must also be readily available.

Precautions

Aluminum has become increasingly popular for use in engines, due to its low weight and excellent heat transfer characteristics. The following precautions must be observed when handling aluminum (or any other) engine parts:

—Never hot-tank aluminum parts.

—Remove all aluminum parts (identification tags, etc.) from engine parts before hot-tanking (otherwise they will be removed during the process).

—Always coat threads lightly with engine oil or anti-seize compounds before installation, to prevent seizure.

—Never over-torque bolts or spark plugs in aluminum threads. Should stripping occur, threads can be restored using any of a number of thread repair kits available (see next section).

Inspection Techniques

Magnaflux and Zyglo are inspection techniques used to locate material flaws, such as stress cracks. Magnaflux is a magnetic process, applicable only to ferrous materials. The Zyglo process coats the material with a fluorescent dye penetrant, and any material may be tested using Zyglo. Specific checks of suspected surface cracks may be made at lower cost and more readily using spot check dye. The dye is sprayed onto the suspected area, wiped off, and the area is then sprayed with a developer. Cracks then will show up brightly.

Overhaul

The section is divided into two parts. The first, Cylinder Head Reconditioning, assumes that the cylinder head is removed from the engine, all manifolds are removed, and the cylinder head is on a workbench. The camshaft should be removed from overhead cam cylinder heads. The second section, Cylinder Block Reconditioning, covers the block, pistons, connecting rods and crankshaft. It is assumed that the engine is mounted on a work stand, and the cylinder head and all accessories are removed.

Procedures are identified as follows:

Unmarked—Basic procedures that must be performed in order to successfully complete the rebuilding process.

Starred (*)—Procedures that should be performed to ensure maximum performance and engine life.

Double starred (**)—Procedures that may be performed to increase engine performance and reliability.

When assembling the engine, any parts that will be in frictional contact must be pre-lubricated, to provide protection on initial start-up. Any product specifically formulated for this purpose may be used. NOTE: *Do not use engine oil.* Where semi-permanent (locked but removable) installation of bolts or nuts is desired, threads should be cleaned and located with Loctite® or a similar product (non-hardening).

Repairing Damaged Threads

Several methods of repairing damaged threads are available. Heli-Coil® (shown here), Keenserts® and Microdot® are among the most widely used. All involve basically the same principle—drilling out stripped threads, tapping the hole and installing a pre-wound insert—making welding, plugging and oversize fasteners unnecessary.

Two types of thread repair inserts are usually supplied—a standard type for most Inch Coarse, Inch Fine, Metric Coarse and Metric Fine thread sizes and a spark plug type to fit most spark plug port sizes. Consult the individual manufacturer's catalog to determine exact applications. Typical thread repair kits will contain a selection of pre-wound threaded inserts, a tap (corresponding to the outside diameter threads of the insert) and an installation tool. Spark plug inserts usually differ because they require a tap equipped with pilot threads and a combined reamer/tap section. Most manufacturers also supply blister-packed thread repair inserts separately in addition to a master kit containing a variety of taps and inserts plus installation tools.

Before effecting a repair to a threaded hole, remove any snapped, broken or damaged bolts or studs. Penetrating oil can be used to free frozen threads; the offending item can be removed with locking pliers or with a screw or stud extractor. After the hole is clear, the thread can be repaired, as follows:

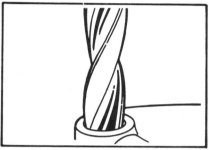

Drill out the damaged threads with specified drill. Drill completely through the hole or to the bottom of a blind hole

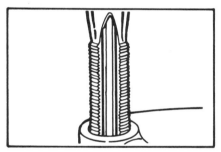

With the tap supplied, tap the hole to receive the thread insert. Keep the tap well oiled and back it out frequently to avoid clogging the threads

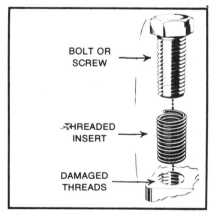

Damaged bolt holes can be repaired with thread repair inserts

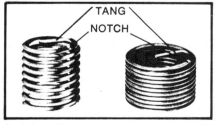

Standard thread repair insert (left) and spark plug thread insert (right)

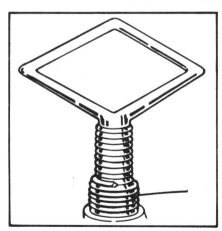

Screw the threaded insert onto the installation tool until the tang engages the slot. Screw the insert into the tapped hole until it is ¼–½ turn below the top surface. After installation break off the tang with a hammer and punch

Standard Torque Specifications and Fastener Markings

The Newton-metre has been designated the world standard for measuring torque and will gradually replace the foot-pound and kilogram-meter. In the absence of specific torques, the following chart can be used as a guide to the maximum safe torque of a particular size/grade of fastener.

- There is no torque difference for fine or coarse threads.
- Torque values are based on clean, dry threads. Reduce the value by 10% if threads are oiled prior to assembly.
- The torque required for aluminum components or fasteners is considerably less.

U. S. BOLTS

SAE Grade Number	1 or 2			5			6 or 7		

Bolt Markings

Manufacturer's marks may vary—number of lines always 2 less than the grade number.

Usage	Frequent			Frequent			Infrequent		
Bolt Size (inches)—(Thread)	Maximum Torque			Maximum Torque			Maximum Torque		
	Ft-Lb	kgm	Nm	Ft-Lb	kgm	Nm	Ft-Lb	kgm	Nm
¼—20	5	0.7	6.8	8	1.1	10.8	10	1.4	13.5
—28	6	0.8	8.1	10	1.4	13.6			
⁵⁄₁₆—18	11	1.5	14.9	17	2.3	23.0	19	2.6	25.8
—24	13	1.8	17.6	19	2.6	25.7			
⅜—16	18	2.5	24.4	31	4.3	42.0	34	4.7	46.0
—24	20	2.75	27.1	35	4.8	47.5			
⁷⁄₁₆—14	28	3.8	37.0	49	6.8	66.4	55	7.6	74.5
—20	30	4.2	40.7	55	7.6	74.5			
½—13	39	5.4	52.8	75	10.4	101.7	85	11.75	115.2
—20	41	5.7	55.6	85	11.7	115.2			
⁹⁄₁₆—12	51	7.0	69.2	110	15.2	149.1	120	16.6	162.7
—18	55	7.6	74.5	120	16.6	162.7			
⅝—11	83	11.5	112.5	150	20.7	203.3	167	23.0	226.5
—18	95	13.1	128.8	170	23.5	230.5			
¾—10	105	14.5	142.3	270	37.3	366.0	280	38.7	379.6
—16	115	15.9	155.9	295	40.8	400.0			
⅞— 9	160	22.1	216.9	395	54.6	535.5	440	60.9	596.5
—14	175	24.2	237.2	435	60.1	589.7			
1— 8	236	32.5	318.6	590	81.6	799.9	660	91.3	894.8
—14	250	34.6	338.9	660	91.3	849.8			

METRIC BOLTS

NOTE: *Metric bolts are marked with a number indicating the relative strength of the bolt. These numbers have nothing to do with size.*

Description	Torque ft-lbs (Nm)			
Thread size x pitch (mm)	Head mark—4		Head mark—7	
6 x 1.0	2.2–2.9	(3.0–3.9)	3.6–5.8	(4.9–7.8)
8 x 1.25	5.8–8.7	(7.9–12)	9.4–14	(13–19)
10 x 1.25	12–17	(16–23)	20–29	(27–39)
12 x 1.25	21–32	(29–43)	35–53	(47–72)
14 x 1.5	35–52	(48–70)	57–85	(77–110)
16 x 1.5	51–77	(67–100)	90–120	(130–160)
18 x 1.5	74–110	(100–150)	130–170	(180–230)
20 x 1.5	110–140	(150–190)	190–240	(160–320)
22 x 1.5	150–190	(200–260)	250–320	(340–430)
24 x 1.5	190–240	(260–320)	310–410	(420–550)

NOTE: *This engine rebuilding section is a guide to accepted rebuilding procedures. Typical examples of standard rebuilding procedures are illustrated. Use these procedures along with the detailed instructions earlier in this chapter, concerning your particular engine.*

Cylinder Head Reconditioning

Procedure	Method
Remove the cylinder head:	See the engine service procedures earlier in this chapter for details concerning specific engines.
Identify the valves:	Invert the cylinder head, and number the valve faces front to rear, using a permanent felt-tip marker.
Remove the camshaft:	See the engine service procedures earlier in this chapter for details concerning specific engines.
Remove the valves and springs:	Using an appropriate valve spring compressor (depending on the configuration of the cylinder head), compress the valve springs. Lift out the keepers with needlenose pliers, release the compressor, and remove the valve, spring, and spring retainer. See the engine service procedures earlier in this chapter for details concerning specific engines.
Check the valve stem-to-guide clearance:	Clean the valve stem with lacquer thinner or a similar solvent to remove all gum and varnish. Clean the valve guides using solvent and an expanding wire-type valve guide cleaner. Mount a dial indicator so that the stem is at 90° to the valve stem, as close to the valve guide as possible. Move the valve off its seat, and measure the valve guide-to-stem clearance by rocking the stem back and forth to actuate the dial indicator. Measure the valve stems using a micrometer, and compare to specifications, to determine whether stem or guide wear is responsible for excessive clearance. NOTE: *Consult the Specifications tables earlier in this chapter.*

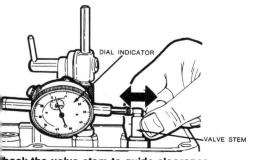

DIAL INDICATOR

VALVE STEM

Check the valve stem-to-guide clearance

Cylinder Head Reconditioning

Procedure	*Method*
De-carbon the cylinder head and valves: 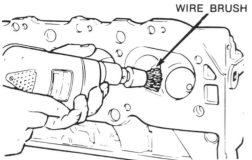 WIRE BRUSH **Remove the carbon from the cylinder head with a wire brush and electric drill**	Chip carbon away from the valve heads, combustion chambers, and ports, using a chisel made of hardwood. Remove the remaining deposits with a stiff wire brush. **NOTE:** *Be sure that the deposits are actually removed, rather than burnished.*
Hot-tank the cylinder head (cast iron heads only): **CAUTION:** *Do not hot-tank aluminum parts.*	Have the cylinder head hot-tanked to remove grease, corrosion, and scale from the water passages. **NOTE:** *In the case of overhead cam cylinder heads, consult the operator to determine whether the camshaft bearings will be damaged by the caustic solution.*
Degrease the remaining cylinder head parts:	Clean the remaining cylinder head parts in an engine cleaning solvent. Do not remove the protective coating from the springs.
Check the cylinder head for warpage: 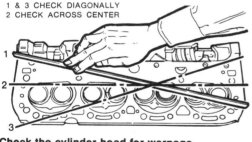 1 & 3 CHECK DIAGONALLY 2 CHECK ACROSS CENTER **Check the cylinder head for warpage**	Place a straight-edge across the gasket surface of the cylinder head. Using feeler gauges, determine the clearance at the center of the straight-edge. If warpage exceeds .003″ in a 6″ span, or .006″ over the total length, the cylinder head must be resurfaced. **NOTE:** *If warpage exceeds the manufacturer's maximum tolerance for material removal, the cylinder head must be replaced.* When milling the cylinder heads of V-type engines, the intake manifold mounting position is altered, and must be corrected by milling the manifold flange a proportionate amount.
*Knurl the valve guides: 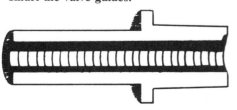 **Cut-away view of a knurled valve guide**	*Valve guides which are not excessively worn or distorted may, in some cases, be knurled rather than replaced. Knurling is a process in which metal is displaced and raised, thereby reducing clearance. Knurling also provides excellent oil control. The possibility of knurling rather than replacing valve guides should be discussed with a machinist.
Replace the valve guides: **NOTE:** *Valve guides should only be replaced if damaged or if an oversize valve stem is not available.*	See the engine service procedures earlier in this chapter for details concerning specific engines. Depending on the type of cylinder head, valve guides may be pressed, hammered, or shrunk in. In cases where the guides are shrunk into the head, replacement should be left to an equipped machine shop. In other

Cylinder Head Reconditioning

Procedure	Method

A—VALVE GUIDE I.D.   B—LARGER THAN THE VALVE GUIDE O.D.

WASHERS

B–A

A—VALVE GUIDE I.D.   B—LARGER THAN THE VALVE GUIDE O.D.

Valve guide installation tool using washers for installation

cases, the guides are replaced using a stepped drift (see illustration). Determine the height above the boss that the guide must extend, and obtain a stack of washers, their I.D. similar to the guide's O.D., of that height. Place the stack of washers on the guide, and insert the guide into the boss.

NOTE: *Valve guides are often tapered or beveled for installation.* Using the stepped installation tool (see illustration), press or tap the guides into position. Ream the guides according to the size of the valve stem.

Replace valve seat inserts:

Replacement of valve seat inserts which are worn beyond resurfacing or broken, if feasible, must be done by a machine shop.

Resurface (grind) the valve face:

FOR DIMENSIONS, REFER TO SPECIFICATIONS

CHECK FOR BENT STEM

DIAMETER

VALVE FACE ANGLE

1/32" MINIMUM   THIS LINE PARALLEL WITH VALVE HEAD

Critical valve dimensions

Using a valve grinder, resurface the valves according to specifications given earlier in this chapter.

CAUTION: *Valve face angle is not always identical to valve seat angle.* A minimum margin of 1/32" should remain after grinding the valve. The valve stem top should also be squared and resurfaced, by placing the stem in the V-block of the grinder, and turning it while pressing lightly against the grinding wheel.

NOTE: *Do not grind sodium filled exhaust valves on a machine. These should be hand lapped.*

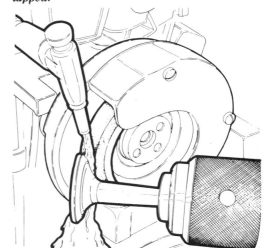

Valve grinding by machine

Cylinder Head Reconditioning

Procedure	Method

Resurface the valve seats using reamers or grinder:

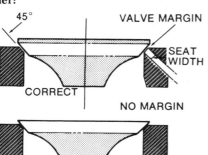

Valve seat width and centering

Reaming the valve seat with a hand reamer

Select a reamer of the correct seat angle, slightly larger than the diameter of the valve seat, and assemble it with a pilot of the correct size. Install the pilot into the valve guide, and using steady pressure, turn the reamer clockwise.

CAUTION: *Do not turn the reamer counterclockwise.* Remove only as much material as necessary to clean the seat. Check the concentricity of the seat (following). If the dye method is not used, coat the valve face with Prussian blue dye, install and rotate it on the valve seat. Using the dye marked area as a centering guide, center and narrow the valve seat to specifications with correction cutters.

NOTE: *When no specifications are available, minimum seat width for exhaust valves should be $5/64''$, intake valves $1/16''$.*

After making correction cuts, check the position of the valve seat on the valve face using Prussian blue dye.

To resurface the seat with a power grinder, select a pilot of the correct size and coarse stone of the proper angle. Lubricate the pilot and move the stone on and off the valve seat at 2 cycles per second, until all flaws are gone. Finish the seat with a fine stone. If necessary the seat can be corrected or narrowed using correction stones.

Check the valve seat concentricity:

Check the valve seat concentricity with a dial gauge

Coat the valve face with Prussian blue dye, install the valve, and rotate it on the valve seat. If the entire seat becomes coated, and the valve is known to be concentric, the seat is concentric.

*Install the dial gauge pilot into the guide, and rest of the arm on the valve seat. Zero the gauge, and rotate the arm around the seat. Run-out should not exceed .002″.

Cylinder Head Reconditioning

Procedure	Method

*Lap the valves:
NOTE: *Valve lapping is done to ensure efficient sealing of resurfaced valves and seats.*

Invert the cyclinder head, lightly lubricate the valve stems, and install the valves in the head as numbered. Coat valve seats with fine grinding compound, and attach the lapping tool suction cup to a valve head.
NOTE: *Moisten the suction cup.* Rotate the tool between the palms, changing position and lifting the tool often to prevent grooving. Lap the valve until a smooth, polished seat is evident. Remove the valve and tool, and rinse away all traces of grinding compound.

**Fasten a suction cup to a piece of drill rod, and mount the rod in a hand drill. Proceed as above, using the hand drill as a lapping tool.
CAUTION: *Due to the higher speeds involved when using the hand drill, care must be exercised to avoid grooving the seat.* Lift the tool and change direction of rotation often.

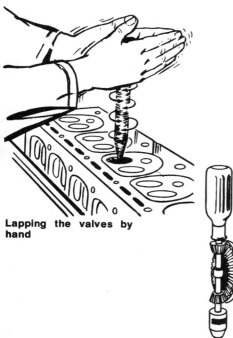

Lapping the valves by hand

HAND DRILL

ROD

Home-made valve lapping tool

SUCTION CUP

Check the valve springs:

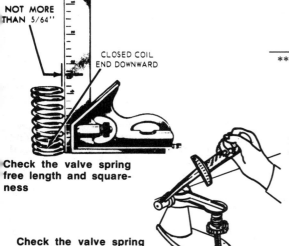

NOT MORE THAN 5/64"

CLOSED COIL END DOWNWARD

Check the valve spring free length and squareness

Check the valve spring test pressure

Place the spring on a flat surface next to a square. Measure the height of the spring, and rotate it against the edge of the square to measure distortion. If spring height varies (by comparison) by more than $1/16''$ or if distortion exceeds $1/16''$, replace the spring.

**In addition to evaluating the spring as above, test the spring pressure at the installed and compressed (installed height minus valve lift) height using a valve spring tester. Springs used on small displacement engines (up to 3 liters) should be ∓ 1 lb of all other springs in either position. A tolerance of ∓ 5 lbs is permissible on larger engines.

Cylinder Head Reconditioning

Procedure	Method

*Install valve stem seals:

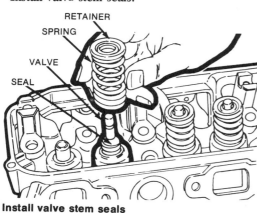

RETAINER
SPRING
VALVE
SEAL

Install valve stem seals

*Due to the pressure differential that exists at the ends of the intake valve guides (atmospheric pressure above, manifold vacuum below), oil is drawn through the valve guides into the intake port. This has been alleviated somewhat since the addition of positive crankcase ventilation, which lowers the pressure above the guides. Several types of valve stem seals are available to reduce blow-by. Certain seals simply slip over the stem and guide boss, while others require that the boss be machined. Recently, Teflon guide seals have become popular. Consult a parts supplier or machinist concerning availability and suggested usages.

NOTE: *When installing seals, ensure that a small amount of oil is able to pass the seal to lubricate the valve guides; otherwise, excessive wear may result.*

Install the valves:

See the engine service procedures earlier in this chapter for details concerning specific engines.

Lubricate the valve stems, and install the valves in the cylinder head as numbered. Lubricate and position the seals (if used) and the valve springs. Install the spring retainers, compress the springs, and insert the keys using needlenose pliers or a tool designed for this purpose.

NOTE: *Retain the keys with wheel bearing grease during installation.*

Check valve spring installed height:

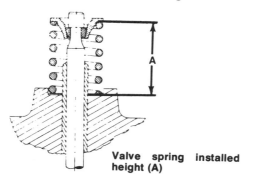

A

Valve spring installed height (A)

Measure the distance between the spring pad the lower edge of the spring retainer, and compare to specifications. If the installed height is incorrect, add shim washers between the spring pad and the spring.

CAUTION: *Use only washers designed for this purpose.*

GRIND OUT THIS PORTION

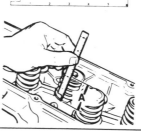

A

Measure the valve spring installed height (A) with a modified steel rule

Clean and inspect the camshaft:

Degrease the camshaft, using solvent, and clean out all oil holes. Visually inspect cam lobes and bearing journals for excessive wear. If a lobe is questionable, check all lobes as indicated below. If a journal or lobe is worn, the camshaft must be reground or replaced.

Cylinder Head Reconditioning

Procedure	Method

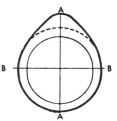

NOTE: *If a journal is worn, there is a good chance that the bushings are worn.*

If lobes and journals appear intact, place the front and rear journals in V-blocks, and rest a dial indicator on the center journal. Rotate the camshaft to check straightness. If deviation exceeds .001″, replace the camshaft.

*Check the camshaft lobes with a micrometer, by measuring the lobes from the nose to base and again at 90° (see illustration). The lift is determined by subtracting the second measurement from the first. If all exhaust lobes and all intake lobes are not identical, the camshaft must be reground or replaced.

Check the camshaft for straightness

Camshaft lobe measurement

Install the camshaft:	See the engine service procedures earlier in this chapter for details concerning specific engines.
Install the rocker arms:	See the engine service procedures earlier in this chapter for details concerning specific engines.

Cylinder Block Reconditioning

Procedure	Method

Checking the main bearing clearance:

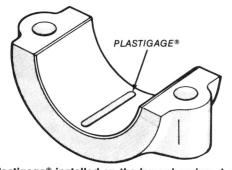

PLASTIGAGE®

Plastigage® installed on the lower bearing shell

Invert engine, and remove cap from the bearing to be checked. Using a clean, dry rag, thoroughly clean all oil from crankshaft journal and bearing insert.

NOTE: *Plastigage® is soluble in oil; therefore, oil on the journal or bearing could result in erroneous readings.* Place a piece of Plastigage along the full length of journal, reinstall cap, and torque to specifications.

NOTE: *Specifications are given in the engine specifications earlier in this chapter.*

Remove bearing cap, and determine bearing clearance by comparing width of Plastigage to the scale on Plastigage envelope. Journal taper is determined by comparing width of the Plastigage strip near its ends. Rotate crankshaft 90° and retest, to determine journal eccentricity.

NOTE: *Do not rotate crankshaft with Plastigage installed.* If bearing insert and journal appear in-

Cylinder Block Reconditioning

Procedure	Method

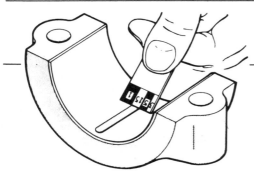

Measure Plastigage® to determine main bearing clearance

tact, and are within tolerances, no further main bearing service is required. If bearing or journal appear defective, cause of failure should be determined before replacement.

* Remove crankshaft from block (see below). Measure the main bearing journals at each end twice (90° apart) using a micrometer, to determine diameter, journal taper and eccentricity. If journals are within tolerances, reinstall bearing caps at their specified torque. Using a telescope gauge and micrometer, measure bearing I.D. parallel to piston axis and at 30° on each side of piston axis. Subtract journal O.D. from bearing I.D. to determine oil clearance. If crankshaft journals appear defective, or do not meet tolerances, there is no need to measure bearings; for the crankshaft will require grinding and/or undersize bearings will be required. If bearing appears defective, cause for failure should be determined prior to replacement.

Check the connecting rod bearing clearance:

Connecting rod bearing clearance is checked in the same manner as main bearing clearance, using Plastigage. Before removing the crankshaft, connecting rod side clearance also should be measured and recorded.

* Checking connecting rod bearing clearance, using a micrometer, is identical to checking main bearing clearance. If no other service is required, the piston and rod assemblies need not be removed.

Remove the crankshaft:

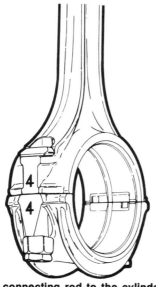

Using a punch, mark the corresponding main bearing caps and saddles according to position (i.e., one punch on the front main cap and saddle, two on the second, three on the third, etc.). Using number stamps, identify the corresponding connecting rods and caps, according to cylinder (if no numbers are present). Remove the main and connecting rod caps, and replace sleeves of plastic tubing or vacuum hose over the connecting rod bolts, to protect the journals as the crankshaft is removed. Lift the crankshaft out of the block.

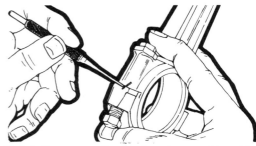

Match the connecting rod to the cylinder with a number stamp

Match the connecting rod and cap with scribe marks

Cylinder Block Reconditioning

Procedure	Method
Remove the ridge from the top of the cylinder: RIDGE CAUSED BY CYLINDER WEAR  CYLINDER WALL TOP OF PISTON **Cylinder bore ridge**	In order to facilitate removal of the piston and connecting rod, the ridge at the top of the cylinder (unworn area; see illustration) must be removed. Place the piston at the bottom of the bore, and cover it with a rag. Cut the ridge away using a ridge reamer, exercising extreme care to avoid cutting too deeply. Remove the rag, and remove cuttings that remain on the piston. **CAUTION:** *If the ridge is not removed, and new rings are installed, damage to rings will result.*
Remove the piston and connecting rod: **Push the piston out with a hammer handle**	Invert the engine, and push the pistons and connecting rods out of the cylinders. If necessary, tap the connecting rod boss with a wooden hammer handle, to force the piston out. **CAUTION:** *Do not attempt to force the piston past the cylinder ridge* (see above).
Service the crankshaft:	Ensure that all oil holes and passages in the crankshaft are open and free of sludge. If necessary, have the crankshaft ground to the largest possible undersize.
	**Have the crankshaft Magnafluxed, to locate stress cracks. Consult a machinist concerning additional service procedures, such as surface hardening (e.g., nitriding, Tuftriding) to improve wear characteristics, cross drilling and chamfering the oil holes to improve lubrication, and balancing.
Removing freeze plugs:	Drill a small hole in the middle of the freeze plugs. Thread a large sheet metal screw into the hole and remove the plug with a slide hammer.
Remove the oil gallery plugs:	Threaded plugs should be removed using an appropriate (usually square) wrench. To remove soft, pressed in plugs, drill a hole in the plug, and thread in a sheet metal screw. Pull the plug out by the screw using pliers.
Hot-tank the block: **NOTE:** *Do not hot-tank aluminum parts.*	Have the block hot-tanked to remove grease, corrosion, and scale from the water jackets. **NOTE:** *Consult the operator to determine whether the camshaft bearings will be damaged during the hot-tank process.*

Cylinder Block Reconditioning

Procedure	*Method*
Check the block for cracks:	Visually inspect the block for cracks or chips. The most common locations are as follows: Adjacent to freeze plugs. Between the cylinders and water jackets. Adjacent to the main bearing saddles. At the extreme bottom of the cylinders. Check only suspected cracks using spot check dye (see introduction). If a crack is located, consult a machinist concerning possible repairs.
	** Magnaflux the block to locate hidden cracks. If cracks are located, consult a machinist about feasibility of repair.
Install the oil gallery plugs and freeze plugs:	Coat freeze plugs with sealer and tap into position using a piece of pipe, slightly smaller than the plug, as a driver. To ensure retention, stake the edges of the plugs. Coat threaded oil gallery plugs with sealer and install. Drive replacement soft plugs into block using a large drift as a driver.
	* Rather than reinstalling lead plugs, drill and tap the holes, and install threaded plugs.
Check the bore diameter and surface: 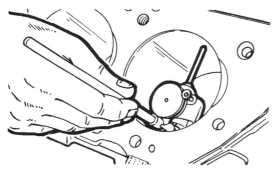 **Measure the cylinder bore with a dial gauge**	Visually inspect the cylinder bores for roughness, scoring, or scuffing. If evident, the cylinder bore must be bored or honed oversize to eliminate imperfections, and the smallest possible oversize piston used. The new pistons should be given to the machinist with the block, so that the cylinders can be bored or honed exactly to the piston size (plus clearance). If no flaws are evident, measure the bore diameter using a telescope gauge and micrometer, or dial gauge, parallel and perpendicular to the engine centerline, at the top (below the ridge) and bottom of the bore. Subtract the bottom measurements from the top to determine taper, and the parallel to the centerline measurements from the perpendicular measurements to determine eccentricity. If the measurements are not within specifications, the cylinder must be bored or honed, and an oversize piston installed. If the measurements are within specifications the cylinder may

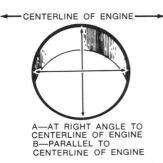

A—AT RIGHT ANGLE TO CENTERLINE OF ENGINE
B—PARALLEL TO CENTERLINE OF ENGINE

Cylinder bore measuring points

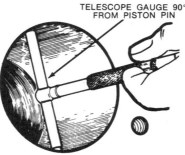

Measure the cylinder bore with a telescope gauge

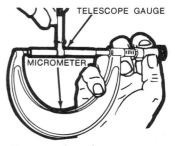

Measure the telescope gauge with a micrometer to determine the cylinder bore

Cylinder Block Reconditioning

Procedure	Method
	be used as is, with only finish honing (see below). NOTE: *Prior to submitting the block for boring, perform the following operation(s).*
Check the cylinder block bearing alignment: 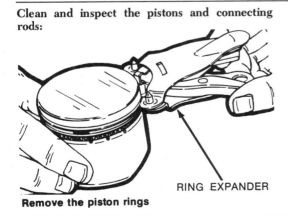 Check the main bearing saddle alignment	Remove the upper bearing inserts. Place a straightedge in the bearing saddles along the centerline of the crankshaft. If clearance exists between the straightedge and the center saddle, the block must be alignbored.
*Check the deck height:	The deck height is the distance from the crankshaft centerline to the block deck. To measure, invert the engine, and install the crankshaft, retaining it with the center maincap. Measure the distance from the crankshaft journal to the block deck, parallel to the cylinder centerline. Measure the diameter of the end (front and rear) main journals, parallel to the centerline of the cylinders, divide the diameter in half, and subtract it from the previous measurement. The results of the front and rear measurements should be identical. If the difference exceeds .005″, the deck height should be corrected. NOTE: *Block deck height and warpage should be corrected at the same time.*
Check the block deck for warpage:	Using a straightedge and feeler gauges, check the block deck for warpage in the same manner that the cylinder head is checked (see Cylinder Head Reconditioning). If warpage exceeds specifications, have the deck resurfaced. NOTE: *In certain cases a specification for total material removal (cylinder head and block deck) is provided. This specification must not be exceeded.*
Clean and inspect the pistons and connecting rods: RING EXPANDER Remove the piston rings	Using a ring expander, remove the rings from the piston. Remove the retaining rings (if so equipped) and remove piston pin. NOTE: *If the piston pin must be pressed out, determine the proper method and use the proper tools; otherwise the piston will distort.* Clean the ring grooves using an appropriate tool, exercising care to avoid cutting too deeply. Thoroughly clean all carbon and varnish from the piston with solvent. CAUTION: *Do not use a wire brush or caustic solvent on pistons.* Inspect the pistons for scuffing, scoring, cracks, pitting, or excessive ringsgroove wear. If wear is evident, the piston must be replaced. Check the connecting rod length by measuring

Cylinder Block Reconditioning

Procedure	Method

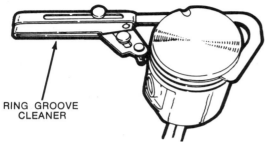

RING GROOVE
CLEANER

Clean the piston ring grooves

the rod from the inside of the large end to the inside of the small end using calipers (see illustration). All connecting rods should be equal length. Replace any rod that differs from the others in the engine.

* Have the connecting rod alignment checked in an alignment fixture by a machinist. Replace any twisted or bent rods.

* Magnaflux the connecting rods to locate stress cracks. If cracks are found, replace the connecting rod.

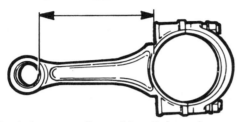

Check the connecting rod length (arrow)

Fit the pistons to the cylinders:

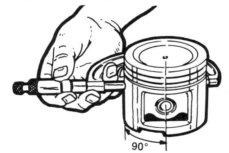

90°

Measure the piston prior to fitting

Using a telescope gauge and micrometer, or a dial gauge, measure the cylinder bore diameter perpendicular to the piston pin, 2½" below the deck. Measure the piston perpendicular to its pin on the skirt. The difference between the two measurements is the piston clearance. If the clearance is within specifications or slightly below (after boring or honing), finish honing is all that is required. If the clearance is excessive, try to obtain a slightly larger piston to bring clearance within specifications. Where this is not possible, obtain the first oversize piston, and hone (of if necessary, bore) the cylinder to size.

Assemble the pistons and connecting rods:

Install the piston pin lock-rings (if used)

Inspect piston pin, connecting rod small end bushing, and piston bore for galling, scoring, or excessive wear. If evident, replace defective part(s). Measure the I. D. of the piston boss and connecting rod small end, and the O. D. of the piston pin. If within specifications, assemble piston pin and rod.
CAUTION: *If piston pin must be pressed in, determine the proper method and use the proper tools; otherwise the piston will distort.*
Install the lock rings; ensure that they seat properly. If the parts are not within specifications, determine the service method for the type of engine. In some cases, piston and pin are serviced as an assembly when either is defective. Others specify reaming the piston and connecting rods for an oversize pin. If the connecting rod bushing is worn, it may in many cases be replaced. Reaming the piston and replacing the rod bushing are machine shop operations.

Cylinder Block Reconditioning

Procedure	Method

Finish hone the cylinders:

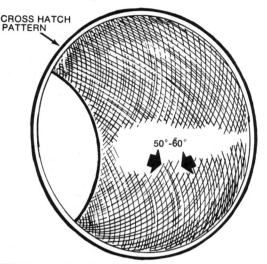

CROSS HATCH PATTERN

50°-60°

Chuck a flexible drive hone into a power drill, and insert it into the cylinder. Start the hone, and move it up and down in the cylinder at a rate which will produce approximately a 60° cross-hatch pattern.

NOTE: *Do not extend the hone below the cylinder bore.* After developing the pattern, remove the hone and recheck piston fit. Wash the cylinders with a detergent and water solution to remove abrasive dust, dry, and wipe several times with a rag soaked in engine oil.

Check piston ring end-gap:

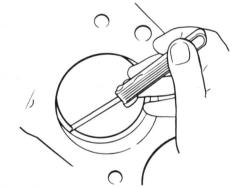

Check the piston ring end gap

Compress the piston rings to be used in a cylinder, one at a time, into that cylinder, and press them approximately 1″ below the deck with an inverted piston. Using feeler gauges, measure the ring end-gap, and compare to specifications. Pull the ring out of the cylinder and file the ends with a fine file to obtain proper clearance.

CAUTION: *If inadequate ring end-gap is utilized, ring breakage will result.*

Install the piston rings:

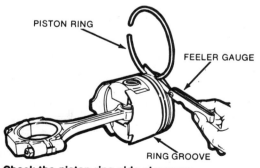

PISTON RING

FEELER GAUGE

RING GROOVE

Check the piston ring side clearance

Inspect the ring grooves in the piston for excessive wear or taper. If necessary, recut the groove(s) for use with an overwidth ring or a standard ring and spacer. If the groove is worn uniformly, overwidth rings, or standard rings and spaces may be installed without recutting. Roll the outside of the ring around the groove to check for burrs or deposits. If any are found, remove with a fine file. Hold the ring in the groove, and measure side clearance. If necessary, correct as indicated above.

NOTE: *Always install any additional spacers above the piston ring.*

The ring groove must be deep enough to allow the ring to seat below the lands (see illustration). In many cases, a "go-no-go" depth gauge will be provided with the piston rings. Shallow grooves may be corrected by recutting, while deep

Cylinder Block Reconditioning

Procedure	Method
	grooves require some type of filler or expander behind the piston. Consult the piston ring supplier concerning the suggested method. Install the rings on the piston, lowest ring first, using a ring expander.
	NOTE: *Position the rings as specified by the manufacturer.* Consult the engine service procedures earlier in this chapter for details concerning specific engines.
Install the rear main seal:	See the engine service procedures earlier in this chapter for details concerning specific engines.
Install the crankshaft:	Thoroughly clean the main bearing saddles and caps. Place the upper halves of the bearing inserts on the saddles and press into position.

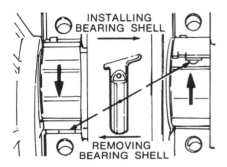

Remove or install the upper bearing insert using a roll-out pin

NOTE: *Ensure that the oil holes align.* Press the corresponding bearing inserts into the main bearing caps. Lubricate the upper main bearings, and lay the crankshaft in position. Place a strip of Plastigage on each of the crankshaft journals, install the main caps, and torque to specifications. Remove the main caps, and compare the Plastigage to the scale on the Plastigage envelope. If clearances are within tolerances, remove the Plastigage, turn the crankshaft 90°, wipe off all oil and retest. If all clearances are correct, remove all Plastigage, thoroughly lubricate the main caps and bearing journals, and install the main caps. If clearances are not within tolerance, the upper bearing inserts may be removed, without removing the crankshaft, using a bearing roll out pin (see illustration). Roll in a bearing that will provide proper clearance, and retest. Torque all main caps, excluding the thrust bearing cap, to specifications. Tighten the thrust bearing cap finger tight. To properly align the thrust bearing, pry the crankshaft the extent of its axial travel several times, the last movement held toward the front of the engine, and torque the thrust bearing cap to specifications. Determine the crankshaft end-play (see below), and bring within tolerance with thrust washers.

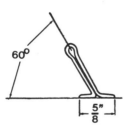

Home-made bearing roll-out pin

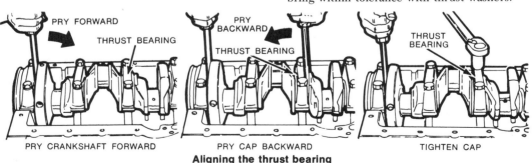

Aligning the thrust bearing

Measure crankshaft end-play:	Mount a dial indicator stand on the front of the block, with the dial indicator stem resting on the

Cylinder Block Reconditioning

Procedure	Method

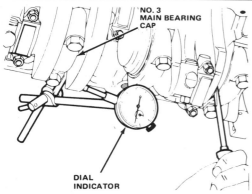

Check the crankshaft end-play with a dial indicator

Check the crankshaft end-play with a feeler gauge

nose of the crankshaft, parallel to the crankshaft axis. Pry the crankshaft the extent of its travel rearward, and zero the indicator. Pry the crankshaft forward and record crankshaft end-play.

NOTE: *Crankshaft end-play also may be measured at the thrust bearing, using feeler gauges (see illustration).*

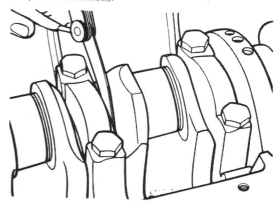

Install the pistons:

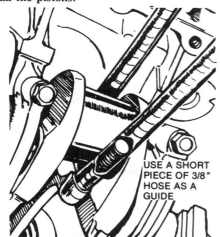

Use lengths of vacuum hose or rubber tubing to protect the crankshaft journals and cylinder walls during piston installation

Press the upper connecting rod bearing halves into the connecting rods, and the lower halves into the connecting rod caps. Position the piston ring gaps according to specifications (see car section), and lubricate the pistons. Install a ring compresser on a piston, and press two long (8″) pieces of plastic tubing over the rod bolts. Using the tubes as a guide, press the pistons into the bores and onto the crankshaft with a wooden hammer handle. After seating the rod on the crankshaft journal, remove the tubes and install the cap finger tight. Install the remaining pistons in the same manner. Invert the engine and check the bearing clearance at two points (90° apart) on each journal with Plastigage.

NOTE: *Do not turn the crankshaft with Plastigage installed.*

If clearance is within tolerances, remove *all* Plastigage, thoroughly lubricate the journals, and torque the rod caps to specifications. If clearance is not within specifications, install different thickness bearing inserts and recheck.

CAUTION: *Never shim or file the connecting rods or caps.*

Always install plastic tube sleeves over the rod bolts when the caps are not installed, to protect the crankshaft journals.

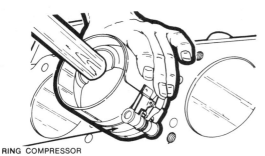

RING COMPRESSOR   **Install the piston using a ring compressor**

Cylinder Block Reconditioning

Procedure	Method
Check connecting rod side clearance: 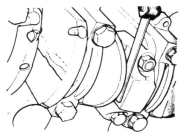 **Check the connecting rod side clearance with a feeler gauge**	Determine the clearance between the sides of the connecting rods and the crankshaft using feeler gauges. If clearance is below the minimum tolerance, the rod may be machined to provide adequate clearance. If clearance is excessive, substitute an unworn rod, and recheck. If clearance is still outside specifications, the crankshaft must be welded and reground, or replaced.
Inspect the timing chain (or belt):	Visually inspect the timing chain for broken or loose links, and replace the chain if any are found. If the chain will flex sideways, it must be replaced. Install the timing chain as specified. Be sure the timing belt is not stretched, frayed or broken. NOTE: *If the original timing chain is to be re-used, install it in its original position.* See the engine service procedures earlier in this chapter for details concerning specific engines.

Completing the Rebuilding Process

Following the above procedures, complete the rebuilding process as follows:

Fill the oil pump with oil, to prevent cavitating (sucking air) on initial engine start up. Install the oil pump and the pickup tube on the engine. Coat the oil pan gasket as necessary, and install the gasket and the oil pan. Mount the flywheel and the crankshaft vibration damper or pulley on the crankshaft. NOTE: *Always use new bolts when installing the flywheel.* Inspect the clutch shaft pilot bushing in the crankshaft. If the bushing is excessively worn, remove it with an expanding puller and a slide hammer, and tap a new bushing into place.

Position the engine, cylinder head side up. Install the cylinder head, and torque it as specified. Install the rocker arms and adjust the valves.

Install the intake and exhaust manifolds, the carburetor(s), the distributor and spark plugs. Adjust the point gap and the static ignition timing. Mount all accessories and install the engine in the car. Fill the radiator with coolant, and the crankcase with high quality engine oil.

Break-in Procedure

Start the engine, and allow it to run at low speed for a few minutes, while checking for leaks. Stop the engine, check the oil level, and fill as necessary. Restart the engine, and fill the cooling system to capacity. Check the point dwell angle and adjust the ignition timing and the valves. Run the engine at low to medium speed (800–2500 rpm) for approximately ½ hour, and retorque the cylinder head bolts. Road test the car, and check again for leaks.

Follow the manufacturer's recommended engine break-in procedure and maintenance schedule for new engines.

Emission Controls and Fuel System

EMISSION CONTROLS

Positive Crankcase Ventilation (PCV) System

The positive crankcase ventilation (PCV) valve is located on the intake manifold below the carburetor. In the case of the rotary engine the word "crankcase" is not quite correct, as the Mazda rotary engine has no crankcase in the normal sense of the term. Rather, the valve, which is operated by intake manifold vacuum, is used to meter the flow of fuel and air vapors through the rotor housings.

TESTING AND REPLACEMENT

The procedures for PCV valve testing and replacement may be found under "Routine Maintenance," in Chapter One.

Rotary Engine Air Injection System

OPERATION

The air injection system used on the Mazda rotary engine differs from the type used on a conventional piston engine in two respects:

1. Air is not only supplied to burn the gases in the exhaust ports, but it is also used to cool the thermal reactor.

2. A three-way air control valve is used in place of the conventional anti-backfire and diverter valves. It contains an air cutout valve, a relief valve, and a safety valve.

Air is supplied to the system by a normal vane type air pump. The air flows from the pump to the air control valve, where it is routed to the air injection nozzles to cool the thermal reactor or, in the case of a system malfunction, to the air cleaner. A check valve, located beneath the air control valve seat, prevents the back-flow of hot exhaust gases into the air injection system in case of air pressure loss.

Air injection nozzles are used to feed air

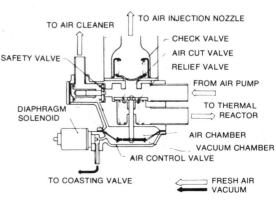

Cross-section of the air control valve

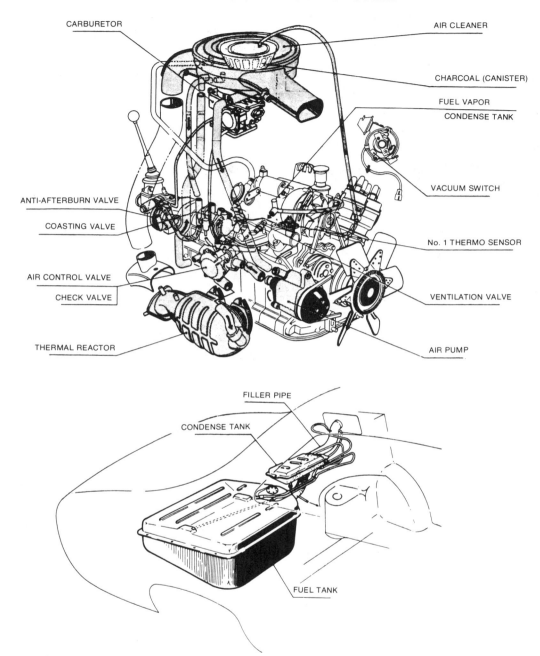

CARBURETOR

AIR CLEANER

CHARCOAL (CANISTER)

FUEL VAPOR
CONDENSE TANK

VACUUM SWITCH

ANTI-AFTERBURN VALVE

COASTING VALVE

No. 1 THERMO SENSOR

AIR CONTROL VALVE

CHECK VALVE

VENTILATION VALVE

THERMAL REACTOR

AIR PUMP

FILLER PIPE

CONDENSE TANK

FUEL TANK

Components of the rotary engine emission control system—1972 (other years similar)

into the exhaust ports, just as in a conventional piston engine.

COMPONENT TESTING

Air Pump

1. Check the air pump drive belt tension by applying 22 lbs of pressure halfway between the water pump and air pump pulleys. The belt should deflect 0.28–0.35 in. Adjust the belt if necessary, or replace it if it is cracked or worn.

2. Remove belt and turn the pump by hand. If it has seized, the pump will be very difficult or impossible to turn.

NOTE: *Disregard any chirping, squealing, or rolling sounds coming from inside the pump; these are normal when it is being turned by hand.*

3. Check the hoses and connections for

Check the belt deflection halfway between the water pump and air injection pump pulleys

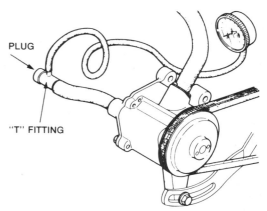

Test connections for the air pump (1977 and later cars)

leaks. Soapy water, applied around the area in question, is a good method of detecting leaks.

4. Connect a pressure gauge between the air pump and the air control valve with a T-fitting.

5. Plug the other hose connections (outlets) on the air control valve, as illustrated.

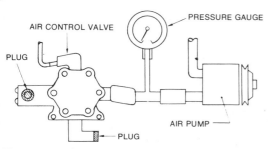

Test connections for the air pump

CAUTION: *Be careful not to touch the thermal reactor; severe burns will result.*

6. With the engine at normal idle speed, the pressure gauge should read 0.93–0.75 psi on 1971–76 cars. On 1977–78 cars, the figures are 800 rpm and 1.64 psi. Replace the air pump if it is less than this.

7. If the air pump is not defective, leave the pressure gauge connected but unplug the connections at the air control valve and proceed with the next test.

Air Control Valve 1971–76

1. Test the air control valve solenoid as follows:

CAUTION: *When testing the air control valve, avoid touching the thermal reactor as severe burns will result.*

a. Turn the ignition switch off and on. A click should be heard coming from the

solenoid. If no sound is audible, check the solenoid wiring.

b. If no defect is found in the solenoid wiring, connect the solenoid directly to the car's battery. If the solenoid still does not click, it is defective and must be replaced. If the solenoid works, then check the components of the air flow control system. See below.

2. Start the engine and run it at idle speed. The pressure gauge should still read 0.37–0.75 psi. No air should leak from the two outlets which were unplugged.

3. Increase the engine speed to 3,500 rpm (3,000 rpm—automatic transmission). The pressure gauge should now read 2.0–2.8 psi and the two outlets still should not be leaking air.

4. Return the engine to idle.

5. Disconnect the solenoid wiring. Air should now flow from the outlet marked (A) in the illustration, but not from the outlet marked (B). The pressure gauge reading should remain the same as in Step Two.

6. Reconnect the solenoid.

7. If the relief valve is faulty, air sent from the air pump will flow into the cooling passages of the thermal reactor with the engine is at idle speed.

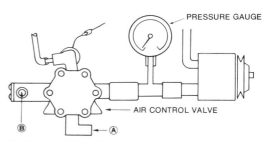

Test connections for the air control valve

8. If the safety valve is faulty, air will flow into the air cleaner when the engine is idling.

9. Replace the air control valve if it fails to pass any one of the above tests. Remember to disconnect the pressure gauge.

Air Control Valve—1977–78

1. Disconnect the air control valve electrical connector. With engine off, connect battery positive terminal in turn to both A and B terminals on the connector leading to the Air control valve. When each connection is made, the solenoid being energized should click.

If a connection at A produces no click, replace solenoid a, and if a connection at B produces no click, replace solenoid b.

2. Disconnect the air line leading from the thermal reactor to the air control valve at the thermal reactor. Also disconnect the air hose leading from the air control valve to the air cleaner at the air cleaner.

3. Connect a tachometer to the engine, and run the engine at idle speed. Check to see that there is practically no air inflow from either outlet.

4. Connect the A terminal to the battery, and increase engine speed to 2,000 rpm. Air should be discharged from the line going to the thermal reactor.

5. Connect the B terminal to the battery, and, with engine speed the same, verify that air is discharged from the hose leading to the air cleaner.

6. If the valve fails either or both tests, replace it.

Check Valve

1. Remove the check valve, as detailed below.

2. Depress the valve plate to see if it will seat properly.

3. Measure the free length of the valve spring; it should be 1.22 in.

NOTE: *The spring free length should be 0.75 in. on automatic transmission equipped models.*

4. Measure the installed length of the spring: it should be 0.68 in.

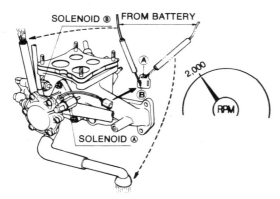

Checking air control valve (1977–78)

Components of the check valve

Air Injection System Diagnosis Chart

Problem	Cause	Cure
1. Noisy drive belt	1a. Loose belt	1a. Tighten belt
	1b. Seized pump	1b. Replace
2. Noisy pump	2a. Leaking hose	2a. Trace and fix leak
	2b. Loose hose	2b. Tighten hose clamp
	2c. Hose contacting other parts	2c. Reposition hose
	2d. Air control or check valve failure	2d. Replace
	2e. Pump mounting loose	2e. Tighten securing bolts
	2g. Defective pump	2g. Replace
3. No air supply	3a. Loose belt	3a. Tighten belt
	3b. Leak in hose or at fitting	3b. Trace and fix leak
	3c. Defective air control valve	3c. Replace
	3d. Defective check valve	3d. Replace
	3e. Defective pump	3e. Replace
4. Exhaust backfire	4a. Vacuum or air leaks	4a. Trace and fix leak
	4b. Defective air control valve	4b. Replace
	4c. Sticking choke	4c. Service choke
	4d. Choke setting rich	4d. Adjust choke

Replace the check valve if it is not up to specifications.

COMPONENT REMOVAL AND INSTALLATION

Air Pump

1. Remove the air cleaner assembly from the carburetor.
2. Loosen, but do not remove, the adjusting link bolt.
3. Push the pump toward the engine to slacken belt tension and remove the drive belt.
4. Disconnect the air supply hoses from the pump.
5. Unfasten the pump securing bolts and remove the pump.

CAUTION: *Do not pry on the air pump housing during removal and do not clamp the housing in a vise once the pump has been removed. Any type of heavy pressure applied to the housing will distort it.*

Installation is performed in the reverse order of removal. Adjust the belt tension by moving the air pump to the specification given in the "Testing" section, above.

Air Control Valve

CAUTION: *Remove the air control valve only after the thermal reactor has cooled sufficiently to prevent the danger of a serious burn.*

1. Remove the air cleaner assembly.
2. Unfasten the leads from the air control valve solenoid or the electrical connector.
3. Disconnect the air hoses from the valve.
4. Loosen the screws which secure the air control valve and remove the valve.

Valve installation is performed in the reverse order of removal.

Arrow indicates position of the air control valve

Check Valve 1971–76

1. Perform the air control valve removal procedure, detailed above. Be sure to pay attention to the CAUTION.
2. Remove the check valve seat.
3. Withdraw the valve plate and spring.

Install the check valve in the reverse order of removal.

Check Valve—1977–78

1. Perform the air control valve removal procedure as described above.
2. Remove the check valve and gasket by unscrewing the valve from the manifold.
3. Install check valve in reverse order, and reinstall air control valve.

Air Injection Nozzle

1. Remove the gravel shield from underneath the car.
2. Perform the oil pan removal procedure as detailed in "Engine Lubrication," above.
3. Unbolt the air injection nozzles from both of the rotor housing.

Nozzle installation is perfromed in the reverse order of removal.

Piston Engine Air Injection System

OPERATION

Most Mazda piston engines use the conventional air injection system. This sytem uses a belt driven vane type pump to force air through air injection nozzles into the exhaust manifold or thermal reactor. The system employs a check valve near the exhaust manifold or thermal reactor to keep exhaust gases from traveling back into the air lines if the air pump fails. The system also uses an air control valve which regulates the amount of air sent to the exhaust manifold, increasing it when the vehicle is overrunning (throttle closed at speeds beyond about 20 mph), at which time extra fuel is admitted to the manifold.

Various models replace the air pump with a pulse type system which utilizes pressure waves in the exhaust system and a reed valve to pump air into the exhaust manifold. Models not using pulse air employ a conventional air pump, a catalytic converter, and a system which protects the converter from overheating by interrupting airflow at high converter temperatures.

CHECKING THE AIR PUMP

1. Disconnect the hose from the air pump outlet.
2. Connect a pressure gauge to the outlet.
3. Check the drive belt for proper tension and run engine at 1500 rpm. Gauge reading should be at least 1 psi. If not, replace the pump.

CHECKING THE REED VALVE

1. Run the engine until it is hot. Disconnect the air hose at the reed valve.
2. Run the engine at idle speed, and place a finger over the inlet of the reed valve. Air should be sucked into the valve.
3. Increase speed to 1,500 rpm and make sure no exhaust gas is discharged from the reed valve inlet.

CHECKING THE RELIEF VALVE

1. Run the engine at idle.
2. At idle, no air should be felt at the relief valve. If air flow is felt, replace the valve.
3. Increase the idle to 2000 rpm on 1600 engine, 4000 rpm on other engines. If air flow is felt, valve is working properly.

CHECKING THE CHECK VALVE

1. Run the engine until it is hot. Disconnect the air hose at the check valve on the exhaust manifold.
2. Gradually increase the engine speed to 1,500 rpm while carefully checking for exhaust (hot) gas leakage from the check valve. Replace the valve if exhaust gases are present.

AIR CONTROL VALVE TEST

1. Start the engine and run it at idle.
2. Hold a finger over the relief valve port of the air control valve. Discharge air should be felt.
3. Disconnect the vacuum sensing tube from the air control valve and plug the tube. No air should be felt at the relief port.

AIR CONTROL VALVE CHECK VALVE TEST

1. Disconnect the vacuum sensing tube from the air control valve solenoid.
2. Blow through the vacuum tube. Air should pass through the valve. Suck on the tube. No air should pass through the valve.

PUMP REPLACEMENT

1. Disconnect the inlet and outlet hoses at the pump.
2. Remove the adjusting bolt and lift off the drive belt.
3. Support the pump and remove the mounting bolts. Lift out the pump.
4. Installation is the reverse of removal. Adjust drive belt to specification. Correct belt adjustment will give a 5″ flex at the midpoint with thumb pressure.

REPLACING AIR CONTROL VALVE

1. Disconnect the vacuum lines from the valve.
2. Disconnect the wiring from the valve.
3. Disconnect the air hoses from the valve.
4. Unbolt and remove the valve.
5. Install in reverse of removal.

CHECK VALVE OR REED VALVE REPLACEMENT

1. Disconnect inlet air hose and unscrew valve from exhaust manifold.
2. To replace, screw in new valve and connect inlet air hose.

Thermal Reactor (Rotary Engine)

A thermal reactor is used in place of a conventional exhaust manifold. It is used to oxidize unburned hydrocarbons and carbon monoxide before they can be released into the atmosphere.

If the engine speed exceeds 4,000 rpm, or if the car is decelerating, the air control valve diverts air into passages in the thermal reactor housing in order to cool the reactor. On later models, air flow into the reaction chamber is cut off under these conditions.

A one-way valve prevents hot exhaust gases from flowing back into the air injection system. The valve is located at the reactor air intake.

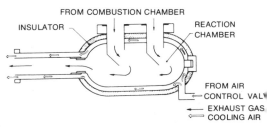

Thermal reactor cooling circuit

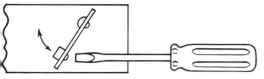

Check one-way valve operation, as illustrated

INSPECTION

CAUTION: *Perform thermal reactor inspection only after the reactor has cooled sufficiently to prevent the danger of being severely burned.*

1. Examine the reactor housing for cracks or other signs of damage.
2. Remove the air supply hose from the one-way valve. Insert a screwdriver into the valve and test the butterfly for smooth operation. Replace the valve if necessary.
3. If the valve is functioning properly, connect the hose to it.

NOTE: *Remember to check the components of the air injection system which are related to the thermal reactor.*

REMOVAL AND INSTALLATION

Thermal reactor removal and installation are given in the "Engine Mechanical" section.

Rotary Engine Deceleration Control System

OPERATION

The deceleration control system uses an anti-afterburn valve, a coasting valve, and an air supply valve. In addition, either a throttle positioner (1971) or an idle sensing switch (1972–76) is fitted to the carburetor.

1971 models have a throttle positioner to keep idle speed at about 950 rpm during deceleration.

1972–76 models do not have a throttle positioner, but have an idle sensing switch attached to the carburetor in its place. When the throttle closes, its linkage contacts a plunger on the switch which completes the circuit from the No. 1 control box to the coasting valve, thus causing the coasting valve to operate. On automatic transmission equipped models, it also determines trailing distributor operation.

A solenoid-operated air supply valve opens when the ignition is shut off to prevent the engine from dieseling (running on).

On 1977 models, these systems are replaced by a combination anti-afterburn and coasting valve, idle switch, and control unit.

When the throttle is closed, a signal travels from the idle switch through the control box to a solenoid valve on the deceleration valve which supplies extra air to the intake manifold in order to reduce emissions.

These systems are highly complex and are covered by an extended warranty. Therefore, only simple adjustments are included here.

COMPONENT TESTING

Throttle Positioner—1971

1. Remove the air supply hose from the costing valve and plug up its intake.
2. Start the engine and increase its speed to 2,000 rpm.
3. Connect the solenoid on the costing valve directly to the car's battery.
4. Release the throttle so that it snaps shut. The idle speed should go no lower than 950 rmp (±50 rpm). If it does, adjust the throttle positioner, as outlined below.

Idle Switch—1972–76

1. Unfasten the idle switch leads.
2. Connect a test meter to the switch terminals ("A" and "C"—1973).
3. With the engine at idle, the meter should indicate a completed circuit.
4. Depress the plunger on the idle switch; the circuit should be broken (no meter reading).

If the idle switch is not functioning properly adjust it as described below.

ADJUSTMENTS

Throttle Positioner

1. Disconnect the wiring from the costing valve solenoid and connect the solenoid directly to the car battery.

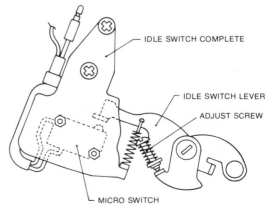

IDLE SWITCH COMPLETE

IDLE SWITCH LEVER

ADJUST SCREW

MICRO SWITCH

1972 idle switch—the 1973 switch uses a multi-connector

2. Loosen the locknut on the solenoid adjuster.

3. Rotate the adjuster until an idle speed of 950 ± 50 rpm is obtained when the throttle is released from an engine speed of 2,000 rpm.

4. Tighten the locknut carefully once the proper idle speed has been obtained.

5. Disconnect the coasting valve solenoid from the battery and reconnect it as found.

NOTE: *As soon as the solenoid is disconnected from the battery, idle speed should drop to 800 rpm.*

Idle Switch

1. Warm up the engine until the water temperature is at least 159°F.

2. Make sure that the mixture and idle speed are adjusted properly.

3. Adjust the idle speed to 1,075–1,100 rpm (1,200–1,300 rpm—automatic transmission) by rotating the throttle adjusting screw.

4. Rotate the idle switch adjusting screw until the switch changes from off to on position.

5. Slowly turn the idle switch adjusting screw back to the point where the switch just changes from on to off.

6. Turn the throttle screw back so that the engine returns to normal idle.

NOTE: *Be sure that the idle switch turns on when the idle speed is still above 1,000 rpm.*

Piston Engine Deceleration Control System

Accelerator Switch Adjustment 1600 Engine

1. Remove the air cleaner. If the engine is not warm, open the throttle and choke and then release the throttle to ensure that throttle is at normal idle speed position (off the fast idle cam).

2. Fully loosen the adjusting screw of the switch (turning out until switch just clicks off), and then tighten very gradually until switch just clicks back on.

3. Turn the screw exactly an additional 1½ turns.

VACUUM THROTTLE OPENER ADJUSTMENT 1977–78 GLC

1. Connect a tachometer to the engine. Run the engine until hot, and stop it and remove the air cleaner.

2. Disconnect the vacuum sensing tube

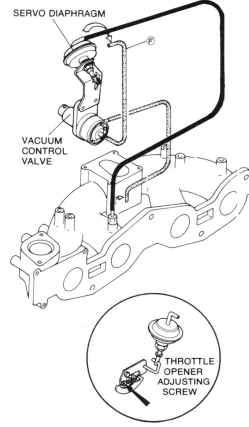

SERVO DIAPHRAGM

VACUUM CONTROL VALVE

THROTTLE OPENER ADJUSTING SCREW

Adjusting the vacuum throttle opener system —1977–78 GLC

"F" from the servo diaphragm, and connect a vacuum hose between the vacuum tap on the manifold and the diaphragm. Disconnect the vacuum line going from carburetor to distributor and plug the open end.

3. Start the engine and read the tachometer. Engine speed should be 1300–1500 rpm. If not to specification, adjust the throttle opener adjusting screw to bring engine speed to within the range.

4. Reconnect distributor and servo diaphragm vacuum lines, and then disconnect and plug the vacuum line going to the anti-afterburn valve. Disconnect the vacuum line going from the manifold to the vacuum control valve, and Tee in a vacuum gauge as shown.

5. Start the engine and accelerate to 3,000 rpm. Watch the vacuum gauge and release the throttle. After a rapid rise in vacuum, the gauge should stabilize at 22.0–22.8 in. for a few seconds while the system gradually closes the throttle, and then fall off.

6. If vacuum does not stabilize in the right range, loosen the locknut and turn the adjusting screw in the end of the vacuum control valve until vacuum is in the specified range. Turn the screw clockwise to increase the vacuum reading, and counterclockwise to decrease it.

7. Tighten the locknut, and restore all vacuum connections. Replace the air cleaner and remove the tachometer.

SERVO DIAPHRAGM ADJUSTMENT

1. Connect a tachometer to the engine.
2. Run the engine at idle to normal operating temperature.
3. Stop the engine and remove the air cleaner.
4. Disconnect the vacuum sensing tube F at the servo diaphragm.
5. Connect the inlet manifold and the servo diaphragm with a suitable tube so that the inlet manifold vacuum can be led directly to the servo diaphragm.
6. Disconnect the vacuum sensing tube from the carburetor to the distributor at the distributor and plug the tube.
7. Start the engine and check to see that the engine speed increases to 1100–1300 rpm (GLC), 1000–1200 rpm (626).
8. Turn the throttle positioner adjuster screw in or out to adjust to specifications.

THREE WAY SOLENOID VALVE CHECK

1. Disconnect the vacuum sensing tube A from the servo diaphragm.
2. Disconnect the vacuum sensing tube B from the three way solenoid valve.
3. Disconnect the connector (brown-white wire) from the engine speed switch and ground the three way solenoid valve using a jumper wire.
4. Turn the ignition switch on.

Engine speed switch check

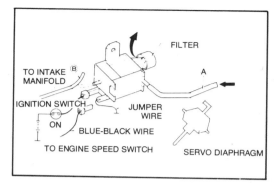

Three way solenoid valve check—with ignition switch on

5. Blow through the three way solenoid valve from the disconnected tube in step 1 and make sure the air comes out from the air filter of the valve.
6. Turn the ignition switch off.
7. Blow through the valve through the disconnected tube A in step 1, and make sure that the air comes through the port a.
8. Replace the three way solenoid valve if it does not operate properly.

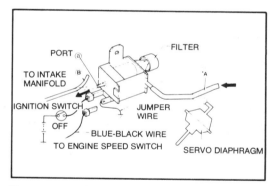

Three way solenoid valve check—with ignition switch off

ENGINE SPEED SWITCH CHECK

1. Disconnect the engine speed switch connector.
2. Connect a voltmeter to the connection.
3. Increase the engine speed to 2,000 rpm then slowly decrease the engine speed.
4. Record the engine speed at which the current flows to the circuit. The engine speed should be 1,600–1,800 rpm (California A/T) and 1,400–1,600 rpm (Canada M/T).
5. Slowly increase the engine speed again and record the engine speed at which the current does not flow to the circuit. The dif-

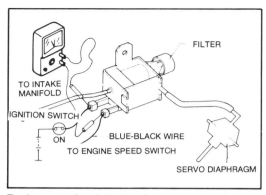

Engine speed switch check

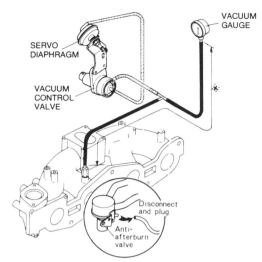

※ —USE TEST TUBE OF 3.0mm (0.12 in)
INNER DIAMETER. LENGTH SHOULD
BE WITHIN 2.0m (6.6 ft).

Adjusting the vacuum control valve—1977–78 GLC

ference between the engine speed recorded in step 3 and 5 should be 150–250 rpm.

6. The engine speed switch must be replaced if found defective.

Exhaust Gas Recirculation System

OPERATION

This system is used to meter a small amount of exhaust gas back into the intake manifold to slow the combustion process, slightly reduce the maximum temperatures in the combustion chambers, and thus reduce nitrogen oxides. A water temperature switch or three way solenoid valve may stop exhaust gas recirculation when the engine is cold. On most models, the EGR Control Valve must be serviced periodically, and on some models, a meaintenance warning system reset. Also, the EGR valve is by far the most sensitive part of the system, as it can become carbon clogged.

EGR CONTROL VALVE TEST

1. Remove the air cleaner.
2. Run the engine at idle.
3. Disconnect the vacuum sensing tube from the EGR control valve, and make connections directly to an intake manifold (not carburetor) tap with a vacuum hose.
4. Connect this vacuum tube to the EGR control valve. The engine should stop. If not, clean or replace the EGR control valve.

REPLACING EGR CONTROL VALVE

1. Remove air cleaner.
2. Disconnect the vacuum sensing tube from the EGR control valve.
3. Disconnect the EGR control valve-to-exhaust manifold pipe.

4. Disconnect the pipe between the EGR control valve and the intake manifold.
5. Unbolt and remove the EGR control valve.
6. If old valve is to be reused, it should be cleaned with a wire brush before installation.
7. To install, reverse the above procedure.

RESETTING EGR MAINTENANCE WARNING SYSTEM

This system is used on rotary engine cars. After the passages of the EGR valve have been cleaned with solvent and the outlet of the valve has been wire brushed, reset the maintenance warning system. On models to 1976, remove the cover from the switch and slide the knob in the opposite direction. On later models, disconnect the connector, which is located under the left of the dash, turn one side 180 degrees, and reconnect it.

Evaporative Emission Control System

The evaporative emission control system is designed to control the emission of gasoline vapors into the atmosphere. On all models except the GLC and the 626 the vapors rising from the gasoline in the fuel tank are vented into a separate condensing tank which is located in the luggage compartment. There they condense and return to the fuel tank in

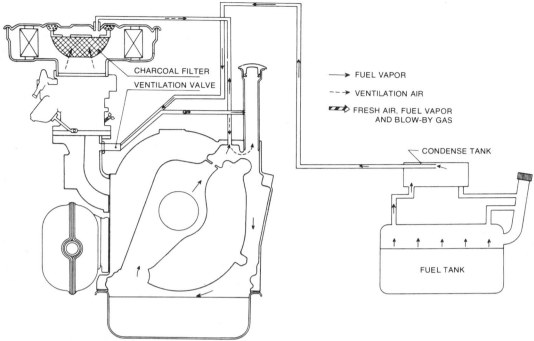

Rotary engine emission control system—1972 (other years similar)

Arrow shows location of the condensing tank in the luggage compartment

liquid form when the engine is not running.

When the engine is running, the fuel vapors are sucked directly into the engine through the PCV valve and are burned along with the air/fuel mixture.

Any additional fuel vapors which are not handled by the condensing tank are stored in a charcoal canister or a filter which is incorporated into the air cleaner (1972–73). When the engine is running, the charcoal is purged of its stored fuel vapor. On some models, a check valve vents the fuel vapor into the atmosphere if pressure becomes too excessive in the fuel tank. The check valve is located in the luggage compartment, next to the condensing tank. On the GLC models the sys-

tem consists of a charcoal canister, cut and check valve, liquid separater (wagon only), and purge control valves. The system on the model 626 consists of a charcoal canister, check and cut valve, purge control valves, Evaporator shutter valve in air cleaner.

SYSTEM TESTING

There are several things to check if a malfunction of the evaporative emission control system is suspected.

1. Leaks may be traced by using an infrared hydrocarbon tester. Run the test probe along the lines and connections. The meter will indicate the presence of a leak by a high hydrocarbon (HC) reading. This method is much more accurate than a visual inspection which would indicate only the presence of a leak large enough to pass liquid.

2. Leaks may be caused by any of the following, so always check these areas when looking for them:

   a. Defective or worn lines
   b. Disconnected or pinched lines
   c. Improperly routed lines
   d. A defective check valve

NOTE: *If it becomes necessary to replace any of the lines used in the evaporative emission control system, use only those hoses which are fuel resistant or are marked "EVAP."*

3. If the fuel tank has collapsed, it may be the fault of clogged or pinched vent lines, a defective vapor separator, or a plugged or incorrect check valve.

Catalytic Converter

REMOVAL AND INSTALLATION

GLC—Rear Wheel Drive

1. Raise the vehicle and support with jack stands.
2. Remove the four bolts and remove the heat insulator.
3. Disconnect the two hangers from the muffler and move the muffler assembly rearward.
4. Disconnect the exhaust pipes from the catalytic converter.
5. Remove the catalytic converter.
6. To install reverse the above.

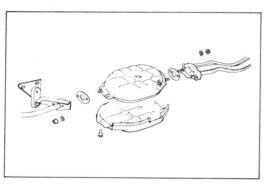

Catalytic converter installation—GLC

GLC—Front Wheel Drive

1. Raise the car and safely support it on jackstands.
2. Remove the heat shield from the front (at exhaust manifold) and rear (under car) converters.
3. Unbolt the front converter from the exhaust manifold and exhaust pipe.
4. Remove the sensor tube from the rear converter. Disconnect the hangers, loosen and remove the front and rear mounting bolts. Remove the converter.
5. Installation is in the reverse order of removal. Always use new flange gaskets.

626 and 808 (1600)

1. Raise the vehicle and support with jack stands.

2. Remove the heat insulator from the catalytic converter.
3. Remove the nuts from the front and rear flanges of the converter and remove it from the vehicle.
4. To install reverse the above.

808 (1300)

1. Raise the vehicle and support with jack stands.
2. Disconnect the sensor wire connector at the converter.
3. Loosen and remove the sensor from the converter.
4. Remove the heat insulator from the converter.
5. Remove the nuts from the front and rear flanges of the converter.
6. Remove the nuts and rubber bushings between the converter and the body and remove the converter.
7. To install reverse the above procedure.

CATALYST THERMO SENSOR CHECK

808 (1300)

1. Remove the passenger's side trim plate and floor mat.
2. Disconnect the wire connector at the sensor.
3. Check the sensor with a circuit tester. If there is no current replace the sensor.

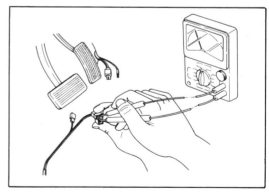

Checking catalyst thermo sensor

FUEL SYSTEM

Mechanical Fuel Pump

This pump is used on all GLC models. The pump is located on the right side of the engine block on rear wheel drive models and on the left side of the intake manifold on front wheel drive models.

REMOVAL AND INSTALLATION

1. Slide the two fuel line clips back off the pump connectors. Then, pull fuel lines off the pump. Mark inlet and outlet lines.
2. Remove the two mounting bolts from the block, and remove the pump, gaskets, and spacer.
3. Reverse the removal procedure to install.

TESTING

1. Disconnect the fuel inlet line going to the carburetor. Install a pressure gauge into the line coming from the pump. Be careful not to spill fuel or, if it does spill, to remove spillage before starting the engine.
2. Start the engine and run it at idle on the fuel in the carburetor float bowl until the pressure gauge reaches a maximum reading. Note the pressure reading—specifications are 2.84–3.84 psi.
3. To test the volume of fuel discharged by the pump, the engine must be run at idle for one minute. Remove the pressure gauge, reinstall the fuel line into the carburetor, and run the engine until the carburetor float bowl is full of fuel. Procure a durable container (preferably metal) of well over 1 qt. capacity. Disconnect the fuel line at the carburetor, and put the open end into the container. Idle the engine until it stops (or for one minute) and time how long it has run. Then, reconnect the fuel line to the carburetor and run the starter or idle the engine until float bowl is full. Repeat the operation involving fuel discharge and timing until the engine has run for total of one full minute at idle speed and all the fuel discharged by the pump has been collected. Th pump must discharge at least 1.1 qts. per minute.
4. If the pump fails either the pressure or volume test, replace it.

Electric Fuel Pump

The electric fuel pump is located in the luggage compartment of the RX-2, RX-3, RX-4, Cosmo and 308 coupes and sedans. On RX-3 and RX-4 station wagons, it is located behind the left-hand trim panel in the cargo compartment. The 626 and GLC wagon fuel pump is located under the floor of the car in front of the fuel tank.

Fuel pump location—sedans and coupes

REMOVAL AND INSTALLATION
Sedans and Coupes—1971–75

1. Open the luggage compartment lid.
2. Remove the rear inside trim panel, after unfastening its two securing screws.
3. Disconnect the wiring and the fuel lines from the pump.
4. Unfasten the nuts and bolts which secure the pump assembly. Remove the pump.

Installation is performed in the reverse order of removal.

Sedans and Coupes—1976–78

1. Open the trunk and remove the partition board or, on the Cosmo, the floor mat.
2. Disconnect the bullet type electrical connector.
3. Raise the Cosmo rear end upward and place on axle stands for access from underneath.
4. Remove the pump cover attaching bolts and remove the cover.
5. Disconnect inlet and outlet hoses from the pump.
6. Remove the nuts attaching the pump to the car body.
7. Installation is the reverse of the removal procedure.

Station Wagon—Except GLC

1. Remove the left-hand cargo compartment trim panel.
2. Disconnect the wiring and fuel lines from the pump.
3. Unfasten the nuts which secure the pump and remove the pump.

Installation is performed in the reverse order of removal.

626 and GLC Wagons

1. Disconnect the negative battery cable at the battery.
2. Disconnect the fuel pump lead wire in the luggage compartment.

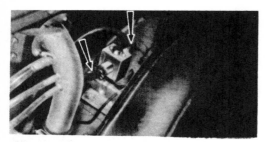

Fuel pump location—RX-3 wagon

3. Raise the vehicle and support with jack stands.

4. Disconnect the fuel pump bracket.

5. Disconnect the fuel inlet and outlet hoses and remove the fuel pump.

6. Installation is the reverse of removal.

TESTING

1. Remove the air cleaner. Procure a durable container (preferably metal) of about 1½ qts. capacity.

2. Disconnect the carburetor fuel inlet hose. Turn the ignition switch on and allow all air to be purged from the system with the hose pointed into the container.

3. Turn off ignition, install a pressure gauge into the line, and turn ignition back on. When pressure has stabilized, note the reading and turn ignition off. Pressure should be: 2.8–3.6 for cars built before 1974; 3.55–4.98 for 1974–75 cars; and 4.3–5.4 for 1976 and later cars.

4. Pull the pressure gauge out of the fuel line and position the line so fuel will be discharged into the container. Turn the ignition switch on for one minute. Volume should be: .9 qts for 1971–73 cars; 1.22 qts. for 1974–78 cars.

5. If the pump fails either or both tests, replace it.

Carburetor

REMOVAL AND INSTALLATION

Rotary—Except Below

1. Remove the air cleaner assembly, complete with its hoses and mounting bracket.

2. Detach the choke and accelerator cables from the carburetor.

3. Disconnect the fuel and vacuum lines from the carburetor.

4. Remove the oil line which runs to the metering oil pump, at the carburetor.

5. Unfasten the idle sensor switch wiring, if so equipped.

6. Remove the carburetor attaching nuts and/or bolts, gasket or heat insulator, and remove the carburetor.

Installation is performed in the reverse order of removal. Use a new gasket. Fill the float bowl with gasoline to aid in engine starting.

1977–78 Cosmo

1. Disconnect battery (−) cable. Disconnect all hoses from the air cleaner and remove it.

2. Disconnect accelerator and choke cables at the carburetor.

3. Disconnect the two electrical connectors at the heater and the air vent solenoid and the vacuum lines.

4. Disconnect the sub-zero starting assist hose at the carburetor (except California cars).

5. Disconnect the metering oil pump hoses at the carburetor. Disconnect the metering oil pump rod at the connecting lever.

6. Disconnect electrical connectors at the idle switch and the power valve solenoid (if so equipped).

7. If the car has a manual transmission, disconnect the connector at the richer solenoid.

8. Disconnect the fuel inlet and return lines at the carburetor.

9. Remove carburetor attaching nuts, and remove the carburetor.

10. Install in reverse order, using new gaskets.

Piston Engines

1. Disconnect the negative battery cable.

2. Remove the air cleaner.

3. Disconnect the acclerator cable.

4. Disconnect all wire connections, vacuum sensing tubes and fuel hoses then remove the carburetor.

5. Reverse the above to install.

OVERHAUL

Carburetor rebuilding kits include specific procedures and exploded views for order of assembly and disassembly, and so only generally applicable rebuilding suggestions are provided here. Efficient carburetion depends greatly on careful cleaning and inspection during overhaul since dirt, gum, water, or varnish in or on the carburetor parts are often responsible for poor performance.

Overhaul your carburetor in a clean, dust-free area. Carefully dissemble the carbu-

CHILTON'S
FUEL ECONOMY
& TUNE-UP TIPS

Tune-Up • Spark Plug Diagnosis • Emission Controls

Fuel System • Cooling System • Tires and Wheels

General Maintenance

55 WAYS TO IMPROVE FUEL ECONOMY

CHILTON'S FUEL ECONOMY & TUNE-UP TIPS

Fuel economy is important to everyone, no matter what kind of vehicle you drive. The maintenance-minded motorist can save both money and fuel using these tips and the periodic maintenance and tune-up procedures in this Repair and Tune-Up Guide.

There are more than 130,000,000 cars and trucks registered for private use in the United States. Each travels an average of 10-12,000 miles per year, and, in total they consume close to 70 billion gallons of fuel each year. This represents nearly ⅔ of the oil imported by the United States each year. The Federal government's goal is to reduce consumption 10% by 1985. A variety of methods are either already in use or under serious consideration, and they all affect your driving and the cars you will drive. In addition to "down-sizing", the auto industry is using or investigating the use of electronic fuel delivery, electronic engine controls and alternative engines for use in smaller and lighter vehicles, among other alternatives to meet the federally mandated Corporate Average Fuel Economy (CAFE) of 27.5 mpg by 1985. The government, for its part, is considering rationing, mandatory driving curtailments and tax increases on motor vehicle fuel in an effort to reduce consumption. The government's goal of a 10% reduction could be realized — and further government regulation avoided — if every private vehicle could use just 1 less gallon of fuel per week.

How Much Can You Save?

Tests have proven that almost anyone can make at least a 10% reduction in fuel consumption through regular maintenance and tune-ups. When a major manufacturer of spark plugs sur-

TUNE-UP

1. Check the cylinder compression to be sure the engine will really benefit from a tune-up and that it is capable of producing good fuel economy. A tune-up will be wasted on an engine in poor mechanical condition.

2. Replace spark plugs regularly. New spark plugs alone can increase fuel economy 3%.

3. Be sure the spark plugs are the correct type (heat range) for your vehicle. See the Tune-Up Specifications.

Heat range refers to the spark plug's ability to conduct heat away from the firing end. It must conduct the heat away in an even pattern to avoid becoming a source of pre-ignition, yet it must also operate hot enough to burn off conductive deposits that could cause misfiring.

The heat range is usually indicated by a number on the spark plug, part of the manufacturer's designation for each individual spark plug. The numbers in bold-face indicate the heat range in each manufacturer's identification system.

Manufacturer	Typical Designation
AC	R **45** TS
Bosch (old)	WA **145** T30
Bosch (new)	HR **8** Y
Champion	RBL **15** Y
Fram/Autolite	**4**15
Mopar	P-**62** PR
Motorcraft	BR**F-42**
NGK	BP **5** ES-15
Nippondenso	W **16** EP
Prestolite	14GR **5** 2A

Periodically, check the spark plugs to be sure they are firing efficiently. They are excellent indicators of the internal condition of your engine.

On AC, Bosch (new), Champion, Fram/Autolite, Mopar, Motorcraft and Prestolite, a higher number indicates a hotter plug. On Bosch (old), NGK and Nippondenso, a higher number indicates a colder plug.

4. Make sure the spark plugs are properly gapped. See the Tune-Up Specifications in this book.

5. Be sure the spark plugs are firing efficiently. The illustrations on the next 2 pages show you how to "read" the firing end of the spark plug.

6. Check the ignition timing and set it to specifications. Tests show that almost all cars

veyed over 6,000 cars nationwide, they found that a tune-up, on cars that needed one, increased fuel economy over 11%. Replacing worn plugs alone, accounted for a 3% increase. The same test also revealed that 8 out of every 10 vehicles will have some maintenance deficiency that will directly affect fuel economy, emissions or performance. Most of this mileage-robbing neglect could be prevented with regular maintenance.

Modern engines require that all of the functioning systems operate properly for maximum efficiency. A malfunction anywhere wastes fuel. You can keep your vehicle running as efficiently and economically as possible, by being aware of your vehicles operating and performance characteristics. If your vehicle suddenly develops performance or fuel economy problems it could be due to one or more of the following:

PROBLEM	POSSIBLE CAUSE
Engine Idles Rough	Ignition timing, idle mixture, vacuum leak or something amiss in the emission control system.
Hesitates on Acceleration	Dirty carburetor or fuel filter, improper accelerator pump setting, ignition timing or fouled spark plugs.
Starts Hard or Fails to Start	Worn spark plugs, improperly set automatic choke, ice (or water) in fuel system.
Stalls Frequently	Automatic choke improperly adjusted and possible dirty air filter or fuel filter.
Performs Sluggishly	Worn spark plugs, dirty fuel or air filter, ignition timing or automatic choke out of adjustment.

Check spark plug wires on conventional point type ignition for cracks by bending them in a loop around your finger.

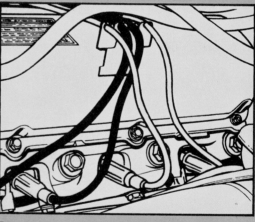

Be sure that spark plug wires leading to adjacent cylinders do not run too close together. (Photo courtesy Champion Spark Plug Co.)

have incorrect ignition timing by more than 2°.

7. If your vehicle does not have electronic ignition, check the points, rotor and cap as specified.

8. Check the spark plug wires (used with conventional point-type ignitions) for cracks and burned or broken insulation by bending them in a loop around your finger. Cracked wires decrease fuel efficiency by failing to deliver full voltage to the spark plugs. One misfiring spark plug can cost you as much as 2 mpg.

9. Check the routing of the plug wires. Misfiring can be the result of spark plug leads to adjacent cylinders running parallel to each other and too close together. One wire tends to pick up voltage from the other causing it to fire "out of time".

10. Check all electrical and ignition circuits for voltage drop and resistance.

11. Check the distributor mechanical and/or vacuum advance mechanisms for proper functioning. The vacuum advance can be checked by twisting the distributor plate in the opposite direction of rotation. It should spring back when released.

12. Check and adjust the valve clearance on engines with mechanical lifters. The clearance should be slightly loose rather than too tight.

SPARK PLUG DIAGNOSIS

Normal

APPEARANCE: This plug is typical of one operating normally. The insulator nose varies from a light tan to grayish color with slight electrode wear. The presence of slight deposits is normal on used plugs and will have no adverse effect on engine performance. The spark plug heat range is correct for the engine and the engine is running normally.

CAUSE: Properly running engine.

RECOMMENDATION: Before reinstalling this plug, the electrodes should be cleaned and filed square. Set the gap to specifications. If the plug has been in service for more than 10-12,000 miles, the entire set should probably be replaced with a fresh set of the same heat range.

Incorrect Heat Range

APPEARANCE: The effects of high temperature on a spark plug are indicated by clean white, often blistered insulator. This can also be accompanied by excessive wear of the electrode, and the absence of deposits.

CAUSE: Check for the correct spark plug heat range. A plug which is too hot for the engine can result in overheating. A car operated mostly at high speeds can require a colder plug. Also check ignition timing, cooling system level, fuel mixture and leaking intake manifold.

RECOMMENDATION: If all ignition and engine adjustments are known to be correct, and no other malfunction exists, install spark plugs one heat range colder.

Photos Courtesy Champion Spark Plug Co.

Oil Deposits

APPEARANCE: The firing end of the plug is covered with a wet, oily coating.

CAUSE: The problem is poor oil control. On high mileage engines, oil is leaking past the rings or valve guides into the combustion chamber. A common cause is also a plugged PCV valve, and a ruptured fuel pump diaphragm can also cause this condition. Oil fouled plugs such as these are often found in new or recently overhauled engines, before normal oil control is achieved, and can be cleaned and reinstalled.

RECOMMENDATION: A hotter spark plug may temporarily relieve the problem, but the engine is probably in need of work.

Carbon Deposits

APPEARANCE: Carbon fouling is easily identified by the presence of dry, soft, black, sooty deposits.

CAUSE: Changing the heat range can often lead to carbon fouling, as can prolonged slow, stop-and-start driving. If the heat range is correct, carbon fouling can be attributed to a rich fuel mixture, sticking choke, clogged air cleaner, worn breaker points, retarded timing or low compression. If only one or two plugs are carbon fouled, check for corroded or cracked wires on the affected plugs. Also look for cracks in the distributor cap between the towers of affected cylinders.

RECOMMENDATION: After the problem is corrected, these plugs can be cleaned and reinstalled if not worn severely.

MMT Fouled

APPEARANCE: Spark plugs fouled by MMT (Methycyclopentadienyl Maganese Tricarbonyl) have reddish, rusty appearance on the insulator and side electrode.

CAUSE: MMT is an anti-knock additive in gasoline used to replace lead. During the combustion process, the MMT leaves a reddish deposit on the insulator and side electrode.

RECOMMENDATION: No engine malfunction is indicated and the deposits will not affect plug performance any more than lead deposits (see Ash Deposits). MMT fouled plugs can be cleaned, regapped and reinstalled.

High Speed Glazing

APPEARANCE: Glazing appears as shiny coating on the plug, either yellow or tan in color.

CAUSE: During hard, fast acceleration, plug temperatures rise suddenly. Deposits from normal combustion have no chance to fluff-off; instead, they melt on the insulator forming an electrically conductive coating which causes misfiring.

RECOMMENDATION: Glazed plugs are not easily cleaned. They should be replaced with a fresh set of plugs of the correct heat range. If the condition recurs, using plugs with a heat range one step colder may cure the problem.

Ash (Lead) Deposits

APPEARANCE: Ash deposits are characterized by light brown or white colored deposits crusted on the side or center electrodes. In some cases it may give the plug a rusty appearance.

CAUSE: Ash deposits are normally derived from oil or fuel additives burned during normal combustion. Normally they are harmless, though excessive amounts can cause misfiring. If deposits are excessive in short mileage, the valve guides may be worn.

RECOMMENDATION: Ash-fouled plugs can be cleaned, gapped and reinstalled.

Detonation

APPEARANCE: Detonation is usually characterized by a broken plug insulator.

CAUSE: A portion of the fuel charge will begin to burn spontaneously, from the increased heat following ignition. The explosion that results applies extreme pressure to engine components, frequently damaging spark plugs and pistons.

Detonation can result by over-advanced ignition timing, inferior gasoline (low octane) lean air/fuel mixture, poor carburetion, engine lugging or an increase in compression ratio due to combustion chamber deposits or engine modification.

RECOMMENDATION: Replace the plugs after correcting the problem.

Photos Courtesy Fram Corporation

EMISSION CONTROLS

13. Be aware of the general condition of the emission control system. It contributes to reduced pollution and should be serviced regularly to maintain efficient engine operation.

14. Check all vacuum lines for dried, cracked or brittle conditions. Something as simple as a leaking vacuum hose can cause poor performance and loss of economy.

15. Avoid tampering with the emission control system. Attempting to improve fuel econ-

FUEL SYSTEM

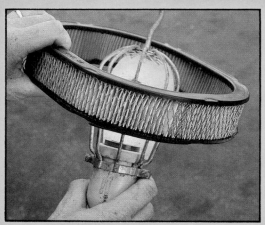

Check the air filter with a light behind it. If you can see light through the filter it can be reused.

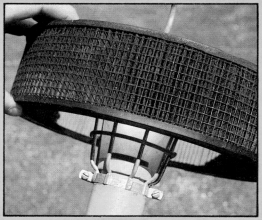

Extremely clogged filters should be discarded and replaced with a new one.

18. Replace the air filter regularly. A dirty air filter richens the air/fuel mixture and can increase fuel consumption as much as 10%. Tests show that ⅓ of all vehicles have air filters in need of replacement.

19. Replace the fuel filter at least as often as recommended.

20. Set the idle speed and carburetor mixture to specifications.

21. Check the automatic choke. A sticking or malfunctioning choke wastes gas.

22. During the summer months, adjust the automatic choke for a leaner mixture which will produce faster engine warm-ups.

COOLING SYSTEM

29. Be sure all accessory drive belts are in good condition. Check for cracks or wear.

30. Adjust all accessory drive belts to proper tension.

31. Check all hoses for swollen areas, worn spots, or loose clamps.

32. Check coolant level in the radiator or expansion tank.

33. Be sure the thermostat is operating properly. A stuck thermostat delays engine warm-up and a cold engine uses nearly twice as much fuel as a warm engine.

34. Drain and replace the engine coolant at least as often as recommended. Rust and scale

TIRES & WHEELS

38. Check the tire pressure often with a pencil type gauge. Tests by a major tire manufacturer show that 90% of all vehicles have at least 1 tire improperly inflated. Better mileage can be achieved by over-inflating tires, but never exceed the maximum inflation pressure on the side of the tire.

39. If possible, install radial tires. Radial tires deliver as much as ½ mpg more than bias belted tires.

40. Avoid installing super-wide tires. They only create extra rolling resistance and decrease fuel mileage. Stick to the manufacturer's recommendations.

41. Have the wheels properly balanced.

omy by tampering with emission controls is more likely to worsen fuel economy than improve it. Emission control changes on modern engines are not readily reversible.

16. Clean (or replace) the EGR valve and lines as recommended.

17. Be sure that all vacuum lines and hoses are reconnected properly after working under the hood. An unconnected or misrouted vacuum line can wreak havoc with engine performance.

23. Check for fuel leaks at the carburetor, fuel pump, fuel lines and fuel tank. Be sure all lines and connections are tight.

24. Periodically check the tightness of the carburetor and intake manifold attaching nuts and bolts. These are a common place for vacuum leaks to occur.

25. Clean the carburetor periodically and lubricate the linkage.

26. The condition of the tailpipe can be an excellent indicator of proper engine combustion. After a long drive at highway speeds, the inside of the tailpipe should be a light grey in color. Black or soot on the insides indicates an overly rich mixture.

27. Check the fuel pump pressure. The fuel pump may be supplying more fuel than the engine needs.

28. Use the proper grade of gasoline for your engine. Don't try to compensate for knocking or "pinging" by advancing the ignition timing. This practice will only increase plug temperature and the chances of detonation or pre-ignition with relatively little performance gain.

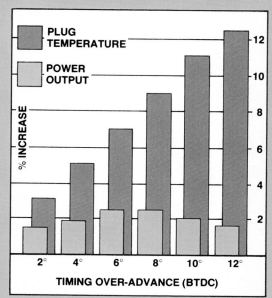

Increasing ignition timing past the specified setting results in a drastic increase in spark plug temperature with increased chance of detonation or preignition. Performance increase is considerably less. (Photo courtesy Champion Spark Plug Co.)

that form in the engine should be flushed out to allow the engine to operate at peak efficiency.

35. Clean the radiator of debris that can decrease cooling efficiency.

36. Install a flex-type or electric cooling fan, if you don't have a clutch type fan. Flex fans use curved plastic blades to push more air at low speeds when more cooling is needed; at high speeds the blades flatten out for less resistance. Electric fans only run when the engine temperature reaches a predetermined level.

37. Check the radiator cap for a worn or cracked gasket. If the cap does not seal properly, the cooling system will not function properly.

42. Be sure the front end is correctly aligned. A misaligned front end actually has wheels going in different directions. The increased drag can reduce fuel economy by .3 mpg.

43. Correctly adjust the wheel bearings. Wheel bearings that are adjusted too tight increase rolling resistance.

Check tire pressures regularly with a reliable pocket type gauge. Be sure to check the pressure on a cold tire.

GENERAL MAINTENANCE

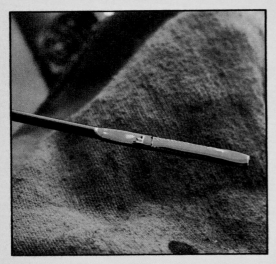

Check the fluid levels (particularly engine oil) on a regular basis. Be sure to check the oil for grit, water or other contamination.

A vacuum gauge is another excellent indicator of internal engine condition and can also be installed in the dash as a mileage indicator.

44. Periodically check the fluid levels in the engine, power steering pump, master cylinder, automatic transmission and drive axle.

45. Change the oil at the recommended interval and change the filter at every oil change. Dirty oil is thick and causes extra friction between moving parts, cutting efficiency and increasing wear. A worn engine requires more frequent tune-ups and gets progressively worse fuel economy. In general, use the lightest viscosity oil for the driving conditions you will encounter.

46. Use the recommended viscosity fluids in the transmission and axle.

47. Be sure the battery is fully charged for fast starts. A slow starting engine wastes fuel.

48. Be sure battery terminals are clean and tight.

49. Check the battery electrolyte level and add distilled water if necessary.

50. Check the exhaust system for crushed pipes, blockages and leaks.

51. Adjust the brakes. Dragging brakes or brakes that are not releasing create increased drag on the engine.

52. Install a vacuum gauge or miles-per-gallon gauge. These gauges visually indicate engine vacuum in the intake manifold. High vacuum = good mileage and low vacuum = poorer mileage. The gauge can also be an excellent indicator of internal engine conditions.

53. Be sure the clutch is properly adjusted. A slipping clutch wastes fuel.

54. Check and periodically lubricate the heat control valve in the exhaust manifold. A sticking or inoperative valve prevents engine warm-up and wastes gas.

55. Keep accurate records to check fuel economy over a period of time. A sudden drop in fuel economy may signal a need for tune-up or other maintenance.

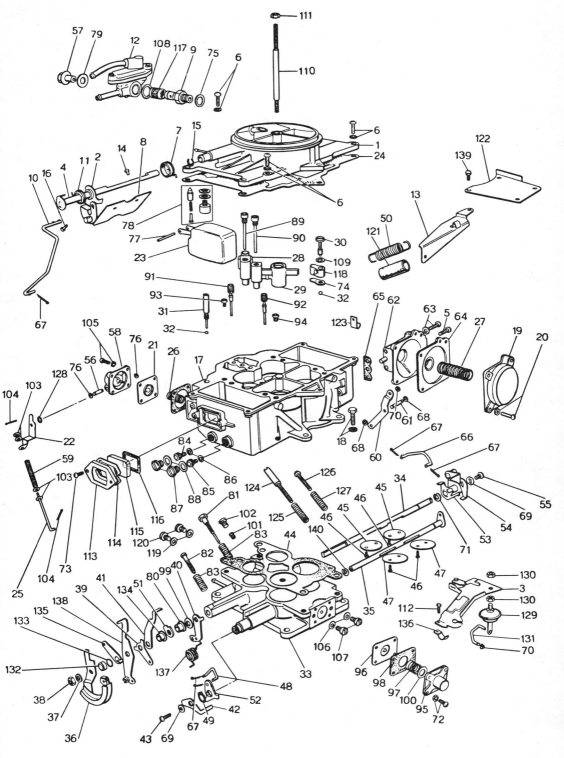

Carburetor—exploded view

1. Air horn	5. Screw	9. Connector	13. Hanger
2. Choke valve lever	6. Setscrew	10. Connecting rod	14. Screw
3. Clip	7. Spring	11. Spring	15. Ring
4. Choke lever shaft	8. Choke valve	12. Fuel return valve	16. Bolt

retor, referring often to the exploded views. Keep all similar and look-alike parts segregated during disassembly and cleaning to avoid accidental interchange during assembly. Make a note of all jet sizes.

When the carburetor is disassembled, wash all parts (except diaphragms, electric choke units, pump plunger, and any other plastic, leather, fiber, or rubber parts) in clean carburetor solvent. Do not leave parts in the solvent any longer than is necessary to sufficiently loosen the deposits. Excessive cleaning may remove the special finish from the float bowl and choke valve bodies, leaving these parts unfit for service. Rinse all parts in clean solvent and blow them dry with compressed air or allow them to air dry. Wipe clean all cork, plastic, leather, and fiber parts with a clean, lint-free cloth.

Blow out all passages and jets with compressed air and be sure that there are no restrictions or blockages. Never use wire or similar tools to clean jets, fuel passages, or air bleeds. Clean all jets and valves separately to avoid accidental interchange.

Check all parts for wear or damage. If wear or damage is found, replace the defective parts. Especially check the following:

1. Check the float needle and seat for wear. If wear is found, replace the complete assembly.

2. Check the float hinge pin for wear and the float(s) for dents or distortion. Replace the float if fuel has leaked into it.

3. Check the throttle and choke shaft bores for wear or an out-of-round condition. Damage or wear to the throttle arm, shaft, or shaft bore will often require replacement of the throttle body. These parts require a close tolerance of fit; wear may allow air leakage, which could affect starting and idling.

NOTE: *Throttle shafts and bushings are not included in overhaul kits. They can be purchased separately.*

4. Inspect the idle mixture adjusting needles for burrs or grooves. Any such condition requires replacement of the needle, since you will not be able to obtain a satisfactory idle.

5. Test the accelerator pump check valves. They should pass air one way but not the other. Test for proper seating by blowing and sucking on the valve. Replace the valve if necessary. If the valve is satisfactory, wash the valve again to remove breath moisture.

6. Check the bowl cover for warped surfaces with a straightedge.

7. Closely inspect the valves and seats for

17. Carburetor body	48. Throttle lever link	80. Collar	111. Nut
18. Bolt	49. Ring	81. Throttle adjusting	112. Screw
19. Diaphragm cover	50. Throttle return spring	screw	113. Cover
20. Screw	51. Arm	82. Idle adjusting screw	114. Gasket
21. Diaphragm	52. Retainer	83. Spring	115. Sight glass
22. Accelerator pump	53. Metering pump lever	84. Main jet	116. Gasket
arm	54. Metering pump arm	85. Main jet	117. Filter
23. Float	55. Screw	86. Gasket	118. Accelerator nozzle
24. Gasket	56. Pin	87. Plug	119. Gasket
25. Connecting rod	57. Union bolt	88. Gasket	120. Plug
26. Spring	58. Cover	89. Air bleed	121. Cover
27. Spring	59. Diaphragm spring	90. Air bleed	122. Coasting valve
28. Small venturi	60. Diaphragm lever	91. Slow jet	bracket
29. Small venturi	61. Diaphragm pin	92. Step jet	123. Clip
30. Bolt	62. Diaphragm chamber	93. Air bleed screw	124. Screw
31. Check ball plug	63. Screw	94. Air bleed step	125. Spring
32. Steel ball	64. Diaphragm	95. Cover	126. Screw
33. Flange	65. Gasket	96. Diaphragm	127. Spring
34. Throttle shaft	66. Connecting rod	97. Spring	128. Shim
35. Throttle shaft	67. Pin	98. Gasket	129. Throttle positioner
36. Throttle lever	68. Ring	99. Washer	130. Nut
37. Spring washer	69. Washer	100. Shim	131. Rod
38. Nut	70. Diaphragm stop ring	101. Jet	132. Collar
39. Lock	71. Diaphragm stop ring	102. Bleed plug	133. Shim
40. Adjusting arm	72. Screw	103. Retainer	134. Collar
41. Starting lever	73. Level gauge screw	104. Pin	135. Arm
42. Arm	74. Gasket	105. Screw	136. Plate
43. Screw	75. Gasket	106. Gasket	137. Retaining spring
44. Gasket	76. Stop ring	107. Plug	138. Lever
45. Valve	77. Float pin	108. Gasket	139. Setscrew
46. Screw	78. Needle valve seat	109. Gasket	140. Ring
47. Throttle valve	79. Gasket	110. Bolt	

wear and damage, replacing as necessary.

8. After the carburetor is assembed, check the choke valve for freedom of operation.

Carburetor overhaul kits are recommended for each overhaul. These kits contain all gaskets and new parts to replace those that deteriorate most rapidly. Failure to replace all parts supplied with the kit (especially gaskets) can result in poor performance later.

Some carburetor manufacturers supply overhaul kits of three basic types: minor repair; major repair; and gasket kits. Basically, they contain the following:

Minor Repair Kits:
- All gaskets
- Float needle valve
- Volume control screw
- All diaphragms
- Spring for the pump diaphragm

Major Repair Kits:
- All jets and gaskets
- All diaphragms
- Float needle valve
- Volume control screw
- Pump ball valve
- Main jet carrier
- Float
- Complete intermediate rod
- Intermediate pump lever
- Complete injector tube
- Some cover hold-down screws and washers

Gasket Kits:
- All gaskets

After cleaning and checking all components, reassemble the carburetor, using new parts and referring to the exploded view. When reassembling, make sure that all screws and jets are tight in their seats, but do not overtighten, as the tips will be distorted. Tighten all screws gradually, in rotation. Do not tighten needle valves into their seats; uneven jetting will result. Always use new gaskets. Be sure to adjust the float level when reassembling.

FLOAT AND FUEL LEVEL ADJUSTMENTS

1971 Models

1. Adjust the amount of the fuel coming through the needle valve by bending the float stop so that the distance between the lowest part of the float and the lower air horn face is 2.1–2.2 in.

2. Invert the air horn and lower the float

"1" is the float seal lip and "A" is the distance to be measured with the float in the raised position

so that the float seat lip is just contacting the needle valve.

3. Adjust the fuel level by adding or subtracting washers at the fuel intake so that the distance between the upper face of the float and the lower face of the air horn is 1.8–1.9 in.

1972–73 Models

1. Perform Steps 1–2 of the 1971 procedure, above.

2. Measure the clearance between the float and the surface of the air horn gasket; it should be 0.22 in.

3. Bend the float seat lip in order to adjust the float setting.

On all models built after 1973, the float level can be checked without removing the carburetor from the car, utilizing a sight glass in a float bowl. In some cases, difficult access may require the use of a mirror.

With the engine operating at normal idle speed (choke off), observe the fuel level. The level of liquid should cross the glass within the diameter of the green dot or the thickness of the line which is printed onto the glass. If the level is incorrect, the carburetor must be removed from the engine and the air horn removed in order to correct the flaot level.

Float lowered—1972–73

1974-76 Rotary Engines

1. Invert the air horn, raise the float, and lower it very gradually until the seat lip on the float just touches the needle valve. Then, measure the clearance between the bottom of the float and the face of the air horn gasket. The clearance should be: '74—.43 in.; '75—.39 in.; '76—.30–.38 in. Bend the float seal lip to obtain the specified clearance.

2. Turn the air horn over into its normal position and allow the float to drop by its own weight. Measure the clearance between the bottom of the float and the air horn gasket. Clearance should be 2.03–2.07 in. If clearance is incorrect, bend the float stop to correct it.

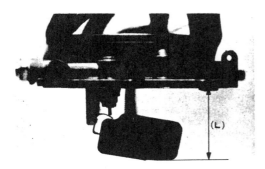

Measuring float drop—1974–76 rotary engines

1977-78 Rotary Engines

1. Invert the air horn and allow the float to drop by its own weight.

2. Measure the clearance between the float and the air horn gasket. It should be .6–.14 in. If necessary, bend the float seal lip until clearance is correct.

3. Turn the air horn over into its normal position, and measure the distance between the bottom of the float and the air horn gasket. The dimension should be 2.03–2.07 in. If necessary, bend the float stop to correct the dimension.

1600 cc Engine

To perform the float adjustment procedure on this carburetor, remove the carburetor assembly from the engine and remove the screws and glass cover from the float bowl.

1. Invert the carburetor and lower the float until the tang just touches the needle valve. Measure the distance between what is normally the top of the float and what is normally the top edge of the carburetor float bowl. The clearance should be .256 in. Bend the float tang to obtain the proper clearance.

1300, 1415, 1490 cc Engine

1. Invert the air horn and lower the float slowly until the seat lip just touches the needle valve. Measure the clearance between the float and air horn gasket surface (remove the gasket). It should be .433 in. Bend the float seat lip as necessary to correct the dimension.

2. With air horn still inverted, lift the float upward until the float stop contacts the air horn. Measure the clearance between the top of the needle valve and the float seat lip. It should be .051–.067 in. If not, bend the *float stop* until the clearance is correct.

1970 cc Engine

1. Invert the air horn and allow the float to lower by its own weight.

2. Measure the clearance between the float and the air horn bowl. The clearance should be .433 in. Bend the float seat lip to adjust.

3. Turn the air horn to the normal position and allow the float to lower by its own weight.

4. Measure the distance between the bottom of the float and the air horn bowl. The distance should be 1.811 in. Bend the float stopper to adjust.

FAST IDLE ADJUSTMENT ROTARY ENGINE

1971-73

1. With the choke valve fully closed, measure the clearance between the primary throttle valve and bore with wire gauge.

2. Compare this measurement with the specifications given in the chart at the end of this section.

3. Bend the fast idle lever, if adjustment of the clearance is required.

4. Test the choke valve to make sure that it operates freely.

5. Open the choke all the way. The throttle valve should be opened less than one degree, when measured with a protractor.

6. Close the choke valve to an angle of 35°. The throttle valve should just begin to open at this point.

7. Start the engine and run it at idle. The choke diaphragm rod should be pulled all the way out. If it is not, check for a clogged or an improperly connected vacuum line.

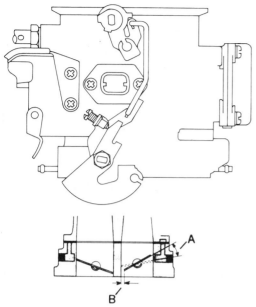

Fast idle adjustments—measure the angle "A" and the clearance "B"

Year	Throttle Valve Clearance
1971	0.047 in.
1972–73 (M/T)	0.045 in.
1973 (A/T)	0.055 in.

throttle and the throttle bore with a wire gauge. Specifications are:
- 1975—.069–.085 in.
- 1976—.067–.079 in.
- 1977–78—8.037–.045 in. 49 states, .050–.058 in. —California

1974

If the carburetor is mounted on the car, center a protractor on the end of the throttle-shaft and then have someone pull the choke knob all the way out. The angle through which the throttle moves should be: 14–17 degrees with manual transmission; 16–19 degrees with automatic. If necessary, bend the connecting rod to correct the angle of movement and recheck.

If the carburetor is off the car, the same measurement can be taken by measuring the clearance between the *lower* edge of the throttle and the throttle bore with a wire gauge of appropriate diameter. Pull the choke lever link out fully. The dimensions are: manual transmission—.0398–.0524 in.; automatic transmission—.0480–.0618 in.

1975–78

If the carburetor is installed on the car, warm the engine up and stop. Pull the choke knob all the way out and install a tachometer. Restart the engine. In ten seconds, engine speed should reach 3,000–3,500 rpm. If necessary, bend the rod connecting the choke shaft to the fast idle cam and recheck fast idle speed in a similar manner.

If the carburetor is off the car, the same measurement can be made by pulling the choke lever link out fully, and measuring the clearance between the lower edge of the

FAST IDLE ADJUSTMENT–PISTON ENGINES

1600 cc Engine

NOTE: *This adjustment can be performed only with the carburetor off the car.*

1. Close the choke valve fully, and measure the clearance between the lower edge of the throttle and the throttle bore with a wire feeler gauge.

2. The clearance should be .07 in. If incorrect, bend the rod connecting the choke shaft to the fast idle cam to correct it.

1300 cc Engine (1976–78)

1. Follow the procedure above, if the carburetor is off the car. The dimension is: .048–.060 in. The dimension can be checked with the carburetor on the car. Center a protractor on the throttle shaft and measure the angle that the throttle shaft moves from no choke to full choke. The angle should be 18.5 degrees.

2. If necessary, bend the rod connecting choke shaft and fast idle cam to adjust

1415, 1490, 1970 cc Engine

1. On the 1415 cc engine remove the bi-metal cover.

2. Using your finger close the choke valve fully.

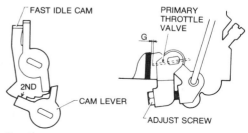

Adjusting fast idle cam—1415 cc engine

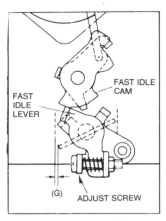

Fast idle cam adjustment—1970 cc engine

3. Make sure the fast idle cam is on the 1st position. 3rd position 1490 cc engine.

4. The throttle valve opening (clearance G) should be 1415 cc engine—.054 in. (1979) and .041 in. (1980), 1490 cc engine—.026 in. 1970 cc engine—.041 in. (1979) and .024 in. (from 1980).

5. Adjust by turning the adjustment screw.

NOTE: *Turn the adjustment screw clockwise to increase the clearance.*

SEMI-AUTOMATIC CHOKE ADJUSTMENT–ROTARY ENGINES

1974–78

1. The engine must be overnight cold. Pull the choke knob all the way out and wire it in this position (or if carburetor is off the car, wire the link in position). Wire the choke vacuum break disphragm in the fully withdrawn position, or, if a vacuum of over 15 in. HG is available, apply vacuum to the diaphragm.

2. Measure the opening angle of the choke by gauging the clearance between the top of

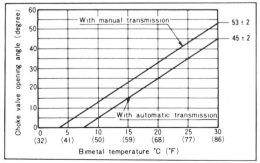

Choke valve clearance—1974

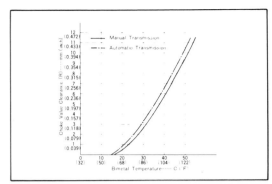

Choke valve clearance—1975

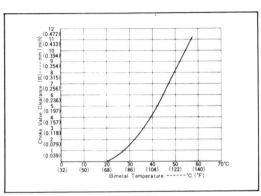

Choke valve clearance—1976

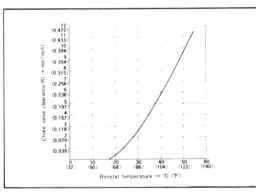

Choke valve clearance—1977–78

the choke and the air horn wall with a wire feeler gauge. Compare the reading to the *appropriate* chart and adjust the adjusting screw, located on the end of the choke shaft, to correct the reading, if necessary.

AUTOMATIC CHOKE CHECK

626 and GLC

1. Fully depress the accelerator pedal to make sure the choke valve closes properly.

2. Check for binding in the choke valve by pushing with your finger.

3. Make sure that the bi-metal cover index

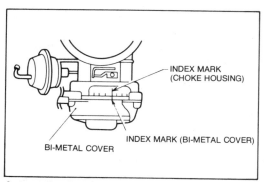

Automatic choke check—models 626 and GLC 1979–80

mark is set at the center of the choke housing index mark.

4. Check the automatic choke heater source wiring for proper connection then start the engine.

5. Make sure the choke valve is opened fully after the engine is warmed up.

6. If the automatic choke heater source wiring is normal and the choke valve does not operate after warm-up, replace the bi-metal cover.

UNLOADER ADJUSTMENT

626 and GLC

1. Close the choke valve fully, then open the primary throttle valve fully.

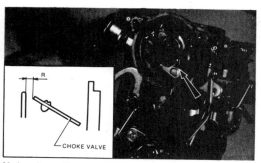

Unloader adjustment—1979–80 GLC

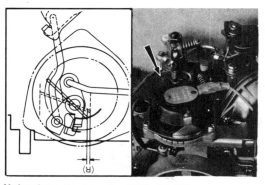

Unloader adjustment—1979–80 626

2. Measure the choke valve clearance. The clearance should be .09 in. (GLC) and 0.118 in. (626).

3. Bend the tab to adjust.

SECONDARY THROTTLE VALVE ADJUSTMENT

626 and GLC

1. The secondary throttle valve starts to open when the primary throttle valve opens 49–51 degrees and completely opens at the same time when the primary throttle valve fully opens.

2. Check the clearance between the primary throttle valve and the wall of the throttle bore when the secondary throttle valve starts to open.

3. The clearance should be .266 in. (626), .236 in. (GLC rear wheel drive) and .311 in. (GLC front wheel drive).

4. To adjust the clearance bend the connecting rod.

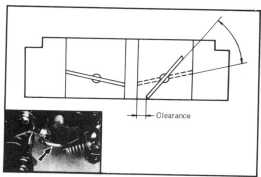

Secondary throttle valve adjustment—1979–80 626 and GLC

ACCELERATOR PUMP ADJUSTMENT

1971–73

1. Remove the air cleaner assembly.

2. Move the primary throttle valve and check pump discharge.

3. If there is no discharge, check for a clogged pump nozzle or a binding pump lever.

Arrow indicates pump adjustment

4. If it is binding, dress the sliding surface of the lever with sandpaper and lubricate it with oil.

5. If pump discharge is still unsatisfactory, adjust the pump lever to one of the two other adjusting holes in the connecting rod.

Fuel Tank

REMOVAL AND INSTALLATION

Except GLC—Front Wheel Drive

On sedans and coupes, the fuel tank is located behind the partition board in the trunk. On wagons, it is under the rear of the car.

1. On sedans and coupes, open the trunk and remove the partition board. On Wagons, raise the vehicle and support securely on axle stands.

2. Disconnect the inlet line from the fuel filter. Remove tank filler hose clamp, and disconnect the hose at the tank.

3. Disconnect condensing tank hoses.

4. Remove mounting bolts and remove the tank.

5. Installation is in reverse order.

GLC—Front Wheel Drive

The fuel tank is located under the rear of the car.

1. Remove the rear seat.

2. Remove the fuel tank gauge unit and drain the gas tank. Siphon if necessary.

3. Raise the rear of the car and safely support it on jackstands.

4. Disconnect all hoses at the tank.

5. Remove the mountings, lower the fuel tank from the car.

6. Installation is in the reverse order of removal.

Chassis Electrical

HEATER

Blower
REMOVAL AND INSTALLATION

All Models

The heater blower is located underneath the dash panel, inside the passenger compartment. On most models, the blower is located next to the heater box and connected to it by a duct. On RX-2 models, it is attached directly to the heater box and therefore no connecting duct is used.

NOTE: *On models equipped with dealer installed air conditioning, blower access may be slightly more difficult.*

1. Disconnect the negative battery cable.
2. Remove the dash undercover if equipped. Disconnect the multiconnector to the blower motor.
3. Remove the right side defroster hose for clearance if necessary.
4. If equipped with sliding heater controls, move the control to the HOT position and disconnect the control wire if in the way.
5. Remove the mounting screws and dismount the blower motor.
6. Installation is the reverse of removal.

Core

REMOVAL AND INSTALLATION
Except RX-2 Models

NOTE: *On models equipped with air conditioning access to the heater core will be more difficult.*

CAUTION: *Do not attempt to discharge the air conditioning system unless you are thoroughly familiar with the system. Escaping refrigerant will freeze any surface it contacts. If you do not have the proper training, have the system discharged and recharged by a professional.*

1. Disconnect the negative battery cable. Drain the coolant from the radiator.
2. Disconnect the heater hoses at the engine firewall.
3. Disconnect the duct which runs between the heater box and the blower motor or, depending on model, remove the crush pad and instrument panel pad from the dash. See following section for pad and panel removal.
4. Disconnect the defroster hose(s) if necessary, set the control to the DEF and HOT position and disconnect the control wires if they are in the way.

5. Unfasten the retaining screws that secure the halves of the heater box together or remove the heater unit and separate the heater box for access to the heater core.

6. Detach the hoses if not already disconnected. Remove the mounting clips and the heater core. Reverse the removal procedure for installation.

RX-2 Models

1. Perform Step 1 of the heater core removal above, then remove the blower motor.

2. Unfasten the screws securing the blower housing to the heater box.

3. Unfasten the screws that attach the bottom half of the heater box to the top.

4. Disconnect the heater hoses from the heater core.

5. Unfasten the clips securing the core to heater box and remove the heater core.

6. Install on the reverse order of removal.

Crush Pad and Instrument Panel

REMOVAL AND INSTALLATION

1. Disconnect the negative battery cable.

2. Remove the steering wheel and the lower steering column cover.

3. Remove the glove box, switch panel and console.

4. Remove the meter (gauge) hood, heater control panel mounting screws and separate the heater controls from the instrument panel frame. Remove the combination meter.

5. Remove the air duct(s) and the steering shaft mounting bracket bolts. Allow the column to lower.

6. Disconnect and label the meter wiring. Remove the mounting bolts and unmount the crush pad and instrument panel.

7. Install in reverse order of removal.

RADIO

REMOVAL AND INSTALLATION

CAUTION: *Never operate the radio with the speaker disconnected or with the speaker leads shorted together. Damage to the output transistors will result. Always replace the speaker with one of the same impedance (ohms) as was removed.*

RX-3 Models

1. Unfasten the two upper and the two lower screws which secure the center panel to the dashboard.

Arrows show location of the four center panel securing screws used on RX-3 models

2. Remove the ashtray.

3. Remove the knobs from both the radio and the heater controls.

4. Tip the center panel forward.

5. Disconnect the power, speaker, and antenna leads from the radio.

6. Slip the radio out from behind the panel.

NOTE: *With the panel tipped forward, access to the gauges, their pilot lights, and the heater controls may also be obtained.*

Installation is performed in the reverse order of removal. Remember to adjust the trimmer screw (condenser) on the radio if a new antenna or a new antenna lead has been used. Select a weak station around 1,400 kHz on the AM band and turn the trimmer until the strongest signal is obtained.

RX-2 Models

1. Remove the knobs from the radio and heater controls.

2. Remove the knob from the hand throttle and its retaining collar.

3. Unfasten the two upper and the two lower screws which secure the center panel.

4. Working from underneath the panel, unfasten the rear brace from the radio.

5. Pivot the center panel sideways (to the left) and remove all the leads which are connected to the radio.

6. Withdraw the radio from the panel.

NOTE: *With the center panel turned sideways, access to the heater controls, clock, switches, and the pilot light may also be obtained.*

Installation is performed in the reverse

order of removal. If a new antenna or antenna lead is installed, remember to adjust the trimmer (condenser) on the radio. Select a weak station around 1,400 kHz on the AM band and turn the trimmer screw until the strongest signal is obtained.

RX-4

1. Remove mounting screws and remove right (passenger's) side console cover.
2. Disconnect power connector and unscrew aerial connector.
3. Remove rear mounting bolt.
4. Pull off radio knobs. Support radio assembly from the rear while removing mounting bezel nuts. Pull the unit back so shafts clear the front of the console, and slide the unit out the right side.
5. Installation is in reverse order.

Cosmo

1. Pull off radio knobs. Remove radio bezel nuts.
2. Disconnect radio power connector and unscrew aerial connector.
3. Support radio while removing rear mounting bolt.
4. If necessary disconnect additional connectors that may be in the way, and then tilt the rear of the radio upward, pull it backward (or toward the front of the car) until the knob shafts clear the console, and remove out one side.
5. Installation is in reverse order.

808

1. Pull off radio knobs. Remove radio bezel nuts.
2. Disconnect radio power connector and unscrew aerial connector.
3. Remove rear radio bracket mounting nut while supporting radio.
4. Pull the back end of the radio slightly downward and to the rear until knob shafts clear the dash panel, and then pull the unit down and out from behind the panel.
5. Install in reverse order.

GLC

1. See the procedure for instrument cluster removal below, and remove the crash pad, meter hood, and wood grain center panel.
2. Disconnect the (−) cable from the battery. Then, remove attaching screws from either side of the dash panel, and pull the radio out. Disconnect aerial wiring, power connec-

tor, and speaker connector, and pull the radio out of the dash.
3. Install in reverse order.

626

1. Disconnect the negative battery cable.
2. Remove the ashtray, Radio knobs, heater control lever knob, and the fan control switch knob.
3. Remove the center panel attaching screws and pull the center panel rearward.
4. Remove the radio attaching screws and disconnect the antenna.
5. Installation is the reverse of removal.

WINDSHIELD WIPERS

Wiper Arm
REMOVAL AND INSTALLATION

The wiper arm is held in place with a screw which runs directly into the wiper arm drive shaft. Note the angle of the wiper arm so that it may be replaced in the same position on the splines on the drive shaft, and then remove the screw and pull the arm off the drive shaft. To install, slide the arm into the splines in the same position, and install the screw.

Wiper Motor
REMOVAL AND INSTALLATION

1. Remove the attaching screws and remove the wiper arms.
2. Raise the hood, and remove the screws from the front of the cowl plate or from the service hole panel on the firewall. Raise the front of the plate and disconnect the windshield washer hose at the nozzle. Then, remove the plate.
3. Disconnect the motor wiring. Remove motor and transmission attaching bolts and remove the motor and transmission.
4. Install the wiper motor in reverse order.

INSTRUMENT CLUSTER

Instrument cluster removal and installation procedures included here are those which can reasonably be performed utilizing the tools and skills possessed by the average do-it-yourself mechanic. Directions for performing this procedure on RX-4, 808, and Cosmo models are not included because of extreme complexity and the required use of certain special tools.

Arrow indicates the screw which secures the instrument cluster to the side of the dashboard on RX-3 models

REMOVAL AND INSTALLATION

RX-3 Models

1. Disconnect the ground cable from the negative (−) battery terminal.

2. Pull the knob off the steering column-mounted headlight switch. Remove the screws which fasten the halves of the steering column shroud and separate the halves.

3. Open the left-hand (driver's side) door to gain access to the screw which is located on the side of the instrument cluster. Remove the screw.

4. Unfasten the three retaining screws which are located underneath the instrument cluster.

5. Tip the top of the cluster toward the steering wheel.

6. Disconnect the wiring and the speedometer cable from the back of the instrument cluster.

7. Remove the cluster assembly completely.

Installation is performed in the reverse order of removal.

RX-2 Models

1. Disconnect the ground cable from the negative terminal (−) of the battery.

2. Unfasten the screws which hold the halves of the steering column shroud together and pull off the headlight switch knob. Separate the halves of the shroud.

3. Working from underneath the instrument cluster, disconnect the speedometer cable.

4. Unfasten the two upper and the two lower screws which secure the instrument cluster.

5. Tip the top of the cluster toward the steering wheel.

6. Disconnect each component by unfastening its electrical connector.

7. Lift the cluster away from the dash panel.

Installation is performed in the reverse order of removal.

GLC—Standard Dash

1. Disconnect the (−) battery terminal. Place masking tape on the instrument panel pad directly below the instrument cluster to prevent damage to the pad during the procedure.

2. Remove the meter hood by removing the screw above either dial, and pulling the hood off the dash.

3. Remove the wood grain center panel cover by removing the screw from the left side and unclipping the panel on the right (see illustration).

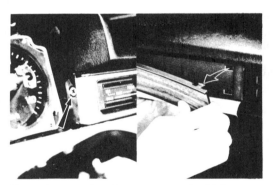

Removing wood grain center panel—GLC

4. Remove the three screws located under the front edge of the crash pad, and remove the pad.

5. Reach behind the speedometer and disconnect the cable by pressing on the flat surface of the connector.

6. Remove the three screws from the instrument cluster, and pull the cluster out of the dash.

7. Disconnect the multiple connectors.

8. Installation is the reverse of removal.

GLC—Sport Dash

1. Disconnect the (−) battery cable.

2. Put masking tape along the panel just below where the cluster will come out to protect it.

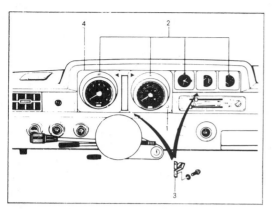

Removing instrument hood, GLC sport dash

3. Remove the meter hood by removing the tripmeter knob (1), screws (2), clips (3), and the hood (4) (see illustration).

4. Remove the wood grain center panel cover as described in Step 3 of the procedure above.

5. Remove the instrument panel pad by removing the three screws located under the front edge and removing the pad.

6. Remove the three screws from the top of the combination instrument cluster, and pull the cluster outward.

7. Disconnect the speedometer cable by pressing on the flat surface of the plastic connector. Disconnect the wiring connectors. Remove the cluster.

8. Installation is the reverse of the removal procedure.

626

1. Disconnect the negative battery cable.
2. Remove the steering wheel.
3. Remove the column cover.
4. Disconnect the speedometer cable.
5. Remove the meter hood.
6. Remove the combination meter attaching screws, disconnect the wire connections and remove the combination meter assembly.
7. Installation is the reverse of removal.

SPEEDOMETER CABLE REPLACEMENT

Reach back behind the dash and disconnect the speedometer cable behind the instrument by depressing the flat portion of the connector, and then pulling the connector off. Then pull the cable core out of the cable housing.

If the entire cable core does not come out due to breakage, it will be necessary to raise and securely support the car, unscrew the speedometer cable housing at the transmission, and pull the lower end of the cable out. Then, reconnect the lower end of the cable housing.

Lubricate the new core with speedometer cable lubricant, and insert it into the top of the cable housing. Work the cable in until it bottoms against the drive gear in the transmission. Then, simultaneously press the core inward while rotating until the square end of the core engages the gear and seats. Reconnect the cable housing to the back of the speedometer.

CIRCUIT PROTECTION

Fusible Links

On all rotary engine cars and the 808, these are located in either one or two boxes next to the battery in the engine compartment. If these links blow, they may be replaced with the specified parts by disconnecting the battery, disconnecting wiring to each link requiring replacement, removing the attaching screws and the link, and installing the new link or links in the reverse of the removal procedure.

On the GLC, there is a connector block located on the radiator panel on the right side of the radiator inside the engine compartment. Two links connected there are color coded red and green and may simply be unplugged to remove them, and replaced by plugging in replacement parts. Make sure to disconnect the battery before replacing them.

Fuse Box Location

The fuse boxes on both the RX-3 and the RX-2 models are located underneath the righthand (passenger's) side of the dash panel.

On the RX-3, RX-4, and Cosmo models, the box is located just above the lower parcel shelf and uses a back-hinged cover.

On RX-2 models, the box is located underneath the leading edge of the dash and is equipped with a sliding cover.

On the GLC and 626 the fuse box is located underneath the lefthand side of the dash panel. All covers have the location, amperage, and the circuit protected by each individual fuse, stamped on them.

Arrow shows location of RX-3 fusebox (RX-2 similar)

HEADLIGHTS

REMOVAL AND INSTALLATION

1. Remove the radiator grille and signal light lens if necessary. Unfasten the headlight bezel attaching screws and remove the bezel.

2. Loosen the screws which secure the headlight retainers, but do not remove the screws.

CAUTION: *Do not loosen the headlight aim adjusting screws.*

3. Turn the headlight retainer so that the large portion of the slots clears the heads of the screws.

4. Carefully withdraw the headlight and retainer. Take the retainer off the light.

5. Unplug the connector from the rear of the light.

Installation is performed in the reverse order of removal. Be sure that the headlights are aimed in accordance with your state laws.

NOTE: *Be careful not to mix up the inner and outer lights if both must be replaced at the same time. The inner lights have only one filament, while the outer lights have two.*

WIRING DIAGRAMS

Wiring diagrams have been left out of this book. As cars have become more complex, and available with longer and longer option lists, wiring diagrams have grown in size and complexity also. It has become virtually impossible to provide a readable reproduction in a reasonable number of pages.

Clutch and Transmission

MANUAL TRANSMISSION/ TRANSAXLE

REMOVAL AND INSTALLATION

All Models Except GLC and 626

1. Remove the knob from the gearshift lever.
2. Unfasten the screws which secure the center console to the floor and remove the console over the shift lever.
3. Remove the floor mat.
4. Unfasten the screws which attach the shift lever boot and withdraw the boot over the shift lever.
5. Unbolt the cover and remove it from the gearshift lever retainer.
6. Pull the gearshift lever, complete with shims and bushings, straight up and out of its retainer.
7. Detach the ground lead from the negative (−) battery terminal.
8. Fasten the nuts which secure the clutch release cylinder and tie the cylinder up and out of the way. Do not disconnect the hydraulic line from the clutch release cylinder. On RX-4 and Cosmo, remove the upper starter bolt and loosen the three upper engine-to-transmission bolts.
9. Detach the back-up switch multiconnector which is located near the clutch re-

lease cylinder. On RX-4 and Cosmo, remove the brake booster line bracket from the clutch housing.
10. Raise the car and support it on jackstands.

CAUTION: *Be sure that the car is securely supported. Remember, you will be working underneath it.*

11. Unfasten the transmission drain plug and drain the oil. Wipe the drain plug clean and install it again.
12. Remove the driveshaft, as described below, and plug up the transmission extension housing.

NOTE: *An old U-joint yoke makes an excellent plug. Or, lacking this, secure a plastic bag over the opening with rubber bands.*

13. Detach the exhaust pipe from the thermal reactor flange. On RX-4 and Cosmo, remove the heat insulators first.

CAUTION: *Be sure that the reactor and exhaust pipe have cooled sufficiently to prevent severe burns.*

14. Unfasten the speedometer cable from the extension housing.
15. Detach the starter motor wiring. Remove its securing nuts and bolts and withdraw the starter motor.
16. Support the transmission with a block of wood mounted on a jack.

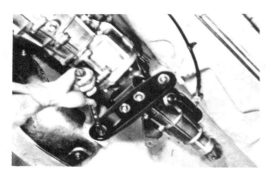

Unfasten the bolts which secure the transmission support to the frame

17. Remove the nuts which attach the transmission support to the frame members.

18. Evenly, and in several stages, remove the bolts which retain the bell housing to the engine.

19. Carefully slide the transmission assembly rearward until the input shaft has cleared the clutch disc.

20. Gently lower the transmission from the car.

Transmission installation is performed in the reverse order of removal. Align the clutch plate with an arbor or an old input shaft. Adjust the clutch and shift linkage as detailed elsewhere. Refill the transmission with gear oil:

- Below 0°F—SAE EP80
- Above 0°F—SAE EP90

GLC—Rear Wheel Drive

1. Disconnect the (−) battery cable.

2. Put the transmission in neutral and remove the console and shift lever.

3. Remove the two upper bolts from the clutch housing.

4. Raise the vehicle and support it securely on axle stands or a lift.

5. Drain the transmission oil and replace the plug.

6. Remove the driveshaft, and plug or cover the hole in the extension housing.

7. Disconnect the speedometer cable and back-up light switch wires.

8. Disconnect the exhaust pipe hanger from the bracket on the clutch housing.

9. Remove the exhaust pipe support bracket from the clutch housing. Disconnect the clutch cable at the release lever.

10. Remove the lower clutch housing cover.

11. Remove the starter electrical connections, remove the bolts, and remove the starter.

12. Disconnect the exhaust pipe hanger at the extension housing.

13. Place a jack under the engine, using a block of wood to protect the oil pan. Make sure the jack can securely support the weight of the engine.

14. Disconnect the transmission support member at the transmission.

15. Remove transmission-to-engine attaching bolts.

16. Carefully slide the transmission rearward until the input shaft has cleared the clutch disc, and lower it out of the car.

17. In installation, reverse above procedures, aligning the clutch plate with an arbor or old input shaft. Adjust clutch and shift linkage. Refill the transmission with the proper grade of gear oil.

GLC—Front Wheel Drive

1. Raise the vehicle and support it safely. Disconnect the negative battery cable.

2. Disconnect all electrical wiring and connections, control linkages from the transaxle. Mark these units to aid in reassembling.

3. Remove the front wheels. Disconnect the lower ball joints from the steering knuckles. Pull the driveshafts from the differential gears.

NOTE: *A circlip is positioned on the driveshaft ends and engages in a groove, machined in the differential side gears. The driveshafts may have to be forced from the differential housing to release the clip from the groove.*

CAUTION: *Do not allow the driveshafts to drop. Damage may occur to the ball and socket joints and to the rubber boots. Wire the shafts to the vehicle body when released from the differential.*

4. Support the engine with a jack. Remove the crossmember and the mounting bolts retaining the transaxle in place. Remove the unit from the vehicle.

5. Installation is the reverse of removal.

CAUTION: *Be sure the rubber mounts are not twisted or distorted and not in contact with the body.*

626

1. Remove the gearshift lever knob.

2. Remove the console box.

3. Remove the gearshift lever boot and the gearshift lever.

4. Disconnect the negative battery cable.

5. Raise the vehicle and support with jack stands.

6. Drain the transmission lubricant.

7. Disconnect the propeller shaft as described in Chapter 7.

8. Disconnect the exhaust pipe hanger.

9. Remove the starter motor.

10. Disconnect the back-up switch wire.

11. Disconnect the speedometer cable.

12. Place a jack under the engine, protecting the oil pan with a block of wood.

13. Remove the transmission attaching bolts and remove the transmission.

14. Transmission installation is performed in the reverse order of removal. Align the clutch plate with an old arbor or an old input shaft. Add lubricant until the level reaches the bottom of the filler plug hole.

SHIFT LEVER ADJUSTMENT

The shift lever on most models, may be adjusted during transmission installation by means of the adjusting shims on the three bolts between the cover plate and the packing. The force required to move the shift knob should be 4.4–8.8 lbs.

CLUTCH

REMOVAL AND INSTALLATION

1. Remove the transmission, as detailed above.

2. Attach a brake to the flywheel.

3. Install a clutch arbor to hold the clutch in place.

NOTE: *An old input shaft makes an excellent arbor.*

4. Unfasten the bolts which secure the clutch cover, one turn at a time in sequence, until the clutch spring tension is released. Do not remove the bolts singly.

5. Remove the clutch disc.

CAUTION: *Be careful not to get grease or oil on the surface of the clutch disc.*

6. Unhook the return spring from the throwout bearing and remove the bearing.

7. Pull out the release fork until its retaining spring frees itself from the ball stud. Withdraw the fork from the housing.

Clutch installation is performed in the following order:

1. Clean the flywheel and pressure plate surfaces with fine emery paper. Be sure that

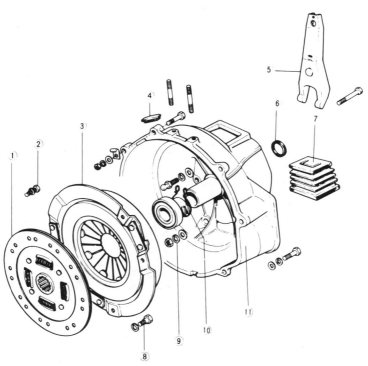

1. Clutch disc	4. Service hole cover 8. Reamer bolt
2. Bolt	5. Release fork 9. Release bearing
3. Clutch cover and pressure plate	6. Oil seal 10. Spring
assembly	7. Dust boot 11. Clutch housing

Clutch components

there is no oil or grease on them. Grease the eccentric shaft needle bearing.

2. Apply Loctite® on the eccentric shaft threads (RX-2 and RX-3 only). Install the flywheel with its keyway over the key on the eccentric shaft.

3. Apply sealer to both sides of the flywheel lockwasher and position the lockwasher on the eccentric shaft.

4. Install the flywheel locknut and on rotary engine cars, tighten it to 350 ft. lbs. or as tight as possible with an extension no longer than three feet long on the wrench, then bend the tabs of the lockwasher up around it.

5. Use an arbor to center the clutch disc during installation. Install the clutch disc with the long end of its hub facing the transmission.

NOTE: *Use an old input shaft to center the clutch disc, if an arbor is not available.*

6. Align the O-mark on the clutch cover with the reamed hole of the O-mark on the flywheel.

7. Tighten the clutch cover bolts evenly, and in two or three stages, to 13–20 ft. lbs.

CAUTION: *Do not tighten the bolts one at a time.*

8. Grease the pivot pin. Insert the release fork through its boot so that its retaining spring contacts the pivot pin.

9. Lightly grease the face of the throwout bearing and its clutch housing retainer.

10. Install the throwout bearing and return spring. Check the operation of the release fork and throwout bearing for smoothness.

11. Install the transmission.

PEDAL HEIGHT ADJUSTMENT

1. Loosen the locknut on the adjusting bolt.

2. Turn the adjusting bolt until the clearance between the pedal pad and the floor mat is 7.28 in. (7.48—GLC rear wheel drive, 9.05 GLC—front wheel drive 7.60–626).

3. Carefully tighten the locknut.

PEDAL FREE-PLAY ADJUSTMENT

RX-2, RX-3

1. Loosen the locknut on the master cylinder pushrod.

2. Rotate the pushrod until the clutch pedal has a travel of 0.8–1.2 in. before clutch disengagement.

3. Carefully tighten the locknut.

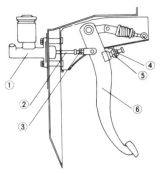

1. Master cylinder
2. Rod
3. Locknut
4. Adjusting bolt
5. Locknut
6. Clutch pedal

Clutch pedal height adjustment

RX-4, Cosmo, 808, 626

The free-play of the clutch pedal before the pushrod contacts the piston in the master cylinder should be 0.02–0.12 in.

To adjust the free-play, loosen the locknut and turn the pushrod until the proper adjustment is obtained. Tighten the locknut after the adjustment is complete.

CLUTCH RELEASE CABLE ADJUSTMENT

GLC—Rear Wheel Drive

Loosen the locknut and put tension on outer cable (pull—do not push) while turning the adjusting nut until the clearance shown in the illustration is .06–.09 in. Then, tighten the locknut.

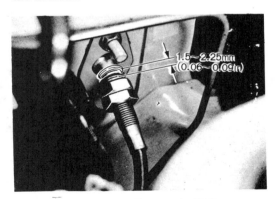

Clutch release cable adjustment—GLC

GLC—Front Wheel Drive

The cable adjustment on the front wheel drive models is accomplished by turning an adjustment nut located on the end of the clutch cable at the release bracket mounted on the top of the transaxle case.

Loosen the locknut and turn the adjusting nut until the gap (clearance) between the roller on the cable and the release bracket is between .08 and .12 in., tighten the locknut.

RELEASE FORK FREE-PLAY ADJUSTMENT

1. Unfasten the return spring from the release fork.
2. Loosen the locknut on the release rod.
3. Turn the adjusting nut on the release rod until the proper release fork free-play obtained:
   - RX-3—0.12–0.16 in.
   - RX-4 and Cosmo
   - RX-2—0.16–0.20 in.
4. Carefully tighten the locknut and hook the return spring back on the release fork.

Clutch Master Cylinder

REMOVAL AND INSTALLATION

1. Unfasten the hydraulic line from the master cylinder outlet.
   CAUTION: *Use care not to drip any hydraulic fluid on the car's painted surfaces, as it is an excellent paint remover.*
2. Remove the nuts which secure the master cylinder assembly to the firewall.
3. Withdraw the master cylinder straight out and away from the firewall.

Installation is performed in the reverse order of removal. Bleed the hydraulic system as detailed below.

OVERHAUL

1. Thoroughly clean the outside of the master cylinder.
2. Drain the hydraulic fluid from the cylinder. Unbolt the reservoir from the cylinder body.

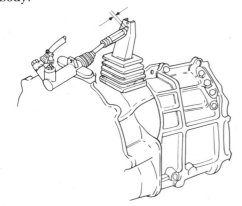

Clutch fork free-play is measured between arrows

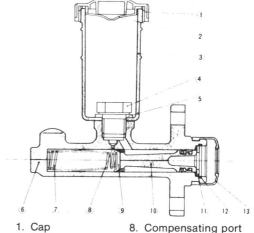

1. Cap	8. Compensating port
2. Baffle	9. Primary cup
3. Reservoir	10. Piston
4. Bolt	11. Stop
5. Washer	12. Stop wire
6. Cylinder	13. Boot
7. Return spring	

Cutaway view of the clutch master cylinder

3. Remove the boot from the cylinder.
4. Release the wire piston stop with a screwdriver and withdraw the stop washer.
5. Withdraw the piston, piston cups, and return spring from the cylinder bore.
6. Wash all the parts in clean hydraulic (brake) fluid.
7. Examine the piston cups. If they are damaged, softened, or swollen, replace them with new ones.
8. Check the piston and bore for scoring or roughness.
9. Use a wire gauge to check the clearance between the piston and its bore. Replace either the piston or the cylinder if the clearance is greater than 0.006 in.
10. Be sure that the compensating port in the cylinder is not clogged.

Assembly of the master cylinder is performed in the following order:

1. Dip the piston and cups in clean hydraulic (brake) fluid.
2. Bolt the reservoir up to the cylinder body.
3. Fit the return spring into the cylinder.
4. Insert the primary cup into the bore so that its flat side is facing the piston.
5. Place the secondary cup on the piston and insert them in the cylinder bore.
6. Install the stop washer and the wire piston stop.
7. Fill the reservoir half-full of hydraulic fluid. Operate the piston with a screwdriver

until fluid spurts out of the cylinder outlet.

8. Fit the boot on the cylinder.

Clutch Release Cylinder
REMOVAL AND INSTALLATION

1. Raise the vehicle and support with jack stands.

2. Unscrew the hydraulic line from the release cylinder.

3. Unhook the release fork return spring from the cylinder.

4. Unfasten the nuts which secure the release cylinder to the transmission.

Installation is performed in the reverse order of removal. Bleed the hydraulic system as detailed below and adjust the release fork free-play as detailed above.

Removing the clutch release cylinder

OVERHAUL

Consult the "Master Cylinder Overhaul" section above for release cylinder overhaul procedures.

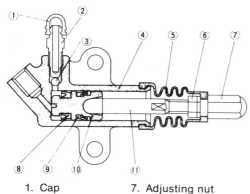

1. Cap	7. Adjusting nut
2. Bleed screw	8. Primary cup
3. Valve	9. Secondary cup
4. Cylinder	10. Piston
5. Boat	11. Pushrod
6. Locknut	

Cutaway view of the clutch release cylinder

SYSTEM BLEEDING

1. Remove the rubber cap from the bleeder screw on the release cylinder.

2. Place a bleeder tube over the end of the bleeder screw.

3. Submerge the other end of the tube in a jar half-filled with hydraulic (brake) fluid.

4. Depress the clutch pedal fully and allow it to return slowly.

5. Keep repeating Step 4 while watching the hydraulic fluid in the jar. As soon as the air bubbles disappear, close the bleeder screw.

NOTE: *During the bleeding procedure, the reservoir must be kept at least ¾ full.*

6. Remove the tube and refit the rubber cap. Fill the reservoir with hydraulic fluid.

AUTOMATIC TRANSMISSION

REMOVAL AND INSTALLATION
RX-3 and RX3-SP

The automatic transmission is filled with Type F fluid.

1. Remove the heat shroud. Remove the exhaust pipe bracket from the torque converter housing.

2. Detach the exhaust pipe.

CAUTION: *The exhaust system on rotary engine-equipped Mazda's gets considerably hotter than a conventional system; be sure to allow enough time for it to cool.*

3. Remove the driveshaft.

4. Detach the speedometer cable.

5. Remove the control rod.

6. Unfasten the vacuum lines from the vacuum modulator.

7. Unfasten the multiconnector from the downshift solenoid and the neutral safety switch.

8. Disconnect the oil cooler lines.

9. Remove the starter.

10. Matchmark the torque converter and the flex-plate.

11. Working through the starter motor mounting hole, remove the four bolts which secure the torque converter to the flex-plate.

12. Support the transmission.

13. Remove the crossmember.

14. Remove the bolts which secure the torque converter housing to the top of the engine.

15. Raise the transmission so that it is level.

16. Use a screwdriver to carefully apply

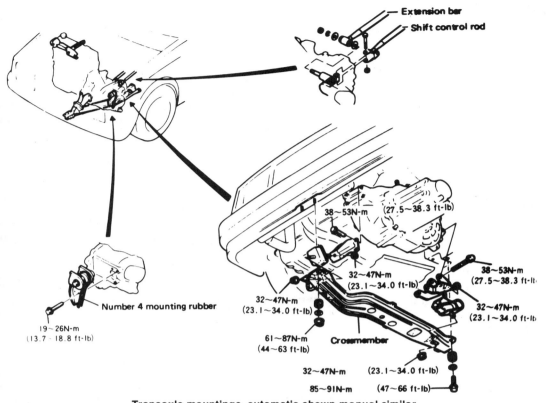

Transaxle mountings, automatic shown-manual similar

pressure between the torque converter and the flex-plate.

17. Slide the transmission rearward and lower it from the car.

CAUTION: *Do not rest the weight of the transmission on the torque converter splines.*

Automatic transmission installation is the reverse of removal. There are several points which should be noted, however:

Before installing the transmission, use a dial indicator to measure flex-plate runout. If runout exceeds 0.020 in., the flex-plate must be replaced.

Hand-tighten the four torque converter installation bolts and then lock the flex-plate with a brake. Next, tighten the four bolts evenly, and in several stages, to 29–36 ft. lbs.

Check the fluid level again and road test the car.

RX-4, RX-7 and Cosmo

The transmission is filled with Type F fluid.

1. Remove the converter access hole cover. Lock the flex-plate by holding the drive pulley lockbolt with a wrench.

2. Matchmark the converter and flex-

plate. Unfasten the four converter-to-flex-plate securing bolts.

3. Remove the exhaust pipe.

4. Remove the driveshaft.

5. Remove speedometer cable.

6. Remove all vacuum lines and electrical leads from the transmission.

7. Remove the starter.

8. Remove the bottom cover from the converter housing.

9. Support the transmission and remove the crossmember.

10. Disconnect the oil cooler.

11. Unbolt the converter housing, raise the transmission to a level place and separate it from the flex-plate.

12. Automatic transmission installation is the reverse of removal. There are several points which should be noted, however.

Before installing the transmission, use a dial indicator to measure flex-plate runout. Runout should be around 0.012 in. If runout exceeds 0.020 in., the flex-plate must be replaced.

After completing transmission installation, rotate the eccentric shaft to be sure that there is no interference in the transmission.

808, 626 and GLC—Rear Wheel Drive

Use only Type F transmission fluid.

1. Drain the transmission.
2. Remove the heat insulator.
3. Disconnect the exhaust pipe.
4. Disconnect the driveshaft at the rear axle flange.
5. Remove the driveshaft.
6. Disconnect the speedometer cable.
7. Disconnect the shift rod.
8. Remove all vacuum hoses.
9. Disconnect all wiring.
10. Disconnect the oil cooler lines.
11. Remove the access cover from the lower end of the converter housing.
12. Matchmark the drive plate and torque converter for realignment and remove the converter bolts.
13. Support the transmission with a jack and remove the crossmember.
14. Remove the converter housing-to-engine bolts.
15. Remove the filler tube.
16. Separate the flex-plate and the converter.
17. Remove the transmission and converter as an assembly.
18. To install the transmission, reverse the removal procedure.

GLC—Front Wheel Drive

1. Raise the vehicle and support it safely. Disconnect the negative battery cable.

NOTE: *When removing or installing the transaxle assembly the rear end of the power plant (engine) must be lifted with the aid of a chain.*

2. Disconnect all electrical wiring and connections, control linkages from the transaxle. Mark these units to aid in reassembling.
3. Remove the front wheels. Disconnect the lower ball joints from the steering knuckles. Pull the driveshafts from the differential gears.

NOTE: *A circlip is positioned on the driveshaft ends and engages in a groove, machined in the differential side gears. The driveshafts may have to be forced from the differential housing to release the clip from the groove.*

CAUTION: *Do not allow the driveshafts to drop. Damage may occur to the ball and socket joints and to the rubber boots. Wire the shafts to the vehicle body when released from the differential.*

4. Support the engine with a jack. Remove the crossmember and the mounting bolts retaining the transaxle in place. Remove the unit from the vehicle.

5. Installation is the reverse of removal.

CAUTION: *Be sure the rubber mounts are not twisted or distorted and not in contact with the body.*

6. To properly install the driveshafts in the differential side gears, position the open end of the circlip in the up position, and with the driveshaft in a horizontal position, push the driveshafts into the side gears. To be sure the circlip engages the groove, a sound may be heard or attempt to pull the driveshaft from the differential. Reconnect the ball joints at the lower arms.

PAN REMOVAL AND INSTALLATION

1. Raise and support the vehicle.
2. Place a drain pan under the transmission pan.
3. Remove the pan attaching bolts (except the two at the front). Loosen the two at the front slightly. Allow the fluid to drain.
4. Remove the pan.
5. Remove and discard the gasket.
6. Install a new pan gasket and install the pan on the transmission.
7. Lower the vehicle and fill the transmission with fluid. Check the transmission operation.

SHIFT LINKAGE ADJUSTMENT

1972–75

1. Unfasten the T-joint on the intermediate lever.
2. Place the range selector lever, which is mounted on the side of the transmission case, in Neutral; i.e., so that the slot in the selector shaft is pointing straight up and down.
3. Adjust the console-mounted gear selector lever by turning the T-joint until it indicates Neutral.
4. Reconnect the T-joint. Check the gear selector operation in all other ranges to see that the linkage has no slack.

1976–82

1. Place the transmission selector lever in Neutral.
2. Disconnect the clevis from the lower end of the selector arm.
3. Move the manual lever to the N position.

NOTE: *The N position is the third detent from the back.*

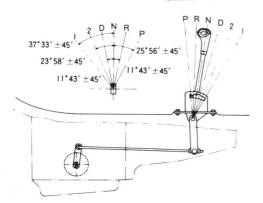

Transmission linkage adjustment

4. Loosen the two clevis retaining nuts and adjust the clevis so that it freely enters the lever hole.

5. Tighten the retaining nuts.

6. Connect the clevis to the lever and secure with the spring washer, flat washer and retaining clip.

NEUTRAL SAFETY SWITCH ADJUSTMENT

RX-2, RX-3

1. Check the shift linkage, as detailed above, before adjusting the neutral safety switch.

2. Remove the nut which secures the gear selector lever and the neutral safety switch attaching bolts.

3. Unfasten the screw which is located underneath the switch body.

4. Place the selector shaft in Neutral by using the gear selector lever.

NOTE: *If the linkage is adjusted properly, the slot in the selector shaft should be vertical.*

5. Move the switch body so that the screw hole in the case aligns with the hole in the internal rotor.

6. Check their alignment by inserting an 0.009 in. diameter pin or a No. 53 drill through the holes.

7. Once the proper alignment is obtained, tighten the switch mounting bolts. Remove the pin or drill and insert the screw back into the hole.

8. Tighten the nut which secures the gearshift selector lever.

9. Check the operation of the neutral safety switch again. If it still is not operating properly, i.e., the car starts in positions other than Park or Neutral or the back-up lights

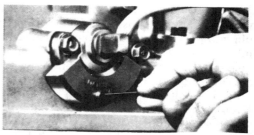

Align the neutral safety switch by inserting a drill through the holes in it

come on in gears other than Reverse, replace the switch.

RX-4, Cosmo and 808

1. Remove the housing from the shift lever.

2. Adjust the shift lever so that there is 0–0.012 in. clearance between the pin and the guide plate, when the lever is in Neutral.

3. Adjust the neutral safety switch so that the pin hole in the switch body is aligned with the pin hole of the sliding plate when the shift lever is in Neutral.

4. Check the adjustment by trying to start the engine in all gears. It should only start in Park or Neutral.

5. Reinstall the housing on the shift lever.

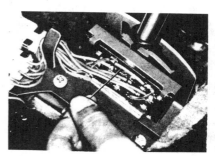

Adjusting RX-4 and Cosmo neutral safety switch

GLC

NOTE: *Front wheel drive models use a hydraulic switch that must be replaced if faulty, it is non-adjustable.*

1. Adjust shift linkage as described above. Put the selector lever in neutral position (3rd detent from the rear).

2. Remove the transmission manual lever retaining nut and pull the lever off the switch.

3. Loosen (do not remove) the two switch retaining bolts and remove the alignment pin hole screw at the bottom of the switch.

4. Gently rotate the switch back and forth while attempting to insert a .078 in. diameter pin into the alignment pin hole. When alignment is correct, the pin will slide through the hole in the internal rotor. Tighten the switch attaching bolts and remove the pin.

5. Reinstall the alignment pin hole screw. Position the manual lever back onto the switch shaft and install the washer and nut.

6. Check the operation of the switch.

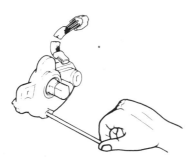

Adjusting GLC neutral safety switch

626

1. Place the transmission selector lever in the neutral position.

2. Loosen the neutral switch attaching screws.

3. Position the manual shift lever shaft in the neutral position by adjusting the range select lever. The proper neutral position is where the slot of the manual shaft is positioned vertically and the detent positions in the shaft correctly with a click sound.

4. Move the neutral switch so that the identification marks on the switch body and the sliding plate are aligned.

5. Tighten the neutral switch adjusting screws.

6. Check the adjustment by trying to start the engine in all gears. It should only start in Park and Neutral.

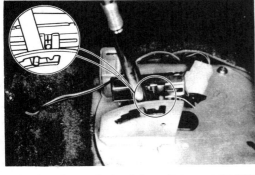

Adjusting the neutral safety switch—model 626

KICKDOWN SWITCH AND DOWNSHIFT SOLENOID ADJUSTMENT

All Except 626

1. Check the accelerator linkage for smooth operation.

2. Turn the ignition on, but do not start the engine.

3. Depress the accelerator pedal fully to the floor. As the pedal nears the end of its travel, a light click should be heard from the downshift solenoid.

4. If the kickdown switch operates too soon, loosen the locknut on the switch shaft. Adjust the shaft so that the acclerator linkage makes contact with it when the pedal is depressed approximately ⅞ of the way to the floor. Tighten the locknut.

5. If no noise comes from the solenoid at all, check the wiring for the solenoid and the switch.

6. If the wiring is in good condition, remove the wire from the solenoid and connect it to a 12V power source. If the solenoid does not click when connected, it is defective and should be replaced.

NOTE: *When the solenoid is removed, about two pints of transmission fluid will leak out; have a container ready to catch it. Remember to add more fluid to the transmission after installing the new solenoid.*

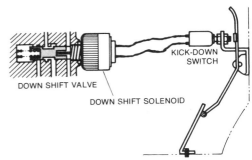

Kickdown switch and downshift solenoid adjustment

626

1. Disconnect the wiring connectors from the kickdown switch.

2. Screw out the kick-down switch a few turns.

3. Fully depress the accelerator pedal.

4. Gradually screw in the kick-down switch until you hear a clicking sound then screw it in ½ turn more.

5. Tighten the locknut and connect the wiring connectors.

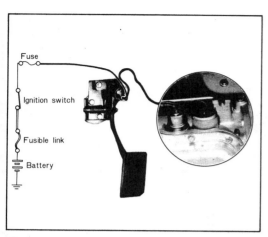

Kickdown switch adjustment—model 626

ADJUSTING BRAKE BAND

Rear Wheel Drive Models

NOTE: *On all cars but the GLC and 626, this adjustment can be made by removing* the cover located on the lower right front of the transmission (three bolts). On the GLC and 626, the transmission pan must be removed—the servo piston stem and locknut are visible at the left front.

Loosen the locknut and then torque the servo piston stem to 9–11 ft. lb. Then, back off exactly two turns. Hold the stem stationary and tighten the locknut to 11–29 ft. lb.

Front Wheel Drive Models

1. Raise the vehicle and support safely.
2. Locate the servo cover and remove from the right side of the transmission case.
3. Loosen locknut and tighten the servo adjusting bolt to 9–11 ft. lbs. torque.
4. Loosen the servo bolt two full turns and tighten the locknut.
5. Install the servo cover and lower vehicle.

Drive Train

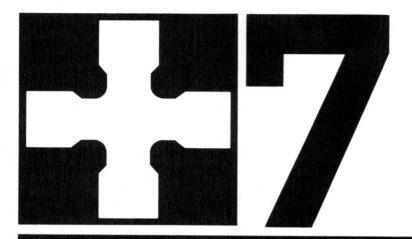

DRIVELINE

Driveshaft and U-Joints
REMOVAL AND INSTALLATION
RX-3 and GLC—Rear Wheel Drive

1. Raise the rear end of the car and support it using jackstands.

CAUTION: *Be sure that the car is securely supported. Remember, you will be working underneath it.*

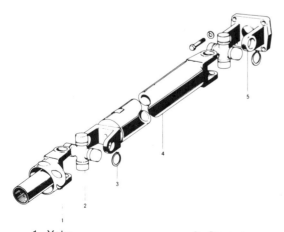

1. Yoke
2. Spider and bearing cup assembly
3. Snap-ring
4. Shaft
5. Yoke

Components of the RX-3 driveshaft

2. Matchmark the flanges on the driveshaft and pinion so that they may be installed in their original position.

3. Remove the four bolts which secure the driveshaft to the pinion flange.

4. Lower the back end of the driveshaft and slide the front end out of the transmission.

5. Plug up the hole in the transmission to prevent it from leaking.

NOTE: *Use an old U-joint yoke or, if none is available, place a plastic bag, secured with rubber bands, over the hole.*

Driveshaft installation is performed in the reverse order of removal. Tighten the driveshaft-to-pinion flange bolts to 22 ft. lbs. on RX-3, and 25–27 ft. lbs. on GLC.

RX-2 and 626 Models

The driveshaft used on RX-2 and 626 models is removed in a manner similar to that outlined for RX-3 and GLC models above. The only difference in the removal procedure is that the center bearing must be unbolted prior to driveshaft removal. Remove the driveshaft and the center bearing as a single unit.

NOTE: *Do not remove the oil seals and the center bearing from the support unless they are defective.*

Installation is performed in the reverse

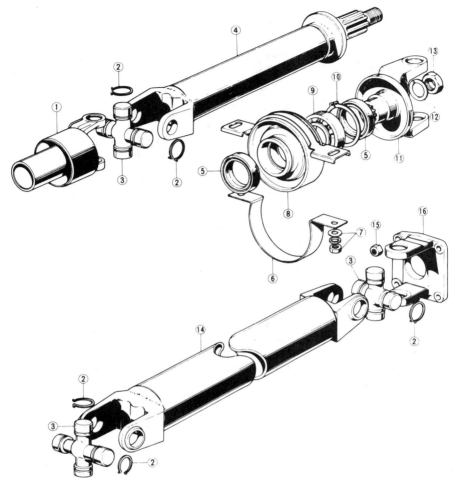

1. Sliding yoke
2. Snap-ring
3. Universal joint
4. Driveshaft
5. Oil seal
6. Protector
7. Nut & washer
8. Center bearing support
9. Ball bearing
10. Snap-ring
11. Yoke
12. Washer
13. Nut
14. Driveshaft
15. Nut
16. Universal joint yoke

Components of the RX-2 driveshaft

order of removal. Tighten the center bearing support bolts to 14–21 ft. lbs.-RX2, 27–38 ft. lbs.-626 and the drive-shaft-to-pinion flange bolts to 25–27 ft. lbs.

RX-4, 808, and Cosmo

Perform this operation only when the exhaust system is *cold*.

1. Remove the front heat insulator.
2. Remove the nuts which secure the downpipe to the thermal reactor flange.
3. Remove the downpipe from the main muffler flange.
4. Matchmark the pinion and driveshaft flanges.
5. Unfasten the center bearing.
6. Remove the driveshaft.
7. Driveshaft installation is the reverse of

removal. Tighten the yoke-to-front driveshaft locknut to 116–130 ft. lbs.

U-JOINT OVERHAUL

Perform this procedure with the driveshaft removed from the car.

1. Matchmark both the yoke and the driveshaft so that they can be returned to their original balancing position during assembly.
2. Remove the bearing snap-rings from the yoke.
3. Use a hammer and a brass drift to drive *in* one of the bearing cups. Remove the cup which is protruding from the other side of the yoke.
4. Remove the other bearing cups by pressing them from the spider. On the GLC

1. Roller bearing (cup)   4. Yoke
2. Spider   5. Driveshaft
3. Oil seal   6. Snap-ring
Components of the U-joint

and 626, bearings may be removed by tapping on the base of the yoke with a hammer.

5. Withdraw the spider from the yoke.

Examine the spider journals for rusting or wear. Check the bearings for smoothness or pitting.

Measure the spider diameter. The standard diameter on RX-2 and RX-3 is 0.5795 in. If the spider wear exceeds 0.0040 in. on RX-2 models or 0.0079 in. on RX-3 models, replace the spider. On RX-4 the minimum diameter is .6472 in., on 808 and 626 it is .5746 in., and on GLC it is .4996 in. If diameter is too small, replace the spider.

NOTE: *The spider and bearing are replaced as a complete assembly only.*

Check the seals and rollers for wear or damage.

Assembly of the U-joint is performed in the following order:

1. Pack the bearing cups with grease.

2. Fit the rollers into the cups and install the dust seals.

3. Place the spider in the yoke and then fit one of the bearing cups into its bore in the yoke.

4. Press the bearing cup home, while guiding the spider into it, so that a snap-ring can be installed.

5. Press-fit the other bearings into the yoke.

6. Select a snap-ring to obtain minimum end-play of the spider. Use snap-rings of the same thickness on both sides to center the spider.

NOTE: *Selective fit snap-rings are available in sizes ranging from 0.048 to 0.054 in.*

7. Install the spider/yoke assembly and bearings into the driveshaft in the same manner as the spider was assembled to the yoke.

8. Test the operation of the U-joint assembly. The spider should move freely with no binding.

DRIVEAXLES

Front Wheel Drive

INSPECTION

1. Loosen the front wheel lugs, raise the car and safely support it on jackstands. Remove the wheels and tires.

2. Check the driveaxle inner and outer boots for cracks or damage, for leaking grease or loose bands. Replace or repair if necessary.

3. Turn the driveaxle by hand, if the splines or joints are excessively loose, replace or repair as necessary.

4. Examine the driveaxle for cracks or twist. Replace if necessary.

REMOVAL AND INSTALLATION

1. See Step 1 of Inspection. Drain the transaxle fluid after removing the splash shields.

2. Loosen the driveaxle locknut at the center of the disc brake hub after raising the lock tab. Apply brake pressure while loosening.

3. Remove the lower ball joint from the steering knuckle (see Chapter 8).

4. Remove the driveaxle from the transaxle case by pulling the brake caliper outward with increasing force. While applying outward force, hit the driveaxle shaft with a brass hammer, if necessary, to help in removal.

5. Remove the locknut and pull the driveaxle from the steering knuckle. Remove the driveaxle and plug the transaxle case with a clean rag to prevent dirt from entering.

6. Installation is in the reverse order of removal. Before installing the driveaxle into the transaxle case, check the oil seals for cuts or damage. Replace the oil seals if necessary. Insert the axle into the transaxle case by pushing on the wheel hub assembly. Always install a new slip on the driveaxle.

JOINT OVERHAUL

NOTE: *The joint on the wheel side of the driveaxle is non-rebuildable. If worn, the joint and axle must be replaced. The boot may be changed if necessary. Do not interfere with the balancer found on the right axle unless necessary for wheel joint boot replacement. If balancer is removed it must be reinstalled in the same position 14.45 ins. from the front of the wheel joint.*

1. Remove the boot band by raising the locking clip and band with a pair of pliers.

2. Remove the lock clip from the inner

edge of the ball joint casting. Remove the casting.

3. Remove the snap-ring from the end of the splines and remove the cage and bearings.

4. Carefully pry the balls from the bearing cage. After the balls are removed turn the cage slightly and remove it from the inner ring.

5. Wash all of the parts in a safe solvent and inspect for wear.

6. A joint kit for the transaxle end and boot kits for both ends are available. The kits are installed in the reverse order of disassembly. Always use the grease supplied with the kits. Tape the spline ends of the shaft when installing the rubber boots.

REAR AXLE

Axle Shafts

REMOVAL AND INSTALLATION

NOTE: *The left and the right rear axle shafts are not interchangeable as the left shaft is shorter than the right. It is, therefore, not a good idea to remove them both at once.*

1. Remove the wheel cover and loosen the lug nuts.

2. Raise the rear of the car and support the axle housing on jackstands.

3. Unfasten the lug nuts and remove the wheel.

4. Remove the brake assembly. (See Chapter 9). On Cosmo, remove the brake disc. Disconnect parking brake cable, if necessary.

5. Unfasten the nuts which secure the brake backing plate and the bearing retainer to the axle housing.

6. Withdraw the axle shaft with a puller.

Axle shaft installation is performed in the following order:

Measure the depth of the bearing seal

1. Apply grease to the oil seal lips and then insert the oil seal into the axle housing.

2. On all models but GLC check the axle shaft end-play in the following manner:

   a. Temporarily install the brake backing plate on the axle shaft.

   b. Measure the depth of the bearing seal and then measure the width of the bearing outer race.

   c. The difference between the two measurements is equal to the overall thickness of the adjusting shims required. Shims are available in thicknesses of 0.004 and 0.016 in.

NOTE: *The maximum permissible endplay is 0.004 in.*

3. Remove the backing plate and apply sealer to the rear axle surfaces which contact it. Install the backing plate again.

4. Install the rear axle shaft, bearing retainer, gasket, and shims through the backing plate and into the axle housing. Coat the shims with a small amount of sealer first.

5. Engage the splines on the differential side gear with those on the end of the axle shaft.

6. On Cosmo, install the brake disc. Install the brake assembly and adjust it. Connect parking brake cable and adjust it if necessary. See Chapter Nine.

7. Install the wheel and lower the car.

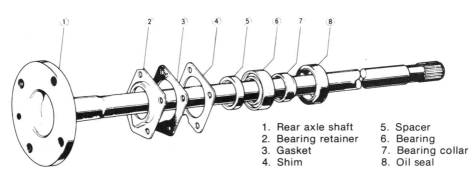

1. Rear axle shaft
2. Bearing retainer
3. Gasket
4. Shim
5. Spacer
6. Bearing
7. Bearing collar
8. Oil seal

Components of the rear axle shaft assembly

Suspension and Steering

REAR SUSPENSION

Springs

REMOVAL AND INSTALLATION

RX-3, RX-4, and GLC Wagon

1. Remove the wheel cover and loosen the lug nuts.

2. Raise the back end of the car and support it with jackstands.

CAUTION: *Be sure that the car is securely supported. Remember, you will be working underneath it.*

3. Remove the lug nuts and the wheel.

4. Support the rear axle housing with jackstands.

5. Disconnect the lower part of the shock from the spring clamp. Unfasten the nuts which secure the U-bolt. Withdraw the U-bolt seat, rubber pad, plate, and the U-bolt itself.

6. Unfasten the two bolts and the nut that secure the spring pin to the front end of the rear spring.

7. Pry the spring pin out with a large, flat pry bar inserted between the spring pin and its body bracket.

8. Unfasten the nuts and the bolts which attach the rear shackle to the car's body.

9. Withdraw the rear spring assembly, complete with its shackle.

10. Remove the shackle assembly from the end of the spring.

11. Pull the rubber bushings out from both ends of the spring.

Rear spring installations is performed in the reverse order of removal. When installing the rubber bushings, do not lubricate them. Tighten the U-bolt securing nuts to 30 ft. lbs., and both the spring pin and the shackle pin to 14 ft. lbs.

RX-2 Models and GLC

Rear coil spring removal is performed as part of the shock absorber removal operation. See the appropriate section following for the combined procedure.

Cosmo

1. Remove the rear wheels.

2. Support the lower arms with a jack.

3. Remove the pivot bolt and nut which secures the rear end of the lower arm to the axle housing.

4. Lower the jack to relieve the spring pressure on the lower arm and remove the spring.

5. If replacing one spring only, a suitable adjusting plate will be necessary to give equal road clearance on each side.

6. Install spring in reverse order of re-

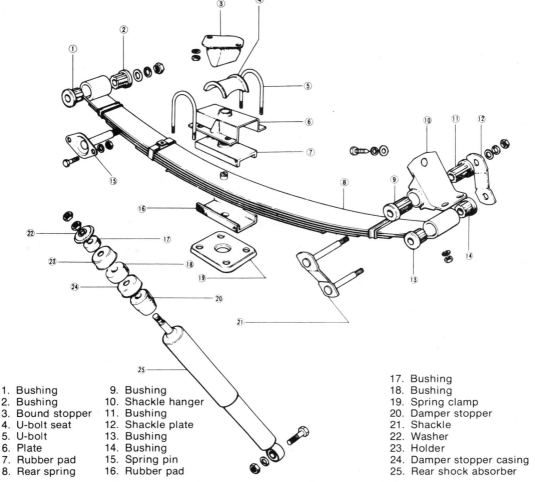

1. Bushing	9. Bushing	17. Bushing
2. Bushing	10. Shackle hanger	18. Bushing
3. Bound stopper	11. Bushing	19. Spring clamp
4. U-bolt seat	12. Shackle plate	20. Damper stopper
5. U-bolt	13. Bushing	21. Shackle
6. Plate	14. Bushing	22. Washer
7. Rubber pad	15. Spring pin	23. Holder
8. Rear spring	16. Rubber pad	24. Damper stopper casing
		25. Rear shock absorber

RX-3 sedan and coupe rear suspension—wagon similar

moval, but do not tighten bolts while car is on stands.

626

1. Raise the rear end of the vehicle and support it with jackstands. Place the jackstands under the bracket on the front sides of the lower arms.

2. Remove the rear wheel.

3. Place a jack under the rear axle housing to support it.

4. Remove the shock absorber lower attaching nut and disengage the shock absorber from the rear axle housing.

5. Remove the lateral rod from the right side of the axle housing.

6. Remove the upper link attaching nut from the rear of the axle housing.

7. Remove the lower arm attaching nut from the rear axle housing.

8. Remove the control rod attaching nut and remove the bushings, spacer and washers. Disengage the rear stabilizer bar from the control rod if so equipped.

9. Slowly lower the jack to relieve the spring pressure on the lower arm, then remove the spring.

10. Installation is the reverse of removal. During installation of the coil spring make sure the open end of the spring faces the rear axle housing. Tighten all bolts temporarily then after the vehicle is lowered to the ground torque to specifications. Upper link and lower arm to axle housing—66 ft. lbs., Lateral rod to axle housing—66 ft. lbs.

Shock Absorbers
BOUNCE TEST

Each shock absorber can be tested by bouncing the corner of the vehicle until maximum up and down movement is obtained. Release

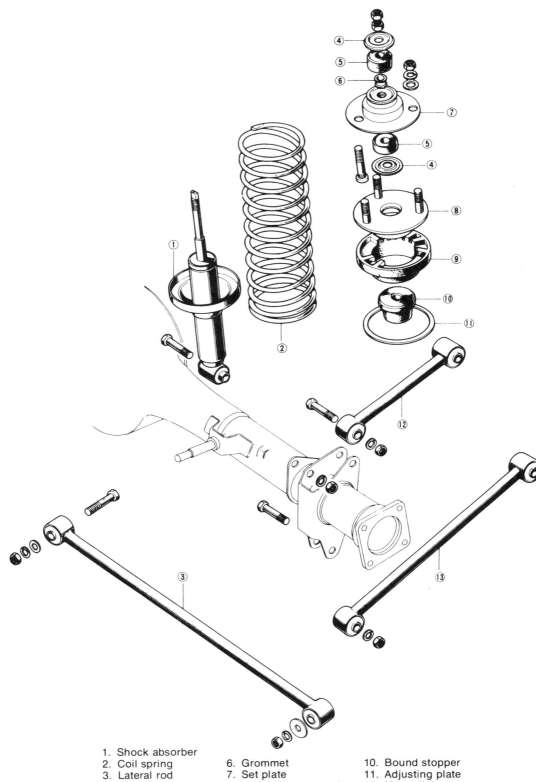

1. Shock absorber
2. Coil spring
3. Lateral rod
4. Retainer
5. Rubber insulator

6. Grommet
7. Set plate
8. Spring seat (upper)
9. Rubber seat

10. Bound stopper
11. Adjusting plate
12. Upper link
13. Lower link

RX-2 rear suspension assembly

the car. It should stop bouncing in one or two bounces. Compare both front corners or both rear corners but do not compare the front to the rear. If one corner bounces longer than the other it should be inspected for damage and possibly be replaced.

REMOVAL AND INSTALLATION

RX-3 RX-4,808 Coupes and Sedans

1. On RX-4, remove the seat. Remove the trim panel from the rear of the luggage compartment.
2. Unfasten the nuts, then remove the washers and rubber bushings from the upper shock absorber mounts.
3. Unfasten the nut and bolt which secures the end of the rear shock to the axle housing.
4. Withdraw the shock from underneath the car.

Installation is performed in the reverse order of removal. Tighten the upper shock mount to 15 ft. lbs. on all models but the 808. On the 808, tighten the upper nuts until a ¼ in. dimension exists between the top of the shock absorber rod and the top of the rod nut.

RX-3, RX-4 and 808 Wagons

1. Raise the back end of the station wagon and support it with jackstands.
   CAUTION: *Be sure that the car is securely supported. Remember, you will be working underneath it.*
2. Remove the locknuts, washers, and rubber bushings from the lower shock absorber mount.
3. Install a compressor on the shock and compress it.
4. Unfasten the bolts which secure the upper shock absorber mount to the body.
5. Withdraw the shock, with the compres-

Arrow show location of upper rear shock mounting nut on RX-3 sedans and coupes

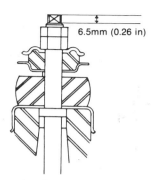

6.5mm (0.26 in)

Tightening dimension for upper shock mounting nut—808 models

Removing the rear shock mounting bracket—RX-3 wagons

sor still attached, from underneath the car.
6. Slowly remove the compressor from the shock.

Shock absorber installation is performed in the reverse order of removal. Tighten the upper shock mount to 15 ft. lbs., except on the 808. On the 808, tighten the upper nuts until a ¼ in. dimension exists between the bottom of the shock absorber rod and the bottom of the nuts.

RX-2 Models

1. Working from inside the luggage compartment, unfasten the nuts which secure the upper end of the shock absorber.
2. Unfasten the nut and bolt at the lower end of the shock absorber.
3. Place a jack underneath the axle housing and raise the car.
4. Place jackstands underneath the frame side rails.
   CAUTION: *Be sure that the jackstands are properly placed under the side rails.*
5. Slowly lower the jack to take the load off the springs.
6. Withdraw the shock/coil spring assembly from underneath the car.

7. Mark the shock for identification during assembly and secure the bottom of the shock in a vise.

8. Fit a spring compressor on the spring.

9. Unfasten the locknuts from the upper end of the shock.

10. Remove the washers, bushings, setplate, spring seat, rubber pad, adjusting plate, and bumper from the top of the shock.

Installation of the rear shock is performed in the reverse order of removal. Be sure to mount the shock with its stone guard facing toward the front of the car. Tighten the bolt and nut which secures the lower end of the shock, to 72–87 ft. lbs.

NOTE: *If a new coil spring is being fitted, match it with an adjusting plate of the correct thickness to obtain equal road clearance on both sides. There are three different size coil springs available.*

GLC—Rear Wheel Drive

1. Raise the rear of the vehicle and support securely via the frame side rails. Remove the wheels.

2. Remove the upper shock absorber bolt from inside the fender well.

3. Remove the lower shock bolt and nut, and remove the shock.

4. To remove the rear spring, support the lower control arm with a jack. Remove the pivot bolt which connects the lower control arm and rear axle.

5. Very slowly lower the jack until the spring pressure has been relieved, and remove the spring.

6. Install the spring in reverse order of removal, but do not fully tighten the pivot bolt. Then, lower the vehicle until it is at normal ride height and torque the bolt to 47–59 ft. lb.

7. Install the shock absorber in the reverse of the removal procedure.

GLC—Front Wheel Drive

1. Remove the side trim panels from inside the "trunk". Loosen and remove the top mounting nuts from the shock absorber assembly.

2. Loosen the rear wheel lugs, raise the car and safely support it on jackstands.

3. Remove the rear wheels. Disconnect the flexible brake hose from the strut.

4. Disconnect the trailing arm from the lower side of the strut: Separate the laterial link and strut by removing the bolt assembly.

5. Remove the strut from the lower unit

by removing the two through nuts and bolts.

6. Remove the strut and brake assembly. Clamp the strut assembly in a vise and loosen the nut at the top of the shock absorber.

CAUTION: *Do not remove the nut at this time.*

7. Compress the coil spring with a compressor tool. Remove the top nut and bracket. Remove the coil spring.

8. Installation is the reverse of removal. After mounting the strut assembly, lower the car to the ground and torque the mountings; Piston rod and mounting block—41–60 ft. lbs. Mounting block and tower mount—16–20 ft. lbs. Lower mounts—40–50 ft. lbs.

626

1. Raise the rear end of the vehicle and place jack stands under the bracket on the front side of the lower arms.

2. Remove the rear wheel.

3. Remove the bracket attaching nuts from the upper end of the shock absorber.

4. Remove the lower shock absorber retaining nut and remove the shock absorber.

CAUTION: *Do not disassemble the gas sealed type shock absorber as it contains highly compressed gas. Defective shocks should be replaced if found defective.*

5. Installation is the reverse of removal. Torque the upper bracket bolts to 28 ft. lbs., the lower bracket bolts to 32 ft. lbs., and the shock absorber attaching nuts to 53 ft. lbs.

FRONT SUSPENSION

MacPherson Struts

REMOVAL AND INSTALLATION

1. Remove the wheel cover and loosen the lug nuts.

2. Raise the front of the vehicle and support it with jackstands. Do not jack it or support it by any of the front suspension members. Remove the wheel.

CAUTION: *Be sure that the car is securely supported. Remember, you will be working underneath it.*

3. Remove the brake caliper and disc as detailed in Chapter 9, on all models except GLC—front wheel drive.

4. Unfasten the nuts which secure the upper shock mount to the top of the wheel arch. Disconnect brake line from strut.

5. Unfasten the two bolts that secure the lower end of the shock to the steering knuckle arm.

6. Remove the shock and coil spring as a complete assembly.

7. Mount the strut (shock/spring) assembly in a vise. Compress the coil spring with a spring compressor.

8. Hold the upper end of the shock piston rod with a pipe wrench and unfasten the locknut.

9. Remove the parts from the top of the shock absorber in the order shown in the appropriate illustration.

CAUTION: *When removing the spring compressor from the coil spring, do so gradually so that spring tension is not released all at once.*

Installation of the MacPherson strut is performed in the reverse order of removal. Tighten the nut on the top of the piston rod to 10 ft. lbs. except on GLC. On GLC and 626, torque to 47–59 ft. lbs.

NOTE: *If a new coil spring is being fitted, match it with an adjusting plate of the correct thickness to obtain equal road clearance on both sides. Do not use more than two adjusting plates on a side.*

Control Arm

REMOVAL AND INSTALLATION

Except Front Wheel Drive

1. Perform the first two steps of the MacPherson strut removal procedure.

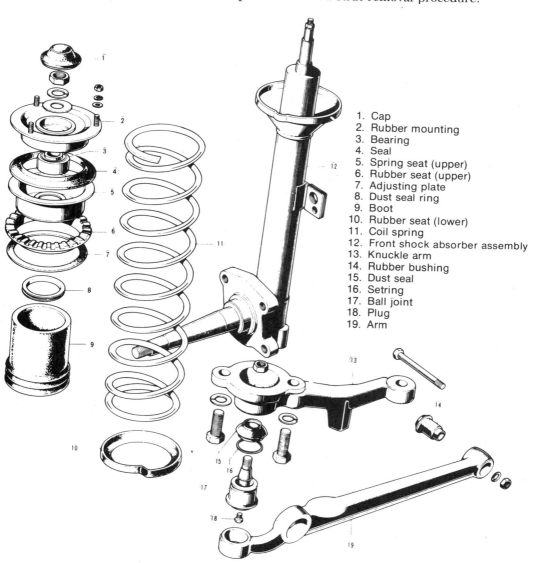

1. Cap
2. Rubber mounting
3. Bearing
4. Seal
5. Spring seat (upper)
6. Rubber seat (upper)
7. Adjusting plate
8. Dust seal ring
9. Boot
10. Rubber seat (lower)
11. Coil spring
12. Front shock absorber assembly
13. Knuckle arm
14. Rubber bushing
15. Dust seal
16. Setring
17. Ball joint
18. Plug
19. Arm

MacPherson strut front suspension—all models except GLC

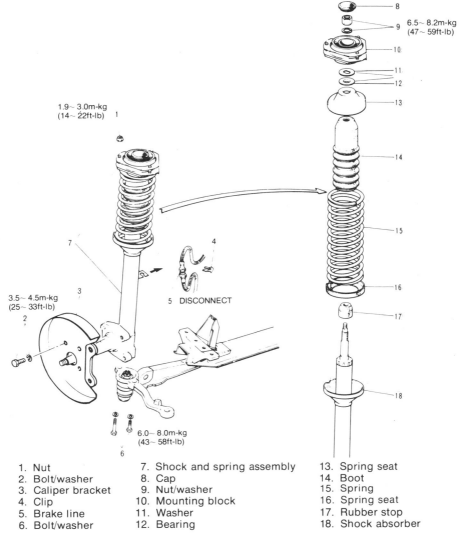

1.9~ 3.0m-kg
(14~ 22ft-lb)

6.5~ 8.2m-kg
(47~ 59ft-lb)

3.5~ 4.5m-kg
(25~ 33ft-lb)

6.0~ 8.0m-kg
(43~ 58ft-lb)

5 DISCONNECT

1. Nut	7. Shock and spring assembly	13. Spring seat
2. Bolt/washer	8. Cap	14. Boot
3. Caliper bracket	9. Nut/washer	15. Spring
4. Clip	10. Mounting block	16. Spring seat
5. Brake line	11. Washer	17. Rubber stop
6. Bolt/washer	12. Bearing	18. Shock absorber

MacPherson strut front assembly-typical GLC rear wheel drive models

Unfasten the three bolts which secure the upper shock mount to the wheel arch (arrows)

2. Remove the cotter pin and nut, which secure the tie-rod end, from the knuckle arm, then use a puller to separate them.

3. Unfasten the bolts which secure the lower end of the shock absorber to the knuckle arm.

4. Remove the nut then withdraw the rubber bushing and washer which secure the stabilizer bar to the control arm.

5. Unfasten the nut and bolt which secure the control arm to the frame member.

6. Push outward on the strut assembly while removing the end of the control arm from the frame member.

7. Remove the control arm and steering knuckle arm as an assembly.

Removing the control arm

8. Install the assembly in a vise. Remove its cotter pin and unfasten the ball joint nut; then separate the knuckle arm from the control arm with a puller.

Installation of the control arm is performed in the reverse order of its removal. Torque the control arm-to-crossmember nut and bolt to: 51–65 ft. lbs. on the RX-2; 34 ft. lbs. on the RX-3; 54–69 ft. lbs. on the RX-4 and Cosmo; and 29–40 ft. lbs. on the GLC 626 and 808.

Front Wheel Drive

1. Loosen the wheel lugs, raise the car and safely support it on jackstands. Remove the front wheel.

2. Remove the through bolt connecting the lower arm to the steering knuckle.

3. Remove the bolts and nuts mounting the control arm to the body (two inner and three outer).

4. Remove the lower control arm. The ball joint can be serviced at this time if necessary.

5. Installation is in the reverse order of removal. Mounting Torque;
- Ball Joint to Steering Knuckle—32–40 ft. lbs.
- Outer Bolts—43–54 ft. lbs.
- Inner Bolts 69–86 ft. lbs.

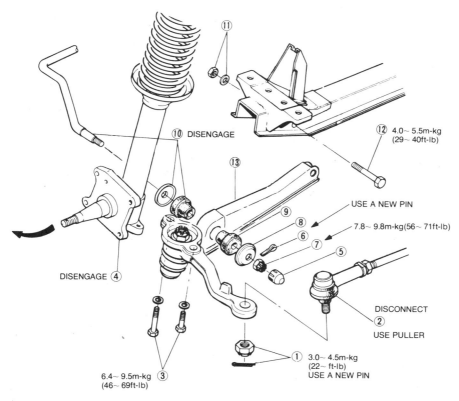

1. Nut/cotter pin
2. Tie rod
3. Bolt/washer
4. Shock absorber
5. Stop
6. Cotter pin
7. Nut
8. Washer
9. Rubber bush
10. Stabilizer bar/washer/rubber bush
11. Nut/washer
12. Bolt
13. Control arm and steering knuckle arm

Removing the control arm—GLC rear wheel drive models

Tension Rod and Stabilizer Bar
REMOVAL AND INSTALLATION
626

1. Raise the vehicle and support with jack stands.

2. Remove the tension rod attaching nuts from the suspension arm.

3. Remove the nuts, washers and rubber bushings holding the tension rod to the tension rod bracket and remove the tension rod.

4. Remove the control rod assembly.

5. Remove the stabilizer bar support plate and bushings.

6. Installation is the reverse of removal.
NOTE: *When installing the stabilizer bushing with the support plate, place the open end of the bushing toward the front.*

Front Hub and Steering Knuckle
REMOVAL AND INSTALLATION
GLC—Front Wheel Drive

1. Loosen the lug nuts, raise the front of the car and safely support it on jackstands. Remove the tire and wheel.

2. Raise the staked tab from the hub center nut, remove the nut from the axle. Apply the brake to help hold the rotor while loosening the nut.

3. Remove the tie-rod end from the steering knuckle. Disconnect the horseshoe clip that retains the brake line to the strut.

4. Remove the mounting bolts that hold the caliper assembly to the knuckle. Wire the caliper out of the way, do not allow the caliper to be supported by the brake hose.

5. Remove the through bolt and nut that retains the lower ball joint to the steering knuckle and disconnect the ball joint.

6. Remove the two bolts and nuts retaining the strut to the steering knuckle. Separate the steering knuckle and hub from the strut and drive axle.

7. The hub is pressed through the wheel bearings into the knuckle. Replacement of the wheel bearings or hub removal requires a special puller and access to a bench press, your dealer or local automotive machine shop can handle the job for you.

8. Remove the inner oil seal and bearing. Remove the wheel hub from the knuckle with a wheel hub puller (Mazda tool 49 F001 726). Remove the outer bearing using a press and Mazda tools 49 F401 368 and 49 F401 365. Drive the outer and inner race from the knuckle with a brass drift and hammer.

9. Install new inner and outer races. Pack the inner and outer bearing and install in knuckle. Use Mazda tool 49 B001 727 tighten the tool nut and measure the preload with a scale connected to the caliper mounting hole on the knuckle. Various spacers are available to increase or decrease the preload. Preload should be 1.7–6.9 in lbs.

10. Install the inner and outer grease seals. Press fit the hub through the bearings into the knuckle. Use 6613.8 lbs. of pressure to install.

11. Installation of the knuckle and hub is in the reverse order of removal. Always use a new axle locknut and tighten it to 116–174 ft. lbs. Stake the locknut after tightening. Knuckle to strut mounting; 58–86 ft. lbs. Knuckle to ball joint; 33–40 ft. lbs. Knuckle to tie rod end; 22–33 ft. lbs.

Ball Joints
INSPECTION
All Except GLC

1. Perform Steps 1–5 of the control arm removal procedure.

2. Check the ball joint dust boot condition. Replace the boot if it will allow water or dirt to enter the ball joint assembly.

3. Check the amount of pressure required to turn the ball stud by hooking a pull scale into the tie-rod hole in the knuckle arm. Pull the spring scale until the arm just begins to turn; this should require: 13–24 lbs.—RX-2 and RX-3; 27–40 lbs.—RX-4 and Cosmo to 1977; 4.4–8.8 lbs.—1978 Cosmo and RX-4; 4.6–9.2—RX-3SP; 17.6–30 lbs.—808.

4. Replace the ball joint, as detailed in the following section, if it is not up to specification.

Checking the pressure required to turn the ball stud with a spring scale

GLC Rear Wheel Drive, Station Wagon and 626

1. Check the dust boot for wear or cracks, and replace if necessary.

2. Raise the vehicle until the wheel is off the ground. Grab the tire at top and bottom, and alternately pull it toward you and push it away to check for ball joint end play. Wear limit is .04 in. If necessary, replace ball joint and control arm assembly. See control arm removal and installation procedure above. When installing ball joint nut, torque to 43–51 ft. lbs.—GLC and 46–69 ft. lbs.—626.

REMOVAL AND INSTALLATION
All Except GLC and 626

1. Complete the control arm removal procedure as detailed above.
2. Remove the set ring and the dust boot from the ball joint.
3. Clean the ball joint and control arm assembly.
4. Press the ball joint out of the control arm.

Installation of a new ball joint is performed in the following order:
1. Clean the ball joint mounting bore and coat it with kerosene.
2. Press the ball joint into the control arm. NOTE: *If the pressure required to press the new ball joint into place is less than 3,300 lbs., the bore is worn and the control arm must be replaced.*
3. Attach the ball joint/control arm assembly to the steering knuckle. Tighten the nut to 60 ft. lbs. and insert the cotter pin. The 60 ft. lbs. figure has been changed on the 1978 RX-3SP, Cosmo, and RX-4; it is now 43–58 ft. lbs. on those models.
4. Install the control arm in the car, as detailed above.

GLC and 626

On the GLC and 626 models refer to the Control Arm removal and installation procedure. When installing the ball joint nut torque to 43–51 lbs.—GLC and 46–69 ft. lbs.—626.

Front End Alignment
CASTER AND CAMBER

Caster and camber are preset by the manufacturer. They require adjustment only if the suspension and steering linkage components are damaged, in which case, repair is accomplished by replacing the damaged part except on RX-4 626 and Cosmo.

On these models, the caster and camber

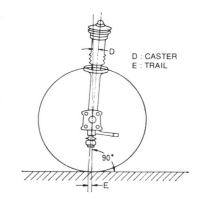

Caster

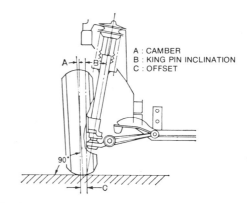

Camber

may be changed by rotating the shock absorber support. If they can't be brought to within specifications, replace or repair suspension parts as necessary.

To check caster and camber, use one of the alignment machines following its manufacturer's instructions. Compare the results obtained, against the specifications in the "Wheel Alignment Specifications" chart.

TOE-IN ADJUSTMENT

Toe-in is the difference in the distance between the front wheels, as measured at both the front and rear of the front tires.

1. Raise the front of the car so that its front wheels are just clear of the ground.
2. Use a scribing block to mark a line at the center of each tire tread while rotating the wheels by hand.
3. Measure the distance between the marked lines at both their front and rear. NOTE: *Take both measurements at equal distances from the ground.*
4. The toe-in is equal to the difference between the front and rear measurements (front figure smaller). See chart below.

Wheel Alignment Specifications

Year	Model	Camber		Caster		Toe-in (in.)	Steering Axis Inclination (deg)
		Range (deg)	Preferred Setting (deg)	Range (deg)	Preferred Setting (deg)		
1972–74	RX-2	$^1/_4$P–$1^3/_4$P	1P	$^1/_2$N–$1^1/_2$P	$^1/_2$P	0–0.24	$8^3/_4$P
1975	RX-3	1P–2P	$1^1/_2$P	$^1/_2$N–$1^1/_2$P	$^1/_2$P	0–0.24	$8^7/_{10}$P
	RX-4	$1^1/_2$P–$2^1/_2$P	2P	0–2P	1P	0–0.24	$9^1/_2$P
	808	$^2/_3$P–$2^1/_6$P	$1^1/_3$P	$^1/_2$N–$1^1/_2$P	$^1/_2$P	0–0.24	$8^3/_4$P
1976	808 (1600)	①	②	③–2P	$^1/_2$P	0–0.24	$8^1/_2$P
1976–77	808 (1300)	④	⑤	$^1/_2$N–$1^1/_2$P	$^1/_2$P	0–0.24	$8^2/_3$P
1976–78	RX-3, RX-3SP	③	⑥	$^1/_2$N–$1^1/_2$P	$^1/_2$P	0–0.24	$8^2/_3$P
	RX-4	1P–2P	$1^1/_2$P	⑦	⑧	0–0.24	$9^2/_3$P ⑨
1977	Cosmo	$1^1/_2$P–3P ⑩	$2^1/_4$P ⑪	0–2P	1P	0–0.24	$9^3/_4$P
1977–78	808 (1600)	⑫	⑬	⑭	⑮	0–0.24	⑯
	GLC	—	$^2/_3$P	$^5/_8$P–$2^1/_3$P	$1^{35}/_{60}$	0–0.24	$8^1/_2$P
1978	Cosmo	0P–2P	1P	$1^1/_2$P–3P ⑰	$2^1/_4$ ⑱	0–0.24	$9^3/_4$P
1979–80	GLC	15′–1°15′ ⑲	45′ ⑳	15′–2°25′ ㉑	1°45′ ㉒	0–0.24	8°45′
	626	45′–1°45′	1°15′	㉓	㉔	0–0.24	10°40′
1981–82	GLC	—	50′P	—	1°25′P	0.12 out-0.12 in	12°20′
1979–82	626	45′–1°45′	1°15′	㉓	㉔	0–0.24	10°40′

①Sedan: $^5/_6$P–$2^1/_3$P
　coupe: 1P–$2^1/_2$P
　wagon: 1P–$2^1/_3$P
②Sedan: $1^1/_2$P
　coupe: $1^5/_6$P
　wagon: $1^2/_3$P
③Sedan & wagon $^5/_6$N–$1^1/_5$P
　coupe: $1^1/_{12}$P–2P
④Sedan: $^2/_3$P–$2^1/_6$P
　coupe wagon: 1P–$2^1/_3$P
⑤Sedan: $1^1/_3$P
　coupe wagon: $1^2/_3$P
⑥Sedan & wagon: $1^2/_3$P
　coupe: $1^1/_2$P

⑦Sedan & hardtop: 0–2P
　wagon: $^1/_3$P–$1^1/_3$P
⑧Sedan & hardtop: 1P
　wagon: $^1/_2$P
⑨Wagon: $9^1/_3$P
⑩Manual: 1P–2P
⑪Manual: $1^1/_2$P
⑫Sedan & wagon: 1P–$2^1/_2$P
　coupe: $1^1/_3$P–$2^5/_6$P
⑬Sedan & wagon: $1^5/_6$P
　coupe: $2^1/_{12}$P
⑭Sedan & coupe: $^1/_{12}$P–$2^1/_2$P
　wagon: $^1/_4$P–$2^1/_4$P

⑮Sedan & coupe: $1^1/_{12}$P
　wagon: $1^1/_4$P
⑯Sedan & coupe: $8^5/_{12}$P
　wagon: $8^1/_4$P
⑰Manual: $1^5/_{60}$–$2^{35}/_{60}$
⑱Manual: $1^5/_8$
⑲Station wagon: 30′–1°30′
⑳Station wagon: 1°
㉑Station wagon: 1°–2°30′
㉒Station wagon: 1°45′
㉓Right side: 2°55′–4°25′
　Left side: 2°25′–3°55′
㉔Right side: 3°45′
　Left side: 3°10′

5. To adjust the toe-in, loosen the tie-rod locknuts and turn both tie-rods an equal amount until the proper measurement is obtained.

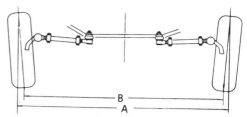

A−B= 0 ~ 6 mm (0 ~ 0.24 in)

Measuring toe-in

STEERING

Steering Wheel

REMOVAL AND INSTALLATION

1. Remove the screws which secure the crash pad/horn button assembly to the steering wheel. If there are no mounting screws, pry the pad off, starting at the top. Remove the assembly.

2. Make matchmarks on the steering wheel and steering shaft.

3. Unfasten the steering wheel hub nut

Removing the steering column shroud

1. Idler bracket
2. Seal
3. Bushing
4. Plug
5. Spring
6. Idler arm
7. Rubber bushing
8. Rubber bushing
9. Washer
10. Nut
11. Cotter pin
12. Center link
13. Ball joint
14. Tie-rod
15. Locknut
16. Ball joint

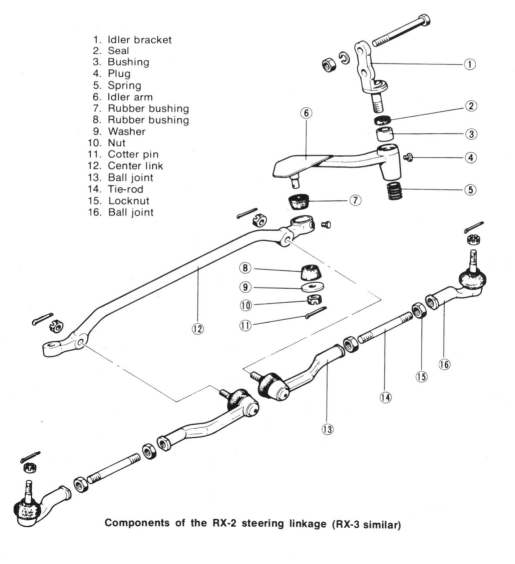

Components of the RX-2 steering linkage (RX-3 similar)

and remove the steering wheel with a puller.

CAUTION: *The steering column is collapsible; pounding on it or applying excessive pressure to it may cause it to deform, in which case the entire column will have to be replaced.*

Installation of the steering wheel is performed in the reverse order of removal. Tighten the steering wheel nut to 25 ft. lbs.

Turn Signal Switch

COMBINATION (TURN SIGNAL) SWITCH REPLACEMENT

RX-2, RX-3, 808

1. Remove the steering wheel.
2. Remove the left-hand column shroud.
3. Remove the retaining ring (screw on 808) from the combination (turn signal) switch.
4. Withdraw the switch over the steering column.
5. Installation is the reverse of removal.

RX-4 and Cosmo

1. Remove the steering wheel.
2. Loosen the nut which secures the vent knob (left side) and allow the knob assembly to drop away from its mounting bracket.
3. Remove choke knob. Remove the choke retaining nut and separate the choke from the panel.
4. Remove the upper column cover.
5. Disconnect the panel light dimmer switch wiring.
6. Disconnect the exhaust temperature warning light wiring.
7. Loosen, but don't remove the screws at either end of the lower panel cover.

NOTE: *The left-hand screw is located in the hole which was covered by the upper column cover and the right-hand screw is above the ashtray opening (ashtray removed).*

8. Pull the upper column cover away from the instrument panel.
9. Disconnect the combination switch connector.
10. Remove the retaining ring from the steering column.
11. Unfasten the combination switch retaining screw and remove the switch.
12. Installation is the reverse of removal.

GLC and 626

1. Disconnect the battery. Remove the horn cover cap.

2. Remove the steering wheel attaching nut, and pull off the wheel with a puller.
3. Remove the attaching screws, and remove the right and left steering column covers.
4. Disconnect the connector for the combination switch or, if the ignition switch is being replaced, disconnect connectors for both that and the combination switch.
5. Remove the retaining ring from the steering column.
6. Remove the combination retaining screw, and remove the switch.
7. To install, reverse the removal procedure, torquing the steering wheel nut to 22–29 ft. lb.

Ignition Lock/Switch Assembly

REMOVAL AND INSTALLATION

RX-2, RX-3, 626, 808, GLC

1. Remove the combination switch as described above. Then, withdraw the ignition switch assembly.
2. Install the new switch and tighten the mounting bolts. Break their heads off to make the switch difficult for a thief to remove.
3. Reverse the remaining steps of the removal procedure.

RX-4 and Cosmo

1. Follow steps under Combination Switch Replacement.
2. Remove the instrument frame brace.
3. Disconnect the switch wires.
4. Remove the switch.
5. Installation is the reverse of removal.

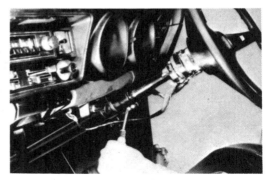

Cut slots in the ignition switch securing bolts and remove them with a screwdriver

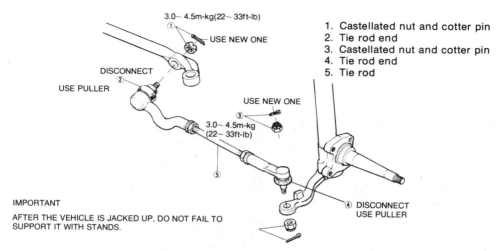

3.0~ 4.5m-kg(22~ 33ft-lb)

USE NEW ONE

DISCONNECT

USE PULLER

USE NEW ONE

3.0~ 4.5m-kg
(22~ 33ft-lb)

1. Castellated nut and cotter pin
2. Tie rod end
3. Castellated nut and cotter pin
4. Tie rod end
5. Tie rod

DISCONNECT
USE PULLER

IMPORTANT

AFTER THE VEHICLE IS JACKED UP, DO NOT FAIL TO
SUPPORT IT WITH STANDS.

Replacing tie rod—GLC

Tie Rods

REMOVAL AND INSTALLATION

1. If an alignment machine is not available, measure the length of the tie rod you'll be working on. Remove cotter pin or pins and castellated nut or nuts from one or both ends of the tie rod, depending upon whether one or both ends requires replacement. Use a puller designed for this purpose to free either or both ends from center link or steering knuckle. If only one end of the rod is to be replaced, loosen the locknut and screw the rod end off the tie rod.

2. To replace, first loosen tie rod locknuts, and then insert rod ends through holes in center link and steering knuckle. If only one end is being replaced, screw the end onto the tie rod and insert pin into center link or steering knuckle. Install nut(s) and torque to 22–33 ft. lb. Install new cotter pins.

3. If an alignment machine is available, adjust toe-in and then torque tie rod locknuts

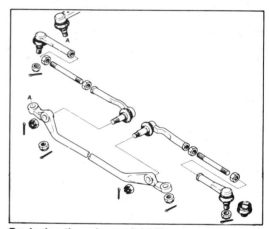

Replacing tie rod—model 626

to 51–58 ft. lb. If the car must be taken to a shop for alignment, turn the tie rod so that the length is the same as it was before part(s) were replaced, torque both locknuts, and then have toe-in adjusted as soon as possible.

Brakes

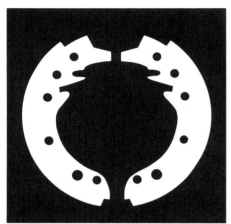

BRAKE SYSTEM

Adjustments

FRONT DISC BRAKES

The front disc brakes are self-adjusting by design. As the brake pads and discs wear, fluid pressure compensates for the amount of wear. Because this action causes the fluid level to go down, its level should be checked and replenished as often as is necessary.

REAR DRUM BRAKES

All Models Except GLC

1. Block the front wheels, raise the car, and support it with jackstands.

CAUTION: *Be sure that the car is securely supported. Remember, you will be working underneath it.*

2. Release the parking brake completely.
3. Remove the adjusting hole plugs from the backing plate.
4. Engage the adjuster with a screwdriver. Turn the adjuster in the direction of the arrow stamped on the backing plate until the brake shoes are fully expanded, i.e., the wheel will not turn.
5. Pump the brake pedal several times to be sure that the brake shoe contacts the drum evenly.

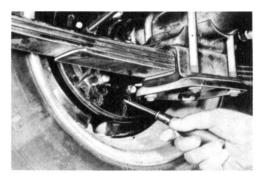

Adjusting the rear brake shoes

NOTE: *If the wheel turns after you remove your foot from the brake pedal, continue turning the adjuster until the wheel will no longer rotate.*

6. Back off on the adjuster about 4–5 notches. The wheel should rotate freely, without dragging. If it does not, turn the adjuster an additional notch.
7. Pump the brake pedal several times and check wheel rotation again.
8. Fit the plug into the adjusting hole and then repeat the adjusting procedure for the three other rear brake shoes.

GLC

NOTE: *Front wheel drive models are equipped with self-adjusting brakes, no external adjustment is possible.*

1. Raise and securely support the vehicle. Make sure parking brake is fully released.

2. Loosen anchor pin locknuts. Hold locknut and turn anchor pin until the wheel locks. Anchor pins on each wheel are turned in opposite directions. On the right side, forward pin turns clockwise, and the rear pin counterclockwise. On the left side, the forward pin turns counterclockwise, the rear pin clockwise.

3. Then turn the anchor pin back until the wheel just turns freely. Hold the adjustment and tighten the locknut.

4. Repeat for the other shoe on the first wheel, and then adjust both shoes on the second wheel.

BRAKE PEDAL

1. Detach the wiring from the brake light switch terminals.

2. Loosen the locknut on the switch.

3. Turn the switch until the distance between the pedal and the floor is: RX-2, RX-3, RX-4, 808, 7.3 in. Cosmo—8.58 in. manual trans., 8.24 in., automatic GLC—7.48 in. manual, 7.68 automatic and 8.46 GLC front wheel drive, 626—8.66 in.

4. Tighten the locknut on switch.

5. Loosen the locknut located on the pushrod.

6. Rotate the pushrod until the pedal free

travel of 0.2–0.6 in. is obtained. (.28–.35 in.—GLC, 626 and Cosmo).

7. Tighten the pushrod locknut.

HYDRAULIC SYSTEM

Master Cylinder
REMOVAL AND INSTALLATION

1. Remove the air cleaner for clearance if necessary.

2. Detach all of the hydraulic lines from the master cylinder. Detach connector for fluid level sensor.

NOTE: *On models which have a fluid reservoir located separately from the master cylinder, remove the lines which run between the two and plug the lines to prevent leakage.*

3. Unfasten the nuts which secure the master cylinder to the power brake unit.

4. Withdraw the master cylinder assembly straight out and away from the power brake unit.

CAUTION: *Be careful not to spill brake fluid on the painted surfaces of the car, as it makes an excellent paint remover.*

Installation of the master cylinder is performed in the reverse order of its removal. Fill its reservoir and bleed the brake system, as detailed below.

OVERHAUL
RX-2, RX-3

1. Clean the outside of the master cylinder and drain any brake fluid remaining in it.

2. Remove the fluid reservoir from the top, if so equipped.

3. Remove the boot from the rear of the cylinder.

4. Depress the primary piston and withdraw the snap-ring from the rear of the cylinder bore.

5. Withdraw the washers, piston, cups, spacer, seat, and return spring from the cylinder bore.

6. Depress the secondary piston, using a rod, and remove the secondary piston bolt from the outside of the cylinder.

7. Remove the secondary piston assembly from the bore.

NOTE: *Blow out the assembly with compressed air, if necessary.*

8. Unfasten the hydraulic line fittings from the master cylinder outlet.

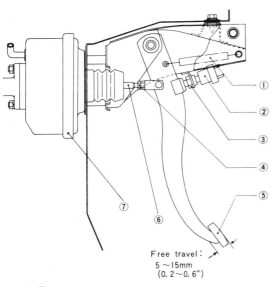

Free travel:
5～15mm
(0.2～0.6″)

1. Return spring
2. Stop lamp switch
3. Locknut
4. Locknut
5. Brake pedal
6. Pushrod
7. Power brake unit

Brake pedal components

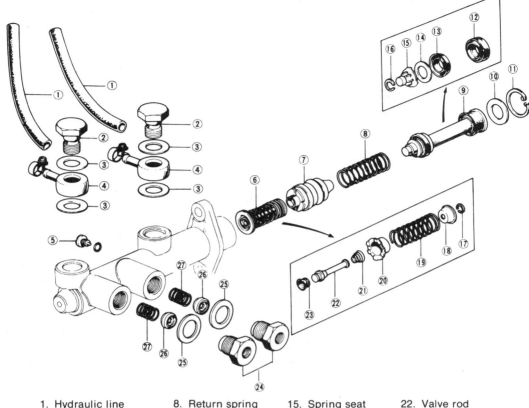

1. Hydraulic line	8. Return spring	15. Spring seat	22. Valve rod
2. Connector bolt	9. Primary piston	16. Stop ring	23. Valve
3. Washer	10. Washer	17. Stop ring	24. Outlet fitting
4. Union	11. Retaining ring	18. Spring seat	25. Washer
5. Stop bolt	12. Secondary cup	19. Return spring	26. Check valve
6. Valve and spring	13. Primary cup	20. Valve case	27. Spring
7. Secondary piston	14. Spacer	21. Spring	

Master cylinder components—RX-2 and RX-3

9. Withdraw the check valves and springs from the outlets.

10. Wash all of the components in clean brake fluid.

CAUTION: *Never use kerosene or gasoline to clean the master cylinder components.*

Examine all of the piston cups and replace any that are worn, damaged, or swollen.

Check the cylinder bore for roughness or scoring. Check the clearance between the piston and cylinder bore with a feeler gauge. Replace either the piston or the cylinder, if the clearance exceeds 0.006 in.

Blow the dirt and the remaining brake fluid out of the cylinder with compressed air.

Master cylinder assembly is performed in the following order:

1. Dip all of the components, except for the cylinder, in clean brake fluid.

2. Install the check valve assemblies in the master cylinder outlets.

3. Insert the return spring and the valve components into the cylinder bore.

4. Fit the secondary cup and the primary cup over the secondary piston. The flat side of the cups should face the piston.

5. Fit the guide pin into the stop bolt hole. Place the secondary piston components into the cylinder bore.

6. Depress the secondary piston as far as it will go and withdraw the guide pin. Screw the stop bolt into the hole.

7. Place the primary cups on the primary piston with the flat side of the cups facing the piston.

8. Insert the return spring and the primary piston into the bore.

9. Depress the primary piston, then install the stop washer and snap-ring.

NOTE: *Be sure that the piston cups do not cover up the compensating ports.*

10. Install the dust boot on the end of the cylinder.

RX-4, 808, Cosmo

1. Clean the outside of the master cylinder with brake fluid and drain the unit thoroughly.

2. Remove connector bolts, unions, and lockwashers from master cylinder inlets.

3. With a screwdriver, remove the piston stop and washer ring, from the cylinder.

4. Remove the primary piston cups, spacer, and spring seat assembly and return spring.

5. Loosen, but DO NOT REMOVE the secondary piston stop bolt.

6. Push the secondary piston in with the screwdriver, remove the stop bolt, and insert the guide pin in its place. If necessary, you can make a guide pin, reading the dimensions off the illustration.

7. Gradually allow the secondary piston and cups and the return spring to come out of the cylinder. If they will not come out under spring pressure, apply compressed air to the outlet hole.

8. Remove all pipe fittings, gaskets, and

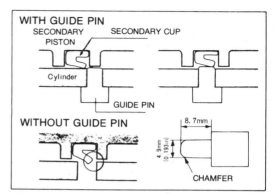

Using a guide pin to remove the secondary piston—RX-4, Cosmo, GLC, 808

check valves and springs from the cylinder.

9. Wash all components in clean brake fluid. NEVER use gasoline or kerosene, as it dissolves rubber parts. Check the cylinder bore for roughness or scoring. Check clearance between piston and cylinder bore—wear limit is .006 in. If necessary, replace parts. Blow remaining dirt out with compressed air. Replace any piston cups that are worn, torn, or swelled. Make sure compensating ports are open.

10. Dip pistons and cups in clean brake fluid.

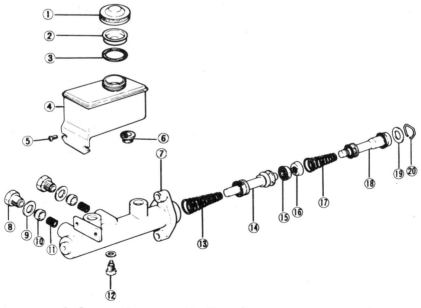

1. Reservoir gap	6. Grommet	11. Check valve	16. Secondary piston cup
2. Fluid baffle	7. Cylinder	12. Secondary piston	17. Primary spring
3. Rubber packing	8. Fluid pipe fitting	13. Secondary spring	18. Primary piston
4. Reservoir tank	9. Gasket	14. Secondary piston	19. Stop washer
5. Screw	10. Check valve	15. Secondary piston cup	20. Stop ring

Exploded view of Cosmo master cylinder (similar to RX-4 and 808)

11. Install check valves and springs into outlet holes. Install pipe fittings and torque to 43–51 ft. lb.

12. Install primary and secondary cups onto secondary piston.

13. Install the guide pin, and then insert the piston assembly and return spring into the master cylinder. Push the piston in as far as it will go with a screwdriver, hold while removing the guide pin and installing the stop bolt and washer and then remove the screwdriver.

14. Install the primary and secondary cups onto the primary piston, and then install the return spring and primary piston assembly. Install stop washer and piston stop ring. MAKE SURE PISTON CUPS DO NOT COVER COMPENSATING PORTS.

15. Install unions, washers, and connector bolts to inlet ports and tighten connector bolts.

GLC and 626

1. See the accompanying illustration and disassemble the master cylinder in num-

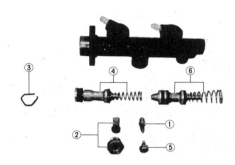

Exploded view of the master cylinder—model 626

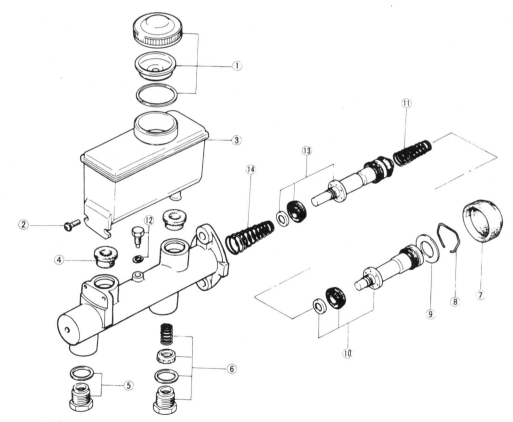

1. Reservoir cap and gasket
2. Screw
3. Fluid reservoir
4. Seal
5. Pipe fitting and packing for front brakes
6. Pipe fitting and packing, check valve and spring, for rear brakes
7. Rubber boot
8. Snap ring
9. Washer
10. Primary piston and cup
11. Primary spring
12. Stop bolt and washer
13. Secondary piston and cup
14. Secondary spring

Exploded view of GLC master cylinder

bered order. See steps 6–7 of the procedure above to remove the secondary piston.

2. See step 9 of the procedure above for inspection.

3. Assemble in reverse order, using the illustration and steps 10, 13, and 14 of the procedure above.

Proportioning Valve
REMOVAL AND INSTALLATION

The proportioning valve regulates the pressure to the rear brakes, reducing it under hard braking, to minimize lockup of the rear wheels. The valve is removed by unfastening the connections, removing the mounting bolts, and removing it. In installation, use the inlet and outlet arrows on the body of the valve to make connections properly from the master cylinder and to the wheels, and note the "F" marking, indicating the port leading to the front brakes. Bleed the system.

CENTERING THE BRAKE FAILURE WARNING VALVE

After a partial failure of the brake system, this valve will go off center and will activate the warning light. Simply bleed the system after repairs are complete, make sure the master cylinder reservoir has plenty of fluid in it, and depress the brake pedal several times until the light goes out.

Bleeding
DISC BRAKES (FRONT)

1. Remove the bleeder screw cap from the wheel cylinder which is furthest from the master cylinder.

NOTE: *Keep the master cylinder reservoir at least ¾ full during the bleeding operation.*

Bleeding the rear wheel cylinders

2. Install a vinyl tube over the bleeder screw. Submerge the other end of the tube in a jar half-full of clean brake fluid.

3. Open the bleeder valve. Fully depress the brake pedal and allow it to return slowly.

4. Repeat this operation until air bubbles cease flowing into the jar.

5. Close the valve, remove the tube, and install the cap on the bleeder valve.

DRUM BRAKES (REAR)

1. Repeat Steps 1–2 of the disc brake bleeding procedure.

2. Depress the brake pedal rapidly several times.

3. Keep the brake pedal depressed and open the bleeder valve. Close the valve without releasing the pedal.

4. Repeat this operation until bubbles cease to appear in the jar.

5. Remove the tube and install the cap on the bleeder valve.

FRONT DISC BRAKES

Disc Brake Pads
INSPECTION

Most models provide an inspection slot in the top of the caliper for checking the pad thickness. However, if the thickness seems marginal, the pads should be removed from the caliper and checked. Models not having an inspection slot will require pad removal to check the thickness of the friction material.

REMOVAL AND INSTALLATION

NOTE: *Prior to the installation of new brake pads, remove ½ of the brake fluid from both sides of the dual master cylinder reservoir(s). This allows for the displaced fluid when the caliper piston is pushed back into the caliper. Discard the fluid and replace the master cylinder reservoir cover.*

1. Loosen the wheel lugs, raise the front of the car and safely support it on jackstands. Remove the front wheels and tires.

2. *On RX-2 (various), RX-3 and 808:* These models use a torque plate single piston floating caliper. To remove the brake pads; Pry the pad protector from the top of the caliper. Remove the spring clip from the holes in the two through pins and outer pad. Remove the inner spring clip, note the difference in the shape of the two clips—they must be reinstalled in the same place. Pull the brake pads

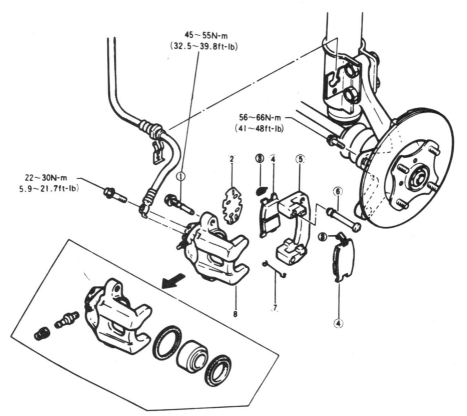

45~55N-m
(32.5~39.8ft-lb)

56~66N-m
(41~48ft-lb)

22~30N-m
5.9~21.7ft-lb)

Disc brake components GLC front wheel drive model

from the caliper. Note any shims between the pads and the caliper, replace them in the same position when installing new pads. Use a piece of hardwood and a "C" clamp to push the caliper piston back into the caliper to provide clearance for the new brake pads.

3. *On GLC Rear Wheel Drive, Cosmo and RX-2 (various):* These models use a single piston caliper that slides on a mounting bracket attached to the steering knuckle. To remove the pads; Remove the clips or pins that hold the caliper guide or retaining key in

Removing the brake pads—RX-3 models

place. Tap out the guide or key. If there is only one key or guide, remember it's position. Lift the caliper from the mounting bracket. Support the caliper with a piece of wire so it is not hanging on the brake hose. Remove the brake pads from the mounting bracket. A support plate is under each pad. They are not interchangeable and must be installed correctly. Use a "C" clamp and push the caliper piston back into the caliper.

4. *626 and GLC-Front Wheel Drive:* These models use a caliper that floats on guide pins and bushings that are threaded into a mounting bracket. To remove the pads; Disconnect the horseshoe clip retaining the brake hose to the front strut. Remove the caliper guide pins and anti-rattle springs or clips.

NOTE: *Variations in pad retainers, anti-rattle and retaining springs occur from year to year. Work on one side at a time, note the position of each spring, etc. for correct installation.*

On 1982 models; remove the upper spring-clip (if equipped) and the lower pin bolt which retains the caliper to the mount. Rotate the caliper upward. On other years, re-

move the mounting pins, lift the caliper up
and away from the disc rotor. Support the
caliper with wire, do not permit it to hang by
the brake hose. All versions slide the out-
board pad from the adapter. Remove the in-
board pad from the caliper or adapter. Note
the location of any shims for reinstallation.
Use a "C" clamp to push the caliper piston
back into the caliper.

5. Pad installation for all models is the reverse of removal. Fill the master cylinder and
bleed the brakes after replacing the brake
pads.

Installing the piston seal retainer on the caliper

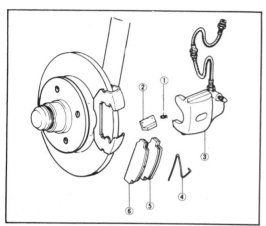

1. Locking clip
2. Stopper plate
3. Caliper
4. Anti-rattle spring
5. Brake shoe
6. Brake shoe

Front disc brake assembly—GLC rear wheel drive

Disc Brake Calipers

REMOVAL AND INSTALLATION

All Models

1. Perform the disc brake pad removal
procedure, as detailed above.

2. Detach the hydraulic line from the caliper. Plug the end of the line to prevent the
entrance of dirt or the loss of fluid.

3. Unfasten the bolts which secure the caliper to the support, and remove the caliper.

Follow the caliper removal procedure in
reverse order for installation. Bleed the hydraulic system after completing installation.

OVERHAUL

All Models

1. Thoroughly clean the outside of the caliper.

2. Remove the dust boot retainer and the
boot.

3. Place a piece of hardwood in front of the
piston.

4. Gradually apply compressed air
through the hydraulic line fitting and withdraw the piston.

NOTE: *If the piston is frozen and cannot
be removed from the caliper, tap lightly
around it, while air pressure is being applied.*

5. Withdraw the piston and seal from the
caliper bore.

6. If necessary, remove the bleeder
screw.

7. Wash all of the parts in clean brake
fluid. Dry them off with compressed air.

CAUTION: *Do not wash the parts in kerosene or gasoline.*

Examine the caliper bore and piston for
scores, scratches, or rust. Replace either
part, as required. Minor scratches or scoring
can be corrected by dressing with crocus
cloth.

NOTE: *Discard the old piston seal and
dust boot. Replace them with new ones.*

Apply clean brake fluid to the piston and
bore. Assemble the caliper in the reverse
order of disassembly. Install it on the car and
bleed the brake system.

Brake Disc Rotor

REMOVAL AND INSTALLATION

1. Remove the caliper assembly, as detailed in the appropriate section above.

NOTE: *It is unnecessary to completely remove the caliper from the car. Leave the
hydraulic line connected to it and wire the
caliper to the underbody of the car so that
it is out of the way.*

2. Check disc runout, as detailed below,
before removing it from the car.

3. Withdraw the cotter pin, nut lock, adjusting nut, and washer from the spindle.

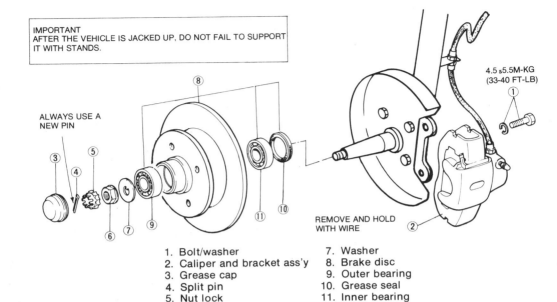

IMPORTANT
AFTER THE VEHICLE IS JACKED UP, DO NOT FAIL TO SUPPORT
IT WITH STANDS.

ALWAYS USE A
NEW PIN

4.5 s5.5M-KG
(33-40 FT-LB)

REMOVE AND HOLD
WITH WIRE

1. Bolt/washer
2. Caliper and bracket ass'y
3. Grease cap
4. Split pin
5. Nut lock
6. Nut
7. Washer
8. Brake disc
9. Outer bearing
10. Grease seal
11. Inner bearing

Front brake caliper, disc and bearing assembly—GLC rear wheel drive

Checking the front brake disc runout

4. Take the thrust washer and outer bearing off the hub.

5. Pull the brake disc/wheel hub assembly off of the spindle.

6. Unbolt and separate the brake disc from the hub, after matchmarking them for proper installation.

CAUTION: *Do not drive the disc off of the hub.*

Installation of the disc and hub is performed in the reverse order of removal. Adjust the bearing preload, as detailed below.

INSPECTION

1. Measure the lateral runout of the disc with a dial indicator while the disc is still installed on the spindle.

NOTE: *Be sure that the wheel bearings are adjusted properly before checking runout.*

2. If runout exceeds specification, replace or resurface the disc.

3. Inspect the surface of the disc for scores or pits and resurface it, if necessary.

4. If the disc is resurfaced, its thickness should be no less than the figure shown in the Brake Specifications Chart.

Wheel Bearings

NOTE: *See Hub and Steering Knuckle in Chapter 8 for the GLC front wheel drive front wheel bearing service.*

REMOVAL AND INSTALLATION

1. Remove the brake disc/hub assembly and separate them, as detailed earlier.

2. Drive the seal out and then remove the inner bearing from the hub.

3. Drive the outer bearing races out with a brass drift applied to the slots provided for this purpose.

4. Clean the inner and outer bearings completely and dry them with compressed air.

CAUTION: *Do not use compressed air to spin the bearings dry.*

5. Clean the spindle and the hub cavity with solvent.

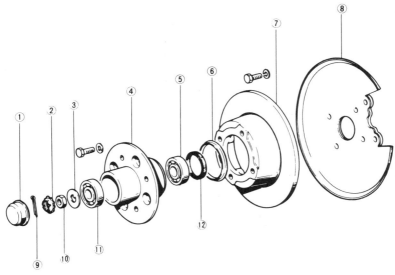

1. Grease cap
2. Nut lock
3. Flat washer
4. Hub
5. Inner bearing
6. Dust ring
7. Brake disc
8. Backing plate
9. Cotter pin
10. Adjusting nut
11. Outer bearing
12. Grease seal

RX-3 front wheel hub assembly—RX-2 similar

Installation is performed in the reverse order of removal. The following points should be noted, however:

1. Repack the bearings and the hub cavity with lithium grease.

CAUTION: *Do not over pack them.*

2. Install the wheel hub-to-brake disc bolts to 36 ft. lbs. torque.

3. Adjust the bearing preload, as described below.

NOTE: *Rear wheel bearing service on GLC front wheel drive model is the same as the previous section.*

PRELOAD ADJUSTMENT

NOTE: *This operation is performed with the wheel, grease cap, nut lock, and cotter pin removed.*

1. On GLC and 626, torque adjusting nut to 14–18 ft. lbs. then rotate the brake disc to seat the bearings. On all other models, rotate the hub/disc assembly while tightening the adjusting nut to seat the bearings.

2. Back off on the adjusting nut about $\frac{1}{6}$ of a turn.

3. Hook a spring scale in one of the bolt holes on the hub.

4. Pull the spring scale squarely, until the hub just begins to rotate. The scale reading should be 0.9–2.2 lbs. except on the GLC and 626. GLC reading is .33–1.32 lbs. 626

Checking front wheel bearing preload

reading is 0.77–1.92 lbs. Tighten the adjusting nut until the proper spring scale reading is obtained.

5. Place the castellated nut lock over the adjusting nut. Align one of the slots on the nut lock with the hole in the spindle and fit a new cotter pin into place.

REAR DISC BRAKES

Rear disc brakes are used on the Cosmo only. Basic design of the caliper and pads is identical to that of the front disc brakes on that car; therefore, for pad removal and installation, caliper removal and installation, and caliper overhaul, see applicable procedures for front disc brakes. Rear disc brake disc removal and installation procedure is provided below.

Brake Discs

1. Securely support the vehicle on stands and remove the wheels. Check the later runout of the disc with a dial indicator—limit is .0039 in.

2. Remove the bolts attaching the caliper bracket, and remove the caliper and bracket as an assembly, and wire it to the rear spring.

3. Fully release the parking brake. Remove the disc attaching screws, install them into the tapped holes about 90 degrees from their normal position, and screw them in evenly to force the disc off the axle shaft flange. Remove screws from disc.

4. To install, position the disc, aligning identification marks on axle shaft flange and disc. Install mounting screws. If a new disc is being installed, install it in each of the four possible positions and check lateral runout with a dial indicator. Install the disc in the position in which runout is minimized, and then match mark disc and axle flange.

REAR DRUM BRAKES

Brake Drums
REMOVAL AND INSTALLATION

NOTE: *On GLC front wheel drive models; disconnect the hand brake cable from the*

---

lever at the backing plate. Move lever toward plate to release brake shoe tension.

1. Remove the wheel disc and loosen the lug nuts.

2. Raise the rear of the car and support it with jackstands.

CAUTION: *Be sure that the car is securely supported. Remember, you will be working underneath it.*

3. Remove the lug nuts and the rear wheel.

4. Be sure that the parking brake is fully released.

5. Remove the bolts which secure the drum to the rear axle shaft flange or center locknut.

NOTE: *If the drum will not come off easily, screw the drum securing bolts into the two tapped holes in the drum. Tighten the bolts evenly in order to force the drum away from the flange.*

Rear brake drum installation is performed in the reverse order of removal. Adjust the shoes after installation is completed or prior to installation on GLC (fwd).

INSPECTION

1. Examine the drum for cracks or overheating spots. Replace the drum if either of these are present.

IMPORTANT
After the vehicle is jacked up, do not fail to support it with stands.

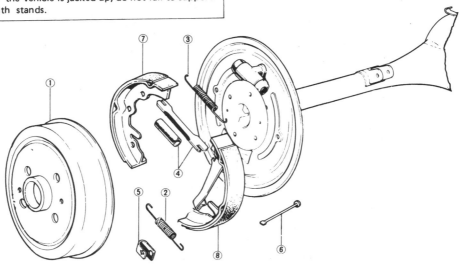

1. Drum	5. Retaining spring
2. Return spring	6. Guide pin
3. Return spring	7. Brake shoe
4. Parking brake strut	8. Brake shoe

Rear brake assembly—GLC

2. Check the drum for scoring. Light scoring can be corrected with sandpaper.

3. Check the drum with a dial indicator for out of roundness; turn the drum if it is beyond the specifications shown in the Brake Specifications Chart.

4. If the drum must be turned because of excessive scoring or out of roundness, the drum's inside diameter should not exceed the specifications shown in the chart.

RX-2 models—7.9135 inches

NOTE: *If one drum is turned, the opposite drum should also be turned to the same size.*

Brake Shoes

REMOVAL AND INSTALLATION

Except GLC-Front Wheel Drive

1. Perform the brake drum removal procedure, as detailed above.

2. Remove the return springs from the upper side of the shoe using a brake spring removal tool.

3. Remove the return springs from the lower side of the shoes in the same manner as Step 2.

4. Remove the shoe retaining spring
   a. On RX-3, RX-4, 808 and Cosmo models by removing the retaining pin with pliers.
   b. On RX-2, 626 and GLC models by compressing the retaining spring while turning the pin 90°.

5. Withdraw the primary shoes and the parking brake link.

6. Disengage the parking brake lever from the secondary shoes by unfastening its retaining clip.

7. Remove the secondary shoe.

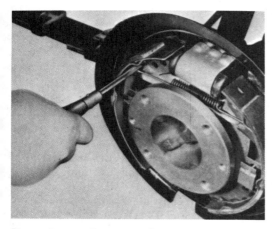

Shoe return spring removal

CAUTION: *Be careful not to get oil or grease on the lining material.*

Inspect the linings and replace them if they are badly burned or worn 0.039 in. beyond the specification for a new lining. (See "Brake Specification" chart)

Replace the linings if they can saturated with oil or grease.

Brake shoe installation is performed in the following manner:

1. Lubricate the threads of the adjusting screw, the sliding surfaces of the shoes, and the backing plate flanges with a small quantity of grease.

CAUTION: *Be careful not to get grease on the lining surfaces.*

2. Install the eye of the parking brake cable through the parking brake lever which has previously been installed on the secondary shoe and secured with its retaining clip.

3. Fit the link between the shoes.

4. Engage the shoes with the slots in the anchor (adjusting screw) and the wheel cylinder.

5. Fasten the shoes to the backing plate with the retaining springs and pins.

6. Install the shoe return springs with the tool used during removal.

7. Install the drums and adjust the shoes as detailed elsewhere.

NOTE: *If a slight amount of grease has gotten on the shoes during installation, it may be removed by light sanding.*

GLC—Front Wheel Drive

1. Loosen the rear wheel lugs, raise the rear of the car and support it safely on jackstands. Remove the rear tire and wheel.

2. Remove the rear brake drum. Clean the dirt from the brake components with a dry brush.

3. Disconnect the parking brake cable from the lever at the rear of the brake mounting plate.

4. Remove the lower return spring from between the two brake shoes. Disconnect the upper return spring from the front brake shoe. Remove the clip that holds the front shoe to the mounting plate and remove the front shoe.

5. Disconnect the adjuster spring from the rear brake shoe. Remove the mounting clip and the rear brake shoe.

6. Push on the adjuster lever while rotating a screwdriver between and quadrant and the knurled pin to retract the self adjuster.

7. Apply a small amount of grease to the

mounting plate brake shoe contact points. Install the shoes, mounting clips and springs in the reverse order of removal.

8. Install the brake drum using a new hub nut (be sure to stake the nut). Connect the parking brake cables. Bleed the brakes if necessary. Pump the pedal several times to adjust the drum to shoe clearance.

Wheel Cylinders
REMOVAL AND INSTALLATION

1. Remove the brake drums and shoes as detailed above.

2. Disconnect the hydraulic line from the wheel cylinder by unfastening the nut on the rear of the backing plate.

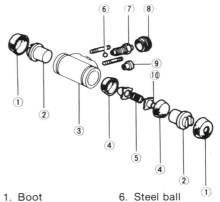

1. Boot
2. Piston
3. Cylinder body
4. Piston cup
5. Return spring
6. Steel ball
7. Bleeder screw
8. Bleeder screw cap
9. Hydraulic line seat
10. Pushrod

Rear wheel cylinder components—typical

Brake Specifications
All measurements given are (in.) unless noted

Model	Lug Nut Torque (ft. lbs.)	Master Cylinder Bore	Brake Disc		Brake Drum			Minimum Lining Thickness	
			Minimum Thickness	Maximum Run-Out	Diameter	Max. Machine O/S	Max. Wear Limit	Front	Rear
RX-2	65–72	0.875	0.433	0.003	7.874	7.90	7.9135	0.276	0.039
RX-3	65	0.875	0.394	0.003	7.874	7.90	7.9135	0.276	0.039
RX-4	65–72	0.875	0.433	0.004	9.0	9.025	9.0395	0.276	0.039
B1600	65–72	0.750	—	—	10.236 ③	10.276 ④	—	0.039	0.039
Rotary Pickup	65–72	0.875	0.433	0.004	10.236	10.275	—	0.276	0.039
808	65–72	0.8125	0.394	0.004	7.874	7.90	7.9135	0.256	0.039
Cosmo	65–72	0.875	0.6693 ①	0.0024 ②	—	—	—	0.276	0.276
GLC (RWD)	65–72 ⑥	13/16	0.4724	0.0024	7.874	⑤	7.9135	0.276	0.039
GLC (FWD)	65–80	13/16	0.039	0.004	7.09	⑤	7.13	0.276	0.039
626	65–80	7/8	0.4724	0.004	7.874	⑤	7.9135	0.256	0.039

① Rear: 0.354   (RWD) Rear Wheel Drive
② Rear: 0.004   (FWD) Front Wheel Drive
③ Front: 10.236
④ Front: 10.276
⑤ No machining maximum given—remove minimum amount which smooths surface, then ensure drum inner diameter meets specification
⑥ 65–80—1979–80

NOTE: *Minimum lining thickness is as recommended by the manufacturer. Due to variations in state inspection regulations, the minimum allowable thickness may be different than recommended by the manufacturer.*

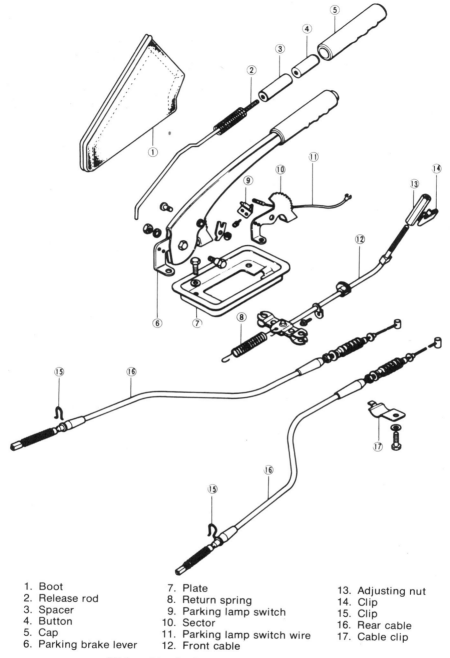

1. Boot
2. Release rod
3. Spacer
4. Button
5. Cap
6. Parking brake lever
7. Plate
8. Return spring
9. Parking lamp switch
10. Sector
11. Parking lamp switch wire
12. Front cable
13. Adjusting nut
14. Clip
15. Clip
16. Rear cable
17. Cable clip

RX-3 parking brake components—RX-2 similar

3. Plug the line to prevent dirt from entering the system or brake fluid from leaking out.

4. Unfasten the nuts which secure the wheel cylinder to the backing plate and remove the cylinder.

Installation of the wheel cylinder is performed in the reverse order of removal.

Bleed the hydraulic system and adjust the brake shoes after installation is completed.

OVERHAUL

1. Remove the boots at either end of the wheel cylinder.

2. Withdraw the pistons, piston cups,

push rods, filling blocks (GLC and 626 only), and return spring.

3. Wash all of the components in clean brake fluid.

CAUTION: *Never use kerosene or gasoline to clean wheel cylinder components.*

Check the cylinder bore and piston for roughness or scoring. Use a wheel cylinder hone, if necessary.

Measure the clearance between the cylinder and the piston with a feeler gauge. If the clearance is greater then 0.006 in., replace either the piston or the cylinder.

Examine the piston cups for wear, softening, or swelling; replace them if necessary.

Assembly is performed as follows:

1. Apply clean brake fluid to the cylinder bore, pistons, and cups.

2. Fit the steel ball into the bleed hole and install the screw, if they were removed.

3. Insert the parts into the cylinder bore in the reverse order of removal.

NOTE: *Install the piston cups so that their flat side is facing outward.*

4. Fit the boots over both ends of the cylinder.

PARKING BRAKE

ADJUSTMENT

1. Adjust the rear brake shoes. Note that on Cosmo, rear (parking) brake shoes are ad-

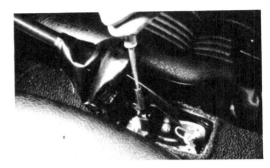

Adjusting the parking brake

justed the same way as ordinary rear drum brakes are adjusted.

2. Adjust the front cable with the nut or screw located at the rear of the parking brake handle. The handle should require 3–7 notches for RX-3, RX-4 GLC (rear wheel drive) and Cosmo models, 3–4 notches for 808, 2–3 notches for RX-2 models and 5–7 notches for 626 models and 5–9 notches for GLC front wheel drive to apply the parking brake.

3. Operate the parking brake several times; check to see that the rear wheels do not drag when it is fully released.

Body

You can repair most minor auto body damage yourself. Minor damage usually falls into one of several categories: (1) small scratches and dings in the paint that can be repaired without the use of body filler, (2) deep scratches and dents that require body filler, but do not require pulling, or hammering metal back into shape and (3) rust-out repairs. The repair sequences illustrated in this chapter are typical of these types of repairs. If you want to get involved in more complicated repairs including pulling or hammering sheet metal back into shape, you will probably need more detailed instructions. Chilton's *Minor Auto Body Repair, 2nd Edition* is a comprehensive guide to repairing auto body damage yourself.

TOOLS AND SUPPLIES

The list of tools and equipment you may need to fix minor body damage ranges from very basic hand tools to a wide assortment of specialized body tools. Most minor scratches, dings and rust holes can be fixed using an electric drill, wire wheel or grinder attachment, half-round plastic file, sanding block, various grades of sandpaper (#36, which is coarse through #600, which is fine) in both wet and dry types, auto body plastic,

primer, touch-up paint, spreaders, newspaper and masking tape.

Most manufacturers of auto body repair products began supplying materials to professionals. Their knowledge of the best, most-used products has been translated into body repair kits for the do-it-yourselfer. Kits are available from a number of manufacturers and contain the necessary materials in the required amounts for the repair identified on the package.

Kits are available for a wide variety of uses, including:

- Rusted out metal
- All purpose kit for dents and holes
- Dents and deep scratches
- Fiberglass repair kit
- Epoxy kit for restyling.

Kits offer the advantage of buying what you need for the job. There is little waste and little chance of materials going bad from not being used. The same manufacturers also merchandise all of the individual products used—spreaders, dent pullers, fiberglass cloth, polyester resin, cream hardener, body filler, body files, sandpaper, sanding discs and holders, primer, spray paint, etc.

CAUTION: *Most of the products you will be using contain harmful chemicals, so be extremely careful. Always read the complete label before opening the containers. When* *you put them away for future use, be sure they are out of children's reach!*

Most auto body repair kits contain all the materials you need to do the job right in the kit. So, if you have a small rust spot or dent you want to fix, check the contents of the kit before you run out and buy any additional tools.

ALIGNING BODY PANELS

Doors

There are several methods of adjusting doors. Your vehicle will probably use one of those illustrated.

Whenever a door is removed and is to be reinstalled, you should matchmark the position of the hinges on the door pillars. The holes of the hinges and/or the hinge attaching points are usually oversize to permit alignment of doors. The striker plate is also moveable, through oversize holes, permitting up-and-down, in-and-out and fore-and-aft movement. Fore-and-aft movement is made by adding or subtracting shims from behind the striker and pillar post. The striker should be adjusted so that the door closes fully and remains closed, yet enters the lock freely.

DOOR HINGES

Don't try to cover up poor door adjustment with a striker plate adjustment. The gap on each side of the door should be equal and uniform and there should be no metal-to-metal contact as the door is opened or closed.

1. Determine which hinge bolts must be loosened to move the door in the desired direction.

2. Loosen the hinge bolt(s) just enough to allow the door to be moved with a padded pry bar.

3. Move the door a small amount and check the fit, after tightening the bolts. Be sure that there is no bind or interference with adjacent panels.

4. Repeat this until the door is properly positioned, and tighten all the bolts securely.

Hood, Trunk or Tailgate

As with doors, the outline of hinges should be scribed before removal. The hood and trunk can be aligned by loosening the hinge bolts in their slotted mounting holes and moving the hood or trunk lid as necessary.

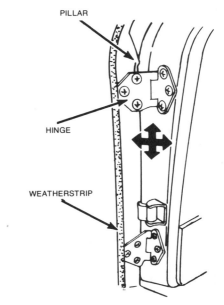

Door hinge adjustment

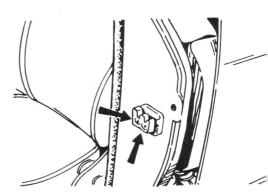

Move the door striker as indicated by arrows

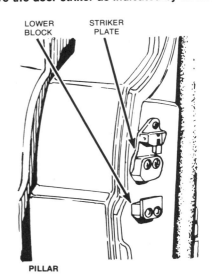

Striker plate and lower block

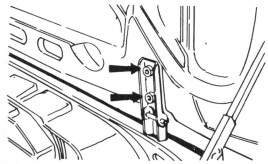

Loosen the hinge boots to permit fore-and-aft and horizontal adjustment

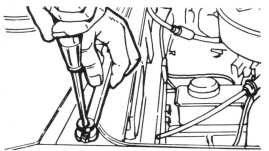

The hood is adjusted vertically by stop-screws at the front and/or rear

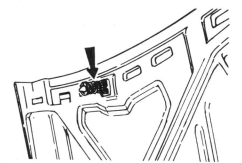

The hood pin can be adjusted for proper lock engagement

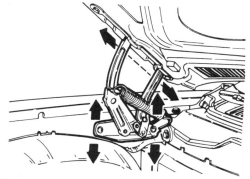

The height of the hood at the rear is adjusted by loosening the bolts that attach the hinge to the body and moving the hood up or down

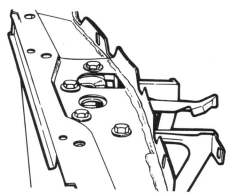

The base of the hood lock can also be repositioned slightly to give more positive lock engagement

The hood and trunk have adjustable catch locations to regulate lock engagement. Bumpers at the front and/or rear of the hood provide a vertical adjustment and the hood lockpin can be adjusted for proper engagement.

The tailgate on the station wagon can be adjusted by loosening the hinge bolts in their slotted mounting holes and moving the tailgate on its hinges. The latchplate and latch striker at the bottom of the tailgate opening can be adjusted to stop rattle. An adjustable bumper is located on each side.

RUST, UNDERCOATING, AND RUSTPROOFING

Rust

Rust is an electrochemical process. It works on ferrous metals (iron and steel) from the inside out due to exposure of unprotected surfaces to air and moisture. The possibility of rust exists practically nationwide—anywhere humidity, industrial pollution or chemical salts are present, rust can form. In coastal areas, the problem is high humidity and salt air; in snowy areas, the problem is chemical salt (de-icer) used to keep the roads clear, and in industrial areas, sulphur dioxide is present in the air from industrial pollution and is changed to sulphuric acid when it rains. The rusting process is accelerated by high temperatures, especially in snowy areas, when vehicles are driven over slushy roads and then left overnight in a heated garage.

Automotive styling also can be a contributor to rust formation. Spot welding of panels creates small pockets that trap moisture and form an environment for rust formation. Fortunately, auto manufacturers have been working hard to increase the corrosion protection of their products. Galvanized sheet metal enjoys much wider use, along with the increased use of plastic and various rust retardant coatings. Manufacturers are also designing out areas in the body where rust-forming moisture can collect.

To prevent rust, you must stop it before it gets started. On new vehicles, there are two ways to accomplish this.

First, the car or truck should be treated with a commercial rustproofing compound. There are many different brands of franchised rustproofers, but most processes involve spraying a waxy "self-healing" compound under the chassis, inside rocker panels, inside doors and fender liners and similar places where rust is likely to form. Prices for a quality rustproofing job range from $100–$250, depending on the area, the brand name and the size of the vehicle.

Ideally, the vehicle should be rustproofed as soon as possible following the purchase. The surfaces of the car or truck have begun to oxidize and deteriorate during shipping. In addition, the car may have sat on a dealer's lot or on a lot at the factory, and once the rust has progressed past the stage of light, powdery surface oxidation rustproofing is not likely to be worthwhile. Professional rustproofers feel that once rust has formed, rustproofing will simply seal in moisture already present. Most franchised rustproofing operations offer a 3–5 year warranty against rust-through, but will not support that warranty if the rustproofing is not applied within three months of the date of manufacture.

Undercoating should not be mistaken for rustproofing. Undercoating is a black, tar-like substance that is applied to the underside of a vehicle. Its basic function is to deaden noises that are transmitted from under the car. It simply cannot get into the crevices and seams where moisture tends to collect. In fact, it may clog up drainage holes and ventilation passages. Some undercoatings also tend to crack or peel with age and only create more moisture and corrosion attracting pockets.

The second thing you should do immediately after purchasing the car is apply a paint sealant. A sealant is a petroleum based product marketed under a wide variety of brand names. It has the same protective properties as a good wax, but bonds to the paint with a chemically inert layer that seals it from the air. If air can't get at the surface, oxidation cannot start.

The paint sealant kit consists of a base coat and a conditioning coat that should be applied every 6–8 months, depending on the manufacturer. The base coat must be applied before waxing, or the wax must first be removed.

Third, keep a garden hose handy for your car in winter. Use it a few times on nice days during the winter for underneath areas, and it will pay big dividends when spring arrives. Spraying under the fenders and other areas which even car washes don't reach will help remove road salt, dirt and other build-ups which help breed rust. Adjust the nozzle to a high-force spray. An old brush will help break up residue, permitting it to be washed away more easily.

It's a somewhat messy job, but worth it in the long run because rust often starts in those hidden areas.

At the same time, wash grime off the door sills and, more importantly, the under portions of the doors, plus the tailgate if you have a station wagon or truck. Applying a coat of wax to those areas at least once before and once during winter will help fend off rust.

When applying the wax to the under part of the doors, you will note small drain holes. These holes often are plugged with under coating or dirt. Make sure they are cleaned out to prevent water build-up inside the doors. A small punch or penknife will do the job.

Water from the high-pressure sprays in car washes sometimes can get into the housings for parking and taillights, so take a close look. If they contain water merely loosen the retaining screws and the water should run out.

Repairing Scratches and Small Dents

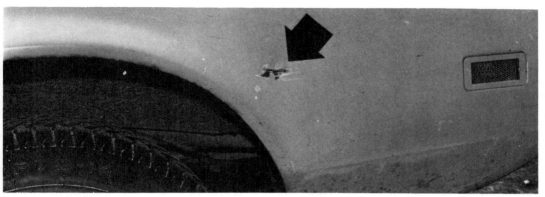

Step 1. This dent (arrow) is typical of a deep scratch or minor dent. If deep enough, the dent or scratch can be pulled out or hammered out from behind. In this case no straightening is necessary

Step 2. Using an 80-grit grinding disc on an electric drill grind the paint from the surrounding area down to bare metal. This will provide a rough surface for the body filler to grab

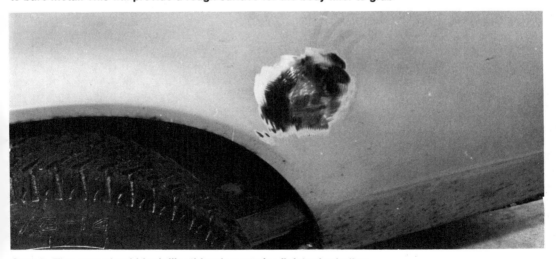

Step 3. The area should look like this when you're finished grinding

Step 4. Mix the body filler and cream hardener according to the directions

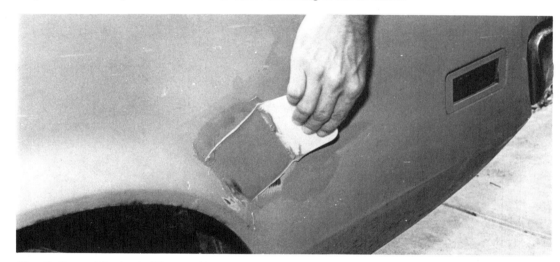

Step 5. Spread the body filler evenly over the entire area. Be sure to cover the area completely

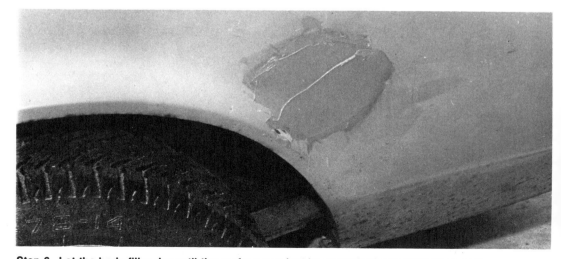

Step 6. Let the body filler dry until the surface can just be scratched with your fingernail

Step 7. Knock the high spots from the body filler with a body file

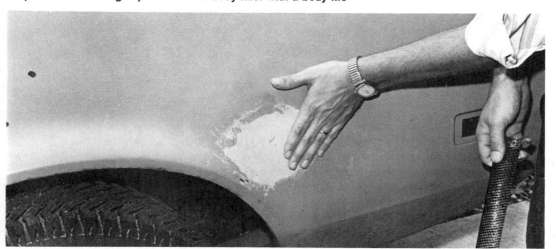

Step 8. Check frequently with the palm of your hand for high and low spots. If you wind up with low spots, you may have to apply another layer of filler

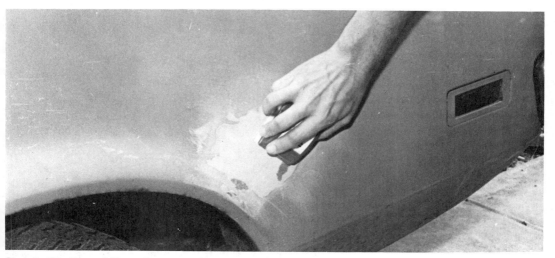

Step 9. Block sand the entire area with 320 grit paper

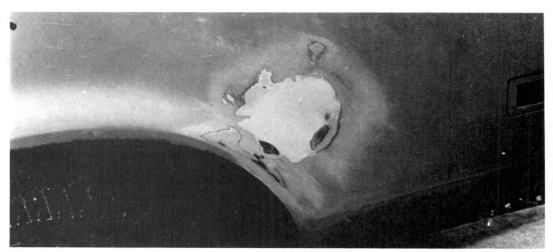

Step 10. When you're finished, the repair should look like this. Note the sand marks extending 2—3 inches out from the repaired area

Step 11. Prime the entire area with automotive primer

Step 12. The finished repair ready for the final paint coat. Note that the primer has covered the sanding marks (see Step 10). A repair of this size should be able to be spotpainted with good results

REPAIRING RUST HOLES

One thing you have to remember about rust: even if you grind away all the rusted metal in a panel, and repair the area with any of the kits available, *eventually* the rust will return. There are two reasons for this. One, rust is a chemical reaction that causes pressure under the repair from the inside out. That's how the blisters form. Two, the back side of the panel (and the repair) is wide open to moisture, and unpainted body filler acts like a sponge. That's why the best solution to rust problems is to remove the rusted panel and install a new one or have the rusted area cut out and a new piece of sheet metal welded in its place. The trouble with welding is the expense; sometimes it will cost more than the car or truck is worth.

One of the better solutions to do-it-yourself rust repair is the process using a fiberglass cloth repair kit (shown here). This will give a strong repair that resists cracking and moisture and is relatively easy to use. It can be used on large or small holes and also can be applied over contoured surfaces.

Step 1. Rust areas such as this are common and are easily fixed

Step 2. Grind away all traces of rust with a 24-grit grinding disc. Be sure to grind back 3—4 inches from the edge of the hole down to bare metal and be sure all traces of rust are removed

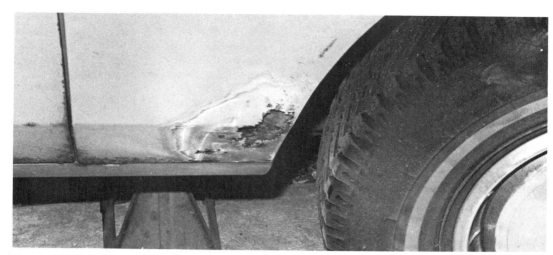

Step 3. Be sure all rust is removed from the edges of the metal. The edges must be ground back to un-rusted metal

Step 4. If you are going to use release film, cut a piece about 2″ larger than the area you have sanded. Place the film over the repair and mark the sanded area on the film. Avoid any unnecessary wrinkling of the film

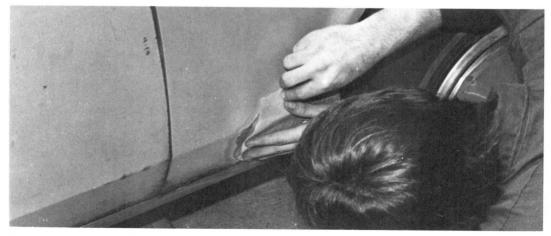

Step 5. Cut 2 pieces of fiberglass matte. One piece should be about 1″ smaller than the sanded area and the second piece should be 1″ smaller than the first. Use sharp scissors to avoid loose ends

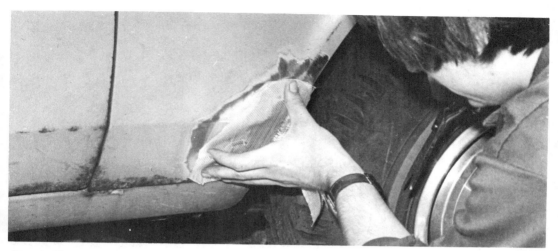

Step 6. Check the dimensions of the release film and cloth by holding them up to the repair area

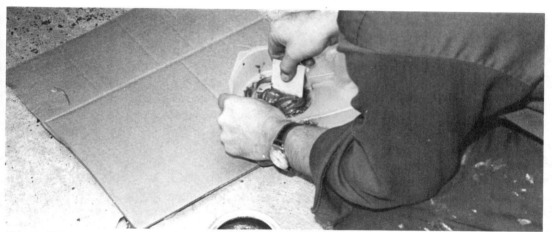

Step 7. Mix enough repair jelly and cream hardener in the mixing tray to saturate the fiberglass material or fill the repair area. Follow the directions on the container

Step 8. Lay the release sheet on a flat surface and spread an even layer of filler, large enough to cover the repair. Lay the smaller piece of fiberglass cloth in the center of the sheet and spread another layer of repair jelly over the fiberglass cloth. Repeat the operation for the larger piece of cloth. If the fiberglass cloth is not used, spread the repair jelly on the release film, concentrated in the middle of the repair

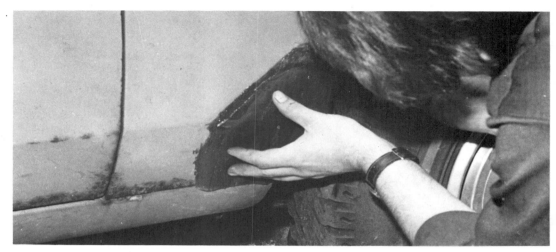

Step 9. Place the repair material over the repair area, with the release film facing outward

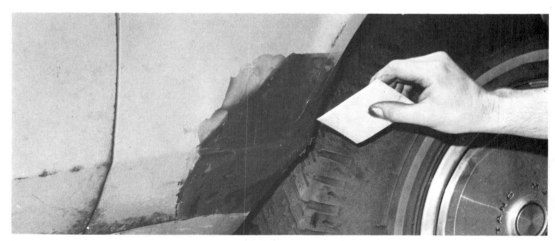

Step 10. Use a spreader and work from the center outward to smooth the material, following the body contours. Be sure to remove all air bubbles

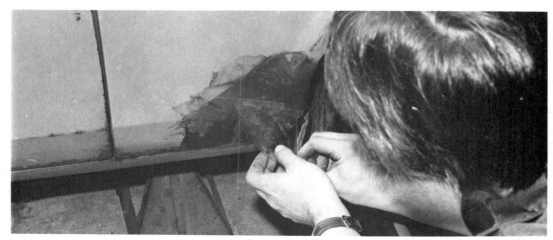

Step 11. Wait until the repair has dried tack-free and peel off the release sheet. The ideal working temperature is 65—90° F. Cooler or warmer temperatures or high humidity may require additional curing time

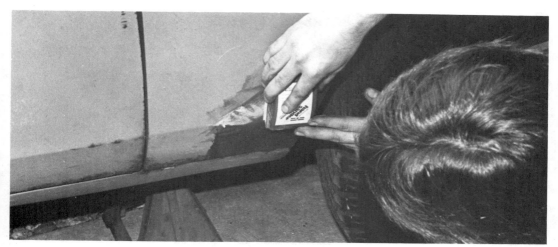

Step 12. Sand and feather-edge the entire area. The initial sanding can be done with a sanding disc on an electric drill if care is used. Finish the sanding with a block sander

Step 13. When the area is sanded smooth, mix some topcoat and hardener and apply it directly with a spreader. This will give a smooth finish and prevent the glass matte from showing through the paint

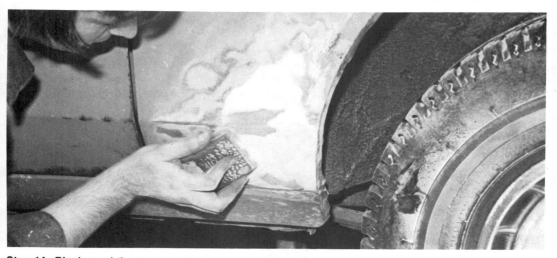

Step 14. Block sand the topcoat with finishing sandpaper

Step 15. To finish this repair, grind out the surface rust along the top edge of the rocker panel

Step 16. Mix some more repair jelly and cream hardener and apply it directly over the surface

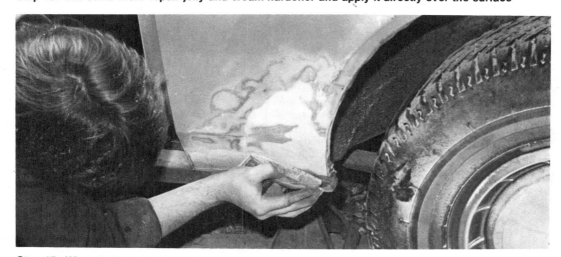

Step 17. When it dries tack-free, block sand the surface smooth

Step 18. If necessary, mask off adjacent panels and spray the entire repair with primer. You are now ready for a color coat

AUTO BODY CARE

There are hundreds—maybe thousands—of products on the market, all designed to protect or aid your car's finish in some manner. There are as many different products as there are ways to use them, but they all have one thing in common—the surface must be clean.

Washing

The primary ingredient for washing your car is water, preferably "soft" water. In many areas of the country, the local water supply is "hard" containing many minerals. The little rings or film that is left on your car's surface after it has dried is the result of "hard" water.

Since you usually can't change the local water supply, the next best thing is to dry the surface before it has a chance to dry itself.

Into the water you usually add soap. Don't use detergents or common, coarse soaps. Your car's paint never truly dries out, but is always evaporating residual oils into the air. Harsh detergents will remove these oils, causing the paint to dry faster than normal. Instead use warm water and a non-detergent soap made especially for waxed surfaces or a liquid soap made for waxed surfaces or a liquid soap made for washing dishes by hand.

Other products that can be used on painted surfaces include baking soda or plain soda water for stubborn dirt.

Wash the car completely, starting at the top, and rinse it completely clean. Abrasive grit should be loaded off under water pressure; scrubbing grit off will scratch the finish. The best washing tool is a sponge, cleaning mitt or soft towel. Whichever you choose, replace it often as each tends to absorb grease and dirt.

Other ways to get a better wash include:

• Don't wash your car in the sun or when the finish is hot.

• Use water pressure to remove caked-on dirt.

• Remove tree-sap and bird effluence immediately. Such substances will eat through wax, polish and paint.

One of the best implements to dry your car is a turkish towel or an old, soft bath towel. Anything with a deep nap will hold any dirt in suspension and not grind it into the paint.

Harder cloths will only grind the grit into the paint making more scratches. Always start drying at the top, followed by the hood and trunk and sides. You'll find there's always more dirt near the rocker panels and wheelwells which will wind up on the rest of the car if you dry these areas first.

Cleaners, Waxes and Polishes

Before going any farther you should know the function of various products.

Cleaners—remove the top layer of dead pigment or paint.

Rubbing or polishing compounds—used to remove stubborn dirt, get rid of minor scratches, smooth away imperfections and partially restore badly weathered paint.

Polishes—contain no abrasives or waxes; they shine the paint by adding oils to the paint.

Waxes—are a protective coating for the polish.

CLEANERS AND COMPOUNDS

Before you apply any wax, you'll have to remove oxidation, road film and other types of pollutants that washing alone will not remove.

The paint on your car never dries completely. There are always residual oils evaporating from the paint into the air. When enough oils are present in the paint, it has a healthy shine (gloss). When too many oils evaporate the paint takes on a whitish cast known as oxidation. The idea of polishing and waxing is to keep enough oil present in the painted surface to prevent oxidation; but when it occurs, the only recourse is to remove the top layer of "dead" paint, exposing the healthy paint underneath.

Products to remove oxidation and road film are sold under a variety of generic names—polishes, cleaner, rubbing compound, cleaner/polish, polish/cleaner, self-polishing wax, pre-wax cleaner, finish restorer and many more. Regardless of name there are two types of cleaners—abrasive cleaners (sometimes called polishing or rubbing compounds) that remove oxidation by grinding away the top layer of "dead" paint, or chemical cleaners that dissolve the "dead" pigment, allowing it to be wiped away.

Abrasive cleaners, by their nature, leave thousands of minute scratches in the finish, which must be polished out later. These should only be used in extreme cases, but are usually the only thing to use on badly oxidized paint finishes. Chemical cleaners are much milder but are not strong enough for severe cases of oxidation or weathered paint.

The most popular cleaners are liquid or paste abrasive polishing and rubbing compounds. Polishing compounds have a finer abrasive grit for medium duty work. Rubbing compounds are a coarser abrasive and for heavy duty work. Unless you are familiar with how to use compounds, be very careful. Excessive rubbing with any type of compound or cleaner can grind right through the paint to primer or bare metal. Follow the directions on the container—depending on type, the cleaner may or may not be OK for your paint. For example, some cleaners are not formulated for acrylic lacquer finishes.

When a small area needs compounding or heavy polishing, it's best to do the job by hand. Some people prefer a powered buffer for large areas. Avoid cutting through the paint along styling edges on the body. Small, hand operations where the compound is applied and rubbed using cloth folded into a thick ball allow you to work in straight lines along such edges.

To avoid cutting through on the edges when using a power buffer, try masking tape. Just cover the edge with tape while using power. Then finish the job by hand with the tape removed. Even then work carefully. The paint tends to be a lot thinner along the sharp ridges stamped into the panels.

Whether compounding by machine or by hand, only work on a small area and apply the compound sparingly. If the materials are spread too thin, or allowed to sit too long, they dry out. Once dry they lose the ability to deliver a smooth, clean finish. Also, dried out polish tends to cause the buffer to stick in one spot. This in turn can burn or cut through the finish.

WAXES AND POLISHES

Your car's finish can be protected in a number of ways. A cleaner/wax or polish/cleaner followed by wax or variations of each all provide good results. The two-step approach (polish followed by wax) is probably slightly better but consumes more time and effort. Properly fed with oils, your paint should never need cleaning, but despite the best polishing job, it won't last unless it's protected with wax. Without wax, polish must be renewed at least once a month to prevent oxidation. Years ago (some still swear by it today), the best wax was made from the Brazilian palm, the Carnuba, favored for its vegetable base and high melting point. However, modern synthetic waxes are harder, which means they protect against moisture better, and chemically inert silicone is used for a long lasting protection. The only problem with silicone wax is that it penetrates all layers of paint. To repaint or touch up a panel or car protected by silicone wax, you have to completely strip the finish to avoid "fish-eyes."

Under normal conditions, silicone waxes will last 4–6 months, but you have to be careful of wax build-up from too much waxing. Too thick a coat of wax is just as bad as no wax at all; it stops the paint from breathing.

Combination cleaners/waxes have become popular lately because they remove the old layer of wax plus light oxidation, while putting on a fresh coat of wax at the same time. Some cleaners/waxes contain abrasive cleaners which require caution, although many cleaner/waxes use a chemical cleaner.

Applying Wax or Polish

You may view polishing and waxing your car as a pleasant way to spend an afternoon, or as a boring chore, but it has to be done to keep the paint on your car. Caring for the paint doesn't require special tools, but you should follow a few rules.

1. Use a good quality wax.

2. Before applying any wax or polish, be sure the surface is completely clean. Just because the car looks clean, doesn't mean it's ready for polish or wax.

3. If the finish on your car is weathered, dull, or oxidized, it will probably have to be compounded to remove the old or oxidized paint. If the paint is simply dulled from lack of care, one of the non-abrasive cleaners known as polishing compounds will do the trick. If the paint is severely scratched or really dull, you'll probably have to use a rubbing compound to prepare the finish for waxing. If you're not sure which one to use, use the polishing compound, since you can easily ruin the finish by using too strong a compound.

4. Don't apply wax, polish or compound in direct sunlight, even if the directions on the can say you can. Most waxes will not cure properly in bright sunlight and you'll probably end up with a blotchy looking finish.

5. Don't rub the wax off too soon. The result will be a wet, dull looking finish. Let the wax dry thoroughly before buffing it off.

6. A constant debate among car enthusiasts is how wax should be applied. Some maintain pastes or liquids should be applied in a circular motion, but body shop experts have long thought that this approach results in barely detectable circular abrasions, especially on cars that are waxed frequently. They advise rubbing in straight lines, especially if any kind of cleaner is involved.

7. If an applicator is not supplied with the wax, use a piece of soft cheesecloth or very soft lint-free material. The same applies to buffing the surface.

SPECIAL SURFACES

One-step combination cleaner and wax formulas shouldn't be used on many of the special surfaces which abound on cars. The one-step materials contain abrasives to achieve a clean surface under the wax top coat. The abrasives are so mild that you could clean a car every week for a couple of years without fear of rubbing through the paint. But this same level of abrasiveness might, through repeated use, damage decals used for special trim effects. This includes wide stripes, wood-grain trim and other appliques.

Painted plastics must be cleaned with care. If a cleaner is too aggressive it will cut through the paint and expose the primer. If bright trim such as polished aluminum or chrome is painted, cleaning must be performed with even greater care. If rubbing compound is being used, it will cut faster than polish.

Abrasive cleaners will dull an acrylic finish. The best way to clean these newer finishes is with a non-abrasive liquid polish. Only dirt and oxidation, not paint, will be removed.

Taking a few minutes to read the instructions on the can of polish or wax will help prevent making serious mistakes. Not all preparations will work on all surfaces. And some are intended for power application while others will only work when applied by hand.

Don't get the idea that just pouring on some polish and then hitting it with a buffer will suffice. Power equipment speeds the operation. But it also adds a measure of risk. It's very easy to damage the finish if you use the wrong methods or materials.

Caring for Chrome

Read the label on the container. Many products are formulated specifically for chrome, but others contain abrasives that will scratch the chrome finish. If it isn't recommended for chrome, don't use it.

Never use steel wool or kitchen soap pads to clean chrome. Be careful not to get chrome cleaner on paint or interior vinyl surfaces. If you do, get it off immediately.

Troubleshooting

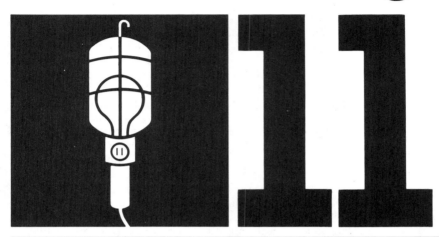

This section is designed to aid in the quick, accurate diagnosis of automotive problems. While automotive repairs can be made by many people, accurate troubleshooting is a rare skill for the amateur and professional alike.

In its simplest state, troubleshooting is an exercise in logic. It is essential to realize that an automobile is really composed of a series of systems. Some of these systems are interrelated; others are not. Automobiles operate within a framework of logical rules and physical laws, and the key to troubleshooting is a good understanding of all the automotive systems.

This section breaks the car or truck down into its component systems, allowing the problem to be isolated. The charts and diagnostic road maps list the most common problems and the most probable causes of trouble. Obviously it would be impossible to list every possible problem that could happen along with every possible cause, but it will locate MOST problems and eliminate a lot of unnecessary guesswork. The systematic format will locate problems within a given system, but, because many automotive systems are interrelated, the solution to your particular problem may be found in a number of systems on the car or truck.

USING THE TROUBLESHOOTING CHARTS

This book contains all of the specific information that the average do-it-yourself mechanic needs to repair and maintain his or her car or truck. The troubleshooting charts are designed to be used in conjunction with the specific procedures and information in the text. For instance, troubleshooting a point-type ignition system is fairly standard for all models, but you may be directed to the text to find procedures for troubleshooting an individual type of electronic ignition. You will also have to refer to the specification charts throughout the book for specifications applicable to your car or truck.

TOOLS AND EQUIPMENT

The tools illustrated in Chapter 1 (plus two more diagnostic pieces) will be adequate to troubleshoot most problems. The two other tools needed are a voltmeter and an ohmmeter. These can be purchased separately or in combination, known as a VOM meter.

In the event that other tools are required, they will be noted in the procedures.

Troubleshooting Engine Problems

See Chapters 2, 3, 4 for more information and service procedures.

Index to Systems

System	To Test	Group
Battery	Engine need not be running	1
Starting system	Engine need not be running	2
Primary electrical system	Engine need not be running	3
Secondary electrical system	Engine need not be running	4
Fuel system	Engine need not be running	5
Engine compression	Engine need not be running	6
Engine vacuum	Engine must be running	7
Secondary electrical system	Engine must be running	8
Valve train	Engine must be running	9
Exhaust system	Engine must be running	10
Cooling system	Engine must be running	11
Engine lubrication	Engine must be running	12

Index to Problems

Problem: Symptom	Begin at Specific Diagnosis, Number ____
Engine Won't Start:	
Starter doesn't turn	1.1, 2.1
Starter turns, engine doesn't	2.1
Starter turns engine very slowly	1.1, 2.4
Starter turns engine normally	3.1, 4.1
Starter turns engine very quickly	6.1
Engine fires intermittently	4.1
Engine fires consistently	5.1, 6.1
Engine Runs Poorly:	
Hard starting	3.1, 4.1, 5.1, 8.1
Rough idle	4.1, 5.1, 8.1
Stalling	3.1, 4.1, 5.1, 8.1
Engine dies at high speeds	4.1, 5.1
Hesitation (on acceleration from standing stop)	5.1, 8.1
Poor pickup	4.1, 5.1, 8.1
Lack of power	3.1, 4.1, 5.1, 8.1
Backfire through the carburetor	4.1, 8.1, 9.1
Backfire through the exhaust	4.1, 8.1, 9.1
Blue exhaust gases	6.1, 7.1
Black exhaust gases	5.1
Running on (after the ignition is shut off)	3.1, 8.1
Susceptible to moisture	4.1
Engine misfires under load	4.1, 7.1, 8.4, 9.1
Engine misfires at speed	4.1, 8.4
Engine misfires at idle	3.1, 4.1, 5.1, 7.1, 8.4

Sample Section

Test and Procedure	Results and Indications	Proceed to
4.1—Check for spark: Hold each spark plug wire approximately ¼" from ground with gloves or a heavy, dry rag. Crank the engine and observe the spark.	→ If no spark is evident:	→**4.2**
	→ If spark is good in some cases:	→**4.3**
	→ If spark is good in all cases:	→**4.6**

Specific Diagnosis

This section is arranged so that following each test, instructions are given to proceed to another, until a problem is diagnosed.

Section 1—Battery

Test and Procedure	Results and Indications	Proceed to
1.1—Inspect the battery visually for case condition (corrosion, cracks) and water level.	If case is cracked, replace battery:	**1.4**
	If the case is intact, remove corrosion with a solution of baking soda and water (**CAUTION:** *do not get the solution into the battery*), and fill with water:	**1.2**

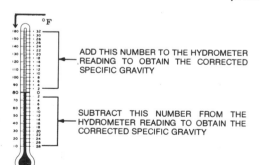

DIRT ON TOP OF BATTERY
CORROSION
PLUGGED VENT
LOOSE CABLE OR POSTS
CRACKS
LOW WATER LEVEL

Inspect the battery case

Test and Procedure	Results and Indications	Proceed to
1.2—Check the battery cable connections: Insert a screwdriver between the battery post and the cable clamp. Turn the headlights on high beam, and observe them as the screwdriver is gently twisted to ensure good metal to metal contact.	If the lights brighten, remove and clean the clamp and post; coat the post with petroleum jelly, install and tighten the clamp:	**1.4**
	If no improvement is noted:	**1.3**

TESTING BATTERY CABLE CONNECTIONS USING A SCREWDRIVER

Test and Procedure	Results and Indications	Proceed to
1.3—Test the state of charge of the battery using an individual cell tester or hydrometer.	If indicated, charge the battery. **NOTE:** *If no obvious reason exists for the low state of charge (i.e., battery age, prolonged storage), proceed to:*	**1.4**

°F

ADD THIS NUMBER TO THE HYDROMETER READING TO OBTAIN THE CORRECTED SPECIFIC GRAVITY

SUBTRACT THIS NUMBER FROM THE HYDROMETER READING TO OBTAIN THE CORRECTED SPECIFIC GRAVITY

Specific Gravity (@ 80° F.)

Minimum	Battery Charge
1.260	100% Charged
1.230	75% Charged
1.200	50% Charged
1.170	25% Charged
1.140	Very Little Power Left
1.110	Completely Discharged

The effects of temperature on battery specific gravity (left) and amount of battery charge in relation to specific gravity (right)

Test and Procedure	Results and Indications	Proceed to
1.4—Visually inspect battery cables for cracking, bad connection to ground, or bad connection to starter.	If necessary, tighten connections or replace the cables:	**2.1**

Section 2—Starting System
See Chapter 3 for service procedures

Test and Procedure	Results and Indications	Proceed to

Note: Tests in Group 2 are performed with coil high tension lead disconnected to prevent accidental starting.

Test and Procedure	Results and Indications	Proceed to
2.1—Test the starter motor and solenoid: Connect a jumper from the battery post of the solenoid (or relay) to the starter post of the solenoid (or relay).	If starter turns the engine normally:	2.2
	If the starter buzzes, or turns the engine very slowly:	2.4
	If no response, replace the solenoid (or relay).	3.1
	If the starter turns, but the engine doesn't, ensure that the flywheel ring gear is intact. If the gear is undamaged, replace the starter drive.	3.1
2.2—Determine whether ignition override switches are functioning properly (clutch start switch, neutral safety switch), by connecting a jumper across the switch(es), and turning the ignition switch to "start".	If starter operates, adjust or replace switch:	3.1
	If the starter doesn't operate:	2.3
2.3—Check the ignition switch "start" position: Connect a 12V test lamp or voltmeter between the starter post of the solenoid (or relay) and ground. Turn the ignition switch to the "start" position, and jiggle the key.	If the lamp doesn't light or the meter needle doesn't move when the switch is turned, check the ignition switch for loose connections, cracked insulation, or broken wires. Repair or replace as necessary:	3.1
	If the lamp flickers or needle moves when the key is jiggled, replace the ignition switch.	3.3

Checking the ignition switch "start" position

STARTER RELAY (IF EQUIPPED)

Test and Procedure	Results and Indications	Proceed to
2.4—Remove and bench test the starter, according to specifications in the engine electrical section.	If the starter does not meet specifications, repair or replace as needed:	3.1
	If the starter is operating properly:	2.5
2.5—Determine whether the engine can turn freely: Remove the spark plugs, and check for water in the cylinders. Check for water on the dipstick, or oil in the radiator. Attempt to turn the engine using an 18″ flex drive and socket on the crankshaft pulley nut or bolt.	If the engine will turn freely only with the spark plugs out, and hydrostatic lock (water in the cylinders) is ruled out, check valve timing:	9.2
	If engine will not turn freely, and it is known that the clutch and transmission are free, the engine must be disassembled for further evaluation:	Chapter 3

Section 3—Primary Electrical System

Test and Procedure	Results and Indications	Proceed to
3.1—Check the ignition switch "on" position: Connect a jumper wire between the distributor side of the coil and ground, and a 12V test lamp between the switch side of the coil and ground. Remove the high tension lead from the coil. Turn the ignition switch on and jiggle the key.	If the lamp lights:	**3.2**
	If the lamp flickers when the key is jiggled, replace the ignition switch:	**3.3**
	If the lamp doesn't light, check for loose or open connections. If none are found, remove the ignition switch and check for continuity. If the switch is faulty, replace it:	**3.3**

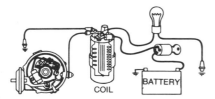

Checking the ignition switch "on" position

3.2—Check the ballast resistor or resistance wire for an open circuit, using an ohmmeter. See Chapter 3 for specific tests.	Replace the resistor or resistance wire if the resistance is zero. **NOTE:** *Some ignition systems have no ballast resistor.*	**3.3**

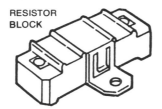

Two types of resistors

3.3—On point-type ignition systems, visually inspect the breaker points for burning, pitting or excessive wear. Gray coloring of the point contact surfaces is normal. Rotate the crankshaft until the contact heel rests on a high point of the distributor cam and adjust the point gap to specifications. On electronic ignition models, remove the distributor cap and visually inspect the armature. Ensure that the armature pin is in place, and that the armature is on tight and rotates when the engine is cranked. Make sure there are no cracks, chips or rounded edges on the armature.	If the breaker points are intact, clean the contact surfaces with fine emery cloth, and adjust the point gap to specifications. If the points are worn, replace them. On electronic systems, replace any parts which appear defective. If condition persists:	**3.4**

Test and Procedure	Results and Indications	Proceed to
3.4—On point-type ignition systems, connect a dwell-meter between the distributor primary lead and ground. Crank the engine and observe the point dwell angle. On electronic ignition systems, conduct a stator (magnetic pickup assembly) test. See Chapter 3.	On point-type systems, adjust the dwell angle if necessary. **NOTE:** *Increasing the point gap decreases the dwell angle and vice-versa.*	**3.6**
	If the dwell meter shows little or no reading;	**3.5**
	On electronic ignition systems, if the stator is bad, replace the stator. If the stator is good, proceed to the other tests in Chapter 3.	

Dwell is a function of point gap

3.5—On the point-type ignition systems, check the condenser for short: connect an ohmeter across the condenser body and the pigtail lead.	If any reading other than infinite is noted, replace the condenser	**3.6**

Checking the condenser for short

3.6—Test the coil primary resistance: On point-type ignition systems, connect an ohmmeter across the coil primary terminals, and read the resistance on the low scale. Note whether an external ballast resistor or resistance wire is used. On electronic ignition systems, test the coil primary resistance as in Chapter 3.	Point-type ignition coils utilizing ballast resistors or resistance wires should have approximately 1.0 ohms resistance. Coils with internal resistors should have approximately 4.0 ohms resistance. If values far from the above are noted, replace the coil.	**4.1**

Check the coil primary resistance

Section 4—Secondary Electrical System

See Chapters 2–3 for service procedures

Test and Procedure	Results and Indications	Proceed to
4.1—Check for spark: Hold each spark plug wire approximately ¼″ from ground with gloves or a heavy, dry rag. Crank the engine, and observe the spark.	If no spark is evident:	**4.2**
	If spark is good in some cylinders:	**4.3**
	If spark is good in all cylinders:	**4.6**

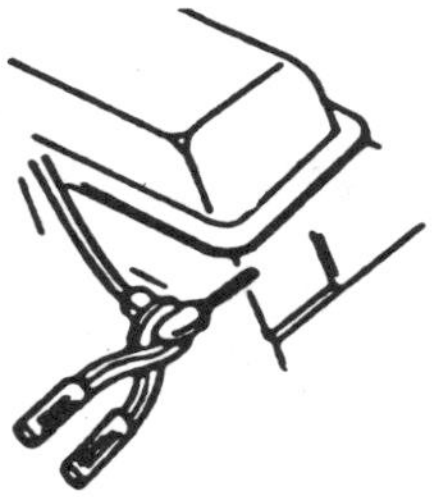

Check for spark at the plugs

4.2—Check for spark at the coil high tension lead: Remove the coil high tension lead from the distributor and position it approximately ¼″ from ground. Crank the engine and observe spark. **CAUTION:** *This test should not be performed on engines equipped with electronic ignition.*	If the spark is good and consistent:	**4.3**
	If the spark is good but intermittent, test the primary electrical system starting at 3.3:	**3.3**
	If the spark is weak or non-existent, replace the coil high tension lead, clean and tighten all connections and retest. If no improvement is noted:	**4.4**
4.3—Visually inspect the distributor cap and rotor for burned or corroded contacts, cracks, carbon tracks, or moisture. Also check the fit of the rotor on the distributor shaft (where applicable).	If moisture is present, dry thoroughly, and retest per 4.1:	**4.1**
	If burned or excessively corroded contacts, cracks, or carbon tracks are noted, replace the defective part(s) and retest per 4.1:	**4.1**
	If the rotor and cap appear intact, or are only slightly corroded, clean the contacts thoroughly (including the cap towers and spark plug wire ends) and retest per 4.1:	
	If the spark is good in all cases:	**4.6**
	If the spark is poor in all cases:	**4.5**

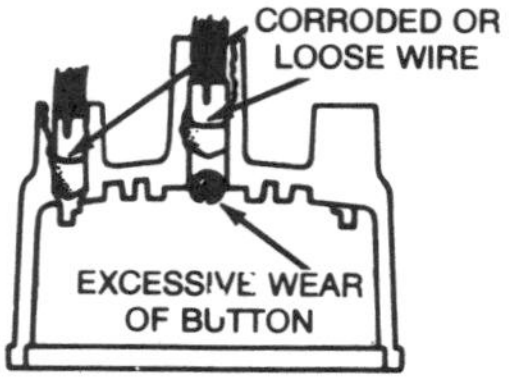

CORRODED OR LOOSE WIRE

EXCESSIVE WEAR OF BUTTON

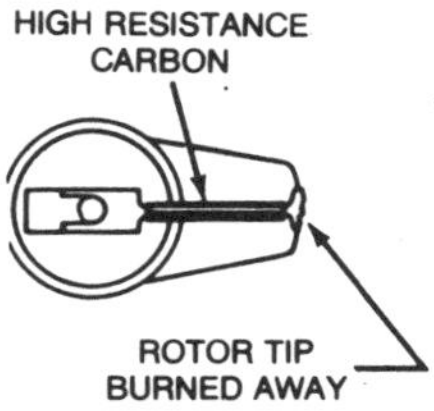

HIGH RESISTANCE CARBON

ROTOR TIP BURNED AWAY

Inspect the distributor cap and rotor

Test and Procedure	Results and Indications	Proceed to
4.4—Check the coil secondary resistance: On point-type systems connect an ohmmeter across the distributor side of the coil and the coil tower. Read the resistance on the high scale of the ohmmeter. On electronic ignition systems, see Chapter 3 for specific tests.	The resistance of a satisfactory coil should be between 4,000 and 10,000 ohms. If resistance is considerably higher (i.e., 40,000 ohms) replace the coil and retest per 4.1. **NOTE:** *This does not apply to high performance coils.*	

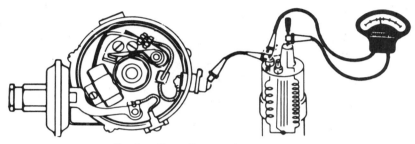

Testing the coil secondary resistance

4.5—Visually inspect the spark plug wires for cracking or brittleness. Ensure that no two wires are positioned so as to cause induction firing (adjacent and parallel). Remove each wire, one by one, and check resistance with an ohmmeter.	Replace any cracked or brittle wires. If any of the wires are defective, replace the entire set. Replace any wires with excessive resistance (over 8000 Ω per foot for suppression wire), and separate any wires that might cause induction firing.	**4.6**

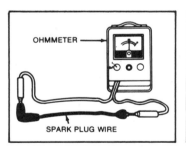

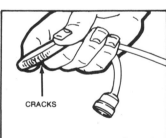

Misfiring can be the result of spark plug leads to adjacent, consecutively firing cylinders running parallel and too close together	**On point-type ignition systems, check the spark plug wires as shown. On electronic ignitions, do not remove the wire from the distributor cap terminal; instead, test through the cap**	**Spark plug wires can be checked visually by bending them in a loop over your finger. This will reveal any cracks, burned or broken insulation. Any wire with cracked insulation should be replaced**

4.6—Remove the spark plugs, noting the cylinders from which they were removed, and evaluate according to the color photos in the middle of this book.	See following.	**See following.**

Test and Procedure	Results and Indications	Proceed to
4.7—Examine the location of all the plugs.	The following diagrams illustrate some of the conditions that the location of plugs will reveal.	**4.8**

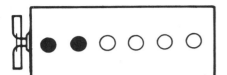

Two adjacent plugs are fouled in a 6-cylinder engine, 4-cylinder engine or either bank of a V-8. This is probably due to a blown head gasket between the two cylinders

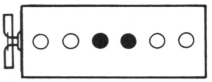

The two center plugs in a 6-cylinder engine are fouled. Raw fuel may be "boiled" out of the carburetor into the intake manifold after the engine is shut-off. Stop-start driving can also foul the center plugs, due to overly rich mixture. Proper float level, a new float needle and seat or use of an insulating spacer may help this problem

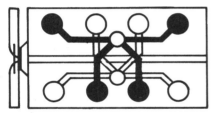

An unbalanced carburetor is indicated. Following the fuel flow on this particular design shows that the cylinders fed by the right-hand barrel are fouled from overly rich mixture, while the cylinders fed by the left-hand barrel are normal

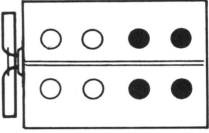

If the four rear plugs are overheated, a cooling system problem is suggested. A thorough cleaning of the cooling system may restore coolant circulation and cure the problem

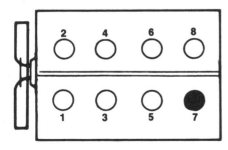

Finding one plug overheated may indicate an intake manifold leak near the affected cylinder. If the overheated plug is the second of two adjacent, consecutively firing plugs, it could be the result of ignition cross-firing. Separating the leads to these two plugs will eliminate cross-fire

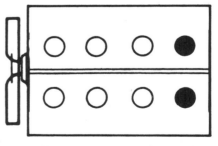

Occasionally, the two rear plugs in large, lightly used V-8's will become oil fouled. High oil consumption and smoky exhaust may also be noticed. It is probably due to plugged oil drain holes in the rear of the cylinder head, causing oil to be sucked in around the valve stems. This usually occurs in the rear cylinders first, because the engine slants that way

Test and Procedure	Results and Indications	Proceed to
4.8—Determine the static ignition timing. Using the crankshaft pulley timing marks as a guide, locate top dead center on the compression stroke of the number one cylinder.	The rotor should be pointing toward the No. 1 tower in the distributor cap, and, on electronic ignitions, the armature spoke for that cylinder should be lined up with the stator.	**4.8**
4.9—Check coil polarity: Connect a voltmeter negative lead to the coil high tension lead, and the positive lead to ground (**NOTE: Reverse the hook-up for positive ground systems**). Crank the engine momentarily.	If the voltmeter reads up-scale, the polarity is correct:	**5.1**
	If the voltmeter reads down-scale, reverse the coil polarity (switch the primary leads):	**5.1**
	Checking coil polarity	

Section 5—Fuel System
See Chapter 4 for service procedures

Test and Procedure	Results and Indications	Proceed to
5.1—Determine that the air filter is functioning efficiently: Hold paper elements up to a strong light, and attempt to see light through the filter.	Clean permanent air filters in solvent (or manufacturer's recommendation), and allow to dry. Replace paper elements through which light cannot be seen:	**5.2**
5.2—Determine whether a flooding condition exists: Flooding is identified by a strong gasoline odor, and excessive gasoline present in the throttle bore(s) of the carburetor.	If flooding is not evident:	**5.3**
	If flooding is evident, permit the gasoline to dry for a few moments and restart. If flooding doesn't recur:	**5.7**
	If flooding is persistent:	**5.5**
	If the engine floods repeatedly, check the choke butterfly flap	
5.3—Check that fuel is reaching the carburetor: Detach the fuel line at the carburetor inlet. Hold the end of the line in a cup (not styrofoam), and crank the engine.	If fuel flows smoothly:	**5.7**
	If fuel doesn't flow (**NOTE: Make sure that there is fuel in the tank**), or flows erratically:	**5.4**

Check the fuel pump by disconnecting the output line (fuel pump-to-carburetor) at the carburetor and operating the starter briefly

Test and Procedure	Results and Indications	Proceed to
5.4—Test the fuel pump: Disconnect all fuel lines from the fuel pump. Hold a finger over the input fitting, crank the engine (with electric pump, turn the ignition or pump on); and feel for suction.	If suction is evident, blow out the fuel line to the tank with low pressure compressed air until bubbling is heard from the fuel filler neck. Also blow out the carburetor fuel line (both ends disconnected):	**5.7**
	If no suction is evident, replace or repair the fuel pump: NOTE: *Repeated oil fouling of the spark plugs, or a no-start condition, could be the result of a ruptured vacuum booster pump diaphragm, through which oil or gasoline is being drawn into the intake manifold (where applicable).*	**5.7**
5.5—Occasionally, small specks of dirt will clog the small jets and orifices in the carburetor. With the engine cold, hold a flat piece of wood or similar material over the carburetor, where possible, and crank the engine.	If the engine starts, but runs roughly the engine is probably not run enough. If the engine won't start:	**5.9**
5.6—Check the needle and seat: Tap the carburetor in the area of the needle and seat.	If flooding stops, a gasoline additive (e.g., Gumout) will often cure the problem:	**5.7**
	If flooding continues, check the fuel pump for excessive pressure at the carburetor (according to specifications). If the pressure is normal, the needle and seat must be removed and checked, and/or the float level adjusted:	**5.7**
5.7—Test the accelerator pump by looking into the throttle bores while operating the throttle.	If the accelerator pump appears to be operating normally:	**5.8**
	If the accelerator pump is not operating, the pump must be reconditioned. Where possible, service the pump with the carburetor(s) installed on the engine. If necessary, remove the carburetor. Prior to removal:	**5.8**

Check for gas at the carburetor by looking down the carburetor throat while someone moves the accelerator

5.8—Determine whether the carburetor main fuel system is functioning: Spray a commercial starting fluid into the carburetor while attempting to start the engine.	If the engine starts, runs for a few seconds, and dies:	**5.9**
	If the engine doesn't start:	**6.1**

Test and Procedure	Results and Indications	Proceed to
5.9—Uncommon fuel system malfunctions: See below:	If the problem is solved:	**6.1**
	If the problem remains, remove and recondition the carburetor.	

Condition	Indication	Test	Prevailing Weather Conditions	Remedy
Vapor lock	Engine will not restart shortly after running.	Cool the components of the fuel system until the engine starts. Vapor lock can be cured faster by draping a wet cloth over a mechanical fuel pump.	Hot to very hot	Ensure that the exhaust manifold heat control valve is operating. Check with the vehicle manufacturer for the recommended solution to vapor lock on the model in question.
Carburetor icing	Engine will not idle, stalls at low speeds.	Visually inspect the throttle plate area of the throttle bores for frost.	High humidity, 32–40° F.	Ensure that the exhaust manifold heat control valve is operating, and that the intake manifold heat riser is not blocked.
Water in the fuel	Engine sputters and stalls; may not start.	Pump a small amount of fuel into a glass jar. Allow to stand, and inspect for droplets or a layer of water.	High humidity, extreme temperature changes.	For droplets, use one or two cans of commercial gas line anti-freeze. For a layer of water, the tank must be drained, and the fuel lines blown out with compressed air.

Section 6—Engine Compression

See Chapter 3 for service procedures

6.1—Test engine compression: Remove all spark plugs. Block the throttle wide open. Insert a compression gauge into a spark plug port, crank the engine to obtain the maximum reading, and record.	If compression is within limits on all cylinders:	**7.1**
	If gauge reading is extremely low on all cylinders:	**6.2**
	If gauge reading is low on one or two cylinders: (If gauge readings are identical and low on two or more adjacent cylinders, the head gasket must be replaced.)	**6.2**

Checking compression

6.2—Test engine compression (wet): Squirt approximately 30 cc. of engine oil into each cylinder, and retest per 6.1.	If the readings improve, worn or cracked rings or broken pistons are indicated:	**See Chapter 3**
	If the readings do not improve, burned or excessively carboned valves or a jumped timing chain are indicated:	**7.1**
	NOTE: *A jumped timing chain is often indicated by difficult cranking.*	

Section 7—Engine Vacuum

See Chapter 3 for service procedures

Test and Procedure	Results and Indications	Proceed to
7.1—Attach a vacuum gauge to the intake manifold beyond the throttle plate. Start the engine, and observe the action of the needle over the range of engine speeds.	See below.	**See below**

INDICATION: normal engine in good condition

Proceed to: 8.1

Normal engine
Gauge reading: steady, from 17–22 in./Hg.

INDICATION: sticking valves or ignition miss

Proceed to: 9.1, 8.3

Sticking valves
Gauge reading: intermittent fluctuation at idle

INDICATION: late ignition or valve timing, low compression, stuck throttle valve, leaking carburetor or manifold gasket

Proceed to: 6.1

Incorrect valve timing
Gauge reading: low (10–15 in./Hg) but steady

INDICATION: improper carburetor adjustment or minor intake leak.

Proceed to: 7.2

Carburetor requires adjustment
Gauge reading: drifting needle

INDICATION: ignition miss, blown cylinder head gasket, leaking valve or weak valve spring

Proceed to: 8.3, 6.1

Blown head gasket
Gauge reading: needle fluctuates as engine speed increases

INDICATION: burnt valve or faulty valve clearance. Needle will fall when defective valve operates

Proceed to: 9.1

Burnt or leaking valves
Gauge reading: steady needle, but drops regularly

INDICATION: choked muffler, excessive back pressure in system

Proceed to: 10.1

Clogged exhaust system
Gauge reading: gradual drop in reading at idle

INDICATION: worn valve guides

Proceed to: 9.1

Worn valve guides
Gauge reading: needle vibrates excessively at idle but steadies as engine speed increases

White pointer = steady gauge hand   Black pointer = fluctuating gauge hand

Test and Procedure	Results and Indications	Proceed to
7.2—Attach a vacuum gauge per 7.1, and test for an intake manifold leak. Squirt a small amount of oil around the intake manifold gaskets, carburetor gaskets, plugs and fittings. Observe the action of the vacuum gauge.	If the reading improves, replace the indicated gasket, or seal the indicated fitting or plug: If the reading remains low:	**8.1** **7.3**
7.3—Test all vacuum hoses and accessories for leaks as described in 7.2. Also check the carburetor body (dashpots, automatic choke mechanism, throttle shafts) for leaks in the same manner.	If the reading improves, service or replace the offending part(s): If the reading remains low:	**8.1** **6.1**

Section 8—Secondary Electrical System
See Chapter 2 for service procedures

Test and Procedure	Results and Indications	Proceed to
8.1—Remove the distributor cap and check to make sure that the rotor turns when the engine is cranked. Visually inspect the distributor components.	Clean, tighten or replace any components which appear defective.	**8.2**
8.2—Connect a timing light (per manufacturer's recommendation) and check the dynamic ignition timing. Disconnect and plug the vacuum hose(s) to the distributor if specified, start the engine, and observe the timing marks at the specified engine speed.	If the timing is not correct, adjust to specifications by rotating the distributor in the engine: (Advance timing by rotating distributor opposite normal direction of rotor rotation, retard timing by rotating distributor in same direction as rotor rotation.)	**8.3**
8.3—Check the operation of the distributor advance mechanism(s): To test the mechanical advance, disconnect the vacuum lines from the distributor advance unit and observe the timing marks with a timing light as the engine speed is increased from idle. If the mark moves smoothly, without hesitation, it may be assumed that the mechanical advance is functioning properly. To test vacuum advance and/or retard systems, alternately crimp and release the vacuum line, and observe the timing mark for movement. If movement is noted, the system is operating.	If the systems are functioning: If the systems are not functioning, remove the distributor, and test on a distributor tester:	**8.4** **8.4**
8.4—Locate an ignition miss: With the engine running, remove each spark plug wire, one at a time, until one is found that doesn't cause the engine to roughen and slow down.	When the missing cylinder is identified:	**4.1**

Section 9—Valve Train
See Chapter 3 for service procedures

Test and Procedure	Results and Indications	Proceed to
9.1—Evaluate the valve train: Remove the valve cover, and ensure that the valves are adjusted to specifications. A mechanic's stethoscope may be used to aid in the diagnosis of the valve train. By pushing the probe on or near push rods or rockers, valve noise often can be isolated. A timing light also may be used to diagnose valve problems. Connect the light according to manufacturer's recommendations, and start the engine. Vary the firing moment of the light by increasing the engine speed (and therefore the ignition advance), and moving the trigger from cylinder to cylinder. Observe the movement of each valve.	Sticking valves or erratic valve train motion can be observed with the timing light. The cylinder head must be disassembled for repairs.	**See Chapter 3**
9.2—Check the valve timing: Locate top dead center of the No. 1 piston, and install a degree wheel or tape on the crankshaft pulley or damper with zero corresponding to an index mark on the engine. Rotate the crankshaft in its direction of rotation, and observe the opening of the No. 1 cylinder intake valve. The opening should correspond with the correct mark on the degree wheel according to specifications.	If the timing is not correct, the timing cover must be removed for further investigation.	**See Chapter 3**

Section 10—Exhaust System

Test and Procedure	Results and Indications	Proceed to
10.1—Determine whether the exhaust manifold heat control valve is operating: Operate the valve by hand to determine whether it is free to move. If the valve is free, run the engine to operating temperature and observe the action of the valve, to ensure that it is opening.	If the valve sticks, spray it with a suitable solvent, open and close the valve to free it, and retest. If the valve functions properly: If the valve does not free, or does not operate, replace the valve:	 **10.2** **10.2**
10.2—Ensure that there are no exhaust restrictions: Visually inspect the exhaust system for kinks, dents, or crushing. Also note that gases are flowing freely from the tailpipe at all engine speeds, indicating no restriction in the muffler or resonator.	Replace any damaged portion of the system:	**11.1**

Section 11—Cooling System
See Chapter 3 for service procedures

Test and Procedure	Results and Indications	Proceed to
11.1—Visually inspect the fan belt for glazing, cracks, and fraying, and replace if necessary. Tighten the belt so that the longest span has approximately ½″ play at its midpoint under thumb pressure (see Chapter 1).	Replace or tighten the fan belt as necessary:	**11.2**

Checking belt tension

Test and Procedure	Results and Indications	Proceed to
11.2—Check the fluid level of the cooling system.	If full or slightly low, fill as necessary:	**11.5**
	If extremely low:	**11.3**
11.3—Visually inspect the external portions of the cooling system (radiator, radiator hoses, thermostat elbow, water pump seals, heater hoses, etc.) for leaks. If none are found, pressurize the cooling system to 14–15 psi.	If cooling system holds the pressure:	**11.5**
	If cooling system loses pressure rapidly, reinspect external parts of the system for leaks under pressure. If none are found, check dipstick for coolant in crankcase. If no coolant is present, but pressure loss continues:	**11.4**
	If coolant is evident in crankcase, remove cylinder head(s), and check gasket(s). If gaskets are intact, block and cylinder head(s) should be checked for cracks or holes.	
	If the gasket(s) is blown, replace, and purge the crankcase of coolant:	**12.6**
	NOTE: *Occasionally, due to atmospheric and driving conditions, condensation of water can occur in the crankcase. This causes the oil to appear milky white. To remedy, run the engine until hot, and change the oil and oil filter.*	
11.4—Check for combustion leaks into the cooling system: Pressurize the cooling system as above. Start the engine, and observe the pressure gauge. If the needle fluctuates, remove each spark plug wire, one at a time, noting which cylinder(s) reduce or eliminate the fluctuation.	Cylinders which reduce or eliminate the fluctuation, when the spark plug wire is removed, are leaking into the cooling system. Replace the head gasket on the affected cylinder bank(s).	

Pressurizing the cooling system

Test and Procedure	Results and Indications	Proceed to
11.5—Check the radiator pressure cap: Attach a radiator pressure tester to the radiator cap (wet the seal prior to installation). Quickly pump up the pressure, noting the point at which the cap releases.	If the cap releases within ± 1 psi of the specified rating, it is operating properly:	**11.6**
	If the cap releases at more than ± 1 psi of the specified rating, it should be replaced:	**11.6**

Checking radiator pressure cap

Test and Procedure	Results and Indications	Proceed to
11.6—Test the thermostat: Start the engine cold, remove the radiator cap, and insert a thermometer into the radiator. Allow the engine to idle. After a short while, there will be a sudden, rapid increase in coolant temperature. The temperature at which this sharp rise stops is the thermostat opening temperature.	If the thermostat opens at or about the specified temperature:	**11.7**
	If the temperature doesn't increase: (If the temperature increases slowly and gradually, replace the thermostat.)	**11.7**
11.7—Check the water pump: Remove the thermostat elbow and the thermostat, disconnect the coil high tension lead (to prevent starting), and crank the engine momentarily.	If coolant flows, replace the thermostat and retest per 11.6:	**11.6**
	If coolant doesn't flow, reverse flush the cooling system to alleviate any blockage that might exist. If system is not blocked, and coolant will not flow, replace the water pump.	

Section 12—Lubrication
See Chapter 3 for service procedures

Test and Procedure	Results and Indications	Proceed to
12.1—Check the oil pressure gauge or warning light: If the gauge shows low pressure, or the light is on for no obvious reason, remove the oil pressure sender. Install an accurate oil pressure gauge and run the engine momentarily.	If oil pressure builds normally, run engine for a few moments to determine that it is functioning normally, and replace the sender.	—
	If the pressure remains low:	**12.2**
	If the pressure surges:	**12.3**
	If the oil pressure is zero:	**12.3**
12.2—Visually inspect the oil: If the oil is watery or very thin, milky, or foamy, replace the oil and oil filter.	If the oil is normal:	**12.3**
	If after replacing oil the pressure remains low:	**12.3**
	If after replacing oil the pressure becomes normal:	—

Test and Procedure	Results and Indications	Proceed to
12.3—Inspect the oil pressure relief valve and spring, to ensure that it is not sticking or stuck. Remove and thoroughly clean the valve, spring, and the valve body.	If the oil pressure improves: If no improvement is noted:	— **12.4**
12.4—Check to ensure that the oil pump is not cavitating (sucking air instead of oil): See that the crankcase is neither over nor underfull, and that the pickup in the sump is in the proper position and free from sludge.	Fill or drain the crankcase to the proper capacity, and clean the pickup screen in solvent if necessary. If no improvement is noted:	**12.5**
12.5—Inspect the oil pump drive and the oil pump:	If the pump drive or the oil pump appear to be defective, service as necessary and retest per 12.1: If the pump drive and pump appear to be operating normally, the engine should be disassembled to determine where blockage exists:	**12.1** **See Chapter 3**
12.6—Purge the engine of ethylene glycol coolant: Completely drain the crankcase and the oil filter. Obtain a commercial butyl cellosolve base solvent, designated for this purpose, and follow the instructions precisely. Following this, install a new oil filter and refill the crankcase with the proper weight oil. The next oil and filter change should follow shortly thereafter (1000 miles).		

TROUBLESHOOTING EMISSION CONTROL SYSTEMS

See Chapter 4 for procedures applicable to individual emission control systems used on specific combinations of engine/transmission/model.

TROUBLESHOOTING THE CARBURETOR

See Chapter 4 for service procedures

Carburetor problems cannot be effectively isolated unless all other engine systems (particularly ignition and emission) are functioning properly and the engine is properly tuned.

Condition	Possible Cause
Engine cranks, but does not start	1. Improper starting procedure 2. No fuel in tank 3. Clogged fuel line or filter 4. Defective fuel pump 5. Choke valve not closing properly 6. Engine flooded 7. Choke valve not unloading 8. Throttle linkage not making full travel 9. Stuck needle or float 10. Leaking float needle or seat 11. Improper float adjustment
Engine stalls	1. Improperly adjusted idle speed or mixture **Engine hot** 2. Improperly adjusted dashpot 3. Defective or improperly adjusted solenoid 4. Incorrect fuel level in fuel bowl 5. Fuel pump pressure too high 6. Leaking float needle seat 7. Secondary throttle valve stuck open 8. Air or fuel leaks 9. Idle air bleeds plugged or missing 10. Idle passages plugged **Engine Cold** 11. Incorrectly adjusted choke 12. Improperly adjusted fast idle speed 13. Air leaks 14. Plugged idle or idle air passages 15. Stuck choke valve or binding linkage 16. Stuck secondary throttle valves 17. Engine flooding—high fuel level 18. Leaking or misaligned float
Engine hesitates on acceleration	1. Clogged fuel filter 2. Leaking fuel pump diaphragm 3. Low fuel pump pressure 4. Secondary throttle valves stuck, bent or misadjusted 5. Sticking or binding air valve 6. Defective accelerator pump 7. Vacuum leaks 8. Clogged air filter 9. Incorrect choke adjustment (engine cold)
Engine feels sluggish or flat on acceleration	1. Improperly adjusted idle speed or mixture 2. Clogged fuel filter 3. Defective accelerator pump 4. Dirty, plugged or incorrect main metering jets 5. Bent or sticking main metering rods 6. Sticking throttle valves 7. Stuck heat riser 8. Binding or stuck air valve 9. Dirty, plugged or incorrect secondary jets 10. Bent or sticking secondary metering rods. 11. Throttle body or manifold heat passages plugged 12. Improperly adjusted choke or choke vacuum break.
Carburetor floods	1. Defective fuel pump. Pressure too high. 2. Stuck choke valve 3. Dirty, worn or damaged float or needle valve/seat 4. Incorrect float/fuel level 5. Leaking float bowl

Condition	Possible Cause
Engine idles roughly and stalls	1. Incorrect idle speed 2. Clogged fuel filter 3. Dirt in fuel system or carburetor 4. Loose carburetor screws or attaching bolts 5. Broken carburetor gaskets 6. Air leaks 7. Dirty carburetor 8. Worn idle mixture needles 9. Throttle valves stuck open 10. Incorrectly adjusted float or fuel level 11. Clogged air filter
Engine runs unevenly or surges	1. Defective fuel pump 2. Dirty or clogged fuel filter 3. Plugged, loose or incorrect main metering jets or rods 4. Air leaks 5. Bent or sticking main metering rods 6. Stuck power piston 7. Incorrect float adjustment 8. Incorrect idle speed or mixture 9. Dirty or plugged idle system passages 10. Hard, brittle or broken gaskets 11. Loose attaching or mounting screws 12. Stuck or misaligned secondary throttle valves
Poor fuel economy	1. Poor driving habits 2. Stuck choke valve 3. Binding choke linkage 4. Stuck heat riser 5. Incorrect idle mixture 6. Defective accelerator pump 7. Air leaks 8. Plugged, loose or incorrect main metering jets 9. Improperly adjusted float or fuel level 10. Bent, misaligned or fuel-clogged float 11. Leaking float needle seat 12. Fuel leak 13. Accelerator pump discharge ball not seating properly 14. Incorrect main jets
Engine lacks high speed performance or power	1. Incorrect throttle linkage adjustment 2. Stuck or binding power piston 3. Defective accelerator pump 4. Air leaks 5. Incorrect float setting or fuel level 6. Dirty, plugged, worn or incorrect main metering jets or rods 7. Binding or sticking air valve 8. Brittle or cracked gaskets 9. Bent, incorrect or improperly adjusted secondary metering rods 10. Clogged fuel filter 11. Clogged air filter 12. Defective fuel pump

TROUBLESHOOTING FUEL INJECTION PROBLEMS

Each fuel injection system has its own unique components and test procedures, for which it is impossible to generalize. Refer to Chapter 4 of this Repair & Tune-Up Guide for specific test and repair procedures, if the vehicle is equipped with fuel injection.

TROUBLESHOOTING ELECTRICAL PROBLEMS

See Chapter 5 for service procedures

For any electrical system to operate, it must make a complete circuit. This simply means that the power flow from the battery must make a complete circle. When an electrical component is operating, power flows from the battery to the component, passes through the component causing it to perform its function (lighting a light bulb), and then returns to the battery through the ground of the circuit. This ground is usually (but not always) the metal part of the car or truck on which the electrical component is mounted.

Perhaps the easiest way to visualize this is to think of connecting a light bulb with two wires attached to it to the battery. If one of the two wires attached to the light bulb were attached to the negative post of the battery and the other were attached to the positive post of the battery, you would have a complete circuit. Current from the battery would flow to the light bulb, causing it to light, and return to the negative post of the battery.

The normal automotive circuit differs from this simple example in two ways. First, instead of having a return wire from the bulb to the battery, the light bulb returns the current to the battery through the chassis of the vehicle. Since the negative battery cable is attached to the chassis and the chassis is made of electrically conductive metal, the chassis of the vehicle can serve as a ground wire to complete the circuit. Secondly, most automotive circuits contain switches to turn components on and off as required.

Every complete circuit from a power source must include a component which is using the power from the power source. If you were to disconnect the light bulb from the wires and touch the two wires together (don't do this) the power supply wire to the component would be grounded before the normal ground connection for the circuit.

Because grounding a wire from a power source makes a complete circuit—less the required component to use the power—this phenomenon is called a short circuit. Common causes are: broken insulation (exposing the metal wire to a metal part of the car or truck), or a shorted switch.

Some electrical components which require a large amount of current to operate also have a relay in their circuit. Since these circuits carry a large amount of current, the thickness of the wire in the circuit (gauge size) is also greater. If this large wire were connected from the component to the control switch on the instrument panel, and then back to the component, a voltage drop would occur in the circuit. To prevent this potential drop in voltage, an electromagnetic switch (relay) is used. The large wires in the circuit are connected from the battery to one side of the relay, and from the opposite side of the relay to the component. The relay is normally open, preventing current from passing through the circuit. An additional, smaller, wire is connected from the relay to the control switch for the circuit. When the control switch is turned on, it grounds the smaller wire from the relay and completes the circuit. This closes the relay and allows current to flow from the battery to the component. The horn, headlight, and starter circuits are three which use relays.

It is possible for larger surges of current to pass through the electrical system of your car or truck. If this surge of current were to reach an electrical component, it could burn it out. To prevent this, fuses, circuit breakers or fusible links are connected into the current supply wires of most of the major electrical systems. When an electrical current of excessive power passes through the component's fuse, the fuse blows out and breaks the circuit, saving the component from destruction.

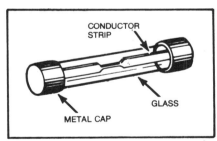

Typical automotive fuse

A circuit breaker is basically a self-repairing fuse. The circuit breaker opens the circuit the same way a fuse does. However, when either the short is removed from the circuit or the surge subsides, the circuit breaker resets itself and does not have to be replaced as a fuse does.

A fuse link is a wire that acts as a fuse. It is normally connected between the starter relay and the main wiring harness. This connection is usually under the hood. The fuse link (if installed) protects all the

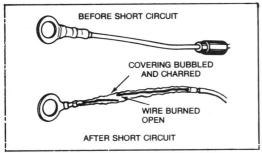

BEFORE SHORT CIRCUIT

COVERING BUBBLED
AND CHARRED

WIRE BURNED
OPEN

AFTER SHORT CIRCUIT

Most fusible links show a charred, melted insulation when they burn out

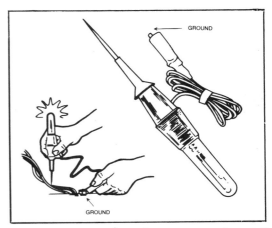

GROUND

GROUND

The test light will show the presence of current when touched to a hot wire and grounded at the other end

chassis electrical components, and is the probable cause of trouble when none of the electrical components function, unless the battery is disconnected or dead.

Electrical problems generally fall into one of three areas:

1. The component that is not functioning is not receiving current.

2. The component itself is not functioning.

3. The component is not properly grounded.

The electrical system can be checked with a test light and a jumper wire. A test light is a device that looks like a pointed screwdriver with a wire attached to it and has a light bulb in its handle. A jumper wire is a piece of insulated wire with an alligator clip attached to each end.

If a component is not working, you must follow a systematic plan to determine which of the three causes is the villain.

1. Turn on the switch that controls the inoperable component.

2. Disconnect the power supply wire from the component.

3. Attach the ground wire on the test light to a good metal ground.

4. Touch the probe end of the test light to the end of the power supply wire that was disconnected from the component. If the component is receiving current, the test light will go on.

NOTE: *Some components work only when the ignition switch is turned on.*

If the test light does not go on, then the problem is in the circuit between the battery and the component. This includes all the switches, fuses, and relays in the system. Follow the wire that runs back to the battery. The problem is an open circuit between the

battery and the component. If the fuse is blown and, when replaced, immediately blows again, there is a short circuit in the system which must be located and repaired. If there is a switch in the system, bypass it with a jumper wire. This is done by connecting one end of the jumper wire to the power supply wire into the switch and the other end of the jumper wire to the wire coming out of the switch. If the test light lights with the jumper wire installed, the switch or whatever was bypassed is defective.

NOTE: *Never substitute the jumper wire for the component, since it is required to use the power from the power source.*

5. If the bulb in the test light goes on, then the current is getting to the component that is not working. This eliminates the first of the three possible causes. Connect the power supply wire and connect a jumper wire from the component to a good metal ground. Do this with the switch which controls the component turned on, and also the ignition switch turned on if it is required for the component to work. If the component works with the jumper wire installed, then it has a bad ground. This is usually caused by the metal area on which the component mounts to the chassis being coated with some type of foreign matter.

6. If neither test located the source of the trouble, then the component itself is defective. Remember that for any electrical system to work, all connections must be clean and tight.

Troubleshooting Basic Turn Signal and Flasher Problems

See Chapter 5 for service procedures

Most problems in the turn signals or flasher system can be reduced to defective flashers or bulbs, which are easily replaced. Occasionally, the turn signal switch will prove defective.

F = Front   R = Rear   ● = Lights off   ○ = Lights on

Condition		Possible Cause
Turn signals light, but do not flash		Defective flasher
No turn signals light on either side		Blown fuse. Replace if defective. Defective flasher. Check by substitution. Open circuit, short circuit or poor ground.
Both turn signals on one side don't work		Bad bulbs. Bad ground in both (or either) housings.
One turn signal light on one side doesn't work		Defective bulb. Corrosion in socket. Clean contacts. Poor ground at socket.
Turn signal flashes too fast or too slowly		Check any bulb on the side flashing too fast. A heavy-duty bulb is probably installed in place of a regular bulb. Check the bulb flashing too slowly. A standard bulb was probably installed in place of a heavy-duty bulb. Loose connections or corrosion at the bulb socket.
Indicator lights don't work in either direction	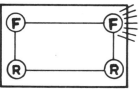	Check if the turn signals are working. Check the dash indicator lights. Check the flasher by substitution.
One indicator light doesn't light		On systems with one dash indicator: See if the lights work on the same side. Often the filaments have been reversed in systems combining stoplights with taillights and turn signals. Check the flasher by substitution. On systems with two indicators: Check the bulbs on the same side. Check the indicator light bulb. Check the flasher by substitution.

Troubleshooting Lighting Problems
See Chapter 5 for service procedures

Condition	Possible Cause
One or more lights don't work, but others do	1. Defective bulb(s) 2. Blown fuse(s) 3. Dirty fuse clips or light sockets 4. Poor ground circuit
Lights burn out quickly	1. Incorrect voltage regulator setting or defective regulator 2. Poor battery/alternator connections
Lights go dim	1. Low/discharged battery 2. Alternator not charging 3. Corroded sockets or connections 4. Low voltage output
Lights flicker	1. Loose connection 2. Poor ground. (Run ground wire from light housing to frame) 3. Circuit breaker operating (short circuit)
Lights "flare"—Some flare is normal on acceleration—If excessive, see "Lights Burn Out Quickly"	High voltage setting
Lights glare—approaching drivers are blinded	1. Lights adjusted too high 2. Rear springs or shocks sagging 3. Rear tires soft

Troubleshooting Dash Gauge Problems

Most problems can be traced to a defective sending unit or faulty wiring. Occasionally, the gauge itself is at fault. See Chapter 5 for service procedures.

Condition	Possible Cause

COOLANT TEMPERATURE GAUGE

Gauge reads erratically or not at all	1. Loose or dirty connections 2. Defective sending unit. 3. Defective gauge. To test a bi-metal gauge, remove the wire from the sending unit. Ground the wire for an instant. If the gauge registers, replace the sending unit. To test a magnetic gauge, disconnect the wire at the sending unit. With ignition ON gauge should register COLD. Ground the wire; gauge should register HOT.

AMMETER GAUGE—TURN HEADLIGHTS ON (DO NOT START ENGINE). NOTE REACTION

Ammeter shows charge Ammeter shows discharge Ammeter does not move	1. Connections reversed on gauge 2. Ammeter is OK 3. Loose connections or faulty wiring 4. Defective gauge

Condition	Possible Cause

OIL PRESSURE GAUGE

Gauge does not register or is inaccurate	1. On mechanical gauge, Bourdon tube may be bent or kinked. 2. Low oil pressure. Remove sending unit. Idle the engine briefly. If no oil flows from sending unit hole, problem is in engine. 3. Defective gauge. Remove the wire from the sending unit and ground it for an instant with the ignition ON. A good gauge will go to the top of the scale. 4. Defective wiring. Check the wiring to the gauge. If it's OK and the gauge doesn't register when grounded, replace the gauge. 5. Defective sending unit.

ALL GAUGES

All gauges do not operate All gauges read low or erratically All gauges pegged	1. Blown fuse 2. Defective instrument regulator 3. Defective or dirty instrument voltage regulator 4. Loss of ground between instrument voltage regulator and frame 5. Defective instrument regulator

WARNING LIGHTS

Light(s) do not come on when ignition is ON, but engine is not started Light comes on with engine running	1. Defective bulb 2. Defective wire 3. Defective sending unit. Disconnect the wire from the sending unit and ground it. Replace the sending unit if the light comes on with the ignition ON. 4. Problem in individual system 5. Defective sending unit

Troubleshooting Clutch Problems

It is false economy to replace individual clutch components. The pressure plate, clutch plate and throwout bearing should be replaced as a set, and the flywheel face inspected, whenever the clutch is overhauled. See Chapter 6 for service procedures.

Condition	Possible Cause
Clutch chatter	1. Grease on driven plate (disc) facing 2. Binding clutch linkage or cable 3. Loose, damaged facings on driven plate (disc) 4. Engine mounts loose 5. Incorrect height adjustment of pressure plate release levers 6. Clutch housing or housing to transmission adapter misalignment 7. Loose driven plate hub
Clutch grabbing	1. Oil, grease on driven plate (disc) facing 2. Broken pressure plate 3. Warped or binding driven plate. Driven plate binding on clutch shaft
Clutch slips	1. Lack of lubrication in clutch linkage or cable (linkage or cable binds, causes incomplete engagement) 2. Incorrect pedal, or linkage adjustment 3. Broken pressure plate springs 4. Weak pressure plate springs 5. Grease on driven plate facings (disc)

Troubleshooting Clutch Problems (cont.)

Condition	Possible Cause
Incomplete clutch release	1. Incorrect pedal or linkage adjustment or linkage or cable binding 2. Incorrect height adjustment on pressure plate release levers 3. Loose, broken facings on driven plate (disc) 4. Bent, dished, warped driven plate caused by overheating
Grinding, whirring grating noise when pedal is depressed	1. Worn or defective throwout bearing 2. Starter drive teeth contacting flywheel ring gear teeth. Look for milled or polished teeth on ring gear.
Squeal, howl, trumpeting noise when pedal is being released (occurs during first inch to inch and one-half of pedal travel)	Pilot bushing worn or lack of lubricant. If bushing appears OK, polish bushing with emery cloth, soak lube wick in oil, lube bushing with oil, apply film of chassis grease to clutch shaft pilot hub, reassemble. NOTE: Bushing wear may be due to misalignment of clutch housing or housing to transmission adapter
Vibration or clutch pedal pulsation with clutch disengaged (pedal fully depressed)	1. Worn or defective engine transmission mounts 2. Flywheel run out. (Flywheel run out at face not to exceed 0.005") 3. Damaged or defective clutch components

Troubleshooting Manual Transmission Problems
See Chapter 6 for service procedures

Condition	Possible Cause
Transmission jumps out of gear	1. Misalignment of transmission case or clutch housing. 2. Worn pilot bearing in crankshaft. 3. Bent transmission shaft. 4. Worn high speed sliding gear. 5. Worn teeth or end-play in clutch shaft. 6. Insufficient spring tension on shifter rail plunger. 7. Bent or loose shifter fork. 8. Gears not engaging completely. 9. Loose or worn bearings on clutch shaft or mainshaft. 10. Worn gear teeth. 11. Worn or damaged detent balls.
Transmission sticks in gear	1. Clutch not releasing fully. 2. Burred or battered teeth on clutch shaft, or sliding sleeve. 3. Burred or battered transmission mainshaft. 4. Frozen synchronizing clutch. 5. Stuck shifter rail plunger. 6. Gearshift lever twisting and binding shifter rail. 7. Battered teeth on high speed sliding gear or on sleeve. 8. Improper lubrication, or lack of lubrication. 9. Corroded transmission parts. 10. Defective mainshaft pilot bearing. 11. Locked gear bearings will give same effect as stuck in gear.
Transmission gears will not synchronize	1. Binding pilot bearing on mainshaft, will synchronize in high gear only. 2. Clutch not releasing fully. 3. Detent spring weak or broken. 4. Weak or broken springs under balls in sliding gear sleeve. 5. Binding bearing on clutch shaft, or binding countershaft. 6. Binding pilot bearing in crankshaft. 7. Badly worn gear teeth. 8. Improper lubrication. 9. Constant mesh gear not turning freely on transmission mainshaft. Will synchronize in that gear only.

Condition	Possible Cause
Gears spinning when shifting into gear from neutral	1. Clutch not releasing fully. 2. In some cases an extremely light lubricant in transmission will cause gears to continue to spin for a short time after clutch is released. 3. Binding pilot bearing in crankshaft.
Transmission noisy in all gears	1. Insufficient lubricant, or improper lubricant. 2. Worn countergear bearings. 3. Worn or damaged main drive gear or countergear. 4. Damaged main drive gear or mainshaft bearings. 5. Worn or damaged countergear anti-lash plate.
Transmission noisy in neutral only	1. Damaged main drive gear bearing. 2. Damaged or loose mainshaft pilot bearing. 3. Worn or damaged countergear anti-lash plate. 4. Worn countergear bearings.
Transmission noisy in one gear only	1. Damaged or worn constant mesh gears. 2. Worn or damaged countergear bearings. 3. Damaged or worn synchronizer.
Transmission noisy in reverse only	1. Worn or damaged reverse idler gear or idler bushing. 2. Worn or damaged mainshaft reverse gear. 3. Worn or damaged reverse countergear. 4. Damaged shift mechanism.

TROUBLESHOOTING AUTOMATIC TRANSMISSION PROBLEMS

Keeping alert to changes in the operating characteristics of the transmission (changing shift points, noises, etc.) can prevent small problems from becoming large ones. If the problem cannot be traced to loose bolts, fluid level, misadjusted linkage, clogged filters or similar problems, you should probably seek professional service.

Transmission Fluid Indications

The appearance and odor of the transmission fluid can give valuable clues to the overall condition of the transmission. Always note the appearance of the fluid when you check the fluid level or change the fluid. Rub a small amount of fluid between your fingers to feel for grit and smell the fluid on the dipstick.

If the fluid appears:	It indicates:
Clear and red colored	Normal operation
Discolored (extremely dark red or brownish) or smells burned	Band or clutch pack failure, usually caused by an overheated transmission. Hauling very heavy loads with insufficient power or failure to change the fluid often result in overheating. Do not confuse this appearance with newer fluids that have a darker red color and a strong odor (though not a burned odor).
Foamy or aerated (light in color and full of bubbles)	1. The level is too high (gear train is churning oil) 2. An internal air leak (air is mixing with the fluid). Have the transmission checked professionally.
Solid residue in the fluid	Defective bands, clutch pack or bearings. Bits of band material or metal abrasives are clinging to the dipstick. Have the transmission checked professionally.
Varnish coating on the dipstick	The transmission fluid is overheating

TROUBLESHOOTING DRIVE AXLE PROBLEMS

First, determine when the noise is most noticeable.

Drive Noise: Produced under vehicle acceleration.

Coast Noise: Produced while coasting with a closed throttle.

Float Noise: Occurs while maintaining constant speed (just enough to keep speed constant) on a level road.

External Noise Elimination

It is advisable to make a thorough road test to determine whether the noise originates in the rear axle or whether it originates from the tires, engine, transmission, wheel bearings or road surface. Noise originating from other places cannot be corrected by servicing the rear axle.

ROAD NOISE

Brick or rough surfaced concrete roads produce noises that seem to come from the rear axle. Road noise is usually identical in Drive or Coast and driving on a different type of road will tell whether the road is the problem.

TIRE NOISE

Tire noise can be mistaken as rear axle noise, even though the tires on the front are at fault. Snow tread and mud tread tires or tires worn unevenly will frequently cause vibrations which seem to originate elsewhere; *temporarily, and for test purposes only,* inflate the tires to 40–50 lbs. This will significantly alter the noise produced by the tires, but will not alter noise from the rear axle. Noises from the rear axle will normally cease at speeds below 30 mph on coast, while tire noise will continue at lower tone as speed is decreased. The rear axle noise will usually change from drive conditions to coast conditions, while tire noise will not. Do not forget to lower the tire pressure to normal after the test is complete.

ENGINE/TRANSMISSION NOISE

Determine at what speed the noise is most pronounced, then stop in a quiet place. With the transmission in Neutral, run the engine through speeds corresponding to road speeds where the noise was noticed. Noises produced with the vehicle standing still are coming from the engine or transmission.

FRONT WHEEL BEARINGS

Front wheel bearing noises, sometimes confused with rear axle noises, will not change when comparing drive and coast conditions. While holding the speed steady, lightly apply the footbrake. This will often cause wheel bearing noise to lessen, as some of the weight is taken off the bearing. Front wheel bearings are easily checked by jacking up the wheels and spinning the wheels. Shaking the wheels will also determine if the wheel bearings are excessively loose.

REAR AXLE NOISES

Eliminating other possible sources can narrow the cause to the rear axle, which normally produces noise from worn gears or bearings. Gear noises tend to peak in a narrow speed range, while bearing noises will usually vary in pitch with engine speeds.

Noise Diagnosis

The Noise Is:	Most Probably Produced By:
1. Identical under Drive or Coast	Road surface, tires or front wheel bearings
2. Different depending on road surface	Road surface or tires
3. Lower as speed is lowered	Tires
4. Similar when standing or moving	Engine or transmission
5. A vibration	Unbalanced tires, rear wheel bearing, unbalanced driveshaft or worn U-joint
6. A knock or click about every two tire revolutions	Rear wheel bearing
7. Most pronounced on turns	Damaged differential gears
8. A steady low-pitched whirring or scraping, starting at low speeds	Damaged or worn pinion bearing
9. A chattering vibration on turns	Wrong differential lubricant or worn clutch plates (limited slip rear axle)
10. Noticed only in Drive, Coast or Float conditions	Worn ring gear and/or pinion gear

Troubleshooting Steering & Suspension Problems

Condition	Possible Cause
Hard steering (wheel is hard to turn)	1. Improper tire pressure 2. Loose or glazed pump drive belt 3. Low or incorrect fluid 4. Loose, bent or poorly lubricated front end parts 5. Improper front end alignment (excessive caster) 6. Bind in steering column or linkage 7. Kinked hydraulic hose 8. Air in hydraulic system 9. Low pump output or leaks in system 10. Obstruction in lines 11. Pump valves sticking or out of adjustment 12. Incorrect wheel alignment
Loose steering (too much play in steering wheel)	1. Loose wheel bearings 2. Faulty shocks 3. Worn linkage or suspension components 4. Loose steering gear mounting or linkage points 5. Steering mechanism worn or improperly adjusted 6. Valve spool improperly adjusted 7. Worn ball joints, tie-rod ends, etc.
Veers or wanders (pulls to one side with hands off steering wheel)	1. Improper tire pressure 2. Improper front end alignment 3. Dragging or improperly adjusted brakes 4. Bent frame 5. Improper rear end alignment 6. Faulty shocks or springs 7. Loose or bent front end components 8. Play in Pitman arm 9. Steering gear mountings loose 10. Loose wheel bearings 11. Binding Pitman arm 12. Spool valve sticking or improperly adjusted 13. Worn ball joints
Wheel oscillation or vibration transmitted through steering wheel	1. Low or uneven tire pressure 2. Loose wheel bearings 3. Improper front end alignment 4. Bent spindle 5. Worn, bent or broken front end components 6. Tires out of round or out of balance 7. Excessive lateral runout in disc brake rotor 8. Loose or bent shock absorber or strut
Noises (see also "Troubleshooting Drive Axle Problems")	1. Loose belts 2. Low fluid, air in system 3. Foreign matter in system 4. Improper lubrication 5. Interference or chafing in linkage 6. Steering gear mountings loose 7. Incorrect adjustment or wear in gear box 8. Faulty valves or wear in pump 9. Kinked hydraulic lines 10. Worn wheel bearings
Poor return of steering	1. Over-inflated tires 2. Improperly aligned front end (excessive caster) 3. Binding in steering column 4. No lubrication in front end 5. Steering gear adjusted too tight
Uneven tire wear (see "How To Read Tire Wear")	1. Incorrect tire pressure 2. Improperly aligned front end 3. Tires out-of-balance 4. Bent or worn suspension parts

HOW TO READ TIRE WEAR

The way your tires wear is a good indicator of other parts of the suspension. Abnormal wear patterns are often caused by the need for simple tire maintenance, or for front end alignment.

Excessive wear at the center of the tread indicates that the air pressure in the tire is consistently too high. The tire is riding on the center of the tread and wearing it prematurely. Occasionally, this wear pattern can result from outrageously wide tires on narrow rims. The cure for this is to replace either the tires or the wheels.

This type of wear usually results from consistent under-inflation. When a tire is under-inflated, there is too much contact with the road by the outer treads, which wear prematurely. When this type of wear occurs, and the tire pressure is known to be consistently correct, a bent or worn steering component or the need for wheel alignment could be indicated.

Feathering is a condition when the edge of each tread rib develops a slightly rounded edge on one side and a sharp edge on the other. By running your hand over the tire, you can usually feel the sharper edges before you'll be able to see them. The most common causes of feathering are incorrect toe-in setting or deteriorated bushings in the front suspension.

When an inner or outer rib wears faster than the rest of the tire, the need for wheel alignment is indicated. There is excessive camber in the front suspension, causing the wheel to lean too much putting excessive load on one side of the tire. Misalignment could also be due to sagging springs, worn ball joints, or worn control arm bushings. Be sure the vehicle is loaded the way it's normally driven when you have the wheels aligned.

Cups or scalloped dips appearing around the edge of the tread almost always indicate worn (sometimes bent) suspension parts. Adjustment of wheel alignment alone will seldom cure the problem. Any worn component that connects the wheel to the suspension can cause this type of wear. Occasionally, wheels that are out of balance will wear like this, but wheel imbalance usually shows up as bald spots between the outside edges and center of the tread.

Second-rib wear is usually found only in radial tires, and appears where the steel belts end in relation to the tread. It can be kept to a minimum by paying careful attention to tire pressure and frequently rotating the tires. This is often considered normal wear but excessive amounts indicate that the tires are too wide for the wheels.

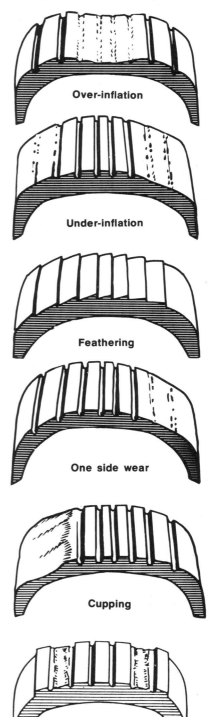

Over-inflation

Under-inflation

Feathering

One side wear

Cupping

Second-rib wear

Troubleshooting Disc Brake Problems

Condition	Possible Cause
Noise—groan—brake noise emanating when slowly releasing brakes (creep-groan)	Not detrimental to function of disc brakes—no corrective action required. (This noise may be eliminated by slightly increasing or decreasing brake pedal efforts.)
Rattle—brake noise or rattle emanating at low speeds on rough roads, (front wheels only).	1. Shoe anti-rattle spring missing or not properly positioned. 2. Excessive clearance between shoe and caliper. 3. Soft or broken caliper seals. 4. Deformed or misaligned disc. 5. Loose caliper.
Scraping	1. Mounting bolts too long. 2. Loose wheel bearings. 3. Bent, loose, or misaligned splash shield.
Front brakes heat up during driving and fail to release	1. Operator riding brake pedal. 2. Stop light switch improperly adjusted. 3. Sticking pedal linkage. 4. Frozen or seized piston. 5. Residual pressure valve in master cylinder. 6. Power brake malfunction. 7. Proportioning valve malfunction.
Leaky brake caliper	1. Damaged or worn caliper piston seal. 2. Scores or corrosion on surface of cylinder bore.
Grabbing or uneven brake action— Brakes pull to one side	1. Causes listed under "Brakes Pull". 2. Power brake malfunction. 3. Low fluid level in master cylinder. 4. Air in hydraulic system. 5. Brake fluid, oil or grease on linings. 6. Unmatched linings. 7. Distorted brake pads. 8. Frozen or seized pistons. 9. Incorrect tire pressure. 10. Front end out of alignment. 11. Broken rear spring. 12. Brake caliper pistons sticking. 13. Restricted hose or line. 14. Caliper not in proper alignment to braking disc. 15. Stuck or malfunctioning metering valve. 16. Soft or broken caliper seals. 17. Loose caliper.
Brake pedal can be depressed without braking effect·	1. Air in hydraulic system or improper bleeding procedure. 2. Leak past primary cup in master cylinder. 3. Leak in system. 4. Rear brakes out of adjustment. 5. Bleeder screw open.
Excessive pedal travel	1. Air, leak, or insufficient fluid in system or caliper. 2. Warped or excessively tapered shoe and lining assembly. 3. Excessive disc runout. 4. Rear brake adjustment required. 5. Loose wheel bearing adjustment. 6. Damaged caliper piston seal. 7. Improper brake fluid (boil). 8. Power brake malfunction. 9. Weak or soft hoses.

Troubleshooting Disc Brake Problems (cont.)

Condition	Possible Cause
Brake roughness or chatter (pedal pumping)	1. Excessive thickness variation of braking disc. 2. Excessive lateral runout of braking disc. 3. Rear brake drums out-of-round. 4. Excessive front bearing clearance.
Excessive pedal effort	1. Brake fluid, oil or grease on linings. 2. Incorrect lining. 3. Frozen or seized pistons. 4. Power brake malfunction. 5. Kinked or collapsed hose or line. 6. Stuck metering valve. 7. Scored caliper or master cylinder bore. 8. Seized caliper pistons.
Brake pedal fades (pedal travel increases with foot on brake)	1. Rough master cylinder or caliper bore. 2. Loose or broken hydraulic lines/connections. 3. Air in hydraulic system. 4. Fluid level low. 5. Weak or soft hoses. 6. Inferior quality brake shoes or fluid. 7. Worn master cylinder piston cups or seals.

Troubleshooting Drum Brakes

Condition	Possible Cause
Pedal goes to floor	1. Fluid low in reservoir. 2. Air in hydraulic system. 3. Improperly adjusted brake. 4. Leaking wheel cylinders. 5. Loose or broken brake lines. 6. Leaking or worn master cylinder. 7. Excessively worn brake lining.
Spongy brake pedal	1. Air in hydraulic system. 2. Improper brake fluid (low boiling point). 3. Excessively worn or cracked brake drums. 4. Broken pedal pivot bushing.
Brakes pulling	1. Contaminated lining. 2. Front end out of alignment. 3. Incorrect brake adjustment. 4. Unmatched brake lining. 5. Brake drums out of round. 6. Brake shoes distorted. 7. Restricted brake hose or line. 8. Broken rear spring. 9. Worn brake linings. 10. Uneven lining wear. 11. Glazed brake lining. 12. Excessive brake lining dust. 13. Heat spotted brake drums. 14. Weak brake return springs. 15. Faulty automatic adjusters. 16. Low or incorrect tire pressure.

Condition	Possible Cause
Squealing brakes	1. Glazed brake lining. 2. Saturated brake lining. 3. Weak or broken brake shoe retaining spring. 4. Broken or weak brake shoe return spring. 5. Incorrect brake lining. 6. Distorted brake shoes. 7. Bent support plate. 8. Dust in brakes or scored brake drums. 9. Linings worn below limit. 10. Uneven brake lining wear. 11. Heat spotted brake drums.
Chirping brakes	1. Out of round drum or eccentric axle flange pilot.
Dragging brakes	1. Incorrect wheel or parking brake adjustment. 2. Parking brakes engaged or improperly adjusted. 3. Weak or broken brake shoe return spring. 4. Brake pedal binding. 5. Master cylinder cup sticking. 6. Obstructed master cylinder relief port. 7. Saturated brake lining. 8. Bent or out of round brake drum. 9. Contaminated or improper brake fluid. 10. Sticking wheel cylinder pistons. 11. Driver riding brake pedal. 12. Defective proportioning valve. 13. Insufficient brake shoe lubricant.
Hard pedal	1. Brake booster inoperative. 2. Incorrect brake lining. 3. Restricted brake line or hose. 4. Frozen brake pedal linkage. 5. Stuck wheel cylinder. 6. Binding pedal linkage. 7. Faulty proportioning valve.
Wheel locks	1. Contaminated brake lining. 2. Loose or torn brake lining. 3. Wheel cylinder cups sticking. 4. Incorrect wheel bearing adjustment. 5. Faulty proportioning valve.
Brakes fade (high speed)	1. Incorrect lining. 2. Overheated brake drums. 3. Incorrect brake fluid (low boiling temperature). 4. Saturated brake lining. 5. Leak in hydraulic system. 6. Faulty automatic adjusters.
Pedal pulsates	1. Bent or out of round brake drum.
Brake chatter and shoe knock	1. Out of round brake drum. 2. Loose support plate. 3. Bent support plate. 4. Distorted brake shoes. 5. Machine grooves in contact face of brake drum (Shoe Knock) 6. Contaminated brake lining. 7. Missing or loose components. 8. Incorrect lining material. 9. Out-of-round brake drums. 10. Heat spotted or scored brake drums. 11. Out-of-balance wheels.

Troubleshooting Drum Brakes (cont.)

Condition	Possible Cause
Brakes do not self adjust	1. Adjuster screw frozen in thread. 2. Adjuster screw corroded at thrust washer. 3. Adjuster lever does not engage star wheel. 4. Adjuster installed on wrong wheel.
Brake light glows	1. Leak in the hydraulic system. 2. Air in the system. 3. Improperly adjusted master cylinder pushrod. 4. Uneven lining wear. 5. Failure to center combination valve or proportioning valve.

Appendix

General Conversion Table

Multiply by	To convert	To	
2.54	Inches	Centimeters	.3937
30.48	Feet	Centimeters	.0328
.914	Yards	Meters	1.094
1.609	Miles	Kilometers	.621
6.45	Square inches	Square cm.	.155
.836	Square yards	Square meters	1.196
16.39	Cubic inches	Cubic cm.	.061
28.3	Cubic feet	Liters	.0353
.4536	Pounds	Kilograms	2.2045
3.785	Gallons	Liters	.264
.068	Lbs./sq. in. (psi)	Atmospheres	14.7
.138	Foot pounds	Kg. m.	7.23
1.014	H.P. (DIN)	H.P. (SAE)	.9861
—	To obtain	From	Multiply by

Note: 1 cm. equals 10 mm.; 1 mm. equals .0394".

Conversion—Common Fractions to Decimals and Millimeters

Common Fractions	Decimal Fractions	Millimeters (approx.)	Common Fractions	Decimal Fractions	Millimeters (approx.)	Common Fractions	Decimal Fractions	Millimeters (approx.)
1/128	.008	0.20	11/32	.344	8.73	43/64	.672	17.07
1/64	.016	0.40	23/64	.359	9.13	11/16	.688	17.46
1/32	.031	0.79	3/8	.375	9.53	45/64	.703	17.86
3/64	.047	1.19	25/64	.391	9.92	23/32	.719	18.26
1/16	.063	1.59	13/32	.406	10.32	47/64	.734	18.65
5/64	.078	1.98	27/64	.422	10.72	3/4	.750	19.05
3/32	.094	2.38	7/16	.438	11.11	49/64	.766	19.45
7/64	.109	2.78	29/64	.453	11.51	25/32	.781	19.84
1/8	.125	3.18	15/32	.469	11.91	51/64	.797	20.24
9/64	.141	3.57	31/64	.484	12.30	13/16	.813	20.64
5/32	.156	3.97	1/2	.500	12.70	53/64	.828	21.03
11/64	.172	4.37	33/64	.516	13.10	27/32	.844	21.43
3/16	.188	4.76	17/32	.531	13.49	55/64	.859	21.83
13/64	.203	5.16	35/64	.547	13.89	7/8	.875	22.23
7/32	.219	5.56	9/16	.563	14.29	57/64	.891	22.62
15/64	.234	5.95	37/64	.578	14.68	29/32	.906	23.02
1/4	.250	6.35	19/32	.594	15.08	59/64	.922	23.42
17/64	.266	6.75	39/64	.609	15.48	15/16	.938	23.81
9/32	.281	7.14	5/8	.625	15.88	61/64	.953	24.21
19/64	.297	7.54	41/64	.641	16.27	31/32	.969	24.61
5/16	.313	7.94	21/32	.656	16.67	63/64	.984	25.00
21/64	.328	8.33						

Conversion—Millimeters to Decimal Inches

mm	inches	mm	inches	mm	inches	mm	inches	mm	inches
1	.039 370	31	1.220 470	61	2.401 570	91	3.582 670	210	8.267 700
2	.078 740	32	1.259 840	62	2.440 940	92	3.622 040	220	8.661 400
3	.118 110	33	1.299 210	63	2.480 310	93	3.661 410	230	9.055 100
4	.157 480	34	1.338 580	64	2.519 680	94	3.700 780	240	9.448 800
5	.196 850	35	1.377 949	65	2.559 050	95	3.740 150	250	9.842 500
6	.236 220	36	1.417 319	66	2.598 420	96	3.779 520	260	10.236 200
7	.275 590	37	1.456 689	67	2.637 790	97	3.818 890	270	10.629 900
8	.314 960	38	1.496 050	68	2.677 160	98	3.858 260	280	11.032 600
9	.354 330	39	1.535 430	69	2.716 530	99	3.897 630	290	11.417 300
10	.393 700	40	1.574 800	70	2.755 900	100	3.937 000	300	11.811 000
11	.433 070	41	1.614 170	71	2.795 270	105	4.133 848	310	12.204 700
12	.472 440	42	1.653 540	72	2.834 640	110	4.330 700	320	12.598 400
13	.511 810	43	1.692 910	73	2.874 010	115	4.527 550	330	12.992 100
14	.551 180	44	1.732 280	74	2.913 380	120	4.724 400	340	13.385 800
15	.590 550	45	1.771 650	75	2.952 750	125	4.921 250	350	13.779 500
16	.629 920	46	1.811 020	76	2.992 120	130	5.118 100	360	14.173 200
17	.669 290	47	1.850 390	77	3.031 490	135	5.314 950	370	14.566 900
18	.708 660	48	1.889 760	78	3.070 860	140	5.511 800	380	14.960 600
19	.748 030	49	1.929 130	79	3.110 230	145	5.708 650	390	15.354 300
20	.787 400	50	1.968 500	80	3.149 600	150	5.905 500	400	15.748 000
21	.826 770	51	2.007 870	81	3.188 970	155	6.102 350	500	19.685 000
22	.866 140	52	2.047 240	82	3.228 340	160	6.299 200	600	23.622 000
23	.905 510	53	2.086 610	83	3.267 710	165	6.496 050	700	27.559 000
24	.944 880	54	2.125 980	84	3.307 080	170	6.692 900	800	31.496 000
25	.984 250	55	2.165 350	85	3.346 450	175	6.889 750	900	35.433 000
26	1.023 620	56	2.204 720	86	3.385 820	180	7.086 600	1000	39.370 000
27	1.062 990	57	2.244 090	87	3.425 190	185	7.283 450	2000	78.740 000
28	1.102 360	58	2.283 460	88	3.464 560	190	7.480 300	3000	118.110 000
29	1.141 730	59	2.322 830	89	3.503 903	195	7.677 150	4000	157.480 000
30	1.181 100	60	2.362 200	90	3.543 300	200	7.874 000	5000	196.850 000

To change decimal millimeters to decimal inches, position the decimal point where desired on either side of the millimeter measurement shown and reset the inches decimal by the same number of digits in the same direction. For example, to convert 0.001 mm to decimal inches, reset the decimal behind the 1 mm (shown on the chart) to 0.001; change the decimal inch equivalent (0.039″ shown) to 0.000039″.

Tap Drill Sizes

Screw & Tap Size	National Fine or S.A.E. Threads Per Inch	Use Drill Number
No. 5	44	37
No. 6	40	33
No. 8	36	29
No. 10	32	21
No. 12	28	15
1/4	28	3
5/16	24	1
3/8	24	Q
7/16	20	W
1/2	20	29/64
9/16	18	33/64
5/8	18	37/64
3/4	16	11/16
7/8	14	13/16
1 1/8	12	1 3/64
1 1/4	12	1 11/64
1 1/2	12	1 27/64

Tap Drill Sizes

Screw & Tap Size	National Coarse or U.S.S. Threads Per Inch	Use Drill Number
No. 5	40	39
No. 6	32	36
No. 8	32	29
No. 10	24	25
No. 12	24	17
1/4	20	8
5/16	18	F
3/8	16	5/16
7/16	14	U
1/2	13	27/64
9/16	12	31/64
5/8	11	17/32
3/4	10	21/32
7/8	9	49/64
1	8	7/8
1 1/8	7	63/64
1 1/4	7	1 7/64
1 1/2	6	1 11/32

Decimal Equivalent Size of the Number Drills

Drill No.	Decimal Equivalent	Drill No.	Decimal Equivalent	Drill No.	Decimal Equivalent
80	.0135	53	.0595	26	.1470
79	.0145	52	.0635	25	.1495
78	.0160	51	.0670	24	.1520
77	.0180	50	.0700	23	.1540
76	.0200	49	.0730	22	.1570
75	.0210	48	.0760	21	.1590
74	.0225	47	.0785	20	.1610
73	.0240	46	.0810	19	.1660
72	.0250	45	.0820	18	.1695
71	.0260	44	.0860	17	.1730
70	.0280	43	.0890	16	.1770
69	.0292	42	.0935	15	.1800
68	.0310	41	.0960	14	.1820
67	.0320	40	.0980	13	.1850
66	.0330	39	.0995	12	.1890
65	.0350	38	.1015	11	.1910
64	.0360	37	.1040	10	.1935
63	.0370	36	.1065	9	.1960
62	.0380	35	.1100	8	.1990
61	.0390	34	.1110	7	.2010
60	.0400	33	.1130	6	.2040
59	.0410	32	.1160	5	.2055
58	.0420	31	.1200	4	.2090
57	.0430	30	.1285	3	.2130
56	.0465	29	.1360	2	.2210
55	.0520	28	.1405	1	.2280
54	.0550	27	.1440		

Decimal Equivalent Size of the Letter Drills

Letter Drill	Decimal Equivalent	Letter Drill	Decimal Equivalent	Letter Drill	Decimal Equivalent
A	.234	J	.277	S	.348
B	.238	K	.281	T	.358
C	.242	L	.290	U	.368
D	.246	M	.295	V	.377
E	.250	N	.302	W	.386
F	.257	O	.316	X	.397
G	.261	P	.323	Y	.404
H	.266	Q	.332	Z	.413
I	.272	R	.339		

Anti-Freeze Chart

Temperatures Shown in Degrees Fahrenheit +32 is Freezing

Cooling System Capacity Quarts	Quarts of ETHYLENE GLYCOL Needed for Protection to Temperatures Shown Below													
	1	2	3	4	5	6	7	8	9	10	11	12	13	14
10	+24°	+16°	+4°	−12°	−34°	−62°								
11	+25	+18	+8	−6	−23	−47								
12	+26	+19	+10	0	−15	−34	−57°							
13	+27	+21	+13	+3	−9	−25	−45							
14			+15	+6	−5	−18	−34							
15			+16	+8	0	−12	−26							
16		+17	+10	+2	−8	−19	−34	−52°						
17		+18	+12	+5	−4	−14	−27	−42						
18		+19	+14	+7	0	−10	−21	−34	−50°					
19		+20	+15	+9	+2	−7	−16	−28	−42					
20			+16	+10	+4	−3	−12	−22	−34	−48°				
21			+17	+12	+6	0	−9	−17	−28	−41				
22			+18	+13	+8	+2	−6	−14	−23	−34	−47°			
23			+19	+14	+9	+4	−3	−10	−19	−29	−40			
24			+19	+15	+10	+5	0	−8	−15	−23	−34	−46°		
25			+20	+16	+12	+7	+1	−5	−12	−20	−29	−40	−50°	
26				+17	+13	+8	+3	−3	−9	−16	−25	−34	−44	
27				+18	+14	+9	+5	−1	−7	−13	−21	−29	−39	
28				+18	+15	+10	+6	+1	−5	−11	−18	−25	−34	
29				+19	+16	+12	+7	+2	−3	−8	−15	−22	−29	
30				+20	+17	+13	+8	+4	−1	−6	−12	−18	−25	

For capacities over 30 quarts divide true capacity by 3. Find quarts Anti-Freeze for the ⅓ and multiply by 3 for quarts to add.

For capacities under 10 quarts multiply true capacity by 3. Find quarts Anti-Freeze for the tripled volume and divide by 3 for quarts to add.

To Increase the Freezing Protection of Anti-Freeze Solutions Already Installed

Cooling System Capacity Quarts	Number of Quarts of ETHYLENE GLYCOL Anti-Freeze Required to Increase Protection													
	From +20° F. to					From +10° F. to					From 0° F. to			
	0°	−10°	−20°	−30°	−40°	0°	−10°	−20°	−30°	−40°	−10°	−20°	−30°	−40°
10	1¾	2¼	3	3½	3¾	¾	1½	2¼	2¾	3¼	¾	1½	2	2½
12	2	2¾	3½	4	4½	1	1¾	2½	3¼	3¾	1	1¾	2½	3¼
14	2¼	3¼	4	4¾	5½	1¼	2	3	3¾	4½	1	2	3	3½
16	2½	3½	4½	5¼	6	1¼	2½	3½	4¼	5¼	1¼	2¼	3¼	4
18	3	4	5	6	7	1½	2¾	4	5	5¾	1½	2½	3¾	4¾
20	3¼	4½	5¾	6¾	7½	1¾	3	4¼	5½	6½	1½	2¾	4¼	5¼
22	3½	5	6¼	7¼	8¼	1¾	3¼	4¾	6	7¼	1¾	3¼	4½	5½
24	4	5½	7	8	9	2	3½	5	6½	7½	1¾	3½	5	6
26	4¼	6	7½	8¾	10	2	4	5½	7	8¼	2	3¾	5½	6¾
28	4½	6¼	8	9½	10½	2¼	4¼	6	7½	9	2	4	5¾	7¼
30	5	6¾	8½	10	11½	2½	4½	6½	8	9½	2¼	4¼	6¼	7¾

Test radiator solution with proper hydrometer. Determine from the table the number of quarts of solution to be drawn off from a full cooling system and replace with undiluted anti-freeze, to give the desired increased protection. For example, to increase protection of a 22-quart cooling system containing Ethylene Glycol (permanent type) anti-freeze, from +20° F. to −20° F. will require the replacement of 6¼ quarts of solution with undiluted anti-freeze.

Index

Chilton's Repair & Tune-Up Guides

The complete line covers domestic cars, imports, trucks, vans, RV's and 4-wheel drive vehicles.

BOOK CODE	TITLE	BOOK CODE	TITLE
#7199	AMC 75-82; all models inc. Eagle	#6937	Granada 75-80
#7163	Aries 81-82	#5905	GTO 68-73
#7032	Arrow Pick-Up 79-81	#5821	GTX 68-73
#6637	Aspen 76-80	#6980	Honda 73-82
#5902	Audi 70-73	#6845	Horizon 78-82
#7028	Audi 4000/5000 77-81	#5912	International Scout 67-73
#6337	Audi Fox 73-75	#5998	Jaguar 69-74
#5807	Barracuda 65-72	#7136	Jeep CJ 1945-81
#6931	Blazer 69-82	#6739	Jeep Wagoneer, Commando, Cherokee 66-79
#5576	BMW 59-70	#6962	Jetta 1980
#6844	BMW 70-79	#6931	Jimmy 69-82
#5821	Belvedere 68-73	#7059	J-2000 1982
#7027	Bobcat	#5905	Le Mans 68-73
#7045	Camaro 67-81	#7055	Lynx 81-82 inc. EXP & LN-7
#6695	Capri 70-77	#6634	Maverick 70-77
#6963	Capri 79-82	#6981	Mazda 71-82
#7059	Cavalier 1982	#7031	Mazda RX-7 79-81
#5807	Challenger 65-72	#6065	Mercedes-Benz 59-70
#7037	Challenger (Import) 71-81	#5907	Mercedes-Benz 68-73
#7041	Champ 78-81	#6809	Mercedes-Benz 74-79
#6316	Charger 71-75	#7128	Mercury 68-71 all full sized models
#7162	Chevette 76-82 inc. diesel	#6696	Mercury Mid-Size 71-81 inc. T-Bird,
#7135	Chevrolet 68-81 all full size models		Montego & Cougar
#6936	Chevrolet/GMC Pick-Ups 70-82	#6780	MG 61-81
#6930	Chevrolet/GMC Vans 67-82	#6973	Monarch 75-80
#7051	Chevy Luv 72-81 inc. 4wd	#6542	Mustang 65-73
#7056	Chevy Mid-Size 64-82 inc. El Camino,	#6812	Mustang II 74-78
	Chevelle, Laguna, Malibu & Monte Carlo	#6963	Mustang 79-82
#6841	Chevy II 62-79	#6841	Nova 69-79
#7059	Cimarron 1982	#7049	Omega 81-82
#7049	Citation 80-81	#6845	Omni 78-82
#7037	Colt 71-81	#5792	Opel 64-70
#6634	Comet 70-77	#6575	Opel 71-75
#6316	Coronet 71-75	#5982	Peugeot 70-74
#6691	Corvair 60-69 inc. Turbo	#7049	Phoenix 81-82
#6576	Corvette 53-62	#7027	Pinto 71-80
#6843	Corvette 63-82	#6552	Plymouth 68-76 full sized models
#6933	Cutlass 70-82	#6934	Plymouth Vans 67-82
#6324	Dart 68-76	#5822	Porche 69-73
#6962	Dasher 74-80	#7048	Porche 924 & 928 76-81 inc. Turbo
#5790	Datsun 61-72	#6962	Rabbit 75-80
#7196	Datsun F10, 310, Nissan Stanza 77-82	#6331	Ramcharger/Trail Duster 74-75
#7170	Datsun 200SX, 510, 610, 710, 810 73-82	#7163	Reliant 81-82
#7197	Datsun 210 and 1200 73-82	#5821	Roadrunner 68-73
#6932	Datsun Z & ZX 70-82	#5988	Saab 69-75
#7050	Datsun Pick-Ups 70-81 inc. 4wd	#7041	Sapporo 78-81
#6324	Demon 68-76	#5821	Satellite 68-73
#6554	Dodge 68-77 all full sized models	#6962	Scirocco 75-80
#6486	Dodge Charger 67-70	#7059	Skyhawk 1982
#6934	Dodge Vans 67-82	#7049	Skylark 80-81
#6326	Duster 68-76	#6982	Subaru 70-82
#7055	Escort 81-82 inc. EXP & LN-7	#5905	Tempest 68-73
#6320	Fairlane 62-75	#6320	Torino 62-75
#6965	Fairmont 78-80	#5795	Toyota 66-70
#6485	Fiat 64-70	#7043	Toyota Celica & Supra 71-81
#7042	Fiat 69-81	#7036	Toyota Corolla, Carina, Tercel, Starlet 70-81
#6846	Fiesta 78-80	#7044	Toyota Corona, Cressida, Crown, Mark II 70-81
#7046	Firebird 67-81	#7035	Toyota Pick-Ups 70-81
#7059	Firenza 1982	#5910	Triumph 69-73
#7128	Ford 68-81 all full sized models	#7162	T-1000 1982
#7140	Ford Bronco 66-81	#6326	Valiant 68-76
#6983	Ford Courier 72-80	#5796	Volkswagen 49-71
#6696	Ford Mid-Size 71-78 inc. Torino,	#6837	Volkswagen 70-81
	Gran Torino, Ranchero, Elite & LTD II	#6637	Volaré 76-80
#6913	Ford Pick-Ups 65-82 inc. 4wd	#6529	Volvo 56-69
#6849	Ford Vans 61-82	#7040	Volvo 70-80
#6935	GM Sub-compact 71-81 inc. Vega,	#6965	Zephyr 78-80
	Monza, Astre, Sunbird, Starfire & Skyhawk		

Chilton's Repair & Tune-Up Guides are available at your local retailer or by mailing a check or money order for **$9.95** plus **$1.00** to cover postage and handling to:

Chilton Book Company
Dept. DM
Radnor, PA 19089

NOTE: When ordering be sure to include your name & address, book code & title.